Tourism, Crime and International Security Issues

Tourism, Crime and International Security Issues

Edited by

ABRAHAM PIZAM
YOEL MANSFELD

JOHN WILEY & SONS

Chichester · New York · Brisbane · Toronto · Singapore

Copyright © 1996 by John Wiley & Sons Ltd,
Baffins Lane, Chichester,
West Sussex PO19 1UD, England

National   01243 779777
International (+44) 1243 779777

Other Wiley Editorial Offices

John Wiley & Sons, Inc., 605 Third Avenue,
New York, NY 10158-0012, USA

Jacaranda Wiley Ltd, 33 Park Road, Milton,
Queensland 4064, Australia

John Wiley & Sons (Canada) Ltd, 22 Worcester Road,
Rexdale, Ontario M9W 1L1, Canada

John Wiley & Sons (SEA) Pte Ltd, 37 Jalan Pemimpin #05-04,
Block B, Union Industrial Building, Singapore 2057

Library of Congress Cataloging-in-Publication Data
Tourism, crime, and international security issues / edited by Abraham
  Pizam and Yoel Mansfeld.
     p.   cm.
   Includes bibliographical references and index.
   ISBN 0-471-96107-8 (alk. paper)
   1. Tourist trade — Safety measures. 2. Crime. 3. Violence.
I. Pizam, Abraham. II. Mansfeld, Y. (Yoel)
G155.A1T5897 1995
338.4'791 — dc20   95-20449
                                                            CIP

British Library Cataloguing in Publication Data

A catalogue record for this book is available from the British Library

ISBN 0-471-96107-8

Typeset in 10/12pt Times by MHL Typesetting Ltd, Coventry
Printed and bound in Great Britain by Bookcraft (Bath) Ltd, Midsomer Norton

This book is printed on acid-free paper responsibly manufactured from sustainable forestation,
for which at least two trees are planted for each one used for paper production.

Contents

List of contributors

Susan A. Bach, Department of Hospitality Management, University of Central Florida, P.O. Box 161400, Orlando, FL 32816-1400, USA

Raphael R. Bar-On, 94 Herzl Boulevard, Jerusalem 96347, Israel

Jonathan Bloom, Faculty of Commerce and Administration, University of Stellenbosch, Private Bag X5018, 7599 Stellenbosch, South Africa

Eric Cohen, Department of Sociology and Anthropology, Hebrew University of Jerusalem, Mount Scopus, Jerusalem, Israel

John Crotts, Advanced Business Program, University of Otago, P.O. Box 56, Dunedin, New Zealand

C. Michael Hall, Tourism Program, University of Canberra, P.O. Box 1, Belconnen ACT 2616, Australia

R.C. Hollinger, Department of Sociology, University of Florida, Gainesville, FL 32611, USA

Rachael Kinder, Department of Management Systems, Massey University, Private Bag 11222, Palmerston North, New Zealand

Nurit Kliot, Department of Geography, University of Haifa, Haifa 31905, Israel

Samuel V. Lankford, Department of Health, Physical Education and Recreation, University of Hawaii at Manoa, Honolulu, HI 968922, USA

John Lea, Faculty of Architecture, The University of Sydney, Sydney NSW 2006, Australia

Stephen LeBruto, Department of Hospitality Management, University of Central Florida, P.O. Box 161400, Orlando, FL 32816-1400, USA

Yoel Mansfeld, Department of Geography, University of Haifa, Haifa 31905, Israel

Tanja Mihalič, Faculty of Economics, University of Ljubljana, Kardeljeva ploščad 17, 61000 Ljubljana, Slovenia

Mitchell J. Muehsam, Department of Economics and Business Analysis, Sam Houston University, Huntsville, Texas 77341, USA

Vanessa O'Sullivan, Tourism Program, University of Canberra, P.O. Box 1, Belconnen ACT 2616, Australia

Wayne Pitts, Department of Sociology, University of New Mexico, Center for Applied Research & Analysis, 2808 Central Avenue, SE, Albuquerque, NM 87106, USA

Abraham Pizam, Department of Hospitality Management, University of Central Florida, P.O. Box 161400, Orlando, FL 32816-1400, USA

Bruce Prideaux, Department of Business Studies, the University of Queensland, Gaton College, Lawes QLD 4343, Australia

Chris Ryan, Department of Management Systems, Massey University, Private Bag

11222, Palmerston North, New Zealand
Susan A. Schiebler, Department of Recreation, Parks and Tourism, University of Florida, Gainseville, FL 32611-0550, USA
Valene S. Smith, Department of Anthropology, California State University, Chico, CA 95929-0400, USA
Peter Tarlow, Department of Economics and Business Analysis, Sam Houston University, Huntsville, TX 77341-2118, USA
Salah E.A. Wahab, Tourismplan, 16 Mamal Al-Sukkar St, Garden City, Cairo, Egypt
Geoffrey Wall, Department of Geography, University of Waterloo, Waterloo, Ontario N2L 3G1, Canada

Introduction

ABRAHAM PIZAM AND YOEL MANSFELD

This book is about the relationship between safety, tranquility and peace and successful tourism. More specifically it is about the effects of the absence of safety, security and peace on domestic and international tourism throughout the world. To no one's surprise, the evidence accumulated in many parts of the world and reported in some of the case studies in this book brings us to the conclusion that safety, tranquility and peace are a necessary condition for prosperous tourism. Leisure tourism is a discretionary activity, and most tourists will not spend their hard earned money to go to a destination where their safety and well-being may be in jeopardy. Even business tourism, which is not considered to be a totally discretionary activity, is affected by incidences of violence and crimes against tourists, since most companies would be extremely reluctant to endanger their employees by sending them to unsafe destinations.

The effects of wars, criminal activities, terrorist attacks and violent acts aimed specifically against tourists have been devastating to tourism destinations. In Florida, an outbreak of crimes against tourists in 1993 caused a decline of 11 per cent in the number of overseas tourists and a 16 per cent decline in the number of Canadian tourists in the first seven months of 1994. The number of European visitors declined nearly 20 per cent — from 1.3 million to 1.05 million. Tourism from Great Britain and Germany, the top European markets for Florida and the two countries that had a number of their citizens who visited Florida attacked or murdered, declined by 22 per cent. Altogether, Florida's total share of foreign visitors to the USA declined from 23 per cent to 20 per cent in the first seven months of 1994 (*Orlando Sentinel*, 1995). Similar cases occurred in other destinations that are plagued by crimes such as Rio de Janeiro, Brazil; Papua New Guinea; Johannesburg, South Africa and others.

International terrorism, and especially the kind that is specifically aimed at tourists, has caused the world tourism industry billions of dollars in lost revenues. For example, it is estimated that following the 1992–3 terrorist attacks against international tourists in Egypt, the country's tourism industry has lost more than US$1 billion in tourism revenues. Similarly, the *Achille Lauro* piracy incident, the TWA hijacking and the attacks on the Rome and Vienna airports have caused serious reductions in the number of American visitors to Europe and the Middle East (60 per cent decline). Armed political conflicts such as in Northern Ireland, Chiapas, Mexico and Cyprus, to name just a few, have also had disastrous impacts on the tourism economies of the affected destinations. Civil unrest in tourism destinations has also had its share of negative impacts on tourism

Tourism, Crime and International Security Issues, edited by
A. Pizam and Y. Mansfeld. © 1996 John Wiley & Sons Ltd.

arrivals and receipts, as evidenced by the 1992 Los Angeles riots that have cost the city billions of dollars in lost revenues. The same effects occurred in the late 1980s in Fiji, New Caledonia and Vanuatu as a result of military coups and political instability.

Last but not least, wars between nations have caused long-term damage or even total destruction of the tourism economies of the countries involved in wars as well as other countries in their proximity. Such was the case during the Gulf War when most countries around the world, not just those directly involved in the war, suffered serious declines in their tourism arrivals and receipts. Similarly, the prolonged war in the former Yugoslavia has seriously damaged the tourism industries of Slovenia, Croatia and Serbia and all but eradicated tourism to Bosnia-Hercegovina.

By now it must be evident even to the most skeptical of readers that tourism can only thrive under peaceful conditions. We can possibly assert that most acts of violence occurring at tourist destinations and all acts of violence or threats of violence aimed specifically against tourists will affect tourist visitation and income.

The 20 chapters in this book represent the work of 25 authors from eight countries who analyze case studies relating to tourism and violence in 16 countries or territories. They address conceptually and empirically the causes and effects of violence against tourists and the tourism industry and provide the reader with possible measures to contain and minimize the negative effects.

In Part 1 of the book the seven chapters describe and analyze the relationship between tourism and crime. In Chapter 1 Tarlow and Muehsam attempt to explain the relationship between crime and tourism by focusing on some of the major sociological theories of the 19th and 20th centuries. They start by analyzing the works of Durkheim on deviance as a natural social phenomenon and the Chicago School of Sociology on the effects of urbanization on crime. From there they continue with a review of the doctrines of conflict theorists (Marxists) who assume that crime is a manifestation of class frustration and connect these to the writings of Veblen on "conspicuous consumption" and the "leisure class," followed by an analysis of the works of Tannenbaum on "labeling," Ditton on "control", Tönnies on "*Gemeinschaft* and *Gesellschaft*" and Mestrovic on "habits of the heart." Finally they use the works of post- modernist sociologists such as Baudrillard, Eco, Rojek and Urry to propose that "tourism is an industry that not only blurs reality but emphasizes . . . a 'barbaric culture' or . . . a 'hedonistic culture'." The authors conclude with a listing of the social phenomena relating to crimes against tourists that occur in the world of tourism make-believe.

Ryan and Kinder in Chapter 2 write about tourists as clients of prostitutes. They discuss the definition of deviance, especially as it relates to tourism and propose that as clients of prostitutes, tourists are neither criminals nor victims of criminals but "marginals" who "are operating at the fuzzy edge of criminality in such a way as to be potentially vulnerable to either criminal or police action." They advance the notion that tourism creates opportunities for sex and possible exploitation, though they admit that in most cases it is difficult to assess how much of the demand for prostitution is generated by leisure or business tourists. From there, they propose a model that explains how the need for prostitution services is translated into specific behavior and conclude with a description of Auckland's Fort Street "crimogenic" place "where likely offenders and suitable targets will be present and capable guardians against crimes will be absent."

In Chapter 3 Schiebler, Crotts and Hollinger report on a study intended to examine the incidence, location and types of crimes perpetrated against tourists in the 10 most visited counties in the state of Florida during 1993 and to explore the underlying causal influences of some social and environmental factors on crimes against tourists. The study analyzed the relationship between the above factors and crime, using two ecologically based theories of crime causation, the "routine activities approach" and the "hot spots theory." The results showed that crimes against tourists are more likely to occur in counties that already have high levels of conventional crimes. From the positive association that was found between the number of security personnel and the number of crimes reported, the authors conclude that the introduction of additional security personnel in an area without the simultaneous reduction in the number of motivated offenders will not reduce the level of crimes.

Lankford in Chapter 4 reports on an empirical study conducted in the northwest USA (Columbia River Gorge), intended to analyze the relationship between tourism development and crime as perceived by residents in tourism communities. The results indicated that rural residents, long-term residents, farmers and some recreationists feared that tourism may cause an increase in crimes in their communities. Younger residents perceived tourism development as causing higher levels of crimes than was perceived by their older counterparts.

In Chapter 5 Prideaux analyzes crime statistics in three popular Australian beach tourist destinations — Sunshine Coast, Cairns and Gold Coast — in order to explain the different crime rates occurring in the three communities. He suggests that the crime rates were higher in Cairns and the Gold Coast because of the "hedonistic" image adopted by these two communities as opposed to the "family wholesome" image that was adopted by the Sunshine Coast. The enhancement of this image through marketing and advertising not only attracted tourists to these destinations but also stimulated the migration of young job seekers having no emotional ties to the area but possessing a large appetite for fun and night-time entertainment. In turn, this mix of youth, money and desire to have fun led to excessive use of alcohol and drugs which ultimately resulted in high levels of crimes.

Cohen in Chapter 6 attempts to show the connection between some basic traits of contemporary Thai society and one prevalent type of tourist-oriented crime, the sale of low-quality gems at exorbitant prices to unsuspecting tourists. He suggests that ambiguity — the coexistence of conflicting cultural themes such as looseness versus rigidity or formality versus informality; opacity — a term indicating the existence of complex and conflicting social institutions; and duality — a preference for form over content (ie "saving face") are possibly related to these tourist-oriented crimes.

In Chapter 7 Bloom analyzes the incidences of increasing crimes against tourists in South Africa and estimates their cost in loss of tourist revenue. He examines the role of negative media reporting on South African tourism and on the image of the country as a whole and suggests the following initiatives to combat tourism-related crimes and violence: empowering community role-players in regional tourism structures; formulating tourism-linked human resource development objectives; reconstructing sub-sectors of the tourism industry in terms of future challenges and opportunities; compiling fast-track programs for capacity building in human and financial resources; providing guidelines for potential tourism entrepreneurs to become a part of the tourism industry; stipulating community responsibilities and self-initiatives; and addressing transparency and control issues.

Part 2 of the book deals with tourism and political instability. The first chapter in this part by Michael Hall and Vanessa O'Sullivan (Chapter 8) provides a theoretical framework which illustrates the role of the media, government policies and tourists' perceptions of destinations in determining attitudes towards the political characteristics of a given tourist destination. Furthermore the impact of political instability is analyzed from two different angles. The first, using the cases of China and Croatia, is an analysis of the indirect impact on tourism; the second focuses on the tourist as a victim of terror. Using a variety of recent cases, Hall and O'Sullivan characterize the devastating effects terror has on tourists and on their propensity to travel. In order to reduce the ramifications of terrorism and political instability on the tourism industry and on tourists, Hall and O'Sullivan suggest that planners and tourism managers take a more sophisticated approach regarding crisis management.

Using the South Pacific as a laboratory, John Lea in Chapter 9 evaluates the tourism development process in this region since the beginning of the 1990s and examines how the changing tourist landscape was affected by violence and created violence as a result of reaching development levels beyond locals' tolerated social caring capacity. He concludes that while tourism has suffered from occasional political instability and violence, it recovered from these disturbances very soon after the threat had passed. However, Lea anticipates future social unrest as a result of poor development planning, the alienation of customary land and the "capturing" of good locations for tourism development.

The interrelation between tourism and terror activities is also examined by Geoffrey Wall, who in Chapter 10 uses in a comparative manner the cases of the Republic of Ireland and Northern Ireland to analyze the impact of terrorism on tourism. Wall claims that tourism is an effective target for terrorists wishing to expose their goals world-wide. This is because of the multi-national nature of the visitor mix in a given tourist attraction. As the media never ignore terror activities, operating against tourists guarantees a world-wide media coverage and thus an effective channeling of information on the terrorists, their activities and their social – political goals. Wall claims that by attacking tourists, terror organizations achieve not just world-wide exposure but direct impact on the country's economic base, as tourists immediately react to these negative events and cancel their bookings and/or choose alternative tourist destinations. By comparing yearly figures of inbound tourist flows and tourist expenditures, Wall demonstrates the distinctive effect of terror on Northern Ireland. While the Republic of Ireland receives tourists whose prime motivation is to tour the country in a relaxed atmosphere, those attracted to the North are mostly visiting friends and relatives and are less affected by the threat of terror existing in this part of the island. The result of terrorism activities in tourist destinations, according to Wall, is a differential economic impact, as people visiting the Republic tend to spend more than those staying with their families in the North.

Another perspective on tourism and international conflicts is provided in Chapter 11 by Raphael Raymond Bar-On who measures the impact of security events on tourist arrivals and the effectiveness of promotion following these incidents. Using seasonally adjusted monthly data on tourist arrivals Bar-On characterizes and measures in detail the impact of regional hostility on tourist arrivals in selected Mediterranean destinations: Israel, Spain, Egypt and Turkey.

The impact of terrorism on tourism is illustrated by Salah Wahab in Chapter 12 who first theoretically differentiates between terrorism and other similar violent activities such as guerrilla warfare, political violence, state dictatorship or organized crime. Within the context of a theoretical framework on the relations between terrorism and tourism, Wahab examines the negative impact of Islamic terror on tourists visiting Egypt between 1992 and 1994. Wahab's analysis shows that this negative impact is magnified by the international media, which tend to take such events and paint them in the darkest possible colors. The Egyptian case shows that when a government is determined to provide the tourist industry with drastic defensive and preventive measures and simultaneously provides certain solutions to socially and economically deprived regions, terror against tourists can be deterred and stopped. Wahab concludes that while a government's direct measures are a prerequisite for fighting the negative effects of terror on tourists, new and innovative marketing measures have to be budgeted for and implemented by the Ministry of Tourism in order to defuse the biased impression of the actual risks tourists face.

National and international conflicts leading to warfare usually leave a distinctive imprint on countries' tourism infrastructure. An example of such results is illustrated by Yoel Mansfeld and Nurit Kliot in Chapter 13, where they examine the evolving tourist map of the partitioned island of Cyprus. The political landscape of Cyprus has changed as a result of the 1974 Civil War, which divided the island into two politically and socially separated entities. This chapter provides in a comparative manner an overview on the way tourism as a major economic sector was destroyed and redeveloped in the two parts of the island. Mansfeld and Kliot conclude that in both parts of the island, tourism has become the leading exporting industry and a main economic tool for the reactivation and rehabilitation of the Greek and Turkish communities living there. However, the evolving tourist map of the two parts is different as a result of the international policy towards this on-going dispute. The self-proclaimed "Turkish Republic of Northern Cyprus" has been facing an economic boycott, as it is considered an illicit country which occupies territories belonging to the Republic of Cyprus. Due to this embargo the development of the Turkish-occupied North was constrained. On the other hand, the Greek South enjoyed international sympathy with its struggle for reunification of the island. Thus, with the help of developed countries and with its strong internal efforts to rehabilitate its society and economy, the South has managed to develop a modern and attractive tourism system. In this case, the war is not just a destructive force but a catalyst for rapid tourism development.

Tourism is often used as a means for achieving better understanding between unfriendly nations. This hypothesis has been tested by Abraham Pizam in Chapter 14, dedicated to the question of whether tourism can change tourists' attitudes as a result of visiting an unfriendly country. Using four case studies and the same methodology, the perceptions and attitudes of Israelis visiting Egypt, Americans visiting the Soviet Union, Turks visiting Greece and Greeks visiting Turkey were examined to check if these were changed as a result of the visit. In each case a control group of people who did not intend to make such visits was also employed. Pizam's commutative findings are that as a result of the tour only small changes in opinions and attitudes took place. The majority of those changes occurred in the negative direction. This chapter suggests that the kind of terms, conditions and/or constraints imposed in the tour have a bearing on the possibility to change one's view of the people in the host community. Pizam believes in the potential of tourism as an instrument for peace promotion, but to achieve this end, tours in previously hostile countries have to be carefully planned and organized in both generating and receiving countries.

In Chapter 15, Pitts provides an in-depth analysis of how the recent uprising in Chiapas, Mexico affected domestic and international tourism in this country. In the

Chiapas region, a deprived peripheral community of Mexicans decided to fight for their rights. Their uprising caused a sharp drop in the number of inbound tourist flows. This dramatic drop affected the region's economy. However, the effect of this uprising did not deter travelers from visiting Chiapas altogether. The drop in the number of visitors was accompanied by a shift from ethnic tourists to what Pitts calls "war tourists" visiting the region because of the political events. A strategy for recovery from the decline of the region's tourism sector was to regain the confidence of the domestic market in the stability of Chiapas. According to Pitts such confidence can be achieved only if the Mexican government deals with the reasons for the uprising and not just with the efforts to change the image of the Chiapas region from an unsafe to a safe tourism attraction.

Part 3 examines the effects of war on tourism. In Chapter 16 Mihalic analyzes the negative effects of wars on tourism in general and on Slovenia in particular. As a result of the war in the former Yugoslavia, Slovenia encountered in 1991 an overall decrease of 44 per cent in the number of tourists and a 39 per cent decline in the number of nights spent. The reduction in tourist arrivals continued for the next two years, and by 1993 Slovenia was still below the pre-war level. Following this analysis, the author computed the pre- and post-war trends for tourism demand in Slovenia and rejected the hypothesis that foreign tourism trends after 1991 would move steeply upwards. The results showed that different countries reacted in a different manner in the post-war era. While tourist arrivals from German-speaking countries and especially Austria increased sharply, the image of the country in more remote countries was still negative and the level of increase was relatively modest.

Smith's Chapter 17 on "war as a tourist attraction" is unique in this book since it is the only chapter to examine the positive rather than the negative effects of an act of violence on tourism. She suggests that the common theme for all war-related tourism activities is commemoration — victory or defeat — and proposes a classification composed of five war-related tourism groupings. These are the "heroic phase" — visits to statues, monuments and museums commemorating national heroes, victories etc.; "remember the fallen" — visits to battlefields and cemeteries; "lest we forget" — visits to holocaust sites and certain museums such as Anne Frank's museum in Amsterdam; "when we were young" — revisiting battlefields by veterans, reunions of military units of famous battle sites, etc.; "reliving the past" — military re-enactments of historic battles at their original sites.

Based on an analysis of international tourist flows to the countries of the Middle East, in Chapter 18 Mansfeld examines (a) the magnitude of the effect of the Arab–Israeli conflict on inbound tourist flow to the region and (b) whether this effect was geographically differentiated. The analysis showed that, although the general trend was similar among all countries, not every security event that caused a decline in tourist arrivals affected all the countries in the same way. It appears that declines in tourist arrivals resulting from security events were highly correlated with the level of involvement of each Middle Eastern country in the given security event. Countries that took an active part in a security event suffered an immediate decline in arrivals, while those that were not involved in the event did not encounter a "spill-over" decline. The study dispelled the existence of a "Middle East factor" — a commonly held perception that the whole region is a "no go" area for tourists.

In Part 4 of the book, two chapters analyze the incidence of crimes in hotels, describe the legal responsibility of hoteliers towards their guests and suggest measures of crime prevention through environmental design.

Based on the events of crime against tourists in Florida and the way they were exposed by the media, Susan Bach in Chapter 19 claims that travelers are more aware of their security and safety needs while staying in hotels or motels. Hoteliers show also a growing awareness of their responsibilities for guests' security. In her chapter, Bach provides a review of the literature which deals with strategies to improve and ensure high levels of security to hotel guests. These are based on the combination of physical and behavioral means of security. In a critical review of the literature, Bach concludes that although numerous recommendations for establishing safety and security measures are available, no empirical evidence is provided to validate their effectiveness. She also calls for an intensive interaction and involvement of hoteliers with the community surrounding them. Such involvement will enhance cooperation on issues of security and crime prevention where both hotels and the community will benefit.

Finally, in Chapter 20 Stephen LeBruto discusses the legal aspects of safety in hospitality operations. Using cases from around the US, but particularly from the state of Florida, he examines the question of innkeepers' liability in cases of negligence or malpractice. LeBruto makes a distinction between the responsibilities of the innkeepers to ensure safety and the various criminal activities by guests or against guests which might influence the hotel and its ability to sell itself in the future. LeBruto provides a comprehensive legal review of the various types of negligence for which the hotel is responsible and the various types of crime committed by or against guests of the hospitality industry.

We would like to thank all our colleagues for their contributions to this volume. We thoroughly appreciate their cooperation and ability to submit their invaluable contributions within a relatively short time. We would also like to thank all those involved in the financial and technical support given to us. Special thanks go to the Research Authority of the University of Haifa for financing all the technical production of this book. We were fortunate to have the assistance of Mrs Genoveba Breitstein who was responsible for the typing of the book; Mrs Olga Sagi who was responsible for the English editing and Mrs Shoshi Mansfeld who (re)produced all the graphic material appearing in some of the chapters. We extend our special thanks to these three highly professional and efficient ladies.

References

Orlando Sentinel (1995). Florida sees sharp drop in visits from foreign tourists. January 13: B1 – B4.

Part 1

Tourism and crime

1 Theoretical aspects of crime as they impact the tourism industry

P. TARLOW AND M. MUEHSAM

Driving across the state of Florida, visitors and local citizens alike daily see signs advising motorists that there are 24-hour armed guards at almost every state rest stop. Those viewing the guards remember a simpler age, when 24-hour protection at public rest areas was never even considered, and cannot help but agree with the Italian commentator, Giuseppe Sacco, who wrote that the last decades of the 20th century have manifested the "vietnamization" of crime (Eco, 1983: 76—7) where decentralized cities become centers for violence. Although international writers have long classified the United States as a dangerous place, never before has violence against visitors created such consternation and world-wide publicity as it has in the 1990s. This concern, placed in a desert-like theoretical gap, cries out for attention by both tourism academics and tourism practitioners. Crimes against tourists have received international attention and put the travel industry in a position of allocating its scarce resources to convince tourists that it is safe to travel. Sociologically, we may state that there are two broad categories of crimes which affect the tourist: (1) planned crimes such as terrorism, illustrated by the hijacking of international airline flights and the bombing of tourism sites such as the Uffizi Gallery in Florence, Italy and (2) crimes of opportunity such as those which have occurred in New York, Washington DC, and Florida. In the former case, the perpetrator seeks to make a statement through the use of violence; in the latter, the crime occurs against an unknown victim as a means by which the criminal gains some form of gratification: be that gratification psychological, sexual, or economic (Katz, 1992). Actions against tourists in the United States, Europe, Latin America, Africa, and Asia both of a collective nature such as terrorism and of an individualistic—opportunistic nature have caused concern not only throughout the tourism/visitor industry but also within the halls of government throughout the world. Violence in the United States has reached the level about which the French social commentator, often hailed as the father of postmodernism, Jean Baudrillard, has stated that America is a land where "everything is charged with somnambulic violence and you must avoid contact to escape its potential discharge" (Baudrillard, 1988: 60). Furthermore, tourism ironically suffers from "crimes in the present" while incorporating as attractions "crimes of the past." To illustrate this point, we offer as an example of such an incorporation of "crimes of the past" the city of Waxahachie, Texas. To the delight of tourists from around the world, the Bonnie and

Tourism, Crime and International Security Issues, edited by
A. Pizam and Y. Mansfeld. © 1996 John Wiley & Sons Ltd.

Clyde bank hold-ups are annually "re-enacted" during the city's Gingerbread Festival (Waxahachie, Texas Convention & Visitors Bureau). Thus, crime itself becomes a form of tourism (Rojek, 1993: 137−45).

What has caused the news media and government agencies to focus so much attention onto this one aspect of crime? One is tempted to state that it is merely a question of economics. Tourism is by most accounts the world's largest peacetime industry (Tarlow and Muehsam, 1992: 28). On the other hand, a social−psychological perspective would be to view travel as "the industry that binds people together." In this necessarily interconnected and travel-dependent world (Giddens, 1990), crimes against travelers touch many more people than just the injured party and his/her family. To be unable to travel safely means that families are torn asunder; interurban, state or national commerce is in peril; and local feelings of claustrophobia on both the micro and macro levels begin to emerge. Media experts may claim that crimes against tourists sell and that the more crimes are reported the more they move to center stage as state, national and international issues. For example, although the O.J. Simpson case is not an act against tourists, it does serve as an example of being as much a media event as a murder trial.

Although crimes against tourists seem to affect the perception of safety of almost everyone who travels, crimes against tourists or visitors are not new. Reaching back to Biblical days we may assume that there were always some people who were willing or desirous of taking advantage of the visitor (*Genesis* 19). Taking unfair advantage of tourists, such as raising the price of an item under the assumption that the tourist knew no better, was so common that the English language coined the term "tourist- trap." In earlier times, travelers needed to fear pirates and kidnappers. To travel then was work, so much so that English derives the word "travel" from the French word "travail" which originates in the Latin noun "tripalium," — a three-stake instrument used for torture (Mish, 1993: 1257). In a like manner, there are few who do not know that airports, bus stations, amusement parks or museums can be fertile ground for crimes of opportunity such as pickpocketing. These institutionalized crimes of the past were considered part and parcel of travel. Travel was known to be hard and risky, and a robbery, a stage-coach hold-up, or even a mugging was more often than not taken as part of the price for adventure (Eco, 1983: 79).

This chapter first focuses on some of the major sociological theories that may lead to one explanation of crime in tourism. We use the United States as a paradigm, assuming that its problems are either representative of other developed nations' problems or foreshadow problems that are yet to come. To quote Baudrillard: "Americans are not wrong in their idyllic conviction that they are the center of the world . . . the absolute model for everyone" (Baudrillard, 1988: 77). This chapter points to the theoretical advantages and problems in explaining the special relationship between crime and tourism. We examine how different theoretical designs raise questions and issues such as: (1) are there ways that criminals act against tourism installations that differ from the way they act against the general public? (2) who gains and loses from these crimes? and (3) does publicity incite further acts of violence? We then provide our own theoretical design which links the various sociological theories already discussed into a theory concerning the special relationship between crime and tourism.

Despite the prominent publicity given to acts of terrorism or criminal acts against individual tourists, little theoretical work has been generated to explain this new−old form of violence. Pizam has noted: "only a small number of empirical studies have explored the relationship between tourism and crime" (Pizam, 1982: 7−10). Even fewer sociological theorists have entered into this theoretical desert on the interaction between these two phenomena. Classical (19th−20th) turn-of-the-century social theorists do not directly address the issues of crime and tourism, nor do they distinguish among deviant actions taken randomly against unknown victims, actions taken against a specific person, and acts of violence against one or more people for political purposes.

Although there is a paucity of theoretical literature and research concerning the relationship between crime and tourism, the study of crime and deviance has long fascinated and occupied sociologists. During sociology's nascent period, often called the *fin de siècle*, sociologists within Europe and the United States began to view deviance as an unavoidable part of social life. For example, in writing about and citing from (David) Emile Durkheim's work, Robert A. Jones has stated:

> . . . Durkheim observed, crime exists in all societies of all kinds, and, despite centuries of effort at its annihilation, has rather increased with the growth of civilization; thus, "there is no phenomenon which represents more incontrovertibly all the symptoms of normality, since it appears to be closely bound up with the conditions of a collective life" (Jones, 1986).

The Durkheimian scholar, Stjepan Mestrovic, expands the concepts of Sacco's vietnamization of crime when he quotes Durkheim to illustrate that civilization is concentrated in the great cities, and similarly crime and suicide are concentrated in urban areas:

> the average number of suicides, of crimes of all sorts, can effectively serve to mark the intensity of immorality in a given society. If we make this experiment, it does not turn out creditably for civilization, for the number of these morbid phenomena seems to increase as the arts, sciences, and industry progress (Mestrovic, 1991: 191).

What was true in Europe was to a great measure also true in the United States. Scull has stated that: "In the very earliest years of American Sociology, the study of deviance and its linkages with efforts at social control occupied a central place, being seen as theoretically and empirically fundamental to the future development of the discipline" (Scull, 1988: 667−8). Studies of crime and deviance intensified in the United States in the early 20th century with the rise of the Chicago School of Sociology, and these studies often paralleled the sociological work done in Europe. Thus, Rosenberg et al. (1982: 7) write: "Like Durkheim, members of the Chicago school . . . looked upon deviance as a natural phenomenon. Thus it [deviance] was to be 'appreciated' rather than corrected." Under the scrutiny of classical urban sociologists, such as Park and Burges, the city of Chicago was treated as a "laboratory of study" (Park and Burges, 1969). The sociologist and philosopher Georg Simmel, writing on urban life and crime, influenced the Chicago School as well as an entire generation of critical theorists (Simmel, 1971). Urban sociologists wanted to understand how so many people could live together, what social controls governed them and how deviance from that control was tolerated or punished. In the middle part of the 20th century, pure functionalist sociologists such as Robert Merton sought to demonstrate how "the patently negative (effects of deviance) was secretly a positive glue holding the social order together" (Scull, 1988: 675).

These explanations of deviance as given above do little, however, to explain the special significance between crime and tourism, nor do they offer a formula for how a tourism industry faced with world-wide communication of news stories handles criminal acts that can destroy that industry. Furthermore, taking a "fatalistic" approach to crime, many of these theories offer little solace to the victim.

Marxists or, as they often are called, "conflict theorists," provide a different perspective. Under the assumption that the majority of violent crime is committed by those in the lower classes, conflict theorists assume that crime is a manifestation of class frustration. Due to society's maldistribution of wealth, crime is an outgrowth of bourgeois greed and the mimicking of that greed by those in the lower classes. Worsley has written about Marx:

> To Marx, the relationship between employer and workers, then, was by no means one of mutual advantage or of complementary "contribution" to a joint activity. All workers . . . were exploited and therefore constituted a category: a social class of exploited producers (Worsley, 1982: 44).

Under such a scenario, it is not the underclass which is committing the crime, but rather due to that class's suffering from economic exploitation and social frustration, crime occurs as an almost "Robin Hood" societal correction factor. Conflict theorists, therefore, posit that the upper classes pass laws that act as: "a means for protecting group rights, privileges, and interests" (Rosenberg et al., 1982: 10). Indeed, Marxists contend that crime in a capitalistic society creates fear, especially among members of the bourgeoisie, of bodily harm and of economic loss. Furthermore, for Marxists, crime symbolizes the ephemerality of a consumer society (Worsley, 1982). A Marxist analysis of crime in tourism is that tourism, being a visible form of the consumer society's ephemeralism, constantly irritates the proletariat and eventually leads to a working-class reaction which the bourgeoisie defines as crime. Conflict theory, although attractive to some because it is sympathetic to the plight of the underclasses, suffers from tautological problems in which victims such as tourists are now held accountable for their victimization. Not all victims are part of the "bourgeois class" who freely flaunt their unfairly gained wealth nor are all victimizers necessarily acting out hostility toward an unjust ruling oligarchy. In fact, in the United States there is a large number of criminals who commit crimes against those in the "proletarian class."

The celebrated turn-of-the-century socio-economist Thorstein Veblen is helpful in translating Marxist thought and provides a bridge between classical theory and a sociology of crime and tourism (Riesman, 1953). For example, in writing about the conspicuous consumption of goods as promoted in a capitalist society, Veblen holds that as wealth increases some people will move to the top of society, in the end developing a new barbarian society in which the wealthiest do nothing, produce nothing and live from the gleanings of those whom they repress. Thus, in analyzing male domination of women and children Veblen has stated:

> unproductive consumption of goods is honorable, primarily as a mark of prowess and a prerequisite of human dignity; secondarily it becomes substantially honorable in itself, especially the consumption of the more desirable things. The consumption of choice articles of food, and frequently also of rare articles of adornment, becomes

tabu [sic] to the women and children; and if there is a base (servile) class of men, the tabu holds for them (Veblen, 1953: 61).

In the introduction to Veblen's *Theory of the Leisure Class*, C. Wright Mills notes that Veblen's theories seem to be opposed to much of the Protestant work ethic (Veblen, 1953: XV). Yet a closer examination of Veblen's writing demonstrates that quite the opposite may be the case. We suggest that Veblen is neither opposed to labor nor to the accumulation of goods resulting from labor. Instead Veblen opposes an aristocratic sense of leisure in which the many serve the few. For example, Veblen writes: "it has already been remarked that the term 'leisure' as here used, does not connote indolence or quiescence. What it connotes is non-productivity (1) from a sense of the unworthiness of productive work, (2) as an evidence of pecuniary ability to afford a life of idleness" (Veblen, 1953: 46). It is unclear, however, where the tourist industry, working to provide recreation and leisure to the many fits into Veblen's scheme (Rojek, 1990: 7−20; Rojek and Turner, 1993). Is the leisure industry nothing more than the merging of Marxian thought with Veblen's ideas? Under that scenario we may ask if tourism is not an industry where the proletariat works at poor-paying professions, such as waiters or airline flight attendants, so as to provide the luxury of leisure to those who exploit them by enticing the proletariat's labor through a false-consciousness called "glamor." Another interpretation of Veblen is that today's leisure industry has little to do with the aristocracy of leisure but rather serves as a necessary psychological opportunity for renewal to allow for efficient production. David Riesman, in writing about Veblen , has suggested that the leisure industry is now one of the major motors that drives the economy and therefore not idleness. According to Riesman:

> The possibility that the industries and services catering to leisure would one day be scanned hopefully for the signs of a new product. To throw into a Keynesian multiplier as a pump-primer of capital goods expenditure never occurred to him [Veblen] — and who, indeed, could have foreseen the abundance with which America would be showered in the twentieth century? The role of the radio, the pleasure car, television, the movies, the beauty parlor in sustaining American income levels has still not been fully grasped (Riesman, 1953: 178).

Is the travel and leisure industry then a world in which some work hard so that many can enjoy, or is it a necessary part of modern capitalism? Certainly, it can be argued that in the developed nations of the latter half of the 20th century one does not need to be rich to have a vacation, and often vacations are provided as one of the benefits of work. Veblen's work inspires the student of crime and tourism to ask a number of key questions. Does tourism act as a "Barbarian bait" for criminals? Do these people see tourists as individuals who have too much leisure, too much money and who freely flaunt their wealth? If so, does the criminal who gazes on the tourist see him/her as a mere Barbarian?

Toward the latter half of the 20th century the work of Frank Tannenbaum began to be developed as "labeling theory." Tannenbaum stated that: "the process of making the criminal ... is a process of tagging, defining, identifying, segregating, describing, emphasizing, making conscious, and self-conscious; it becomes a way of stimulating, suggesting, emphasizing, and evoking the very traits that are complained of " (Rosenberg et al., 1982: 9−10). Using this theoretical approach some people are almost forced to be deviant because they are so "labeled." This theoretical approach can be helpful in thinking about mass killings used as a political weapon. However, once again, the theory may fall into tautological error and leaves little room for any form of individual voluntary decision process.

Controlologists claim that crime is not as much a function of the criminal personality as it is a function of changes in law enforcement procedures. For example, Ditton has written: "Control rather than 'crime' is the vital element . . . the rise or fall in crime rates have to be sought elsewhere than in the motives and intentions of those eventually called 'criminal'" (Ditton, 1979). Controlologists argue that for political or economic reasons, police at times become stricter, judicial attitudes harden and new legislation develops that turns previous standards into deviant behavior. Under this scenario, the media play a vital role. It is the media that either draw attention to crime or choose not to report it, thus influencing public pressure for greater or lesser control of "deviant" elements within society.

Prior to examining the writings of the postmodernists, we examine the work of several other classical social thinkers whose work, although not directly related to the issue of crime and tourism, will aid in the construction of our theoretical design.

The work of the German 19th-century student of society, Ferdinand Tönnies, complements much of the sociology of the *fin de siècle* period and serves as one of the pillars of the postmodernist sense of alienation. Tönnies asserted that societies pass through two stages of inter-human associations, one he called *Gemeinschaft* or a social unit that is *sui generis* in nature and often places its members in a variety of differing roles. An example of a pure *Gemeinschaft* association would be being born into a rural farm family, where the family members must work and play together. On the other hand a *Gesellschaft* association is contractual in nature and often exists because a number of individuals have banded together for a particular purpose. An athletic team composed of people who see each other only for the purpose of practicing their sport is an example of a pure *Gesellschaft* association. Tönnies did not necessarily view this inevitable development as 'progress.' Tönnies then argues that as societies become more complex they move from a *Gemeinschaft* to a *Gesellschaft* society (Pappenheim, 1959: 67). Pappenheim develops Tönnies' pessimistic *Weltanschauung* when he writes:

> So deep is the separation between man and man in *Gesellschaft* that "everybody is by himself and isolated, and there exists a condition of tension against all others." Thus *Gesellschaft* becomes a social world in which latent hostility and potential war are inherent in the relationship of one to another (Pappenheim, 1959: 67).

Tönnies provides us with several major tourism dilemmas. If societies which reach greater levels of *Gesellschaft* experience greater amounts of alienation, violence and uncaring, then is not the potential for violence against those with whom the host society has neither a *Gemeinschaft* relationship nor the collective memory of such a relationship ever increasing? Tönnies asserts that those who live in an industrially developed or modern Westernized society function in a world of tension and latent hostility. Therefore, as a society enters into a postmodern state of hyperreality we may predict that its levels of violence are likely to increase; and simultaneously its sense of shame for committing that act of violence is likely to decrease or be open to easy rationalizations. Lastly, it should not be overlooked that there is a strong affinity between the ideas expressed in Tönnies and those expressed by Marx. In analyzing this interrelationship of ideas, Pappenheim has written:

> we believe that the strongest likeness between the two writers lies in their treatment of
> the structure of modern society . . . [Marx] also uses it [capitalistic society] to describe
> the structure of a social order in which the strong communal organization of previous
> society — for example, the tribal communities or medieval towns — no longer exists.
> In such societies individuals have become so separated and isolated that they establish
> contact only when they can use each other as a means to particular ends: bonds
> between human beings are supplanted by useful associations not of whole persons but
> of particularized individuals (Pappenheim, 1959: 81).

The student of tourism cannot help but notice many of the aspects of modern tourism in
the words cited above. Perhaps no one is as separated from the host society as a tourist,
and students of tourism science know all too well that the relationship between a tourist
and a local person is, in most cases, only for utilitarian purposes. In such a world, it
should not surprise tourism officials that it may be easier for criminals to depersonalize
unsuspecting tourists and thus harm them than to depersonalize someone within the
victimizer's own society.

Bridging the sociological spectrum by uniting classical theory with aspects of
postmodernism is the work of Stjepan Mestrovic. Like Tönnies, Mestrovic's work does
not speak directly to the issue of crime and tourism. Yet, just as in the case of Tönnies,
Mestrovic develops a theoretical design that adds insights and sagacity to our problem.
Mestrovic presents the case that it is our understanding of the emotions or cultural base of
a society, which he calls "the heart," rather than the empirical statistics of a society,
called by him "the mind," that provides the theoretical insights necessary to understand a
societal problem. In explaining what we call Mestrovic's "classical yet post-positivistic"
methodological approach to his analysis of the Balkans, he has written:

> Theory was used [by the founding fathers of sociology] as a context for the
> interpretation of social reality, not as the basis for the generation of hypotheses to be
> falsified . . . the positivistic program cannot give a final account or explanation of any
> phenomenon because its finds are contingent and subject to being proved false . . .
> Such assumptions are of little use . . . to understand . . . what is occurring . . . or what
> the future might hold in store (Mestrovic, 1993: 15).

Mestrovic argues along with Spengler, Sorokin, and Toynbee that there is a violent
legacy left over from the 19th century that permeates Western society (Mestrovic, 1993:
9). He then agrees with such postmodernists as Umberto Eco or Jean Baudrillard and with
cultural sociologists such as Daniel Bell or James Q. Wilson. For example, few will
disagree with Eco when he writes of the legacy of insecurity found in New York City:

> Insecurity is a key word: . . . In the Middle Ages a wanderer in the woods at night saw
> them peopled with maleficent presences; one did not lightly venture beyond the town
> . . . This condition is close to that of the white middle-class inhabitant of New York,
> who doesn't set foot in Central Park after five in the afternoon or who makes sure not
> to get off the subway in Harlem . . . (Eco, 1983: 79).

Mestrovic, in citing both Baudrillard and Tocqueville in describing the United States,
develops what we call a "terra-duplex." In other words, there is a good and bad United
States of America: the USA of culture, of scientific achievement and of freedom; and the
USA of racism, of violence and of uncontrollable capitalist selfishness and greed
(Mestrovic, 1993: 12). This terra-duplex is not far from the analyses of Bell or Wilson.

For example, Bell has written about the 20th century's fascination with marketing: "a hedonistic age is a marketing age, defined by the fact that knowledge becomes coded in messages organized as formulas, slogans, and binary distinctions" (Bell, 1976: 73). Bell asserts that within American urban culture there has been an eclipse of distance between the good and the bad, crime and honesty, morality and responsibility in which the words of the *Book of Judges*: " יעשה בעיניו הישר איש [each man would do that which was right in his own eyes]" (The *Book of Judges* 21: 25). This verse is not far from the thoughts of James Q. Wilson. Wilson contends that without a moral sense society soon falls apart:

> Having thought about the matter [rising crime rates] for many years, I can find no complete explanation for the worldwide increase in crime rates that does not assign an important role to a profound cultural shift in the strength of either social constraints or internal conscience or both, and I can find no complete explanation of that cultural shift that does not implicate to some important degree our convictions about the sources and importance of the moral sentiments (Wilson, 1993: 9).

Interpreting Mestrovic through the prism of these other social thinkers, it would appear that violence forms one of the "habits of the American heart." In other words, in citing William James' essay on habit, Mestrovic implies that although there are many personality types within any society, certain national characteristics dominate and form not only a nation's civic religion but also its civic shame. Mestrovic seems to connote that the collective conscience takes hold even as the population experiences modernistic changes. He writes:

> William James reminds us that without force of habit, anarchy and chaos would rule the social world . . . Without the conservative force of habits, even the modernist project, the Enlightenment, and the principles of liberal democracy could not exist, for these phenomena, like all others, are maintained by habits and are not calculated rationally and anew with each passing event (Mestrovic, 1993: 17).

If that concept is true, then juxtaposing Baudrillard's postmodern analysis with Mestrovic's "habits of the heart" reveals a schizophrenic nature within the American national character. For example, according to Baudrillard: "we shall never resolve the enigma of the relationship between the negative foundation of greatness and that greatness itself. America is powerful and original; America is violent and abominable . . . This is a world that has shown irrepressible development of equality, banality and indifference" (Baudrillard, 1988: 88, 89). Viewing this statement in the light of Mestrovic's ideas leads us to expect a nation of anomic mobility in which we should expect to live with an ever increasing amount of crime towards those who are least rooted within society, and one of these major transient populations is: the tourist.

The last major theoretical ingredient that will be used for our development of a sociological theoretical basis of crime in tourism comes from the world of postmodernism. Postmodernism is a theory/style most typical of the arts. However, starting in the 1980s we can trace the seepage of postmodernistic techniques into tourism science. We have already mentioned the work of Baudrillard and Eco. These two postmodernist writers, although not tourism scholars, offer insights into the question of crime in tourism. Their work lays the foundation for the work of both Chris Rojek and John Urry: tourism scholars who have adapted the postmodernist genre to tourism science. By examining these latter scholars' work we can apply their ideas to the construction of a sociological theory that explains, at least in part, the phenomenon of crimes against tourists. Postmodernism, as first developed in the arts, maintains that seeing should not always be believing, that things are not what they seem, and that positivistic methodologies are not always the most useful of tools in analyzing the world (Roseman, 1990). Postmodernists create a distinction between the "modern" world in which scholars develop clear and precise categories in the best Cartesian sense and the postmodern world in which these categories are blurred. Recently, tourism scientists have begun to assimilate this postmodernist idea and incorporate its principles into their discipline. Rojek perhaps demonstrates this process of de-differentiation best when he asserts:

> Postmodernists speak of the generalized 'de-differentiation' of Modernist categories . . . De-differentiation may be formally defined as a condition in which former social, economic, and political distinctions cease to obtain . . . the Cartesian separation of body and mind ceases to hold good . . . the division between work and leisure is no longer clear-cut; in short, the divisions which gave stability to the Modernist order of things seem to be untenable — they do not correspond with people's actual experience of things (Rojek, 1993: 4–5).

Postmodernism then recognizes that the blurring of categories in a world of de-differentiation theory is a major help in our understanding of crime in tourism. Urry's academic work is most useful in this area, stating that: "postmodernism problematises the distinction between representations and reality . . ." (Urry, 1990: 85). Urry quotes Lash in stating: "modernism conceives of representations as being problematic whereas postmodernism problematises reality" (Urry, 1990: 85). Moving directly toward an analysis of tourism, Urry contends that tourism lives in a postmodern paradigm; it emphasizes a "combination of the visual, the aesthetic, and the popular" (Urry, 1990: 87). Furthermore, Urry cites the blurring of social and economic classes causing a paradigm shift from a life based on morality, fear, and duty to one of fun. Urry bolsters this point by quoting Bourdieu who, in writing of the change in middle class values, declares that their new morality:

> urges a morality of pleasure as duty. This doctrine makes it a failure, a threat to self-esteem, not to "have fun" . . . Pleasure is not only permitted but demanded, on ethical as much as on scientific grounds. The fear of not getting enough pleasure . . . is combined with the search for self-expression and "bodily expression and for communication with others" (1984: 367) (Urry, 1990: 90).

If tourism is based on a postmodernist paradigm in which the real merges with the make-believe, brochures describe what we would like to believe rather than what in reality does exist, then in a post-tourism age we move to the realm of dreams. From creating "dreams," it is not hard to jump to "nightmares."

We now argue that crime in tourism is just one more component, although it may be seen as the coin's flip side, of a postmodern paradigm. Assuming that Mestrovic's reading of Tocqueville is correct: that nations do have "habits of the heart" and that Eco and Baudrillard are correct in their viewing of violence as one component of the American historical experience, then following the process of dialectical materialism developed by the 19th-century German philosopher G.W. Hegel, one outcome in the tourist's "search for fun" is the criminal realization of the "fun of crime" (Brinton et al., 1964: 537).

We then propose the following theoretical paradigm for crime and tourism. Tourism is an industry that according to writers such as Rojek and Urry not only blurs reality but emphasizes in Veblen's term, a "barbaric culture" or in Bell's terms, a "hedonistic culture." The tourist travels so as to merge the habitual with the unique. His/her trip must produce dreams and offer the opportunity to share those dreams. In this world of make-believe a number of social phenomena relating to crime as it concerns the tourist, the tourism industry and/or the criminal occur.

Concerning the individual tourist we may postulate that:

- Tourists often let down their guard making them easy prey for criminals;
- Tourists will often de-differentiate neighborhoods, thus entering into areas in which locals might dare not go;
- Tourists may often confuse good luck with caution or proper planning. Thus, when tourists pass on their travel tales to their relatives and friends, unrealized risks that do not result in dire consequences by pure chance, may influence others to try the same. Others who repeat these risks may not be fortunate enough to escape unscathed.

In a like manner, we contend that the industry has seduced itself by the gods of postmodernism:

- Transportation terminals, hotels, and restaurants have worked so hard at creating a fantasy that often the industry itself begins to believe only what is in its own promotional materials, and thereby loses its ability to create clear and precise categories;
- The industry by successfully promoting itself implicitly invites criminals to take advantage of what the criminal may perceive to be fertile fields of opportunities;
- If authors such as Baudrillard and Eco are correct, that there is a violent side of the United States' society, then to ignore this aspect of American society is to create the potentially opposite effect to what the tourism industry desires, ie, the tourist's dreams of fun may turn into the nightmare of violence.

A theory that encompasses the "habits of the heart" with postmodernism must also look at the perpetrator of the violence. Although there is a multitude of reasons for and explanations of why human beings choose to be hurtful to each other, certain commonalities exist between crimes committed against masses of people for political or economic reasons, and crimes of opportunity committed by individuals. Basing our assessment of criminal elements on classical and postmodernist theories we suggest the following:

- *Vis-à-vis* tourism, criminals experience reality loss. With the blurring of distinctions it is safe to posit that, at least some perpetrators of violence may no longer distinguish clear moral lines. One need only watch day-time television to note the many gang members who testify to the fact that they enjoy killing. The recent upsurge in gang initiation rites in which an innocent victim must be "sacrificed" so that the "pledge" can obtain full gang membership is testimony to the blurring that has occurred.

- Using Hegel as a model we can see violence as the counter-reaction (antithesis) of the search for security. In a world in which the tourist is placed into an almost sterilized environment (eg, theme parks) can we not expect that, using Durkheim's anomie as our guide, at least a portion of the population will choose the non-normative side of safety plus sterility and turn to the violent habits of American society?

- Violence produces a "gaze." Urry has proposed that an underlying factor of post-tourism is the "gaze" (Urry, 1990: 1 – 15). We want people to see us "gaze" at sites and/or doing actions. We suggest that violence is the negative aspect of that "gaze." It provides the crime's perpetrator with a way of being seen, of gaining publicity and in the case of terrorist acts against tourism, of turning the world into a stage upon which one can state one's cause.

- Tourism produces anger or jealousy among those in the economic underclasses. Tourism as a non-essential use of income has come to symbolize wealth, carefreeness and the eternal search for fun. Pertaining to economic crimes, criminals may view hotels, transportation hubs or amusement centres as places that attract people with high incomes. Criminals may even justify their actions by rationalizing that the tourist's loss can easily be recovered or that they need the money more than the victimized tourist.

- When we analyze Bourdieu's statement that the new morality demands a life of fun through the blurring of postmodernism, we can argue that in a world where moral lines are no longer stringent, some elements in society will view murder as a form of fun. Tourists having predictable travel patterns become easy targets for crime. Furthermore, the media's penchant to publicize crimes against tourists adds a sense of the "gaze."

The tourism industry has been criticized for having entered into the world of the "Mad Hatter" where it seeks to profit from violence committed either in ages past and/or to someone else, while it seeks to protect present-day tourists from the violence that surrounds them. Tourism has turned some aspects of "violence into tourism sites." Examples of this convergence abound. Battle sites such as Vicksburg, Mississippi and Gettysburg, Pennsylvania serve as examples of large-scale violence and D-Day's 50th anniversary became a major "tourist event." Tours of Harlem merge poverty with violence, and the Waco, Texas Convention and Visitor Bureau reports a major upsurge in visits since the siege at Mt. Carmel and the burning of the Branch Davidian complex. The site of the personal/national tragedy of Kennedy's assassination in Dallas has been cleaned up, anesthetized and museumized so that the horror of the assassination is now turned into an audio-visual history spectacle with tourists visiting the spot from around the world.

Being a postmodern industry, where reality and dreams merge, the industry must be careful not to allow America's violent side to deface its dreamlike side. Too many precautions can scare tourists and destroy the illusion upon which the industry lives. Tourism is then on the horns of a dilemma. The price for creating a "positive non-reality" is that some will choose a "negative non-reality." Furthermore, the dream vacation is one of the threads woven into the fabric of American socio-economy. Without the dream most people's work becomes mere drudgery; with the dream our weeks of labor are sweetened with the image of palm trees, beautiful mountains, or adventure. Tourism's challenge will be to create enough safety factors that its nightmare of random violence against innocent vacationers does not destroy the dreams of the many.

References

Baudrillard, J. (1988). *America*, London: Verso, translation.
Bell, D. (1976). *The Cultural Contradictions of Capitalism*. New York: Basic Books: 73.
Book of Judges, 21: 25.
Brinton, C., Christopher, J. and Wolff, R. (1964). *Civilization in the West*. Englewood Cliffs, Prentice-Hall: 537.
Ditton, J. (1979). *Controlology: Beyond the New Criminology*. London: The Macmillan Press.
Eco, U. (1983). *Travels in Hyperreality*. San Diego: Harcourt Brace & Company.
Genesis, 19.
Giddens, A. (1990). *The Consequences of Modernity*. Stanford: Stanford University Press.
Jones, R.A. (1986). *Emile Durkheim*. Newbury Park: Sage.
Katz, J. (1992). *The Seduction of Crime*. New York: Basic Books.
Mestrovic, S.G. (1991). *The Coming Fin de Siècle*. London: Routledge.
Mestrovic, S. (1993). *Habits of the Balkan Heart*, College Station, TX: Texas A&M Press.
Mish, F.C. (ed.) (1993). *The Merriam Webster's Collegiate Dictionary*, Tenth Edition. Springfield, MA: Merriam-Webster.
Pappenheim, F. (1959). *The Alienation of Modern Man*. New York: First Modern Reader Paperbacks.
Park, R. and Burges, E. (1969). *Introduction to the Science of Sociology*. Chicago: University of Chicago Press.
Pizam, A. (1982). Tourism and crime: Is there a relationship? *Journal of Travel Research*, **20** (3): 7−10.
Riesman, David (1953). *Thorstein Veblen*. New York: Charles Scribner & Sons.
Rojek, C. (1990). Baudrillard and leisure. *Leisure Studies* **9** (1): 7−20.
Rojek, C. (1993). *Ways of Escape*. London: The Macmillan Press.
Rojek, C. and Turner, B.S. (1993). *Forget Baudrillard?* London: Routledge.
Roseman, P. (1990). *Postmodernism and the Social Sciences*. Princeton: Princeton University Press.
Rosenberg, M.M., Stebbins, R. and Turowetz, A. (1982). *The Sociology of Deviance*. New York: St. Martin's Press.
Scull, A.T. (1988). Deviance and social control. In Smelser, J. (ed.), *Handbook of Sociology*. Newbury Park: Sage.
Simmel, G. (1971). *Individuality and its Social Forms*. Chicago: University of Chicago Press.
Tarlow, P. and Muehsam, M. (1992). Wide horizons: Travel and tourism in the coming decades. *The Futurist*, **26** (5): 28.
Urry, J. (1990). *The Tourist Gaze*. London: Sage.
Veblen, T. (1953). *The Theory of the Leisure Class*, 7th edition, New American Library. New York: The Macmillan Press.
Wilson, J.Q. (1993). *The Moral Sense*. New York: The Free Press: 9.
Worsley, P. (1982). *Marx and Marxism*. Chester (UK): Ellis Horword Ltd.

2 The deviant tourist and the crimogenic place — the case of the tourist and the New Zealand prostitute

CHRIS RYAN AND RACHAEL KINDER

Introduction

This chapter differs from others in this book. Rather than seeking to examine the impact of crime and violence upon tourism, it seeks to explore what is termed deviant tourist behavior and what it might state about society. In short, it reverses the normal direction of, if not causality, then direction of perspective. If there is a "tourist gaze," then it is the "gaze" that reveals deficiencies in "normal," non-touristic life. Additionally, this chapter is about tourists as clients of prostitutes. At first sight such an activity might be thought to have some relation to other forms of deviant tourist behavior such as being drunk or taking drugs. All such tourists might not be defined as criminals, might not be victims of criminals but are operating at the fuzzy edge of criminality in such a way as to be potentially vulnerable to either criminal or police action. It is a process of "marginality" that is being examined and the actors that permit it to happen.

There are a number of themes in this chapter. First, there is a discussion about what constitutes deviancy, both in the abstract and with reference to tourism. Second, and paradoxically, given that the tourists who use sex workers are defined as "marginal" if not actually deviant, a theme emerges that tourist usage of prostitutes is not uncommon. Third, it is argued that tourism creates an opportunity, and an opportunity model is suggested; and fourth, some aspects of the crimogenic place are considered.

The tourist as a deviant — difficulties of definition

There are many theories of motivation and subsequent behavior that locate the sources of tourist needs within the mainstream of society. For example, Mill and Morrison (1985) adopt the marketing theories of Howard and Sheth (1969) where tourist preferences are determined by a social framework engendered by social class, life-cycle and past experiences. Woodside and MacDonald (1993) develop a systems framework of eight choice sets emanating from four principal nodal starting points: namely (a) levels of

Tourism, Crime and International Security Issues, edited by
A. Pizam and Y. Mansfeld. © 1996 John Wiley & Sons Ltd.

income and education; (b) family, friends and social groups; (c) marketing influences and (d) past experience. These, and many other writers, adopt the stance that tourist experience is understood by reference to wider social forces. Thus, it becomes possible for Krippendorf (1987) to note that "sick societies create sick tourists" as he describes an anomic society creating little more than escape needs within tourists.

While not denying that these wider social parameters influence and determine the motivations, goals and needs of tourists, here it is argued that it is perhaps not so much a case of society determining tourist actions, but rather tourist behavior illustrating themes inherent in the wider society. Tourism itself can be regarded as a deviant act as it consists of a series of behavior patterns not normally exhibited by individuals for much of their daily life, if deviancy is simplistically defined as behavior that differs from the norm. However, like the Russian dolls where layer after layer is peeled away to reveal but another doll, so too various forms of deviant behavior can be located one within another. If tourism is regarded as deviant behavior, what then is the deviant tourist? Ryan (1993) notes that both crime and tourism are deviant behaviors — the difference being that crime is not socially tolerated but tourism is. And this tolerance extends to many behaviors which, in a non-tourist context, would be termed socially intolerable. Hence, it might be argued, a matrix of relationships might exist wherein tourists initiate a range of anti-social but tolerated behaviors from drunkenness to patronage of criminal activities such as drug taking (Ryan, 1993). If a behavior is tolerated, however, can it be said to be deviant?

A number of approaches to deviance exist, but one important approach for this chapter is the ethnomethodological perspective where it is argued that marginality imposes an awareness of commonplace arrangements. Downes and Rock (1988) comment that:

> It has been remarked that phenomenological sociology argues that society can be analysed only as a set of experiences, that experiences are experiences by consciousness, and that order is built on a vital framework of categorization . . . social order is a fragile human accomplishment achieved in the face of meaninglessness (1988: 202).

And further:

> Those who deny or defy important separations and definitions within society do more than merely break a rule. They may be thought to challenge the very legitimacy and structure of order, becoming agents or instances of chaos (1988: 203).

In this chapter, the deviant/marginal tourist is the one who breaks the unwritten rules, and it is this rule-breaking that is the essence of much that is marginal or deviant. By an examination of the deviant, the unspoken conventions are challenged; and thus modes of unanalyzed behavior that form an unspoken consensus are illuminated. For example, the businessman can be said to operate at the margin of legality and what might be deemed to be "normal" behavior when, on a business trip, he uses an escort agency or visits a massage parlor. Depending on how the laws relating to prostitution are drawn up, entry into a parlor might not be illegal but having sex might be. On the other hand, sex with an "escort" in his hotel bedroom may not be illegal, but the hotelier might be subject to prosecution if the hotel is used for prostitution. An analysis of the motivation for sex by the businessman might reveal any number of reasons which say something about the roles of males within marriage, deficiencies in marriage, the sexual need of males or the use of economic power to ensure sexual gratification. The nature of the sexual act, which might include, for example, cross dressing or the services of a transsexual, also reveals aspects of behavior not "normally" considered. The lack of "normality" defines a "marginality" which helps in an analysis of that defined as "normal." As will become obvious, while the literature on "deviancy" provided a starting point for the analysis of the situation, increasingly it was felt that the concepts were inappropriate for the majority of activities where tourists are clients of sex workers. The term "marginality" is thought to be more appropriate for a number of reasons described below.

One problem with an argument based upon "deviance" is that it implies there is "one normal" society, and that is obviously not the case. It is not necessary to adopt a postmodernist perspective to argue that contemporary society is both individualistic and yet suffering from a crisis of identity. Society is complex and consists of many societies crowding upon each other. This is also true of tourism. The market has many products, from the eco-tourist to the sex tourist. If sex tourism is a product sold in an open market place, what then of a concept of deviancy? Perhaps, therefore, deviancy is characterized by ambiguity and uncertainty. Simmons (1965) indicates the diversity of social phenomena categorized as being deviant. Theories of deviancy abound, and many imply a normative approach. Thus, on the one hand, Becker (1963, 1974) is concerned with rates of deviant behavior, ie, a perception of broad, social norm breaking, whereas on the other hand, Sutherland (1956) is centered upon circumstances that create individuals as norm breakers. An empirical tradition might look at structures from a value-free position, but others argue that, in this subject, such an approach is deficient. For example, Becker (1963) asks, "whose side are we on?" Quinney (1977) develops an alternative perspective of deviancy based on concepts of power and conflict. Crime is that which conflicts with the interests of the dominant class, and such a definition helps formulate a social reality of crime.

However, are concepts of deviancy borrowed from studies of crime applicable to tourism? The concerns of this chapter are those of the individual tourist, and in that sense an approach based upon that of Sutherland is utilized. Indeed, we seek to examine characteristics of the tourist place that permit an opportunity for what is defined as "deviant behavior." But, examination of the "deviant tourist" poses a paradox in terms of Quinney's work, for the deviancy is not based upon the actions of someone deprived of power. The opposite is the case, for the deviant tourist is empowered by having sufficient income to spend on the exhibited behavior and by the very role of being a tourist. In the model advanced below, in Cohen's terms (Cohen, 1987), while not a victim of the law, neither is the tourist a protégé. The opening paragraphs described the deviant tourist behavior; they did not define it. Yet such behaviors are "deviant" in the sense that they do not represent the behavior of most tourists, even while they, in turn, deviate from their normal life-style. Nor do the actions of tourist drunkenness or patronage of prostitutes necessarily incur the penalties associated with such behaviors. Thus again, in Quinney's terms, the paradox of the "deviant" as a potential "victim" of law enforcement is inappropriate. The concept of deviancy when applied to such a tourist is thus problematical. Yet, even if enigmatic, the concept is still applicable in that it explains much about the nature of mainstream society. Ryan (1991, 1993) utilizes the terminology of irresponsible action, borrowing the concepts of Crompton (1979) that tourism is an escape from the responsibilities of daily life; but, as will be examined in more detail, the motivation of the business tourist who uses a sex worker may, or may not, include a sense of irresponsibility. Indeed, from the viewpoint of the marginal expressing a "truth" about normal "rules," that action can be deemed as being responsible. It acts as a proxy for the "one-night stand" which might threaten a marriage. The action of becoming a client of a sex worker can say much about male roles in society and the burdens placed upon marriage, males and females. The concept of irresponsibility helps little in understanding what at first sight appears to be a clear case of "deviancy." In the case of the business tourist who visits a sex worker while on a business trip, where is the deviancy? Does a visit exhibit deviancy in that the sexual demands made of the prostitute may not be those normally indulged in when involved in sex? Does the visit illustrate deviancy because the visit is seen as little more than "a perk" of the job and which, if thought of, creates feelings of guilt? Or is deviancy defined because the visit defines the norms of unsatisfactory marriages characterized by concealment of innermost needs, whether social or sexual? Or is deviancy defined by concepts of morality? Evidence would seem to suggest that patronage of a brothel is not simply motivated by a need for sex. In interviews for this chapter, one worker in a massage parlor, Louise, commented that a large proportion of clients came to spend a relaxing time, to talk and to escape tensions from work and home. McLeod (1982: 71) quotes Rosa as saying:

> I'd say 90% of men who come to see me are in control of other men all the time and they come to see me to get that burden of responsibility off them and put themselves in my hands and reverse the role.

A wish for concealment would appear to be a common characteristic of the tourist who indulges in this type of behavior. The tourist is enabled to act in this way because he is not at home. This is not to argue that drug taking, drunkenness, hooliganism and the other behaviors with which this chapter is concerned do not happen at the tourist's place of residence, but rather for some people the acts become associated with the circumstances of being a tourist. Travel frees the inhibition, even if it is uncertain if the actual tourist place permits the activity. Again to quote McLeod:

> Martin confined his visits to prostitutes to when he was on one of his frequent overseas business trips. "No, I only use them when I'm abroad. I'd ruin my career and my family, even in London!" (McLeod, 1982: 87).

Defining the concept of the deviant tourist is difficult. The deviant tourist might be defined as a tourist who not only engages in behavior which differs (deviates?) from his normal life-style but who wishes to conceal that behavior from others at his normal place of residence. Such an approach creates a distinction from someone who is deviant at his place of residence and who carries that deviant behavior into the holiday location. By this definition the football (soccer) hooligan who uses the events surrounding football matches as a catalyst for violent action, and who then travels to other matches and engages in similar behavior, is not a deviant tourist. The action is a continuation of that done at the place of residence, and furthermore, since status is gained from participation and acknowledgement by peers, the "tourist" behavior is not something inherent in the tourist experience.

So, various distinctions may be made between:

1. The marginal behavior is undertaken only when on a tourist trip — ie, the activity of being a tourist involves the risk of being deviant.
2. The marginal behavior is undertaken both at and away from home — in this case the action is simply re-located to a new destination. But the fact of being away from home may create new thrills, eg, more "daring" demands upon the prostitute or the thrill of attacking soccer hooligans on their "home patch."

The phenomenon is thus one which, on the whole, is recognized, but which defies definition. That, possibly, is the very nature of deviancy. It is relativistic and ambiguous, and the source of definition may not lie in the *behavior* being examined, but in the *reaction to the behavior*. Deviancy is thus a process of action and reaction. It is a process of individual intent but with social implications. Deviancy in the case of the tourist requiring sexual services can have many hues.

The implications of the demand for sexual services by the deviant tourist is well documented. Studies of the relationship between tourism and prostitution abound, even though the extent to which tourism promotes, encourages and facilitates the practice of prostitution is unclear. The above discussion on deviancy almost implies that if deviancy is in the eye of the beholder, then its consequences are comparatively minor. But that assumes, in the case of prostitution, that both parties to the transaction are equal and consenting partners. Indeed, there is a viewpoint that prostitution is a victimless crime, and that forms in part the case for decriminalization. Again, the argument is complex. From one perspective prostitution is concerned with the unequal economic power between the client and the provider. Within Western societies the working girl may "select" prostitution as a means of earning more than would otherwise be possible to support herself and/or her family. But discussions and reports with clients reveal that the client can feel "ripped off" as the experience is made to feel clinical, hurried and demeaning. Under such circumstances, the discussion of exploiter and exploited becomes less clear. Again, having sex with someone who is under age (however defined) is both exploitative and criminal but does not of itself mean that prostitution should not be decriminalized.

So, how might tourist deviancy/marginality be defined in this specific context? It would seem that there are a number of components involved. The act:

1. Is the one that operates at the fuzzy edge of legality;
2. Is one for which, while there may be limited opportunity at the usual place of residence, the fact of being a tourist creates greater opportunity;
3. Represents a small proportion of total tourist activity;
4. Is often concealed from significant others;
5. Is associated with a wide range of motivations and emotions, some of which may arouse feelings of guilt;
6. May well have social implications not considered by the tourist, yet which would be considered as criminal — eg, the patronage of a prostitute in a brothel where the woman is denied legal rights;
7. When analyzed, reveals much about mainstream conventions and norms.

While, in the literature the term "deviancy" is used to describe these behaviors, as has been noted, it is thought this term is, on the whole, inappropriate, and the term "marginal" is preferred.

The tourist as a client of sex workers

Velten and Kleiber (1992), in a study of 533 German clients of Berlin prostitutes, on the basis of factor analysis, categorized the needs for visiting sex workers as being sexual motives and social reasons. However, these two needs accounted for only 33 per cent of the variance. However, it is worth noting that they state:

> . . . the connection between a sexually unsatisfying partnership (48%) or the absence of one altogether (33.9%), and the seeking of a prostitute's services could not escape notice. In principle, a large number of men in the study (50.3%) actually wanted to live monogamously, which strongly suggests that the use of prostitutes services causes in these men conflicting feelings that they have difficulty coping with (Velten and Kleiber, 1992: 4–5).

Qualitative evidence based on conversations with prostitutes such as that of McLeod's, and in discussions with representatives of the New Zealand Prostitutes' Collective (NZPC), in the opinion of these authors, does question this finding. Many sex workers recognize the need for sex among their clients, and many reports exist of clients' statements of unsatisfactory sex at home. Moreover, Michelle McGill of the NZPC would subscribe to the view that large numbers of men are unable to meet their sexual needs satisfactorily within a monogamous relationship. A number of scenarios can exist. Some men may ideally want sex with only one partner, but find their partner unable to meet their requirements; others may want to protect their marriage but certainly want extra-marital sex. Other men are dissatisfied with their marriage, feel bound to it, but need others for sex; while others have little sense of responsibility to their partners at all. The findings of Velten and Kleiber are not questioned in terms of the expression of the desire, but the statistic is queried; a level of self-justification on the part of respondents is suspected.

What is evident is that tourism does create opportunities for sex, and for possible exploitation. In the case of tourism literature which has concentrated upon the Asian sex tourism industry, the exploitative components would appear clearer, with rural families selling female children into brothels. But even here the relationship between prostitution and tourism needs continuous redefinition. As Cohen (1993) has illustrated, there are distinctions between bar girls and those who work in brothels, between those catering for tourists and those meeting the needs of indigenous markets.

There is less work on prostitution and tourism in developed countries, although there is some reference to, for example, Amsterdam and Nevada. What is not clear is whether there is an exportation of the worst aspects of Thai prostitution into Western markets. Hall (1994) notes the 50 per cent decline in the number of tourists to Hat Yai in 1989 because of concern about HIV. However, while arrivals to Thailand dipped in the late 1980s, by 1994 arrivals to Thailand had increased by 8.1 per cent compared to 1993. The problems of falling profitability for Thai hotels were more due to an over-expansion of hotel stock (Boyd, 1994) than a scare about AIDS. Given the greater sensitivity to sex tourism by the authorities, and the greater willingness of governments in tourist-generating countries to consider prosecution of their own citizens for sex with minors in overseas countries, it can be argued that the Thai sex industry was becoming more constrained.

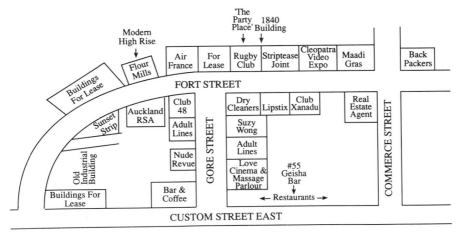

Figure 2.1 The Fort Street red light district

Simultaneously, however, there is an increased number of Asian women being found in massage parlors in other countries. For example, in 1994 the health authorities in Auckland were providing medical services for an increasing number of Asian women that included screening for HIV. In conversations with the authors, Inspector Rod Hodgins, Auckland's Community Relations Coordinator and his colleagues noted the changing nature of Fort Street in Auckland's red light district. In the period 1990 to 1993, there had not only been an increase in the number of massage parlors but a change with more offering "Asian girls." The New Zealand Prostitutes' Collective were suspicious of exploitation with the introduction of the "all inclusive fee," which implies that the sex worker does not receive remuneration, and the fact that their representatives were not admitted to two parlors. Others also expressed concern, and in May 1994 the Auckland police raided these two massage parlors, one in Fort Street and the other in "K" Road with resultant prosecutions for slavery. The women were found to be working 14-hour "shifts" and were being bussed to and from houses in South Auckland with no free movement being permitted to them. Linkages with organized crime were suspected by the police. One area of concern to the police is the linkages that are suspected with groups such as the Wo and 14K triads, and the Auckland police not only have a vice squad but also an Asian Crime Unit. In Auckland there are at least three triad groups operating, the San Yee On, the Wo and 14K gangs, which include members from different Asian nationalities, and some are suspected of having linkages with Russian Mafia groups. Police raids have been undertaken on other night-life clubs besides the massage parlors mentioned above.

It is difficult to assess how much of the demand for the girls' services comes from tourists, but it is believed that a significant proportion of demand does emanate from tourists on business trips. Such tourists have been reported to have much higher patronage of night clubs. Even in Norwich, England, a cathedral town not famed for its exciting night life, business tourists were reported as having a much higher predisposition to use nightclubs than other types of tourists. Ashworth and Tunbridge (1990) report that 26 per cent of business visitors used night-life facilities compared to 12.4 per cent of holidaymakers. In Amsterdam, the role of sex as a tourist attraction is more explicit

(Ashworth et al., 1988). The relationship between tourism and prostitution in part depends upon the place and its level of touristic activity. Kinnell (1989) in her study of Birmingham, UK, concluded that: "It is evident that prostitution in Birmingham is not a service industry to visitors from outside the region who seek commercial sex because they are away from home, or as a form of tourist entertainment." However, although her figures would seem to indicate that not more than 15 per cent of clients came from outside the West Midlands area, there is reason to believe that they may account for more than 15 per cent of revenue. McLeod's (1982) findings replicate those of Stein (1974) that there are parties organized for visiting business tourists. Anecdotal evidence given to one of the authors indicated that this practice was occurring in Nottingham, UK, in 1992.

In the case of Auckland, a small study undertaken by Chetwynd (1991), indicated that the weekly number of clients seen by a working girl was between eight and fourteen. Of the 42 clients seen on the last working day, and categorized by the 20 respondents, the largest single group were businessmen (12). Out-of-towners and tourists numbered eight. Assuming that at least some of these businessmen were visiting Auckland, that could mean that as many as a third of clients were tourists. Helen Frame of NZPC estimated the same figure but pointed out that there was a great variation in business. During major conferences and sporting events, the massage parlors and escort agencies reported very high levels of business. This was confirmed by the Auckland Police quite independently. Members of NZPC also pointed out quite specific differences in markets. Girls worked primarily three ways: through massage parlors, escort agencies and on the streets. It would also seem that Fort Street, where most parlors exist, is not an area where street sex workers operate, but "K- Road" has also changed. Up to 80 per cent of those working off "K-Road" are trans-gender. Some boys also work "K-Road," and some girls will work in the darker streets off "K-Road." Woods (1993) found that the largest group of sex workers in Auckland were those working in parlors.

The number of sex workers in Auckland in 1994 was estimated by Helen Frame of NZPC as being about 1500; and in Wellington, a very conservative estimate by Catherine Healy (again NZPC) is 400. One indication of demand in Wellington is given by the fact that in a three-month period in 1994 the NZPC distributed 17 280 condoms, implying about 2000 sexual liaisons a week (allowing for cases of non-penetrative/non-oral sex). Chetwynd (1991) documents condom distributions by NZPC of 700 per week in Auckland, 1300 per week in Wellington and 100 per week in Dunedin. Of course, the NZPC is not the sole source of supply. Using very conservative estimates, the value of tourist demand for sex workers in Auckland can be calculated as being NZ$4.1 million per annum, a calculation which is thought certainly to underestimate the actual figure. In the case of Wellington, the NZPC condom distribution figures alone imply a business worth NZ$8 million, but the total value of the sex industry and the proportion accounted for by tourists is unknown.

The opportunity

Given that a demand exists for prostitutes, and that this demand is operating at the margin of society, how is the need promoted into a behavior, and do the factors that create opportunity have any lessons for other acts of criminality involving tourists? The event model that Cornish and Clarke (1986) have used to explain the opportunities for burglary might also be applied to tourists visiting prostitutes.

Two stages are conceptualized. The first stage is the "initial involvement" where an individual becomes attracted to the marginal activity. Although presented as a linear model, it is reiterative in process. The needs for sex, affection, the excitement of operating at the margin are generalized needs arising, in part, from situation and how a personality interacts with that situation. Social factors are also important. Income can either facilitate or inhibit the creation of opportunity. The job might create an opportunity for business travel.

Marital situation and perceived sexual identity interact with previous experience and learning. Learning involves not simply an awareness of services through the media but how to access them. In some countries a telephone directory is all that is needed, whereas elsewhere, in the UK for example, a client, or "punter" might require the nerve to go into an adult sex shop to purchase a contact magazine.

One of the aspects that would be associated with the use of sexual services that is akin to some criminal activity is that, on the whole, the act is premeditated. It needs planning. The client must often find the time, make the contact — in short, engage in some planning and search behavior.

Such planning implies evaluation. Is it worth the effort? What is the possibility of discovery? What, if discovered, is the probability of police action involving prosecution and the subsequent loss of reputation? And if, on some overseas trips, the businessman finds himself in an environment where sexual services might be provided by hosts, how strong are the forces that inhibit the sexual action?

Let it be assumed that a decision had been made to visit a prostitute. The second stage of the model is now involved. The area and the actual venue must be chosen. Even if the client telephones an escort agency, some attention has to be paid to the venue. At an anecdotal level, evidence gathered for this chapter included observations on the use of an escort agency as against a massage parlor. The advantage of the hotel was a greater privacy, but it denied the client a choice. Some businessmen would tour the streets on the basis that it provided the widest choice but with the greatest risk of detection.

The crimogenic place

There are distinct geographical patterns of activity. In Auckland, Fort Street offers a high degree of security in many respects. While an area of change, it also possesses mixed use of space. Thus, for example, a flour mill dating from 1928 is still functioning in the street, as is a laundry, the offices of Air France, a block of flats, a high rise for lease and a pub located in a building dating from 1840. In 1994 a police station also located in the street.

The area is representative of many red light districts in that it is an area in transition. As noted, the buildings date from the latter part of the 19th century, and most from before the 1930s, except where older buildings have been demolished to make way for newer buildings. Many are still only two stories in height. In such buildings, to the east of the area, nearest to the railway station, can be found strip joints, while a newer cluster exists in Gore Street, which links Fort Street to Custom Street East. Gore Street is little more than 100 meters in length, yet the transition is clearly marked from the Reserve Bank

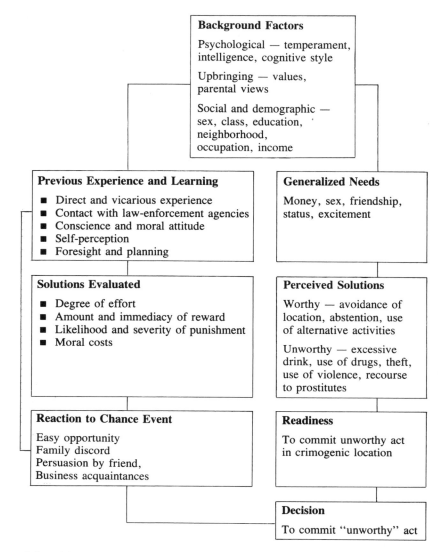

Figure 2.2 Initial involvement model. After Tonoy, M. and Morris, N., *Crime and Punishment*, University of Chicago Press, 1985

multi-story building at the junction of Custom Street East and Gore Street at the northern end, to the Changes Nude Revue, Love Cinema, and Super-star topless bar, to name but a few businesses in the center and southern end of the street. On the corners of Fort and Gore Streets, Club 48 and a dry cleaners face each other, while across the road the pub "The Rugby Club" — advertising itself as the "the party place" lies between vacant premises and a striptease joint and massage parlor.

Many of the sex joints have narrow frontages, but a process of refurbishment is in progress as they are upgrading themselves, while to the east, the buildings along Custom Street East lie closed and littered with posters on shop and office frontages. The whole

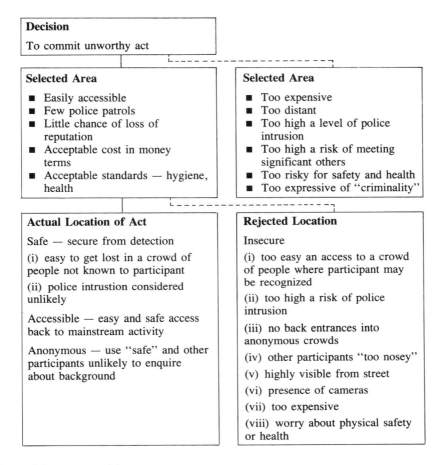

Decision

To commit unworthy act

Selected Area

- Easily accessible
- Few police patrols
- Little chance of loss of reputation
- Acceptable cost in money terms
- Acceptable standards — hygiene, health

Selected Area

- Too expensive
- Too distant
- Too high a level of police intrusion
- Too high a risk of meeting significant others
- Too risky for safety and health
- Too expressive of "criminality"

Actual Location of Act

Safe — secure from detection

(i) easy to get lost in a crowd of people not known to participant

(ii) police intrustion considered unlikely

Accessible — easy and safe access back to mainstream activity

Anonymous — use "safe" and other participants unlikely to enquire about background

Rejected Location

Insecure

(i) too easy an access to a crowd of people where participant may be recognized

(ii) too high a risk of police intrusion

(iii) no back entrances into anonymous crowds

(iv) other participants "too nosey"

(v) highly visible from street

(vi) presence of cameras

(vii) too expensive

(viii) worry about physical safety or health

Figure 2.3 Event model

location is but a few minutes' walk from the bustle of the main central business district, and about 15-minutes' walk at most from the new redevelopment of Hobson's Wharf. To analyze the spatial pattern of sex outlets is only part of a wider picture. As Catherine Healy of NZPC wryly pointed out to the authors, to analyze the spread of sex outlets in terms of vacant premises is insufficient, the main factor is whether there is high enough demand.

From the viewpoint of the tourist seeking a passive or active sexual entertainment (defined by either watching striptease or having the "extras"), Fort Street represents a safe "crimogenic" place. Indeed, in many senses the term is perhaps inappropriate for Fort Street. It offers a high degree of physical safety. The street is frequently patrolled by the police, there is a relatively high level of pedestrian flow even late at night. The clubs and joints have bouncers who, while they hustle for business, have little wish for "trouble." The area is well lit, and from 1994 under surveillance from cameras located at the kink in the road opposite "Sunset Strip."

Physical safety of the client, and to some degree the prostitute, is thus comparatively high. Certainly, the safety of the sex worker is much higher than is the case of the woman or trans-sexual working off "K-Road" or the woman visiting the hotel. But patronage is also dependent upon, it has been argued, concealment. Under New Zealand's 1978 Massage Parlour Act, entering the parlor is not illegal, and hence the client runs little risk from prosecution. The main risk the client might feel is that of being detected by someone he (they are overwhelmingly male) knows, and in this case the role of being a tourist affords a large degree of anonymity. Cohen and Felson's (1979) model of "Routine Activities" argues that crimogenic places are characterized by the presence of a likely offender, a suitable target and the absence of a capable guardian against crime, to which, in 1986, modifications relating to the role of "intimate handlers" and informal social control were added. At first sight the prostitute-seeking tourist might be said to meet the condition of that lack of social control as defined by Felson where: "Lacking commitment to the future, attachments to others, or conventional involvements and beliefs in the rules, an individual has no handle that can be grasped, and informal social control is impossible" (Felson, 1986: 121).

For the tourist, perhaps by definition, under these circumstances, has no intention of creating a long-term relationship or commitment to the place. Indeed, it is the very anonymity that aids the act. But, often, he does adhere to a set of rules, for to do otherwise is to risk the concealment necessary. For many "normal" clients there is an acceptance of the "rules of the house" — ie, the use of condoms, respect for a no kissing norm and not too much hassle about prices. *Siren*, the New Zealand magazine for sex-industry workers, lists 23 tips on how to look after your hooker, so that she can look after you (1994).

As with the concept of "deviancy," which was found to be wanting, so too, as the research for this chapter unfolded, it was felt that the image of the crimogenic place did not quite fit the case of the tourist and the prostitute. The crimogenic place is not only characterized by the factors identified by Felson (1986) but also often possesses quite specific physical characteristics for specific crimes. For the crimes of mugging there may be a lack of light or high pedestrian flow, little police surveillance, run-down housing and many avenues of access for escape. On the other hand, money laundering might require a place of high volume of transactions and high pedestrian flow characterized by many short-term visitors and transactions so as to more easily hide the criminal transactions. Such a place meets the description of a tourist ambience (Ryan, 1991). There is no specific crimogenic area, rather a variety of areas with differing opportunities for different crimes. Thus the attempt of writers such as Cohen and Felson to develop theories more generally applicable to places of different types of criminality.

Yet, many red light districts do exercise their own forms of social control. "Punters," pimps, bouncers, girls and massage parlors don't want trouble — all have much to lose. Also arguably, the police do not want trouble as it becomes easier to monitor activities that might merge into drug dealing and/or organized crime if there is ready accessibility to the margin marking the incidence of more serious crime.

Conclusions

The title of this chapter implies an assumption — that the tourist seeking sexual services and the place at which it occurs is at least deviant if not actually criminal. It is suggested that this is a view many would share. Yet, upon closer examination, this image fades into a concept of marginality defined by legal and social norms. It is legally marginal because in New Zealand as in most countries, the dividing line is, at best, fuzzy. The client in the same massage parlor, under the 1978 Massage Parlour Act, can offer to pay for sex, but the girl cannot ask. Sex might therefore occur, but if the girl has a conviction for prostitution, she cannot legally work in a parlor, and the massage parlor operator might also be prosecuted. It is socially marginal because although the act is not uncommon, it is often not commented upon. From the perspective of sociological theories, it is marginal because, as argued above, it can serve to raise questions about the mainstream of society and its norms.

The patronage of a prostitute is also criminally marginal in that prostitution can be (but it is emphasized, not always nor necessarily) associated with organized crime, drugs, under age sex and slavery. The concept of marginality also has economic ramifications in this instance. The lack of money is a significant motivation for the girls, while men have both the ability and the opportunity to spend their money in this way. Are these women, like Third World tourist destinations, marginal to the mainstream of economic life?

If marginality is a more appropriate concept, then it must be recognized that the margin is not fixed and can be changed. It is therefore appropriate that the legal framework should be examined with a view to assessing the nature of its impact upon sex worker and client alike. Recognition that the use of a prostitute is not a deviant act in the way usually associated with the term, with all its criminal overtones, might be a start, as might the appreciation that as a marginal act the definition is, to a large extent, within the jurisdiction of legal practice. That it is not socially uncommon is known to every sex worker, and if tourist authorities are to see prostitution as a legitimate source of income generation, then legislation that fails to protect the sex worker from the truly criminally deviant needs changing.

Acknowledgements

The authors would wish to thank the following for their time in preparation of this chapter. Inspector Rod Hodgins, Community Relations Coordinator; Inspector Phil Kieber, Staff Officer; Detective Inspector Gavin Jones, Planning Officer; Sergeant Bob Gable, Wharf Police and Senior Sergeant Don Stewart, Planning — all of the Auckland Police; Michelle McGill, Catherine Healy, Helen Frame, Sue and Roxeanne of New Zealand Prostitutes' Collective; and also Jacqui, Louise, Jacky, Zandra and their friends.

References

Anon (1994). The sensitive new age clients guide. *Siren*, April: 7−8, New Zealand Prostitutes' Collective.

Ashworth, G.J. and Tunbridge, J.E. (1990). *The Tourist-Historic City*. Chichester: John Wiley & Sons.

Ashworth, G.J., White, P.E. and Winchester, H. (1988). The Redlight District of the West European City: A Neglected Aspect of the Urban Landscape. *Geoform*, **19**: 201−12.

Becker, H.S. (1963). *Outsiders: Studies in the sociology of deviance*. Glencoe: The Free Press.

Becker, H.S. (1974). Labelling theory reconsidered. In Rock, Paul and McIntosh, Mary (eds), *Deviance and Social Control*, London: Sage: 41−66.

Boyd, A. (1994) Slump in Thai profits. *Asian Hotelier*, July: 1.

Chetwynd, J. (1991). *The New Zealand Prostitutes' Collective — a Process Evaluation of its Formation and Operation*, Christchurch School of Medicine.

Cohen, E. (1987). The tourist as victim and protégé of law enforcing agencies. *Leisure Studies*, **6**, May: 181−98.

Cohen, E. (1993). Open-ended prostitution as a skillful game of luck: Opportunity, risk and security among the tourist oriented prostitutes in a Bangkok *soi*. In Hitchcock, Michael, King, Victor T., and Parnwell, Michael J.G. (eds), *Tourism in South East Asia*, London: Routledge.

Cohen, L.E. and Felson, M. (1979). Social change and crime rate trends: A routine activity approach. *American Sociological Review*, **44**, August: 588−608.

Cornish, D.B. and Clarke, R.V. (1986). *The Reasoning Criminal — Rational Choice Perspectives on Offending*. New York: Springer-Verlag.

Crompton, J.L. (1979). Motivation for pleasure vacation. *Annals of Tourism Research*, **6**,4: 408−24.

Downes, D. and Rock, P. (1988). *Understanding Deviance — a Guide to the Sociology of Crime and Rule-breaking*, Second Edition. Oxford: Clarendon Press.

Felson, M. (1986). Linking criminal choices, routine activities, informal control, and criminal outcomes. In Cornish, D.B. and Clarke, R.V. (eds), *The Reasoning Criminal — Rational Choice Perspectives on Offending*. New York: Springer-Verlag.

Hall, C.M. (1994). *Introduction to Tourism in the Pacific Rim: Development, Impacts and Markets*. Cheshire: Longman.

Heyl, B.S. (1979) *The Madame as Entrepreneur: Career Management in House Prostitution*. New Brunswick, NJ: Transaction Books.

Howard, J.A. and Sheth, J.N. (1969). *Theory of Buyer Behavior*. New York: John Wiley and Sons.

Kinnell, H. (1989). *Prostitutes, Their Clients and Risks of HIV Infection in Birmingham*. Occasional paper. Birmingham: Central Birmingham Health Authority.

Krippendorf, J. (1987). *The Holidaymakers*. Oxford: Heinemann.

McLeod, E. (1982). *Women Working: Prostitution Now*. London: Croom Helm.

Mill, R.C. and Morrison, A.M. (1985). *The Tourist System: An Introductory Text*. Englewood Cliffs, NJ: Prentice Hall.

Quinney, R. (1977). *Class, State and Crime: On the Theory and Practice of Criminal Justice*. New York: David MacKay Co.

Ryan, C.A. (1991). *Recreational Tourism — a Social Science Perspective*. London and New York: Routledge.

Ryan, C.A. (1993). Tourism and crime — an intrinsic or accidental relationship? *Tourism Management*, **14**, (3): 173−83.

Simmons, J.L. (1965). Public stereotypes of deviants. *Social Problems*, **13** (fall): 224.

Stein, M.L. (1974). *Lovers, Friends, Slaves*. New York: Berkley Medallion.

Sutherland, E. (1956). Crime and the conflict process. In Lindemeth, Alfred and Schuessler, Karl (eds). *The Sutherland Papers*. Bloomington: Indiana University Press.

Symanski, R. (1981). *The Immoral Landscape, Female Prostitution in Western Societies*. Toronto: Butterworths.

Winter, M. (1976). *Prostitution in Australia*, Balgowlah, NSW: Purtaboi Publications.

Velten, D. and Kleiber, D. (1992). Characteristics and sexual behavior of clients of female prostitutes, Poster presented at the VIII Internal Conference on AIDS, Amsterdam, July 19−24.

Woods, K.A. (1993). You have to have sex with a condom — you're making love without. *Condom use by parlour workers in and out of work*. Unpublished paper, component of PhD, University of Auckland.

Woodside, A. and MacDonald, R. (1993). General systems framework of customer choice and behavior processes for tourism services. Proceedings, *Decision Making Processes and Preference Changes of Tourists: Intertemporal and Intercountry Perspectives*. Institute of Tourism and Service Economics, University of Innsbruck, November 25−7.

Note in proof — The text refers to a case over alleged slavery charges. At the time of going to press the trial had just taken place and the accused was found guilty not of slavery but of brothel keeping. The sentence has not yet been passed.

3 Florida tourists' vulnerability to crime

SUSAN A. SCHIEBLER, JOHN C. CROTTS AND RICHARD C. HOLLINGER

Foreign embassies routinely issue safety advisories or warnings for residents traveling abroad. The list changes fairly often, but some countries such as Lebanon, Colombia and Afghanistan consistently remain on it (Lunberg and Lunberg, 1993). Third World nations have generally been considered more dangerous than developed nations as travel destinations. However, a new trend has emerged whereby developed nations are also listed among the places where travelers are vulnerable to criminal victimization.

Tourism is generally acknowledged as an industry that only thrives under peaceful conditions. Additionally, the need for safety is a well-recognized innate trait of human nature (Maslow, 1954). Consequently, concern about personal safety has been shown dramatically to restrain travel to hostile destinations (Edgell, 1990). Egypt, for example, lost an estimated $1 billion in tourism revenues due to the publicity surrounding the murder of three and wounding of a dozen foreign tourists by Muslim extremists over a 12-month period (Associated Press, 1993). The 1992 Los Angeles riots are estimated to have cost that city between $1 billion and $2 billion in lost travel revenues (Crystal, 1993). Highly publicized crimes against tourists have been shown to cause destination shifts to safer locales. For example, the *Achille Lauro* ship hijacking caused a sharp drop in cruise travel to the Mediterranean but was attributed to increased cruise bookings for the Caribbean and Alaska lines (*Advertising Age*, 1986). In fact, according to a recent Cruise Line International Association (CLIA) study, cruise travel is still the fastest growing vacation category in North America (*Gainesville Sun*, 1994). Perhaps one factor partially accounting for this growth trend is the issue of safety.

A favorite complaint among travel destination marketers is that the media can take relatively few crime incidents against tourists and through sensationalist reporting create an hysterical overreaction out of proportion to the real level of risk (Crystal, 1993). For example, the tragic murders of a pregnant German mother in Miami and a male English tourist near Tallahassee, followed by a string of other incidents of random violence throughout the remainder of the state, generated considerable national and international media attention suggesting that crime against Florida's tourists was rampant and on the increase. During the same period, however, official state tourist crime statistics told another story. As can be seen in Figure 3.1, the number of reported crimes against non-

Tourism, Crime and International Security Issues, edited by
A. Pizam and Y. Mansfield. © 1996 John Wiley & Sons Ltd.

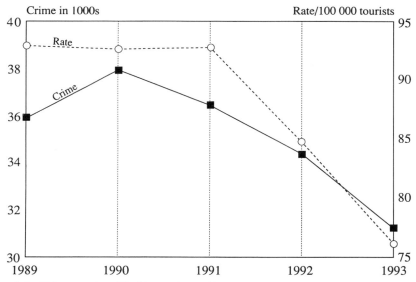

Figure 3.1   Crimes against Florida tourists, 1989–93

residents had declined from a high in 1990 of 37 949 to 31 299 in 1993 (Florida Department of Law Enforcement, 1993). Unfortunately, "perception becomes reality" in the travel business, and these official statistics have done little to calm the apprehensions of those at risk as indicated by the decline in Florida tourism during 1994.

Reliable statistics about crimes against tourists are in short supply. Tourist crime victimization data, if produced at all, are closely guarded by many tourism-reliant destinations (Ambinder, 1992). Obviously, however, if we are to understand the scope of the problem collecting reliable and comparable incidence data is the logical first step. To our knowledge there have been only a few isolated attempts to report scientifically valid tourist crime statistics which could be used for comparison purposes (Jones, 1993; Demos, 1992; Chesney-Lind and Lind, 1986).

Therefore, the purpose of this study is twofold. First, we will report on the prevalence of crimes against tourists in the most popular destinations in Florida during 1993. Specifically, serious crime incidents against those short-term visitors who do not maintain part-time residences in Florida (eg, second homes, condominiums etc.) will be examined since they most closely represent the typical definition of "tourists." Second, we will attempt to identify some of the underlying social and environmental factors correlated with the criminal victimization of tourists using two of the most popular ecologically based theories of crime causation.

The existence of crimes perpetrated against tourists is a topic that few tourism marketing professionals like to discuss. The fact remains, however, that few major tourist destinations in the world today are immune to the problem. Findings of this study will hopefully provide insights to other states and communities regarding more effective approaches to this dilemma.

Human ecology and theories of criminal activity

Previous research attempting to understand the variations of community crime rates historically has drawn from Hawley's (1950) ecological theory of human structures. Hawley viewed a community as an organization of niches and functional roles based upon the principles of symbiotic and commensalistic relationships. The principles of symbiosis connote a mutual dependence among individuals characterized by their functional differences. Predatory crime, as a special case of symbiosis, involves an interdependent relationship between predator and victim in their efforts to adapt to and gain subsistence from the environment. Alternatively, commensalism refers to the relationship among individuals based upon their functional similarities (Hawley, 1950). The criminologists, Felson and Cohen (1980), noted similarities between Hawley's commensalism and Durkheim's (1966) earlier concept of mechanical solidarity, in that societal groups evolve naturally from associations of functionally homogeneous individuals (eg neighborhood, church, school, professions etc). The community, therefore, provides the structure for the symbiotic and commensalistic relationships in which individuals seek subsistence and the satisfaction of needs. It would appear, then, that a human ecology paradigm provides a useful framework in exploring why some community structures seem to generate a greater number of criminal acts than do others. Presently, the two most popular criminological theories based upon human ecology principles are the Routine Activities and the Hot Spots approach.

Routine activities approach

Felson and Cohen (1980) draw heavily from Hawley's human ecology theory in the development of their "routine activities approach" model of criminal acts. Felson and Cohen argued that criminals gain sustenance or satisfy human needs by taking something of value from their victims. In other words, criminal acts can be construed as routine activities which feed upon the routine activities of others. For a criminal act to occur, three required elements must converge in both time and place. According to Felson and Cohen, the minimal elements necessary for a direct predatory crime to happen are: (1) a suitable target or victim, (2) a motivated offender and (3) the inadequacy of effective guardians capable of preventing the interaction between offender and victim. The absence of any one of these three elements is sufficient to prevent a crime from occurring (Cohen and Felson, 1979).

The *suitable targets* element is perhaps the easiest to operationalize. Typically the researcher simply counts the absolute number of potential targets or victims currently at risk to criminal activity. Second, the presence of a *motivated offender* — individuals with both the criminal inclination and the ability to act on their propensity — is also implicit in the nexus of criminality. And third, the most common measure of *capable guardians* focuses on the proximity of persons to deter the criminal act from occurring, usually operationalized by the deployed number of law enforcement officers available in the particular jurisdiction. While the presence of municipal police represents a major component of capable guardians available to tourists, they are by no means the only guardians capable of deterring a crime. Currently in the United States, private security guards greatly outnumber public law enforcement personnel.

Hot spots theory

Routine activities is not the only ecologically based crime causation theory that is concerned with the locus of the offense. According to advocates of what has come to be called "hot spots theory," the research focuses on the relatively few places in each community that are associated with grossly disproportionate levels of crime. These places, or "hot spots," are unique physical locations which provide convergent opportunities in which predatory crimes can occur. For example, Sherman et al. (1989) tracked calls summoning police for a one-year period in Minneapolis and found that over half of all police cars for predatory crimes were dispatched to only 3.3 per cent of the addresses in the metropolitan area. Furthermore, 90 per cent of all robberies were located along only seven main avenues. Sherman et al. (1989) contend that although these hot spots cluster in particular geographical areas, it is the type of place which concentrates opportunities for predatory crime.

Similarly, in a study of the clustering of crimes in Cleveland, Roncek and Maier (1991) found that city blocks with taverns and cocktail lounges had a higher incidence of property and violent crimes as opposed to those city blocks with no such establishments. Moreover, the city block with the highest crime rate was found in a large public-housing complex.

In summary, drawing from the evidence associated with hot spots theory, it can be expected that crimes against tourists will most likely cluster in particular types of physical locations. These particular places are characterized by the fact that they each provide the convergence of potential victims and offenders maximizing the opportunities for predatory crime such as hotels, motels, airports, parking lots, bars, restaurants, tourist attractions, beaches and convenience stores (Roncek and Maier, 1991; Miethe et al. 1987). According to Ryan, tourist destinations create

> . . .centres of populations where visitors are obvious by their dress and the areas they visit. They also carry easily disposed of items of wealth such as cameras, cash and credit cards. They are temporary visitors, and as such are unable to place much pressure on the law enforcement agencies to take action against criminals, or indeed, if the criminals are caught and taken to court, are unlikely to appear as a prosecution witness. Tourist zones (therefore) are areas of criminal opportunity (1993: 14).

Although similar in basic assumptions about the role of the environment in crime causation, hot spots theory differs from the routine activities approach in the types of variables examined. With routine activities' theory one looks at the combined effect of suitable targets, motivated offenders and the absence of capable guardians on the rates of criminality in a given community. The hot spots' explanation determines instead the particular types of physical locations which put victims and offenders in greatest proximity to each other, thereby allowing the opportunity for crime to occur. We will examine both of these theories to evaluate their individual explanatory utility regarding the problem in question, namely, crimes against tourists.

Methodology

As we have stated earlier, the purpose of this study was to examine the incidence, location and types of crimes perpetrated against tourists in the 10 most visited counties in Florida during 1993 and to explore the underlying causal influences of tourist criminal victimization. To achieve this end, quantitative data from a variety of secondary sources were utilized to measure the study's dependent and independent variables. Limiting the focus to only 10 of Florida's 67 counties was made to insure that the subsequent analysis would not be biased by the state's many rural counties that receive only a small proportion of the overall annual tourist volume.

Dependent variable: crimes against tourists

In order to measure annual tourist criminal victimization levels, data were acquired from the Florida Department of Law Enforcement (1993). Federal law requires that local law enforcement agencies collect and regularly report crime to the Federal Bureau of Investigation. To insure the accuracy and completeness of these data for the state, the Florida Department of Law Enforcement (FDLE) coordinates the collection of data among the various state, county and local municipal police agencies. Therefore, the FDLE crime reports provide a uniform and reasonably accurate depiction of the nature, volume and location of crimes reported to the police in each of the state's 67 counties. Unfortunately, no separate category exists in the FDLE report which delineates criminal incidents where the victim was a "tourist." Therefore, for purposes of generating a dependent variable for this study, we defined a tourist as a non-resident of Florida who does not maintain a permanent residence in the state.

Since the risk of criminal victimization is a function of the ratio of the available number of offenders to potential victims, in studies of this nature it is common to convert raw crime incidence data into standardized crime rates (eg, the number of crimes per 100 000 persons). Crime rates effectively control for varying size differences among communities and represent a standardized level of victimization. In Table 3.1 we present the "tourist crime rate" for the top 10 visited counties in Florida during 1993. This statistic was created by dividing the total number of reported crimes against Florida non-residents in 1993 by the estimated number of tourists visiting a given county in the same year. As Table 3.1 indicates, tourist crime rates ranged from a high of 150 per 100 000 visitors in Dade County to a low of 13 per 100 000 in Hillsborough County.

Independent variables

We employed a number of different variables with which to measure the three necessary elements included in the Routine Activities Approach theory.

Suitable targets As our empirical measure of suitable targets, the total number of tourists visiting each of the 10 counties was estimated from the Florida Division of Tourism's annual visitor intercept studies. Approximately 10 000 highway and 10 000 airport interviews are annually conducted with non-resident visitors prior to their departure from the state, employing a random cluster sampling technique. During the interview, subjects are asked to name each city or county in Florida they visited. If, for example, 10 per cent of auto visitors indicated that they visited Dade County, then 10 per cent of non-resident highway visitors to the state (produced through telemetry counters

Table 3.1 Descriptive characteristics of counties

Study Variables	County Name									
	Brevard	Broward	Dade	Duval	Hillsborough	Orange	Palm Beach	Pinellas	Sarasota	Volusia
Tourist Crime Rates**	33.73	77.18	150.35	82.92	12.97	40.52	40.82	28.36	26.40	62.67
Visitor total estimates (in 100 000s)	15.97	43.74	58.13	15.82	18.41	76.86	29.56	25.27	11.87	25.39
Crime rate**	6132	8971	13 268	9956	10 117	8819	8765	6690	6082	6055
Population density* (per sq. km)	151	401	385	336	306	288	164	1173	188	129
% Population white (European origin)	89.8	81.7	72.9	72.8	82.8	79.6	84.8	90.5	94.6	88.6
% Population ages 15–24	12.1	11.3	14.0	15.1	14.5	16.3	10.4	10.4	8.8	12.7
Per capita income (in $1000 US)	15.1	16.9	13.7	13.9	14.2	14.6	19.99	15.7	18.4	13.3
Median income (in $1000 US)	30.5	30.6	26.9	28.5	28.5	30.2	32.5	26.3	29.9	24.8
% Population with income above $100 000*	2.8	4.7	4.9	2.9	3.5	3.5	7.2	3.4	5.2	2.4
% Population below federal poverty level*	9.1	10.2	17.9	12.8	13.3	11.2	9.3	9.5	6.9	12.1
Income inequality	6.3	5.5	13.0	9.9	9.8	7.7	23.1	6.1	1.7	9.7
Number of Law Enforcement Officers (F/T)**	873	3602	5450	1477	1955	811	2518	2000	610	984
Number of security guards***	1260	7175	18 795	3943	4642	3420	56 298	2866	739	1326
Capable guardians' rate	536	858	1252	805	790	772	905	571	485	623

*1990 US Census
**Florida Department of Law Enforcement
***Florida Department of Professional Regulation

and observations) would become the estimate of auto visitors to Dade County. A similar approach was used to estimate, for each of the counties, the number of visitors who arrived on domestic airlines and who arrived from overseas locations using the Florida division of Tourism's Airport Intercept Survey and the US Travel and Tourism Administration's "Inflight Survey" respectively (Crotts, 1993).

Motivated offenders   The measurement of the required motivated offender element of the routine activities model was not nearly as straightforward as simply counting numbers of tourists. A variety of statistics was assembled to serve as proxy measures of the number of motivated offenders present in each of the counties of interest. First, the rate of crimes known to the police calculated as a rate per 100 000 residents was generated for each county. Both violent and property Part 1 UCR offences were included in this statistic. As proxy measures of other potential coerrelates of tourist criminality, Table 3.1 also presents a group of environmental and social economic characteristics of the 10 counties derived from the 1990 Census of US Population and Households. In the criminological literature a number of factors have long been associated with disproportionately higher levels of criminals in a particular community. We have operationalized eight of these crime indicators for each of our counties, namely: (1) population density, (2) per cent of the population that is racially white, (3) per cent of the population that is aged 15 to 24, (4) mean per capita income, (5) median household income, (6) per cent of the population with household incomes over $100 000 per year, (7) per cent of the population with household incomes below the federal poverty level and (8) the relative degree of household income disparity. All of these measures are self-explanatory with the exception of the last. Income disparity, or the range of income difference between the upper and lower income categories of residents, was approximated by subtracting the per cent of households earning over $100 000 per year from the per cent of households living below the poverty level. The greater the residual proportion of people living at the bottom of the socio-economic ladder after subtracting out the very wealthy should yield a proxy measure of income disparity for each county.

Capable guardians   Measuring the number of capable guardians was accomplished by using the Florida Department of Law Enforcement's 1993 count of municipal and county law enforcement officers in combination with the Florida Department of Licensing annual count of private security officers for each county. Given the vastly different population sizes of the particular counties in question, the number of full time law enforcement officers was combined with the number of private security guards, the sum of which was then divided by each county's estimated number of visitors in order to generate a standardized "capable guardian rate."

Results

Routine activities approach

As can be seen in Table 3.2 the routine activities approach variables yielded mixed results in predicting levels of tourist crime. Since only 10 counties are included in this analysis, the small N precluded the use of multivariate statistical techniques. Instead, Table 3.2 presents both the Pearson's R (interval level) and Kendall's Tau (ordinal level)

Table 3.2 Pearson correlation and Kendall's Tau coefficients with tourist crime rate for all independent variables

Independent Variable	Pearson's R	Kendall's Tau-b
Visitors	0.44	0.33
FDLE/UCR county crime rate	0.72*	0.33
Pop. density (/sq. km)	−0.03	0.07
% Population white	−0.73*	−0.56
% Population 15−24	0.29	0.27
Mean per capita $ income	−0.32	−0.29
Median household income	−0.24	0.00
% Population household income over $100 K/yr	0.12	0.00
% Households below poverty level	0.74*	0.42
Relative inequality measure	0.58	0.38
# Law enforcement	0.79*	0.38
# Security guards	0.86**	0.47
Capable guardian rate	0.80*	0.51

*Significant at the $p \leq 0.01$ level
**Significant at the $p \leq 0.001$ level

correlation coefficients for each of the independent variables with the Tourist Crime Rate statistic.

Our suitable targets measure, the estimated number of visitors to each of the 10 counties, was positively related to the rate of tourist crime but was not statistically significant. Similarly, a number of our motivated offender measures were related to the dependent variable in the predicted direction but were not statistically significant. For example, the strongest of these was the degree of inequality measure which was moderately related to tourist crime at nearly the .60 level. Five of the other demographic characteristics of the community which we predicted should be good proxy indicators of the number of motivated offenders also were found not to be statistically significant. Specifically, county population density, per cent between 15 and 24 years of age, per capita annual income, median household and per cent of the population earning over $100K were found to be unrelated to the level of tourist crime in the counties studied.

Only three of the community-level proxy measures of motivated offenders were found to be highly related to tourist crime levels, namely, FDLE/UCR county crime rates, per cent white (in the expected negative direction) and per cent of the population living under the federal poverty level. Since the latter two factors are known to be strong predictors of conventional criminality, it is not surprising that they should also be related to a specific sub-category of offenses like crime against tourists.

Finally, when we examined our capable guardian measures we discovered the strongest set of statistical relationships. All three of our measures, namely, number of police officers, number of private security guards and the composite guardian per visitor rate, were strongly related to the rate of tourist crime. However, correlation coefficients for all three were in the positive direction. Even though the routine activities approach predicts that capable guardians will have a depressant effect on crime rates, research results often demonstrate just the opposite finding. This does not mean that the increased presence of the police and guards is causing more crime. Rather, this result is commonly attributed to the reactive nature of police and guard hirings. In other words, numbers of police officers and guards are increased in response to higher levels of crime. And conversely, in communities where crime is not such a problem there is usually found a much lower police and guard presence. This means that crime is bringing about more police, not vice versa.

Although this finding is an apparent contradiction to the routine activities theoretical approach, it is nevertheless a common finding in crime research. We simply do not have sophisticated enough measures of the capable guardian component to be able to examine the marginal deterrent effects on the crime rate from small increases in the numbers of police and private security forces.

Hot spots theory

Our principal objective was simultaneously to examine two theoretical models, both of which emphasize ecological effects on criminality. As we have discussed earlier, the second of these ecological approaches is called "hot spots" theory. Table 3.3 is a tabulation of violent crimes perpetrated against Florida tourists in the 31 UCR physical location categories.

Two major conclusions can be drawn from Table 3.3. First, a high degree of conformity exists between the counties in terms of the types of locations in which violent crimes against tourists are perpetrated. Specifically, these data revealed that only three of the 31 types of locations accounted for the majority of violent crimes against tourists. Among the overall incidents, nearly 43 per cent of violent crimes against tourists were perpetrated along highway/roadways, followed by 16 per cent at parking lots/garages and 12 per cent at hotels/motels. Only in Brevard County did we find violent crime against tourists to be less of a problem at hotel/motel locations but more of a problem at parks, waterways and in motor vehicles.

Although violent crime is viewed as the more serious problem, statistically there were more than six property crimes committed for every violent crime reported against a Florida tourist in 1993. Though property crime locations were somewhat more evenly distributed across all of the 31 UCR categories than was the case for violent crime, Table 3.4 shows that hotels/motels accounted for 28 per cent of all incidents, followed by parking lots/garages at nearly 21 per cent and highway/roadways at almost 12 per cent. Property crimes involving motor vehicles were particularly prevalent (26 per cent) for visitors in Brevard County, while 29 per cent of Hillsborough County's property crimes against visitors were perpetrated at the airport.

Conclusions

The purpose of this study was to introduce two contemporary criminological theories — Routine Activities Approach and Hot Spots Theory — to a topic of criminality previously devoid of theoretical grounding. Given the limited sample size, this analysis should not be considered a definitive empirical test of either theory. Nevertheless, this exploratory

Table 3.3 Location of violent crimes by county (in percentages)

Location Type	County Name										Row Totals	Ranking
	Brevard	Broward	Dade	Duval	Hillsborough	Orange	Palm Beach	Pinellas	Sarasota	Volusia		
Residence — Single	0.139	0.069	0.072	0.079	0.120	0.034	0.042	0.034	0.167	0.023	0.067	4
Apt/Condo	0.083	0.033	0.020	0.070	0.000	0.017	0.017	0.052	0.100	0.047	0.028	6
Residence — Other	0.000	0.009	0.010	0.000	0.040	0.010	0.025	0.000	0.000	0.000	0.009	13
Hotel/Motel	0.028	0.113	0.017	0.154	0.120	0.345	0.084	0.241	0.100	0.217	0.120	3
Convenience Store	0.000	0.003	0.002	0.005	0.000	0.007	0.008	0.017	0.000	0.000	0.003	
Gas Station	0.000	0.015	0.082	0.037	0.040	0.003	0.025	0.017	0.067	0.008	0.055	5
Liquor Store	0.000	0.000	0.000	0.000	0.000	0.000	0.000	0.000	0.033	0.000	0.000	
Bar/Nightclub	0.000	0.018	0.002	0.042	0.040	0.021	0.050	0.000	0.033	0.031	0.013	10
Supermarket	0.000	0.000	0.002	0.000	0.000	0.000	0.000	0.017	0.000	0.000	0.001	
Specialty Store	0.000	0.006	0.011	0.005	0.000	0.000	0.000	0.000	0.000	0.000	0.007	14
Drug Store/Hospital	0.028	0.000	0.001	0.000	0.000	0.000	0.000	0.000	0.000	0.000	0.001	
Bank	0.000	0.009	0.002	0.000	0.000	0.000	0.000	0.000	0.000	0.000	0.002	
Office Bldg	0.000	0.018	0.004	0.000	0.000	0.041	0.017	0.017	0.000	0.031	0.011	11
Manufacturing Site	0.000	0.000	0.001	0.009	0.000	0.000	0.000	0.000	0.000	0.000	0.000	
Storage	0.000	0.000	0.000	0.000	0.000	0.000	0.000	0.000	0.000	0.000	0.000	
Govt/Public Bldg	0.028	0.003	0.001	0.000	0.000	0.003	0.000	0.000	0.000	0.008	0.002	
School/University	0.000	0.000	0.002	0.000	0.000	0.000	0.000	0.017	0.000	0.000	0.001	
Jail/Prison	0.000	0.000	0.001	0.009	0.000	0.000	0.000	0.000	0.000	0.000	0.001	
Religious Bldg	0.000	0.000	0.000	0.000	0.000	0.000	0.000	0.000	0.000	0.000	0.000	
Airport	0.000	0.000	0.003	0.000	0.040	0.000	0.000	0.000	0.000	0.000	0.002	
Bus Terminal	0.000	0.09	0.004	0.009	0.000	0.003	0.000	0.000	0.000	0.000	0.004	15
Construction Site	0.000	0.000	0.002	0.000	0.000	0.000	0.000	0.000	0.000	0.000	0.004	15
Other Structure	0.028	0.006	0.004	0.014	0.000	0.000	0.008	0.017	0.000	0.000	0.001	
Parking Lot/Garage	0.139	0.31	0.116	0.181	0.240	0.150	0.328	0.293	0.067	0.093	0.159	2
Highway/Roadway	0.194	0.313	0.508	0.270	0.20	0.317	0.345	0.259	0.433	0.465	0.429	1
Park/Woodlands/Field	0.083	0.015	0.012	0.033	0.040	0.008	0.008	0.000	0.000	0.008	0.014	9
Lake/Waterway	0.111	0.003	0.013	0.005	0.040	0.003	0.017	0.000	0.000	0.000	0.011	11
Motor Vehicle	0.111	0.021	0.023	0.047	0.040	0.034	0.025	0.000	0.000	0.015	0.026	7
Other Mobile	0.028	0.000	0.001	0.000	0.000	0.000	0.000	0.000	0.000	0.008	0.001	
Other	0.000	0.024	0.026	0.019	0.040	0.003	0.000	0.017	0.000	0.039	0.018	8
Column Totals*	1.00	1.00	1.00	1.00	1.00	1.00	1.00	1.00	1.00	1.00	1.00	
Total Number Incidences	36	336	1658	215	25	293	119	58	30	129	2899	

(*May not sum up to 100% due to rounding error)

47

Table 3.4 Location of property crimes by county (in percentages)

Location Type	County Name										Row Totals	Ranking
	Brevard	Broward	Dade	Duval	Hillsborough	Orange	Palm Beach	Pinellas	Sarasota	Volusia		
Residence — Single	0.082	0.070	0.032	0.128	0.070	0.037	0.083	0.065	0.226	0.033	0.053	5
Apt/Condo	0.046	0.053	0.028	0.051	0.042	0.017	0.049	0.059	0.053	0.025	0.035	7
Residence — Other	0.006	0.010	0.004	0.013	0.000	0.002	0.006	0.012	0.025	0.002	0.006	
Hotel/Motel	0.195	0.290	0.236	0.205	0.154	0.419	0.124	0.367	0.145	0.462	0.281	1
Convenience Store	0.000	0.002	0.002	0.005	0.000	0.001	0.001	0.001	0.003	0.002	0.002	
Gas Station	0.004	0.006	0.018	0.010	0.000	0.000	0.005	0.001	0.000	0.000	0.009	
Liquor Store	0.000	0.000	0.000	0.000	0.000	0.000	0.000	0.000	0.033	0.000	0.000	
Bar/Nightclub	0.012	0.011	0.010	0.004	0.014	0.007	0.018	0.021	0.014	0.016	0.011	15
Supermarket	0.000	0.004	0.003	0.004	0.005	0.003	0.005	0.001	0.003	0.000	0.003	
Specialty Store	0.010	0.016	0.021	0.010	0.000	0.017	0.010	0.005	0.018	0.005	0.016	10
Drug Store/Hospital	0.006	0.001	0.001	0.006	0.005	0.001	0.002	0.005	0.000	0.001	0.002	
Bank	0.000	0.001	0.002	0.000	1.000	0.001	0.000	0.000	0.000	0.000	0.001	
Office Bldg	0.014	0.018	0.013	0.009	0.009	0.072	0.017	0.009	0.003	0.008	0.022	9
Manufacturing Site	0.004	0.001	0.002	0.003	0.000	0.000	0.001	0.000	0.000	0.001	0.001	
Storage	0.010	0.005	0.001	0.005	0.000	0.003	0.003	0.003	0.003	0.002	0.003	
Govt/Public Bldg	0.008	0.003	0.004	0.000	0.000	0.003	0.001	0.000	0.003	0.002	0.003	
School/University	0.000	0.001	0.002	0.005	0.005	0.001	0.002	0.001	0.000	0.000	0.001	
Jail/Prison	0.000	0.006	0.000	0.009	0.000	0.000	0.000	0.001	0.000	0.000	0.001	
Religious Bldg	0.000	0.000	0.001	0.001	0.005	0.001	0.000	0.003	0.003	0.000	0.001	
Airport	0.000	0.004	0.081	0.001	0.294	0.066	0.031	0.000	0.003	0.001	0.048	6
Bus Terminal	0.002	0.001	0.001	0.012	0.014	0.002	0.000	0.000	0.000	0.001	0.003	
Construction Site	0.002	0.001	0.001	0.000	0.000	0.001	0.000	0.001	0.003	0.000	0.002	
Other Structure	0.008	0.023	0.010	0.045	0.033	0.014	0.006	0.005	0.014	0.003	0.014	13
Parking Lot/Garage	0.195	0.239	0.209	0.155	0.154	0.207	0.352	0.123	0.226	0.122	0.209	2
Highway/Roadway	0.936	0.062	0.191	0.049	0.084	0.034	0.168	0.047	0.064	0.122	0.117	3
Park/Woodlands/Field	0.003	0.009	0.010	0.006	0.014	0.015	0.028	0.012	0.042	0.166	0.013	14
Lake/Waterway	0.041	0.019	0.023	0.005	0.000	0.002	0.012	0.005	0.011	0.001	0.015	11
Motor Vehicle	0.264	0.077	0.028	0.221	0.107	0.047	0.028	0.172	0.042	0.166	0.073	4
Other Mobile	0.008	0.004	0.001	0.004	0.000	0.000	0.008	0.001	0.003	0.000	0.002	
Other	0.016	0.047	0.039	0.027	0.028	0.019	0.012	0.073	0.078	0.013	0.034	8
Column Totals*	1.00	1.00	1.00	1.00	1.00	1.00	1.00	1.00	1.00	1.00	1.00	
Total Number Incidences	503	3032	7083	1097	214	2821	1086	656	283	1027	17 982	

(*May not sum up to 100% due to rounding error)

effort provides several provocative findings which beg future research involving larger samples.

While no single statistic by itself provides a full understanding of the factors contributing to tourists being criminally victimized, several interesting conclusions can be drawn from these results. First, crimes against tourists are more likely to occur in those counties that already are experiencing a disproportionately high level of conventional crime. Put another way, introducing higher rates of tourism in a low crime rate county will not automatically lead to higher rates of tourist victimization. However, increasing the numbers of tourists in an already high crime county does have a significant effect on the rates of crime committed against tourists.

From years of criminological analysis, we know that the highest levels of conventional crime are traditionally found in urban communities populated with disproportionately large numbers of impoverished people many of whom come from non-white racial groups. Not surprisingly, these counties are also where most tourist crime is likely to be found. Even with sizable forces of capable guardians, like police officers and private security guards, crime continues to thrive. Introducing large numbers of unsuspecting tourists into these communities will inevitably result in their becoming victimized at levels similar to those experienced by the year-long resident members of the community. In short, tourism safety does not coexist well with ecological conditions conducive to high levels of criminality.

The above may help explain why Dade County was such a particularly dangerous place for tourists to visit in 1993. A close second to Orange County for the state's most popular tourist destination title, Dade County also is noted for 39 per cent of all reported property crimes and 57 per cent of violent crimes perpetrated in 1993 against tourists. Dade County's 150.35 per 100 000 tourist victimization rate was by far the highest among all the counties analyzed and was almost twice that of the closest second, Duval County, which experienced 83 victimizations per 100 000 tourists. Both violent and property crimes tended to concentrate around Dade County's tourist- and transportation-intensive loci such as hotels/motels, highways, parking lots/garages and motor vehicles.

Therefore, the situation which poses the greatest threat to the safety of the tourist is the convergence of suitable visitor targets in those places where they are most likely to come in contact with indigenous offenders who are already involved in high levels of criminality. If we can assume that predatory crimes against tourists are rational acts, our preventative energies should be invested in exploring ways in which we can make hotels/ motels, parking lots and garages safer for tourists, particularly in those communities which already have a disproportionately high level of non-tourist victimization. In addition, policy makers may wish to devise methods to minimize the exposure of tourists to the risk of being criminally victimized by physically isolating tourist zones from those economically depressed areas where we know the overall crime rate is high. For example, public transportation systems for visitors' use should be encouraged over rental cars and personal vehicles, in order to minimize the unintentional exposure of tourists to high crime neighborhoods.

Furthermore, the physical characteristics of tourist accommodations will likely play a part in limiting risk in high crime areas. Older-style motel rooms that open directly onto dimly lit parking lots should be avoided in favor of hotels and resorts where room access by outsiders is limited through design of physical structures and monitored by private security officers. According to CPTED (Crime Prevention Through Environmental

Design) principles, potential criminals are likely to perceive detection chances greater and opportunities of escape more limited in those properties that are purposely designed with prevention in mind.

Lastly, tourists should not be lulled into a false sense of security due to the mere presence of capable guardians present at the facility. Without simultaneously reducing the number of motivated offenders from the area, simply adding security personnel may not yield the intended deterrent effect. For example, these data showed clearly that levels of capable guardians deployed appeared to be more of a reactive rather than a proactive response to tourist criminal victimization. Law enforcement and private security personnel are obviously important to deterring crime against visitors. However, at the aggregate level we simply do not yet understand the nature of the relationship between the rate of capable guardian deployment and criminal offenses in order to bring about an actual lowering of the rate of tourist victimization. This question will obviously require further research inquiry.

References

Advertising Age. (1986). Caribbean and Alaska cruise report record demand, January: 1.

Ambinder, E. (1992). Urban violence raises safety fears. *Corporate Travel*, **9** (6): 10.

Associated Press. (1993). Tourism falls prey to terrorism. *Gainesville Sun*, May 6.

Bureau of the Census. (1992). *1990 Census of Population and Housing*. Washington, DC: Department of Commerce, US Government Printing Office.

Chesney-Lind, M. and Lind, I. (1986). Visitors as victims. Crimes against tourists in Hawaii. *Annals of Tourism Research*, **13**: 167–91.

Cohen, L.E. and Felson, M. (1979). Social change and crime rate trends: A routine activities approach. *American Sociological Review*, **44**: 588–608.

Crotts, J. (1993). *1992 International Visitors to Florida and Selected Cities*. Gainesville, FL: University of Florida, Center for Tourism Research and Development.

Crystal, S. (1993). Welcome to downtown USA. *Meetings and Conventions*, **28** (3): 42–59.

Demos, E. (1992). Concern for safety: A potential problem in the tourist industry. *Journal of Travel & Tourism Marketing*, **1**: 81–8.

Durkheim, E. (1966). *The Division of Labor in Society*. New York: Free Press.

Edgell, D.L. (1990). *International Tourism Policy*. New York: Van Nostrand Reinhold.

Felson, M. and Cohen, L.E. (1980). Human ecology and crime: A routine activity approach. *Human Ecology*, **8**: 389–405.

Florida Department of Law Enforcement. (1993). *Uniform Crime Reports — 1993*. Tallahassee: State of Florida.

Gainesville Sun. (1994, August 14). Study: Interest in cruises at all time high. pp. D1, D9.

Hawley, A. (1950). *Human Ecology: A Theory of Community Structure*. New York: Ronald Press.

Jones, C.B. (1993). *Tourism Impacts of the Los Angeles Civil Disturbances*. Unpublished paper presented at the 24th Annual Conference of the Travel and Tourism Research Association, Vancouver, June 11.

Lunberg, D. and Lunberg, C. (1993) *International Travel and Tourism*. New York: John Wiley and Sons.

Maslow, A. (1954). *Motivation and Personality*. New York: Harper.

Miethe, T.D., Stafford, M.C. and Long, J.S. (1987). Social differentiation in criminal victimization: A test of routine activities approach. *American Sociological Review*, **52**: 184–94.

Pizam, A. (1982). Tourism and crime: Is there a relationship? *Journal of Travel Research*, **20**: 7–10.

Roncek, D. and Maier, P. (1991). Bars, blocks, and crimes revisited: Linking the theory of routine activities to the empiricism of "hot spots." *Criminology*, **29**: 725–60.

Ryan, C. (1993). Crime, violence, terrorism and tourism. An accidental or intrinsic relationship? *Tourism Management*, **14**: 173–83.

Sherman, L.W., Gartin, P.R. and Beurger, M.E. (1989). Hot spots of predatory crime: Routine activities and the criminology of place. *Criminology*, **27**: 27–55.

Washnis, G.J. (1976). *Citizen Involvement in Crime Prevention*. Lexington, MA: D.C. Heath.

4 Crime and tourism: a study of perceptions in the Pacific northwest

SAMUEL V. LANKFORD

Residents hold varying views and perceptions of tourism and tourists. Many residents acknowledge that tourism, as an industry, creates jobs and supports the local economy. Many, however, feel that their traditional way of life and the socio-cultural structure of their community will be adversely impacted by tourism. Specifically, they feel that tourism may facilitate crowded, noisy and congested conditions in their community. In addition, many people feel that tourism will create more crime and generally lower the quality of community life. Consequently, a full understanding of these real and perceived impacts is necessary in order for local leaders effectively to mitigate impacts, as well as to educate the resident population about the importance of the local tourism industry.

The literature contains numerous studies related to tourism. Many are contradictory in their findings and not conclusive. However, a number of studies have found crime to be related to resident perceptions of tourism development (Rothman, 1978; Runyan and Wu, 1979; Belisle and Hoy, 1980; Sethna, 1980; Pizam and Pokela, 1985; Liu et al., 1987; Milman and Pizam, 1988; Long et al., 1990; Lankford 1991a and b; Lankford and Tanselli, 1990; Ross, 1992). However, other studies (Pizam, 1982; Allen et al., 1993; McCool and Martin, 1994) have not shown direct relationships between crime and tourism.

Pizam (1982) found in a nation-wide (United States) study that very little correlation existed between crime and its relationship to tourism. A later cross-cultural comparative study of perceptions of tourism in seven countries found that crime-related issues were among the concerns of each country studied relative to tourism (Pizam and Telisman-Kosuta, 1989). Another cross-cultural study compared perceptions of residents in central Florida and Nadi, Fiji. The findings suggest that tourism was perceived to contribute toward an increase in organized crime (crimes which are the products of groups or organizations) and individual crime (planned and conducted by individuals) (Pizam et al., 1994).

Another study found that residents felt noise, crime, litter and environmental impacts have increased due to tourism and tourists visiting their community (Lankford, 1994). Specifically, government employees, elected/appointed leaders and business owners

Tourism, Crime and International Security Issues, edited by
A. Pizam and Y. Mansfeld. © 1996 John Wiley & Sons Ltd.

(who felt tourism did not contribute as much to these impacts) significantly differed with residents (who felt tourism created these impacts) on all these quality-of-life issues. Furthermore, crime has been found to be an integral variable in the development of an attitudinal scale designed to measure resident attitudes toward tourism and rural regional development (Lankford, 1991a and 1991b; Lankford and Howard, 1994; Lankford et al., 1994).

Davis et al. (1988) segmented residents based on their attitudes, interests and opinions toward tourism. They identified five groups; haters (extremely negative opinions, representing 16 per cent of the sample); lovers (very positive about tourism, representing 20 per cent of the sample); cautious romantics (representing 21 per cent of the sample are basically in support but hold anti-growth sentiments); in-betweeners (18 per cent of the sample) were characterized as holding moderate opinions; and finally the "love-em for a reason" group (26 per cent of the sample), which supported the industry due to the jobs and economic benefits. What was most interesting about the Davis et al. study is that each group expressed concerns about crime as a disadvantage of tourism development. Specifically, about 30 per cent of each of the above segments were concerned about increases in crime, no matter what their initial inclinations and level of support.

Another study found that the most significant (statistically) changes in resident perceptions across levels of tourism development were the impacts on local quality of life and increasing crime problems (Long et al., 1990). Specifically, the study indicated that as towns became more dependent upon tourism, the more residents felt crime was increasing.

In light of the literature, and in order to gain a better understanding of crime and tourism, the purpose of this study was to explore the perception of crime from a socio-demographic perspective. A number of socio-demographic variables were tested using appropriate statistical tests (chi-square and anova) to determine if relationships and associations existed between crime and tourism development.

Study region

Gunn (1986) noted that tourism has emerged as a powerful economic force and nearly every state and city engage in its promotion. This is especially true in the Pacific northwest where tourism growth has helped offset declines in the traditional industries of commercial fishing, agriculture and forestry (Morse and Anderson, 1989: 1). Visits to Oregon in the past two years have grown substantially, with lodging at capacity throughout much of the state (Goldschmidt 1989). Travelers to the State of Oregon spent $1.8 billion on lodging, attractions, dining and retail purchases in 1988 (Runyan and Conway, 1989). Travel and tourism are currently tied with high-technology manufacturing for third place among export-oriented sectors of the Oregon economy, following forest products and agriculture (Runyan and The Lyon Group, 1989). The State of Oregon has also substantially increased its commitment to the development of the tourism industry, as evidenced by nearly two-thirds of the state's counties having emphasized tourism-related projects as part of the state's regional economic development strategies program.

One area of the Pacific northwest which is experiencing the effects of rapid tourism growth is the Columbia River Gorge. The Gorge, recently designated a National Scenic

Area, managed by the US National Forest, has been attracting visitors from around the world, in turn producing a demand on existing services and facilities.

The establishment of the National Scenic Area provides opportunity for tourism growth and funding of tourism facilities. In addition, these opportunities could create a scenic area with world-class drawing power (Morse and Anderson, 1989). There is additional evidence that tourism is growing and becoming an economic force in the Gorge. The Port of Hood River is developing its waterfront, picnic areas and expanding the marina, while the Port of Cascade Locks is operating the Columbia Gorge sternwheel steamer for visitors to tour the river (Guppy, 1985). There is greater competition for the resources of the Gorge. It is a source of regional and inter-state hydro-electric power, used extensively for transportation, flood control, irrigation, water supply, flow augmentation, fishing, recreation and wildlife habitat. The main industries in the Columbia River Gorge in order of importance are: timber, agriculture and tourism.

Most recently the Gorge has been the site of intensive outdoor recreation and tourism use. The growing number of tourists from around the world choosing to sailboard near Hood River is one example. Hood River, Oregon on the Columbia River ''has become the Aspen of Windsurfing,'' as it was billed on an NBC Nightly News piece (Moses, 1989: 76). Moses (1989: 77) suggested that sailboarders, loggers and orchardists have a ''nice live-in'' relationship with a minimum of tension. However, some residents are not sure this relationship is conducive to enhancing the local quality of life. One resident lamented that ''I can't go down to the river and fish at my favorite spot because it's overrun with sailboarders'' (Moses, 1989: 79). A developer of the Hood River Village Resort says, ''we got surf humans and regular people, and they don't mix'' (Moses, 1989: 79). The same developer predicts that it will get more expensive, and that locals will no longer be able to afford to live in Hood River (Moses, 1989). The Port of Hood River manager does not think that local people are prepared for the inevitable changes to come. He noted that there will have to be a lot of planning in order to deal with the influx of visitors (Moses, 1989). The interest in the Columbia river gorge as a tourist destination has provided a unique opportunity to identify issues of crime and tourism development and the moderating effects of key socio-demographic variables.

Methods

A tourism impact attitudinal scale (TIAS) (Lankford, 1991b; Lankford and Howard, 1994) was utilized in this research. The scale is designed to identify the attitudes and perceptions of government employees and elected/appointed government officials, residents and business owners toward tourism development. The TIAS consists of 27 items measured on a five-point Likert-type scale: 5 = strongly agree; 4 = agree; 3 = neutral; 2 = disagree; 1 = strongly disagree. In addition, 17 socio-demographic questions were included. A two-factor solution accounted for 58 per cent of the total variation in the data (pairwise correlation of .62504). Factor one (labeled as the 'concern for local tourism promotion and development' dimension) is comprised of 18 items (.9612 alpha); and factor two (labeled as the ''personal and community benefits'' dimension) is comprised of nine items (.8884 alpha). The alpha scale coefficient was .9643 for the 27-item attitude scale.

Data collection procedures

The TIAS was administered to 2583 randomly selected residents (proportionate to the population of the 13 cities and six counties) of the Columbia River Gorge in the spring and summer of 1991. Three separate mailings were used to collect the responses. A coding system was used to track non-respondents. Non-respondents were sent an additional survey and a new cover letter at each mailing. The response rate (adjusted for non-deliverables) was 74.71 per cent (n = 1436). According to Babbie (1986: 221), a response rate of 70 per cent is very good. Residents of the Columbia River Gorge were drawn from two independent sample frames: (a) a list of Oregon residents was randomly selected from the Oregon Department of Motor Vehicles' computer tape of registered drivers over age 18; and (b) a list of Washington residents was randomly selected from the Washington Department of Licensing computer tape of registered drivers over age 18. No businesses or public agencies were included in the random sample. The region is serviced by numerous telephone companies, water districts and electric companies. Due to the diversity in service area, geographic distribution of subjects and the fact that the driver license files are updated monthly, Department of Motor Vehicle lists were deemed the most comprehensive list of residents available for this research. Comparison of resident characteristics from this research with US Census data showed no significant differences in age and gender.

   Three groups were formed around the question: "Tourism has increased crime in my community." The groups were formed as follows: group one consisted of respondents who did not think tourism increased crime (disagree or strongly disagree on the five-point scale); group two consisted of residents who were neutral or had no opinion (neutral on the five-point scale); and group three felt that crime levels are related to tourism (agree or strongly agree on the five-point scale).

   To explore the crime issue within this sample, appropriate tests were conducted on the characteristics of age, length of residence, number of community organizations affiliated with, sex, rural or urban residence, occupation, recreational pursuits in the outdoors and whether or not the respondent was born within the region. In previous studies, these variables have been shown to influence attitudes toward tourism and in some cases crime.

Results

To help explain the differences in group attitudes, various socio-demographic characteristics were analyzed (Table 4.1). Significance was found among the groups on a number of the variables tested. A significant association was found between rural and urban residents ($X^2 = 11.34$; $p < .003$). Urban residents tended to believe that crime was not an issue or was negligible, while rural residents felt tourism did increase crime. While not significant, those employed in tourism indicated crime did not increase as a result of tourism. However, when examining other specific occupations (not shown in Table 4.1), farmers felt that crime increased as a result of tourism ($X^2 = 50.66$; $p < .001$).

   A significant association was also found between the three groups and whether or not the respondent was born within the region of study ($X^2 = 18.15$; $p < .001$). A disproportionate number of respondents who were born in the area indicated that tourism did increase crime. A significant difference between the groups (F = 3.50; df = 1380;

Table 4.1 Socio-demographic characteristic analysis of groups

	Agree Crime Increases		Neutral		Disagree Crime Increases		
	N	(%)	N	(%)	N	(%)	
Sex							
Male	242	(17.3)	256	(18.3)	227	(16.2)	$X^2 = 1.77$
Female	208	(14.9)	233	(16.7)	232	(16.6)	
Occupation in Tourism							
Yes	40	(2.9)	51	(3.7)	60	(4.4)	$X^2 = 4.59$
No	406	(29.6)	426	(31.9)	387	(28.2)	
Urban/Rural Resident							
Rural	203	(15.1)	239	(17.8)	252	(18.8)	$X^2 = 11.34$
Urban	232	(17.3)	232	(17.3)	183	(13.6)	
Born in Area							
Yes	130	(9.4)	109	(7.8)	77	(5.5)	$X^2 = 18.15$
No	321	(23.1)	376	(27.1)	377	(27.1)	
Participate in Outdoor Recreation							
Yes	421	(31.2)	435	(32.2)	417	(30.9)	$X^2 = 6.05*$
No	17	(1.3)	36	(2.7)	24	(1.8)	
Means							
Age	44.89 years		48.33 years		49.49 years		$F = 10.19*^a$
Length of Residence	24.81 years		24.16 years		21.72 years		$F = 3.50*^a$
Number of Civic Organizations	2.00		2.06		2.04		$F = 0.1302$

Notes: Where significant differences exist among groups on the F statistic, a Scheffe test was conducted to determine which groups differed from one another.
[a]Indicates residents who think that tourism brings more crime differ significantly from those who do not feel crime is related to tourism.
*$p < 0.01$
**$p < 0.001$

p < .03) was noted in the length of residence. The group indicating crime did increase had the longest length of residence (25 years), significantly differing (p < .05) from those respondents who thought crime did not increase as a result of tourism (mean length of residence = 21 years). What was most curious is that a significant difference (F = 10.19; df = 1380; p < .001) was found among the groups' ages. The group indicating tourism increased crime had a mean age of 44 years, while the group indicating no effect on crime and no opinion had mean ages of 49.5 and 48 years old, respectively.

Recreational pursuits also helped to explain some of the concern about crime. A disproportionate number of respondents who pursue outdoor recreation activities felt tourism increased crime. Specifically, people involved in boating, fishing and horseback riding indicated that tourism increased crime (all significant and the p < .001 level; not shown in Table 4.1). As mentioned earlier, the Gorge is also a popular windsurfing area. As might be expected, windsurfers did not feel crime was a consequence of tourism development ($X^2 = 15.56$; p < .001).

Summary and conclusions

The findings of the present study are consistent with Belisle and Hoy's (1980) research which indicated rural residents are more negative about tourism. Rural residents, long-term residents, farmers and some recreationists may fear that tourism will bring unwanted types of behavior to their communities or their leisure environments. The fear might be that increased tourism may disrupt the quiet and peaceful way of life inherent within these rural areas. The finding that older residents feel crime is not an issue, while younger residents are concerned, cannot be explained. However, the indication that crime is an issue may be that residents hear anti-tourism groups using crime as an issue. Some evidence may support this notion in that the Gorge, recently designated a National Scenic Area, experienced considerable protest from most communities and special-interest groups. Another possibility may be the new members of the community who are attracted to the business opportunities being presented within the region as a result of increased tourism. The findings may support this notion, in that the surge in business and government activity has centered around windsurfing-related businesses (Lankford, 1991a and 1991b; Morse and Anderson, 1989; Moses 1989). Finally, there may be a relationship with the urban and rural differences and the newer residents. New businesses are required to operate within the urban growth boundaries of the communities studied: therefore, newer residents would most likely be residing within the urban areas which may also help explain why the urban sample did not think tourism increases crime.

Another interesting finding is that long-term residents feel tourism brings crime. Additionally, when viewing the variable "place of birth," it was found that a disproportionate number of people who were born within the region think there is an increase in crime. This finding is related to community attachment, as noted by McCool and Martin (1994) and Um and Crompton (1987). Therefore, it appears in this study that community attachment may be of help in explaining the relationship of the perceptions of crime and tourism.

A number of studies on community impacts have suggested that outdoor recreation participation is not a significant variable in explaining attitudes toward tourism impacts and development (Allen et al., 1993; Long et al., 1990). However, Lankford and Howard (1994) found that perceptions of outdoor recreation opportunities and participation was the most significant predictor of attitudes toward tourism in a multi-state and multi-community study (n = 1436). The present study further suggests that people who are involved in outdoor recreation pursuits are fearful of tourism from the standpoint of crime. It may be that residents desire to protect the local recreation resources in order to keep them for their own use. Therefore, using the issue of crime as a means to slow growth, and reduce the promotion of tourism, may be one strategy.

It is anticipated that this study will serve as a baseline study to be replicated in the future to monitor changes in attitudes as the number of tourists and scale of tourism increase in the Columbia River Gorge. It would seem appropriate that an attitudinal scale be developed to help understand the dimensions of residents' perceptions of crime. In this way, local leaders and policy makers can develop strategies to help educate the public about the relationship between crime and tourism. In any case, it appears that residents from a number of communities are concerned about the level of crime that may be brought about by tourism. Decision makers have a responsibility to ensure tourism does not profoundly change the level of crime due to tourism development and promotion and that residents understand the dynamics of the situation

References

Allen, L.R., Hafer, H.R., Long, P.T. and Perdue, R.R. (1993). Rural residents' attitudes toward recreation and tourism development. *Journal of Travel Research*, **31** (4): 27−33.

Babbie, E. (1986). *The Practice of Social Research*. (Fourth Edition). Belmont, CA: Wadsworth.

Belisle, F.J. and Hoy, D.R. (1980). The perceived impacts of tourism by residents: A case study in Santa Marta, Columbia, *Annals of Tourism Research*, **7** (1): 83−101.

Davis, D., Allen, J. and Cosenza, R.M. (1988). Segmenting local residents by their attitudes, interests and opinions toward tourism. *Journal of Travel Research*, **27** (2): 2−8.

Goldschmidt, N. (1989). *Oregon Shines — An Economic Strategy for the Pacific Century*. Salem, OR: Oregon Economic Development Department.

Gunn, C.A. (1986). Philosophical relationships: Conservation, leisure, recreation and tourism. In *The President's Commission on Americans Outdoors*, 1−7, Washington, DC: US Government Printing Office.

Guppy, R. (1985) Hood River County: Small but grand. *Landmark*, **2** (1): 19−23.

Lankford, S.V. (1991a). An analysis of resident preferences, attitudes, and opinions toward tourism and rural regional development in the Columbia River Gorge. Unpublished dissertation, University of Oregon, Eugene. *Dissertation Abstracts International*, 52−9: 349A.

Lankford, S.V. (1991b). Resident attitudes toward tourism in the Columbia River Gorge. Prepared for the States of Oregon and Washington Tourism Departments. University of Oregon, Eugene: Community Planning Workshop.

Lankford, S.V. (1994). Attitudes and perceptions toward tourism and rural regional development. *Journal of Travel Research*, **32** (4): 35−43.

Lankford, S.V., Chen, J.S.Y. and Chen, W. (1994). Tourism's impacts in the Penghu national scenic area, Taiwan, *Tourism Management*, **15** (3): 222−7.

Lankford, S.V., and Howard, D.R. (1994). Developing a tourism impact attitude scale. *Annals of Tourism Research*, **21** (1): 121−39.

Lankford, S.V. and Tanselli, L. (1990). *A Study of Resident Attitudes Toward Tourism*. Prepared for the Bend, Oregon Chamber of Commerce, University of Oregon, Eugene: Community Planning Workshop.

Liu, J.C., Sheldon, P.J. and Var, T. (1987). Resident perceptions of the environmental impacts of tourism. *Annals of Tourism Research*, **14** (1): 17−37.

Long, P.T., Perdue, R.R. and Allen, L. (1990). Rural resident tourism perceptions and attitudes by community level of tourism. *Journal of Travel Research*, **28** (3): 3−9.

McCool, S.F. and Martin, S.R. (1994). Community attachment and attitudes toward tourism development. *Journal of Travel Research*, **32** (3): 29−34.

Milman, A. and Pizam, A. (1988). Social impacts of tourism on Central Florida. *Annals of Tourism Research*, **15**: 191−204.

Morse, K.S. and Anderson, R.S. (1989). Tourism in the Columbia River Gorge: A profile of visitor accommodation and economic impacts. *Vancouver, WA: Washington Sea Grant Program*.

Moses, S. (1989). The Hood River. *Outside*, May: 72−80.

Pizam, A. (1982). Tourism and crime: is there a relationship? *Journal of Travel Research*, **20**(3): 7−10.

Pizam, A., Milman, A. and King, B. (1994). The perceptions of tourism employees and their families towards tourism. *Tourism Management*, **15** (1): 53−61.

Pizam, A. and Pokela, J. (1985). The perceived impacts of casino gambling on a community. *Annals of Tourism Research*, **123** (2): 147−65.

Pizam, A. and Telisman-Kosuta, N. (1989). Tourism as a factor of change: Results and analysis. In Bytstrzanowski, J. (ed), *Tourism as a Factor of Change: A Socio-cultural Study*. Vienna Center, Vienna, pp. 69−93.

Rothman, R.A. (1978). Residents and transients: Community reaction to seasonal visitors. *Journal of Travel Research*, **16**: 8−13.

Runyan, D. and Associates and Conway, D. and Associates (1989). *The Economic Impact of Travel in Oregon*. Salem: Tourism Division, Oregon Economic Development Department.

Runyan, D. and Associates and The Lyon Group (1989). *Oregon Travel and Tourism: Visitor Profile, Marketing and Economic Impacts*. Salem: Tourism Division, Oregon Economic Development Department.

Runyan, D. and Wu, C-Tong, (1979). Assessing tourism's more complex consequences. *Annals of Tourism Research*, **6**: 448−63.

Sethna, R.J. (1980). Social impact of tourism, in selected Caribbean countries. In *Tourism Planning and Development Issues*. Hawkins, D.E., Shafer, E.L. and Rovelstad, J.M. (eds), pp. 239−49. Washington, DC: George Washington University.

Um, S. and Crompton, J.L. (1987). Measuring residents' attachment levels in a host community. *Journal of Travel Research*, **26** (1): 27−9.

5 The tourism crime cycle: a beach destination case study

BRUCE PRIDEAUX

Although a number of studies have been undertaken in an attempt to discover the effect that crime has on tourism, researchers have not yet succeeded in identifying those elements within destinations which encourage an increase in criminal activity. In the search for a connection between increased crime and increased tourism this chapter will identify a number of elements which together appear to stimulate criminal activity in some beach destinations but not in others. Analysis of the factors which apparently stimulate criminal activity indicates the existence of an identifiable cause and effect pattern which can be illustrated in the form of a model, the Tourism Crime Cycle. This model and the possible implications it may have for predicting the impact of crime on tourism destinations will be discussed in this chapter.

Many tourists select holiday destinations using a criteria checklist which includes factors such as personal safety, value for money and the image that the destination promotes. To ensure the continued prosperity of domestic and international tourism, planners in both the private and public sectors should be aware that poor personal security may have an adverse effect on the tourist industry. Graphic images of war and violence nightly flash across television screens, ensuring that intending travelers are well aware of the varieties of potential dangers that exist in a large number of countries. Destinations which gain notoriety as crime hot spots are likely to experience difficulty in retaining their tourism industry. In recent years popular destinations including Rio de Janeiro, Florida, Egypt and the former Yugoslavia have all suffered significant declines in overseas visitation in response to widely reported incidents of crime, terrorism and war.

Australia has always regarded itself as a relatively low-crime destination and, as a consequence, only limited research has been conducted into the rate of crime against visitors and into the development of policy measures to identify significant tourism-related crime trends that may be emerging. In the early 1990s a number of well-publicized crimes against overseas visitors had the potential to tarnish Australia's reputation as a safe tourist destination. One particular case, involving serial murders of backpackers in New South Wales, was widely reported in the European press and gave rise to an editorial in one of Australia's leading Sunday papers which stated that "no parent saying goodbye to a son or daughter as they head off to see the sights of Australia can feel secure in the knowledge that they will return" (*Sunday Telegraph*, November 7,

Tourism, Crime and International Security Issues, edited by
A. Pizam and Y. Mansfeld. © 1996 John Wiley & Sons Ltd.

1993: 29). This chapter will examine the impact that the development of mass tourism has had on the three largest tourist destinations in Queensland, in terms of increasing criminal activity, and will seek to identify any underlying relationships that may exist between tourism and crime. The outcome of the analysis undertaken is the construction of a model demonstrating the stages in the development of crime in beach destinations based on observations conducted at Cairns, the Gold Coast and the Sunshine Coast.

In terms of total tourist numbers, the Gold Coast is the state's largest tourist destination, followed by the Sunshine Coast and Cairns, which are about equal in terms of the number of commercial bed nights. Each of the destinations is located on coastal plains flanked by the Pacific Ocean to the east and rainforest-clad mountain ranges to the west. Each location exhibits a tourism-dependent economic base and each destination offers visitors excellent weather,particularly in the Southern Hemisphere's winter months. Lying just beyond the southernmost extent of the Great Barrier Reef, both the Sunshine Coast and the Gold Coast offer visitors many kilometers of excellent surfing beaches and a wide variety of water sports. Cairns on the other hand is protected from the southern Pacific Ocean swells by the Great Barrier Reef and offers, instead, relatively tranquil swimming and ready access to world-class coral reefs. Diving is a major pastime for both local residents and visitors. Each destination has developed a large tourist industry based principally on the domestic market but with a rapidly growing international sector.

An analysis of reported crime rates in Cairns and the Gold Coast over a 10-year period indicates that criminal activity has grown at a rate that exceeds growth in crime in the remainder of the state and at a rate in excess of local population growth. The Sunshine Coast, situated 200 kilometers north of the Gold Coast, offers a range of attractions almost identical to those of the Gold Coast yet exhibits a rate of crime considerably below the average for the State of Queensland.

In spite of the growing size of Australia's international tourism industry, estimated to have generated exports worth $AUS 5.6 billion in 1991−2, little research has been conducted into the impact of crime on the nation's tourism industry. A number of studies conducted in the 1980s (Walmsley et al., 1981; Clark 1988; and Cameron McNamara, 1986) found little evidence of a strong statistical link between tourism and crime. One study (Cameron McNamara, 1986) prepared for the Cairns City Council and Mulgrave Shire Council noted that it appeared that the underlying social problems of the region were associated with drug usage, unemployment and vagrancy which together were significantly more important precursors of crime that tourism *per se*. Apparently, the authors of the Cameron McNamara report failed to note that rapid growth in the region's tourism industry had led to significant social upheaval as large numbers of new residents moved to Cairns in search of employment and investment. One outcome of the rapid surge in residential population and increased tourism has been the increase in the rate of criminal activity, something not experienced in the decades before tourism emerged as Cairns's largest industry.

Recent Australian research (Kelly, 1993; Prideaux, 1994) has tended to support the findings of international research (Chesney-Lind and Lind, 1986; Liu and Var, 1986) which has identified the existence of links between tourism and crime. A continuing problem in crime research, as it pertains to tourism, is the lack of suitable statistical information about victims and perpetrators. Published Queensland crime statistics fail to distinguish between residents and tourists and provide few details about the perpetrators, particularly in respect of their employment and life-style habits. Kelly (1993: 4) identified four broad categories of offenses which are commonly associated with tourism — activities which are directed against tourists, offenses committed by tourists, offenses which occur through the illegal servicing of demands created by tourists and criminal activities which relate to the growth and development of a destination which exhibits a tourism-dependent economic base. Although it is possible to identify certain classes of crimes as originating from a response to demands by tourists, prostitution being one example, most crimes committed in the study area fall into the more traditional categories of Offenses Against the Person and Offenses Against Property.

The necessity for searching for possible causal links between increasing crime and tourism is important if continued growth in tourism is to occur. Papua New Guinea, Australia's nearest northern neighbor, suffers from a popular perception of high crime, particularly Against the Person. Arguably it is this popular perception of the country, reinforced by regular negative media reports, that is one of the main reasons for that country's inability to develop a significant tourist industry (Ruddy, 1993b). Australia currently enjoys a highly favorable image overseas with a recent survey of 30 000 consumers in 21 countries conducted by advertising agency Young and Rubicam (Ruddy, 1994: 43) finding that Australia was one of the most powerful brands in the world. This positive image should not be taken for granted and widely reported incidents such as the Belanglo State Forest serial killing of seven overseas backpackers and media warnings that Australia has one of the world's highest rates of rape (*Australian*, March 31, 1993) can provide powerful disincentives for overseas visitors.

The size of the Gold Coast's and Cairns's tourism industry, in terms of their respective local economies and the disproportionately high levels of reported crime, provides an ideal environment from which to identify underlying factors which give rise to crime. To test the proposition that mass tourism may be a significant factor in the development of high crime rates, crime statistics for the Gold Coast and Cairns were compared to those of the state as a whole and to the Sunshine Coast. The research methodology adopted included analysis of crime statistics published by the Queensland Police Service, interviews with police, local authorities and tourism industry operators and analysis of published statistics compiled by the Australian Bureau of Statistics.

Queensland Police Service statistics enabled time-series analysis of crime trends to be undertaken. Police Regions covering the Sunshine Coast and the Gold Coast are closely aligned to the borders of the tourism regions and in the case of the Gold Coast, statistics were available at Police Division level. In the case of Cairns, small-area Police Divisions' statistics were not made available and the published data for the Cairns Division included a large sparsely populated area north of the main Cairns tourism region. Approximately 13 per cent of the population in the Cairns Police District live outside of the Cairns tourism region, including a number of aboriginal settlements which reportedly exhibit very high rates of Offenses Against the Person. The inclusion of these Police Divisions in the Cairns statistics may distort the true rate of crime in all classes in the Cairns area. Cairns crime data used in this chapter was not adjusted to account for crimes occurring outside of the Cairns tourist area. Significantly, the finding of this study would not be affected if adjustments in the order of 13 per cent to 20 per cent were made to the data.

Table 5.1 Comparative tourism statistics 1992−3. Visitor nights in commercial accommodation ('000s)

Destination	Intrastate	Interstate	International	Total	Total Expenditure $AUD million
Gold Coast	2004	6755	2111	10 870	1104
Cairns	1042	2171	2594	5807	840
Sunshine Coast	2845	2616	397	5857	348
Brisbane (Capital)	1241	1461	900	3602	425
State Total	12 648	16 736	7255	36 639	3553

Source: *Queensland Tourism Bulletin* (1993). June Quarter, QTTC: Brisbane.

Queensland tourism industry

Queensland's tourism industry is dominated by a series of coastal destinations with Cairns being the dominant northern destination and the Gold Coast being the dominant southern destination. Both centers have well-developed airports with Cairns Airport recently achieving the status of the fourth busiest airport in Australia. The Gold Coast receives domestic air travelers through Coolangatta Airport and international visitors through nearby Brisbane International Airport, the nation's third busiest airport in terms of passenger throughput. International and domestic tourism has developed rapidly in the past decade. In 1985 10.3 per cent of short-term overseas visitors visited Cairns and 10 per cent visited the Gold Coast. By 1992 these figures had increased to 21 per cent and 25 per cent respectively (Bureau of Tourism Research). Domestically, Cairns's share of visitor nights for the State of Queensland has grown from 6.3 per cent in 1982−3 to 10.9 per cent in 1992−3. The Gold Coast has shown similar patterns of growth with domestic visitor nights climbing from 15.2 per cent in 1982−3 to 29.8 per cent in 1992−3. In terms of numbers of commercial bed nights, Cairns and the Sunshine Coast are about equal in size, however the Gold Coast market is nearly 50 per cent larger than either Cairns or the Sunshine Coast individually. Combined, the three destinations accounted for 61.5 per cent of the state's total tourism market in 1992−3. In the same period the Gold Coast and Cairns attracted 65 per cent of Queensland's international visitor nights in commercial accommodation as illustrated in Table 5.1. On a national scale Queensland attracted 25 per cent of Australia's international visitor nights in 1992−3.

Incidence of crime

Table 5.2 illustrates and compares the rate of criminal offenses recorded in Cairns, the Gold Coast and the Sunshine Coast with the State average in 1992−3, measured on the basis of crime per 100 000 population. Crimes are categorized into three groups, Offenses Against the Person, Offenses Against Property and Other Offenses. The first two groups of crimes can be classified as predatory crimes because they involve an intent to inflict injury on a person or cause the loss or damage of property. The final group of crimes is generally referred to as "victimless crimes." Analysis of data illustrated in Table 5.2 indicates that all classes of crime in the Gold Coast and Cairns exceed the average for the State of Queensland, while figures for the Sunshine Coast were well below the state average. These figures are further analyzed in Table 5.3, which compares

Table 5.2 Reported crimes committed — Gold Coast District, Cairns District, Sunshine Coast District and remainder of Queensland per 100 000 population, 1992−3

Offense Category	Sunshine Coast District	Gold Coast District	Cairns District	Queensland
Crimes Against the Person				
Homicides	3	10	11	8.2
Serious Assault	63	230	784	218.5
Minor Assault	85	254	547	248.7
Robbery	13	86	65	57.4
Sexual Offenses	66	115	201	139.4
Other	20	48	124	48
Total	250	743	1732	720.2
Offenses Against Property				
Break & Enter	985	2433	2938	1994.2
Stealing	1728	4744	4346	2984.4
Motor Vehicle Theft	170	1001	539	536.7
Other	737	2394	1844	1766
Total	3620	10 572	9667	7281.4
Total All Offenses	3870	11 315	11 399	8001.4

Source: Queensland Police Service (1993) *Statistical Review, 1992−1993.*

Note: Estimated Residential Population is based on residents living in Police Service District boundaries.

the rates of crime between the various destinations on the basis of crime per 100 000 population measured as a percentage above or below the state average.

Analysis of individual statistics reveals that Offenses Against the Person in Cairns, even allowing for the inclusion of offenses committed outside of the region's major tourism areas, are occurring at a rate that is 240 per cent greater than the state average. On the Gold Coast, Offenses Against the Person were only marginally higher (3 per cent) than the state average. However in Cairns, serious and minor assaults were a major problem with the respective rates being 358.8 per cent and 219.9 per cent higher than the state average in 1992−3. Offenses categorized under the heading of Robbery were 150 per cent higher on the Gold Coast than the state average, while in Cairns the rate was 11.69 per cent below the state average. Sexual offenses were lower on the Gold Coast and Cairns in 1992−3 but in the two previous years Cairns recorded a rate of sexual offenses well above the state average. By contrast the Sunshine Coast figures were significantly below those of both the Gold Coast and Cairns for all types of offenses. Offenses categorized as Offenses Against Property reveal a higher rate of offense on the Gold Coast compared with Cairns. While Break and Enter offenses were significantly higher in Cairns compared to the Gold Coast in 1992−3, the rate of Motor Vehicle Theft on the Gold Coast was 186 per cent higher than the state average, whereas in Cairns the rate was almost equal to the state average. The Gold Coast also recorded a higher rate of Stealing (159 per cent) than Cairns (146.6 per cent) in 1992−3. The Sunshine Coast recorded rates of Offenses Against Property that were on average 50 per cent below the state trend. Predatory crimes on the Gold Coast and Cairns occurred at a rate that were on average 42 per cent higher than the state average. In contrast, the Sunshine Coast recorded a rate 52 per cent below the state average in the same year.

Table 5.3 Comparison of crimes reported on the Gold Coast, Cairns and Sunshine Coast with the remainder of Queensland for the period 1991−2 to 1992−3 per 100 000 population (% increase or decrease)

Offense Category	Sunshine Coast	1991−2 Cairns	Gold Coast	Sunshine Coast	1992−3 Cairns	Gold Coast
Crimes Against the Person						
Homicides	−33.34	+200	+122.22	−63.42	+240.48	+121.95
Serious Assault	−51.2	+324.7	+103.78	−71.16	+358.8	+15.26
Minor Assault	−42.55	+210.2	+122.4	−65.82	+219.94	+12.13
Robbery	−70.2	+161.46	+171.17	−77.35	−11.69	+149.82
Sexual Offenses	−5.23	+110.7	−30.03	−52.65	−30.65	−17.5
Other	−31.42	+119.3	+122.11	−58.33	+115.5	+126.9
Total	−40	+230.16	+100.96	−65.29	+240.48	+103.16
Crimes Against Property						
Break and Enter	−29.72	+151.29	+152.64	−50.6	+146.82	+122
Stealing	−7	+154.65	+171.98	−42.1	+145.62	+158.96
Motor Vehicle Theft	−48.66	−9.35	+189.69	−68.33	+100.43	+186.51
Other Property Damage	+40.53	−16.13	−22.2	−58.27	+104.41	+135.56
Total	−22.57	+143.27	+159.29	−50.29	+132.76	+145.19
Total Major Offenses	−23.99	+150.4	+154.53	−51.63	+142.47	+141.42
Other Offenses						
Handling Stolen Goods	−36	+168.6	+172.1	−30.5	+192	+182.6
Drug Offenses	+127	+189.5	+121.8	−12.55	+257.6	184.7
Good Order Offenses	+44.1	+304.5	−17.89	−72.55	+314.45	+145
Traffic and Other Related Offenses	−0.1	+209.3	+76.37	−42.19	+225.8	+171.5

Source: Queensland Police Service (1993) *Statistical Review 1992−1993*.

A similar picture emerges from the crime rates for those offenses grouped under the general title of Other Offenses. These offenses are generally classed as being victimless in nature although it can be argued that Traffic Offenses in all classes do offer the potential for damage to occur to a third party's person and property. Both the Gold Coast and Cairns recorded rates of offenses in the category of Handling Stolen Goods and Drug Offenses that were considerably higher than the state average. In 1992−3 Drug Offenses were particularly high in Cairns with a rate of 257.6 per cent above the state average being recorded. Analysis of Good Order Offenses, which include offenses such as Public Drunkenness and Abusive Language, indicates a very high rate of offense in Cairns (314.4 per cent above the state average), perhaps pointing to a deeper social malaise not found in other destination areas such as the Sunshine Coast. Moreover the rate of Traffic and Other Related Offenses was much higher on the Gold Coast and Cairns.

Analysis of the three groups of offenses indicates that in most categories, the Sunshine Coast consistently recorded a rate of offense at least 50 per cent below the state average. Classes of offenses grouped under the categories of Stealing, Handling Stolen Goods and Drug Offenses were the exception and may give some cause for concern. Anecdotal evidence suggests that many regular drug users resort to crime, particularly stealing, to support their habit. Although not pursued in this chapter, it would appear that there is a strong link between the growth of the drug culture and Offenses Against Property in the study area. It is also possible that a link exists between the type of mass tourism that has emerged in the study area and the growth of a local drug culture.

Kelly (1993: 6) tested crime figures for the Gold Coast, Cairns and Sunshine Coast, using location quotients (LQ) as a means of comparing variables in each area with a specified norm, based on the proposition that a location quotient larger than 1 indicates that a district has a disproportionately higher number of offenses than experienced in the state as a whole. Kelly found that in the period 1986−90 the Gold Coast and Cairns had location quotients of 1.64 and 1.55 respectively, while the Sunshine Coast had a LQ value of 0.73. Results of these comparisons indicate that high levels of tourism alone are not necessarily responsible for increased crime in tourism destinations such as the Gold Coast and Cairns. It now remains to look more closely at the individual destinations to attempt to identify those factors which apparently stimulate the development of an environment conducive to crime.

In the search for possible links between increased crime and increased tourism, an analysis was made of crime statistics for individual Police Divisions on the Gold Coast. Illustrated in Table 5.4, the results for 1991−2 indicate that 73.19 per cent of reported offenses occurred in the Police Divisions of Broadbeach, Coolangatta, Southport and Surfers Paradise. These divisions are located astride the main tourism areas of the Gold Coast and include the area's major shopping, entertainment, accommodation and recreational facilities. Similar data was not available for the Cairns Police District, although discussions with a Police Service spokesperson indicated that a similar situation existed in Cairns with high rates of offenses occurring in those areas where tourists tended to congregate.

In a study of reported offenses in the Surfers Paradise Police District in the period March 1, 1993 to June 30, 1993, Dokter (1993) found that 84.8 per cent of incidents were reported by local residents, 7 per cent by interstate visitors and 8.2 per cent by overseas visitors. The majority of incidents reported by overseas visitors involved Japanese. In the same study, illustrated in Table 5.5, the majority of thefts in the Surfers Paradise Police District were reported from either hotels or units and from motor vehicles. Thefts in entertainment areas also rated highly. The articles most likely to be stolen were handbags (27.88 per cent) followed by cameras (13.38 per cent) and money (11.52 per cent). A large number of passports were also reported stolen.

Analysis of these figures indicates that the items most commonly stolen were articles likely to contain cash (wallets and handbags), money and items such as cameras and jewelry that could be easily sold for cash. Of particular interest was the very low number of incidents involving thefts from persons (3.87 per cent). The type of articles stolen and the location of thefts indicate that more attention should be given to making individuals aware of the need to adopt a more rigorous approach to safeguarding their personal property.

Discussion

Comparison of offense rates between the destinations studied indicates that there are factors at work in both the Gold Coast and Cairns that are not evident in the Sunshine

Table 5.4 Reported serious offenses in the Gold Coast Police Division, 1991–2

| Police District | Homicide | Reported Offenses Against the Person | | | | | Break & Enter | Reported Offenses Against Property | | | | Total |
		Serious Assault	Minor Assault	Robbery	Other Offenses	Total		Motor Vehicle Theft	Stealing	Property Damage	Other	
Broadbeach	7	87	137	39	69	339	2418	682	3434	810	557	7901
Burleigh Heads	1	38	43	14	32	128	744	198	848	240	135	2165
Coolangatta	5	49	53	30	26	163	973	275	1469	332	183	3232
Coomera	3	15	17	2	9	46	255	112	326	84	43	820
Mudgeeraba	0	1	2	0	2	5	48	5	45	10	4	112
Nerang	2	20	33	11	22	88	710	141	532	192	116	1691
Runaway Bay	3	31	34	10	51	129	533	121	783	187	63	1687
Southport	3	95	161	31	60	350	1465	469	2003	581	474	4992
Surfers Paradise	4	131	178	56	29	398	1217	649	3415	684	320	6285

Source: South Eastern Region, Queensland Police Service (1993). Unadjusted Crime Statistics (1991–2).

Note: Mudgeeraba Police District was gazetted by the Queensland Government in April 1992.

Table 5.5 Analysis of thefts committed in Surfers Paradise Police District during the period March 1, 1993 to June 30, 1993

Item Stolen	% of Total Thefts	Place Where Stolen	% of Total Thefts
Camera	13.33	Hotel/Unit	35.91
Video	0.61	Beach	8.84
Wallet	8.48	Motor Vehicle	18.78
Handbag	27.88	Person	3.87
Clothing	0.61	Entertainment Area	12.71
Money	11.52	Shopping	2.21
Passport	6.67	Food Outlet	3.87
Jewelry	7.27	Other	13.81
Other	23.63		

Source: Dokter, L. (1993). Unpublished Report on Crime on the Gold Coast. Prepared with the assistance of the Queensland Police Service.

Table 5.6 Offense rate per 100 000 population, Queensland minor tourism centers, 1992−3

Police District	Offenses Against the Person	Offenses Against Property	Total Offenses Against Persons and Property
Mackay	542	4764	5306
Townsville	751	6962	7713
Rockhampton	600	5923	6523
Queensland	720	7281	8001

Source: Queensland Police Service (1993). *Statistical Review 1992−1993.*

Coast. To attempt to identify those elements which may give rise to high criminal activity in some tourist destinations and not others, offense rates for other beach destinations in Queensland were reviewed with the results illustrated in Table 5.6. While the local economies of these destinations are not as dependent on tourism as those of the Gold Coast and Cairns, tourism is still an important local industry in each of these centers. Measured on the basis of reported offenses per 100 000 population, each of these destinations exhibited rates of offense below the state average and significantly below offense rates experienced on the Gold Coast and Cairns.

Previous research into the relationship between mass tourism destinations and increasing crime has suggested a number of factors that appear to encourage criminal activity. In general, however, previous studies have failed to identify those features of the growth in tourism that stimulate growth in crime. Most studies point to minor and perhaps peripheral factors. It has been suggested (Fujii and Mak, 1980: 34) that tourists may be regarded as tempting crime targets because they carry "portable wealth" in the form of cash, jewelry and cameras. After reviewing crime statistics in Hawaii, Chesney-Lind and Lind (1986: 170−3) found that tourists experienced rates of crime involving property and violence at rates that were significantly higher than residents. Liu and Var (1986) pointed to structural features of the tourist industry that tend to concentrate tourists into well-defined areas that make them "legitimate targets for crime." Crime patterns observed in

Cairns and the Gold Coast are supportive of this assertion. Clark (1988) found that the pleasant tropical climate of Cairns had attracted many non-tourists to the area including a large number of drifters ("dole bludgers" — to use an Australian colloquialism) and drug users (as indicated by Police Service Statistics and drug support agencies). Both groups tend to be associated with increased criminal activities, particularly in the areas of illegal use of drugs, prostitution and vandalism. Garland (1984:59) found that tourist destinations in New Zealand also showed rates of offenses including violence, drugs and sexual offenses that were higher than the national average. While unable to conclude that tourism was the prime cause of increased crime, Garland concluded that rates of crime confirm the residents' belief that tourism brought with it increased criminal activity. Minority issues have also been raised as a possible cause for crime. However, Australia has developed a multi-cultural society that is relatively unaffected by significant minority crime problems and as a consequence crime rates in tourism destinations cannot be attributed to significant cultural or ethnic minorities.

Unfamiliarity with an area may also result in tourists engaging in activities which lead to victimization. Visiting night clubs and bars late at night and engaging in activities such as prostitution and drug taking that would normally be avoided at home, are typical examples of these types of actions. Uzzell (1984:97) suggested that risk taking is a significant element in the fantasy and escape which is often an important element of the holiday experience. On the Gold Coast and in Cairns numerous instances of visitors and local residents finding themselves victims of theft of handbags and wallets and of assaults and robberies as they left night clubs and bars are reported in the press. While local residents are generally familiar with the "safe" and "unsafe" areas of their local area, tourists usually are not. On the Gold Coast several areas in Surfers Paradise have gained notoriety as places where sexual assaults and robberies are common, although recent police action has targeted these areas resulting in significant reductions in the crime rate.

Other factors which may contribute to increased incidents of crime include resentment by locals over the intrusive effects of mass tourism (Pearce, 1982) and conflicting norms of dress, speech and behavior which give rise to increased tension between tourists and residents. Racial and ethnic factors and color may also be a contributing factor. Some Australians who experienced the threat of Japanese invasion in World War II, and veterans who fought in Asia in subsequent campaigns, still find some difficulty in adjusting to the influx of Japanese visitors to Australia in recent years. To some degree these feelings are magnified through talk-back radio programs and Letters to the Editor in local newspapers which enable these minority opinions to receive wide publicity thus supporting observations made by Pearce.

Data collected in this study points to the strong statistical link between tourism and crime on the Gold Coast and Cairns but does not find such a link present at the Sunshine Coast or at other major beach destinations in the state. The search for explanation appears to point to other social and economic factors that are at work in the areas studied. Closer examination of Drug Offenses recorded at the Gold Coast and Cairns indicates levels of activity far above the state average. According to Police Service spokespersons there is a strong link between drug taking and stealing, a situation evident in the study area. A further connection with Drug Offenses can be found in the rate of Offenses for Handling Stolen Goods. In many instances arrests for Drug Offenses lead to further charges being made for Handling Stolen Goods and for Stealing. Conversely many Stealing and Handling Stolen Goods arrests lead to charges for Possession of Drugs. The need for habitual drug users to support their craving for expensive drugs will often force users to turn to criminal activity, particularly where it involves Offenses Against Property. Police Districts which record Drug Offenses at a rate below the state average do not have high offense rates for Offenses Against Property or for Handling Stolen Goods.

If there is a relationship between drug use and crime in certain tourism areas it is probable that other factors are at work apart from the physical presence of increased numbers of tourists. Closer investigation of the strategies that destinations employ to market themselves may provide an answer. Uzzell (1984) noted that some tourism promotional materials "are trying to sell sun, sea, sand and sex," by purposely using images that exhibit a similarity to contemporary soft pornography. In the case of the Gold Coast and Cairns, advertising often focuses on scantily clad models (male and female), night life and a generally hedonistic experience. Prideaux (1994) suggests that "images of this nature and the potential for employment stimulate migration into the area including those who wish to invest, those looking for work and those attracted by the potential for crime."

The lure of a pleasant life-style, potential for employment in an apparently glamorous industry and possible attractions of a hedonistic life-style away from the emotional bonds of family and friends provide strong inducements for young people to move to destinations such as the Gold Coast and Cairns. Unfortunately for many new arrivals the promise does not match reality. Many tourism jobs are comparatively low-paid, service positions which are often worked on a shift basis. Promotion, even for people with post-secondary education, is slow and often requires a period of time spent working behind the bar or counter. Earnings from employment may not always enable newly arrived workers to engage in the life-style that attracted them to the area in the first place, giving rise to a general feeling of frustration. Such frustrations may lead to people departing from the area or turning to other endeavors such as drugs or crime.

With the emergence of a significant tourist industry based on interstate and international marketing and a parallel growth of migration of young workers into the area, another factor appears to emerge that can have a significant impact on crime. The growth of an entertainment industry based on pubs, nightclubs and other late-night entertainment venues leads to an increase in Good Order Offenses usually associated with excessive consumption of alcohol. Excessive drinking often leads to fights and other instances of rowdy behavior including assaults and rape. On the Gold Coast the growth of a distinctive nightclub culture centered around Orchid Avenue, Surfers Paradise has brought with it a noticeable increase in Good Order Offenses usually committed late at night by young males. Associated with the Good Order Offenses are a range of other crimes including assault, theft of handbags and wallets as well as a range of sexual offenses. Anecdotal evidence also indicates that the nightclub scene provides a good contact point for drug pushers. Again anecdotal evidence indicates that the nightclub scene is heavily patronized by locals with tourists generally being in the minority. A similar situation exists in Cairns where the nightclub industry has grown rapidly since the opening of the Cairns International Airport, which stimulated a surge in investment in new resort hotels. Attracted by the prospects of finding work, many young job seekers moved to the area, thereby providing a large market for the nightclub industry. The pattern of offenses is broadly similar to that found on the Gold Coast.

The picture of a relatively young, mobile population is supported by Australian census data which indicates that at the time of the 1991 Australian Census, 57 per cent of the

Gold Coast's population had moved into the area in the five-year period preceding the census. In the same period the area's population had increased by 37.4 per cent compared to the state as a whole which had experienced growth of 15.1 per cent. In the same five-year period Cairns experienced a a population growth of 67.7 per cent almost entirely from migration into the area.

Other Queensland destinations, with the exception of the Sunshine Coast, have not experienced high rates of population growth in the period 1986—91 nor do they exhibit a population mobility on the scale of that experienced by the Gold Coast and Cairns. Promotional literature for all Queensland coastal destinations makes extensive use of images depicting sand, sea and sun but with the exception of the Gold Coast and Cairns generally refrains from depicting images offering an overtly hedonistic experience. Both Cairns and the Gold Coast make extensive use of images involving sand, sun, sex and romance. Analysis of brochures from destinations other than the Gold Coast and Cairns points to the promotion of images aimed at a wide variety of market segments including families, adventure seekers, eco-tourism experiences and seniors. The Sunshine Coast has refrained from promoting an image that points to a hedonistic life-style in spite of its growing sophistication, including direct air linkages to the large national markets of Sydney and Melbourne and the opening of a number of five-star resorts including properties operated by the Hilton and Hyatt groups.

The Tourism Crime Cycle

Analysis of the crime trends in both Cairns and the Gold Coast indicates a similarity that is not replicated in other Queensland Beach destinations, leading to speculation that a range of factors appear to be at work which, together, create an environment that encourages crime to flourish. The most influential factors appear to be the image that is created and the type of marketing that is undertaken. Tourism is often marketed as a glamorous industry appealing to the desires of escapism, romance, adventure and an opportunity for self-indulgence. Creation of images of this type not only attracts tourists but also stimulates migration of young job seekers to the area. An increasingly mobile population with few emotional ties to the area and in search of their own after-work entertainment provides an opportunity for a large night-entertainment industry to emerge. In turn the potent mix of youth, money and desire to have a good time leads to excessive use of alcohol and encourages the growth of a drug sub-culture which in turn leads to rates of crime well in excess of state or national levels.

The Tourism Crime Cycle depicted in Figure 5.1 illustrates the development of crime in beach destinations based on the type of promotion used in marketing that destination. It is highly likely that similar patterns will be found at work in other tourism destinations such as mountain resorts. The model traces the development of crime through the manner in which the destination is marketed, the types of tourist accommodation facilities constructed and the expansion of the marketing hinterland from day trippers to international tourists. Two principal types of destinations are postulated, the Hedonistic destination and the Family Values destination. The Hedonistic destination will market itself with images of adventure, romance, escapism and sex. Cairns and the Gold Coast are typical examples. Destinations classed as belonging to the Family Values group will not emphasis sex or romance but instead promote family holidays for all age groups, as

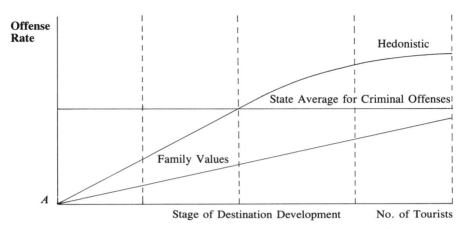

Characteristics of Development	Local Tourism	Regional Tourism	National Tourism (emphasis on hedonistic life-style)	Mass Tourism
Key Developments in the Area's Tourist Industry	• Small tourism industry • Caravan parks, backpackers' hostels, motels are main type of accommodation • Road and air access limited	• Decision made by locals to promote tourism • Roads improved and some air services commenced • Increased investment in tourism facilities • First large resort-style hotel built • Promotion on a larger scale with some national promotion	• Promotion assumes a national focus • Improvements to tourist infrastructure principally in the transport area including scheduled national air services • Resort hotels and manmade attractions move into the area • A nightclub scene develops initially to cater for tourist industry workers as well as tourists	• International promotion including major events — Grand Prix • Improved national access through air and/or rail • Heavy foreign investment • Centre for national/international conferences • Desire to attract casino
Social Characteristics	• Employees are mainly locals • Local ownership • Low crime • Low social mobility	• Migration of workers into the area • Increased outside investment • Crime rate begins to increase in relation to increased mobility of population and type of promotion	• Large number of young single workers who exhibit social mobility, relative deprivation, use of drugs • Increased media awareness of crime • Organised crime increases • Opportunity for corruption of civic officials and police	• Crowding • Citizen fright may occur in hedonistic resorts • Demand for law enforcement
Major Crime Characteristics	• All classes of crime below the state average	• Property crime and drug taking increase in Hedonistic resorts • Low crime in Family Values destinations	• Crime equals then exceeds state average in Hedonistic resorts • Increase in crime in Family Values destinations but still well below state average	• Most classes of crime exceed state average by significant levels in Hedonistic resorts • Increase in Drug Offenses & Stealing in Family Values resorts but generally still below the state average

Figure 5.1 The tourism crime cycle

typified by the Sunshine Coast. The model postulates four stages in the growth of beach destinations commencing with Stage 1, Local Tourism. Growth of destinations is dependent on the development of transport infrastructure and the expansion of the marketing hinterland from the local area in stage one to the international market in stage four. The growth of crime will depend both on the type of marketing adopted and the stage of growth achieved.

During Stage 1, Local Tourism, the tourist industry is developed around day trippers and visitors who stay in caravan parks, inexpensive hotels and motels and in backpackers' hostels. Transport infrastructure is relatively unsophisticated and air services are usually not available. Marketing is generally limited and reliant on the voluntary contributions of local tourist operators. As the size of the destination and its popularity increases, out-of-destination investment begins to occur and larger accommodation facilities are built. At this point in the development of the destination the Tourism Crime Cycle enters Stage 2, Inter-Regional Tourism.

Stage-2 development will commence when the destination refocuses its marketing efforts from the surrounding towns and cities to include a regional or state focus. In the case of Queensland, Stage-2 marketing would be aimed at attracting tourists from other areas of the state. In Stage 2 the destination's larger businesses commence their own promotions and, in an effort to enhance their profitability, pressure the public sector to improve infrastructure facilities, particularly transport networks. Increasing the ease of accessibility to the area, principally by road, but possibly by air and rail, will provide opportunity for further investment in the area. Initially investment in hotels will be made by national operations, however, later into the stage, international chains such as Hilton, Ramada and Sheraton may show interest in the destination. The local economy will grow rapidly during this stage, encouraging an influx of migrant job seekers. At this time the style of promotion to be used to capture a larger share of the state's tourism industry will be decided. If a Hedonistic-type image similar to that used by Cairns and the Gold Coast is adopted the rate of crime can be expected to increase and by the end of the stage it will be nearing the state average. If, on the other hand, a style of promotion based on Family Values is adopted, the rate of crime can be expected to grow but not at a rate that will cause it to exceed the state or national average.

By Stage 3, National Tourism, the destination has commenced marketing on a national scale; and if Hedonistic life-styles are promoted, crime rates will rise sharply, taking them above state averages. During this stage the range of resorts and manmade attractions will expand rapidly. Transport infrastructure will be greatly improved with access to all major national markets being provided by air. In Hedonistic destinations large-scale migration of young job seekers will continue to stimulate the growth of the night-entertainment industry dominated by nightclubs, pubs and late-night bars. The growth of this industry will bring with it a rapid rise in offenses associated with alcohol and drugs. Development in both Cairns and the Gold Coast has closely followed this pattern. If destinations adopt the alternative marketing style based on Family Values, a different pattern of crime will become evident. Although the Sunshine Coast can be classed as a destination in the third stage of development, a significant night-entertainment industry has not emerged. As a consequence Good Order Offenses, particularly those associated with alcohol, and Drug Offenses are still at relatively low levels. It is likely, however, that as the destination's tourist industry continues to increase in size and the night-entertainment industry consolidates, rates of Drug Offenses and Stealing are likely to rise.

During the final stage, Mass Tourism, promotion will assume an international focus and the destination will attempt to attract world-class events such as international conferences and sporting events. It is also likely that a casino will be built to capitalize on the destination's appeal to the national and international market-place. During this stage direct international flights will commence and contribute to the destination's reputation as a mass-tourism market. Crime rates will continue to increase, resulting in citizen fright and increased demand for law enforcement. At this stage the destination must be alert to the impact of crime before crime begins to affect tourists in significant numbers. If the destination gains a reputation as an unsafe place for tourists, there is a strong possibility that tourists will be deterred from considering the destination as a holiday venue.

In reality, the distinction between Stage 3 and 4 is not well defined and will often depend on the access that the destination has to international air services. Cairns gained direct international air services in 1985 prior to the development of a large five-star hotel sector and construction of a casino. The commissioning of the international airport stimulated the growth of a number of five-star resorts and the emergence of a significant nightclub scene. Deregulation of Australia's domestic airline services in 1990 saw an airline price war which resulted in domestic air fares to Cairns falling up to 25 per cent. In spite of the domestic economy being in recession, domestic tourism grew rapidly paralleling the growth in international tourism and increase in crime.

In general terms the Gold Coast has followed the pattern outlined in the model with the exception of the construction of an international airport. Due to Federal Government ownership of most airports in Australia, the Gold Coast has had to rely on Coolangatta Airport at the southern end of the destination for domestic air travel and on the long-established Brisbane Airport 100 kilometers to the north for international arrivals. This arrangement has not proved entirely satisfactory for the Gold Coast because of the distance and ensuing travel times between the Gold Coast and Brisbane. The recent Federal Government announcement that Australian airports will be privatized has encouraged Gold Coast interests to develop a consortium to buy the Coolangatta Airport and redevelop it as an international gateway.

Conclusion

Neither residents nor tourists are exempt from the possibility of becoming a crime victim, an event which can occur at almost any place and at any time. In the normal course of events tourists may expect to have at least the same probability of becoming a crime victim as residents of the area they are visiting. Analysis of the widely different rates of crime experienced by Queensland's major beach destinations indicates that the causes of increased crime are complex and interrelated. An examination of the possible links between the increase in tourism and increase in crime points to the most likely causes being promotional images of the destination, the growth of the night-entertainment industry and the size of the destination's drug sub-culture. There is considerable cause for making a case that these factors are interdependent.

Police Authorities in Australia point to the strong connection between drug taking and property crimes. All recent studies on the subject identify that the major reason for increased property crime in the last two decades has been an increased use of illegal drugs. This relationship is clearly identified in this study. It follows that identification of the factors responsible for the growth of a local drug sub-culture in tourism destinations will suggest a possible connection between the growth of tourism and the growth of crime. In the case of Cairns and the Gold Coast, the most likely connection is the manner in which the area is promoted. The Hedonistic approach to promotion not only attracts tourists, but also attracts internal migration from other areas of the country as people relocate to a seemingly desirable area in search of employment. Concurrently the same promotion may induce criminal elements to turn their attention to these areas, the end result being an upsurge in crime against both residents and tourists. Short of changing a destination's image and taking the risk of suffering a loss of market share, it appears that destinations marketing a Hedonistic image based on glamor, excitement and sex will suffer higher rates of crime than could be expected in destinations which adopt different promotional strategies, experience a lower rate of migration into the area and lack a large drug sub-culture.

To control the problem of crime, authorities at all levels of government and the private sector need to develop a range of strategies including education, new policing methods and policies designed to reduce the opportunity for crime to occur. Allocating significant numbers of additional police to an area may help increase the crime clean-up rate, but without innovative new anti-crime strategies a high crime rate will continue. Analysis of crime figures contained in Table 5.5 indicates that most thefts occur in motels, entertainment areas and from motor vehicles. Many of these thefts are avoidable but require greater efforts in educating both tourists and residents in simple crime prevention strategies. There is also an obvious need to pay greater attention to hotel/motel security.

While the connection between the type of destination marketing and ensuing rates of crime is illustrated in the Tourism Crime Cycle model, the level of crime at which tourism will falter has not been determined. In spite of high crime rates tourists continue to be attracted to both Cairns and the Gold Coast in increasing numbers each successive year. A possible fifth stage of the model may be postulated to describe the effects that may occur if crime rates continue to grow to a level at which tourist numbers commence to decline. Such a stage has not yet been reached in the areas studied. Even in destinations such as New York and Florida which have a reputation for high rates of crime, tourism continues to grow in spite of periodic declines as a consequence of media attention to specific instances of crime.

References

Australian Bureau of Statistics (1992). *Law and Order*, Queensland Catalogue No. 4502.3 ABS.
Bureau of Tourism (1992). *Domestic Tourism Monitor*. Canberra: Bureau of Tourism Research.
Bureau of Tourism Research (1992). *Australian Tourism Trends 1992 Update*. Canberra: Bureau of Tourism Research.
Cameron McNamara (1986). *Cairns Region Joint Tourism Research Study*. Cairns: Cairns City Council and Mulgrave Shire Council.
Carrol, P., Donohue, K., McGovern, M. and McMillan, J. (1991). *Tourism in Australia*. Sydney: Harcourt Brace Jovanovich.
Chesney-Lind, M. and Lind, I. (1986). Visitors as Victims. Crimes against tourists in Hawaii. *Annals of Tourism Research 13*, (2): 167–91.
Chesney-Lind, M., Lind, I. and Schaafsma, H. (1983). Salient factors in Hawaii's crime rate. University of Hawaii-Manoa. *Youth Development and Research Center Report* No. 286.

Clark, L. (1988) Planning for tourism in far north Queensland: A local government response. In *Frontiers of Australian Tourism: The Search for New Perspectives in Policy Development and Research*. Faulkner, W. and Fagence, M. (eds), Canberra: Bureau of Tourism Research: 77–88.

Conley, D. (1993) Safety First. *Gold Coast Weekend Bulletin*, June 12–13.

Dokter, L. (1993). Unpublished Report on Crime on the Gold Coast.

Farrell, B.H. (1987. *The Social and Economic Impacts of Tourism in Pacific Communities*. Santa Cruz CA: Center for South Pacific Studies. University of California at Santa Cruz.

Farrell, B.H. (1982). *Hawaii, the Legend that Sells*. Honolulu: University of Hawaii Press.

Fujii, E. and Mak, J. (1980). Tourism and crime: Implications for regional development policy. *Regional Studies*, **14**: 27–36.

Garland, R. (1984). *New Zealand Hosts and Guests. A Study on the Social Impact of Tourism Research*. Report No. 39, Palmerston North Market Research Centre, Massey University, New Zealand.

Gold Coast Bulletin (1993). Insurance Premiums to Rise. *Gold Coast Bulletin*, 23 June, 1993.

Kelly, I. (1993) Tourist distinction crime rates: An examination of Cairns and the Gold Coast, Australia. *Journal of Tourism Studies*, **4**: 2.

Liu, T. and Var, T. (1986). Residents' attitudes toward tourism impacts in Hawaii. *Annals of Tourism Research*, **13**: 193–213.

Pearce, P.L. (1982). *The Social Psychology of Tourism and Behaviour*. Oxford: Pergamon Press.

Pizam, A. (1982). Tourism and crime: Is there a relationship? *Journal of Travel Research* **20** (3): 8–20.

Prideaux, B.R. (1994) Mass tourism and crime: is there a connection? A study of crime in major Queensland tourism resorts. In Proceedings of the Australian Tourist Research Conference. *Gold Coast Bureau Tourism Research*: Canberra.

Queensland Police Service (1992). *Statistical Review 1991–1992*. Brisbane: Queensland Police Service.

Queensland Police Service (1993). *Statistical Review 1992–1993*. Brisbane: Queensland Police Service.

Ruddy, B. (1993a). Tourism fears of international condemnation. *Sunday Telegraph*, November 7, 1993: 29.

Ruddy, B. (1993b). PNG perceptions all wrong says operator. Brisbane: *Travel Reporter*. October 8, 1993.

Ruddy, B. (1994). Aussie brands names pack a big punch, *The Sunday Mail*, May 8, 1994, Brisbane.

Uzzell, D. (1984). An alternative structuralist approach to the psychology of tourism marketing. *Annals of Tourism Research* **11** (1): 79–99.

Walmsley, D.T., Boshovic, R.M. and Pigram, T.T. (1981). *Tourism and Crime*. Armidale: Department of Geography, University of New England.

6 Touting tourists in Thailand: tourist-oriented crime and social structure

ERIC COHEN

> You have learned of Thailand as the "Land of the Smiles." It is a name frequently used in tourism promotion campaigns in this country . . . You may have no doubt about the truth contained in the statement, since it would boomerang if it were not true. (Suksawat, 1994: 58)

Introduction

Tourist-oriented crime is a little researched topic in tourism studies (Mathieson and Wall, 1982: 150). Moreover, the focus of much research has been fairly limited, with a good deal of the earlier efforts devoted to the establishment of a statistical relationship between an increase in tourism and an increase in crime at a given destination (Mathieson and Wall, 1982: 151; Jud, 1975: McPheters and Strange, 1974; Nicholls, 1976; Pizam, 1982). Other studies sought to explore the question whether crime, and more broadly safety problems at the destination, have an impact on tourism flows (Pizam, 1978, Elliot and Ryan, 1993). A few studies (eg, Chesney-Lind and Lind 1986, Cohen, 1987) focused on the relationship between types of tourists, or tourist behavior and such topics as victimization of tourists and the conduct of local law enforcement agencies towards them. In these studies, the theoretical perspective taken by the researcher was that of the tourist: the specificities of the touristic situation, or differences between tourists, were assumed as the principal explanatory variables in the study of tourism-related crime. In this chapter, "tourism-related crime" refers to all kinds of crime occurring in a touristic context: crimes of locals against tourists, of tourists against locals, tourists against tourists and locals against locals, in so far as the crimes are in some way related to tourism; "tourist-oriented crime" refers specifically to crime committed by locals against tourists. Few if any studies probed the deeper problem of the relationship between basic structural traits of the host society and the nature of tourism-related crime. It appears, however, that it is this problem which promises to open the topic of tourism-related crime to sociological analysis and particularly to its systematic comparative study. This perspective enables us to ask new questions like the following: (1) Do the basic structural

Tourism, Crime and International Security Issues, edited by
A. Pizam and Y. Mansfeld. © 1996 John Wiley & Sons Ltd.

traits of the host society facilitate the emergence of situations conducive to tourism-related crimes? (2) What is the relationship between these traits and the prevalence of certain types of tourism-related crimes? (3) What is the impact of these traits on the manner in which law enforcement agencies deal with tourism-related crimes?

The purpose of this chapter is to demonstrate the theoretical and empirical potential inherent in the perspective here proposed; specifically I shall attempt to show the connection between some basic structural traits of contemporary Thai society and one prevalent type of tourist-oriented crime in that society: confidence tricks. The sale of low-quality gems at exorbitant prices to unsuspecting tourists, a widespread practice in Thailand, will serve to illustrate this type of crime. Since I did not conduct field research on this topic, my material is derived from detailed reports and letters of victims in the English-speaking Thai press.

Basic structural traits of Thai society

Thailand is a complex society and its study is fraught with controversies engendered partly by that complexity (Cohen, 1991: 34—46). Here I shall list only those of its traits which appear to bear directly upon tourist-oriented crime. Three such traits seem to be particularly significant: ambiguity, opacity and the duality of Thai society.

Ambiguity

This is perhaps the most pervasive and distinctive structural trait of Thai society, and one of the keys to its understanding (Cohen, 1991: 8). The ambiguity is essentially the consequence of persistent conflicts between "apparently contradictory motifs" (Anderson, 1978: 231) or cultural themes coexisting in Thai society such as looseness versus rigidity, informality versus formality, individualism versus conformism, private interest versus service to the collectivity, and social hierarchy versus equality. The fact that both themes in each dichotomy are culturally acceptable makes each situation in principle amenable to contrasting interpretations and any conflict resolvable in opposite directions. However, many conflicts aroused by such oppositions remain unresolved; this is especially the case in situations where a resolution would exact a very high price from one of the parties in the conflict. Hence, a "gray zone" of ambiguity between alternative interpretations of social situations emerges. An *ad hoc* compromise, rather than a principled resolution, is then sought in each specific case — a compromise which is itself often sufficiently vague to permit differing interpretations. Thai social structure is permeated by such persistent ambiguities, which are tacitly suffered to prevent the outbreak of overt conflict, while the various groups and factions maneuver behind the scenes to extract maximum benefit from the ambiguous state of affairs. Such zones of ambiguity facilitate the emergence of semi-legal or illegal activities, roles and organizations, which are fairly immune from prosecution by law-enforcing agencies.

Opacity

This is a trait closely related to but not identical with ambiguity. Thai social arrangements, and particularly Thai formal institutions, are highly intricate and, particularly for outsiders, hard to comprehend. Thai bureaucracy is a maze of often conflicting institutions. In the course of their struggle, self-aggrandizing formal institutions, initially formed for specific purposes, seek to broaden their field of activities, generating complex duplications of functions and conflicts of authority over specific issues. Bureaucratic and legal procedures are highly complicated, slow and their outcomes are unpredictable. Personal interests of individual incumbents, and outside influences emanating from important and powerful individuals, often shape bureaucratic decisions.

Duality of "front" and "back" (Goffman: 1959: 22–30)

This is a pervasive characteristic of Thai life; it is closely related to the traditional importance of preserving "face," a common preoccupation in many Asian cultures. This preoccupation leads to a marked preference for form, appearance and image over content and effective action on the level of both institutional practice and personal conduct. The preference for form over content is perceivable throughout the so-called "modernization process" in Thailand, from the second part of the 19th century onward, during which external symbols of modernity were often preferred to fundamental reforms of formal institutions. Even in contemporary Thailand, whenever a new emergency occurs, the government tends to respond by the establishment of a new agency to deal with it or by the promulgation of a new law or regulation, after which, however, little effective action is taken. Thus, while prostitution was outlawed by Marshal Sarit in the 1960s, the number of prostitutes increased, openly and virtually unhindered, in the following period; even as Bangkok came to be known as the "Brothel of Asia," a commander of the Bangkok police in the 1980s announced with a straight face that there is no prostitution in Thailand, since it is an outlawed activity. On the personal level, the preference for "front" over "back" finds expression in a marked reluctance to engage in open confrontation with opponents, even as one fights them covertly and often unabashedly in the rear; and in the general preference for decorous behavior and face-saving devices which cover up inefficiency, failure, deceit and dishonesty. The famous Thai smile thus often hides the reality behind it. The titles of two recent works on different aspects of Thai life, Ekachai's (1990) *Behind the Smile* and Meyer's (1988) *Beyond the Mask* express this duality.

While these traits of Thai society may provide a convenient context for the emergence and proliferation of criminal activity and criminal organizations in general, they appear particularly to encourage certain types of crime against foreigners, especially tourists. Tourists tend to be misled by the appealing, smiling face of Thai society, promoted by the tourist authorities and tourist-oriented publications (Suksawat, 1994). Tourists have serious difficulties in penetrating the opacity of Thai social organization, while the ambiguity and duality pervading most social situations makes it difficult for them to perceive threats of victimization in their environment, and even more so to induce or compel the law-enforcing agencies to nail down the culprits, once they have become victims of a criminal act.

To demonstrate the relationship between these general structural characteristics and criminal acts against tourists in Thailand, I shall in the following present an extended case study of one example of such acts: the widespread confidence game which induces unaware tourists to purchase low-quality gems and-jewels at exorbitant prices.

Gem confidence games

Crime against tourists is on the upswing in contemporary Thailand. If in the mid-1980s, theft, especially bag-snatching, was the principal offense against conventional tourists (Cohen, 1987: 193), in the last decade criminal acts against tourists have become more varied and more serious, ranging from simple cheating about prices and qualities of goods to violent robberies and even murder. The multiplication of crimes against tourists affected Thailand's image, so much so that in a recent British TV program, Thailand was labeled as among the "ten most dangerous holiday destinations" (*The Nation*, 1993: A1) — a description which unleashed a furious denial by the Thai authorities (*Bangkok Post*, 1993b). One of the most prominent tourist-oriented crimes which recently proliferated is confidence trickery — the acquisition by conmen of the victims' trust, in order to cheat them.

The Thai people, apparently friendly, cheerful and hospitable, are a principal tourist attraction. Indeed, tourists generally gain a very positive view of them in the course of their visits. This positive attitude leads tourists to trust Thai people whom they meet on their journey and enables some locals, building upon this propensity to trust them, to engage in confidence games with tourists. The general ability of Thais to present an appealing front and to play different roles, makes it easy for such individuals to convince tourists of the veracity of their intentions and proposals and gain the tourists' confidence. The readiness of many tourists, when abroad, to utilize unexpected opportunities, seek adventures and even engage in risk-taking behavior, facilitates the conmen's job.

Conning in Thailand is not limited to tourists; locals also often fall victim to conmen (Khanphondee, 1994); however, conning of tourists is relatively much more common. Moreover, a different kind of con artist engages in tricking tourists: these individuals appear more sophisticated and refined and belong to a higher class than those who cheat locals. The most prominent con game in which such individuals engage is to convince tourists to purchase gems or jewels in jewelry stores for which they are touting clients. Bernard Trink, a highly experienced reporter on the Bangkok scene, summarizes the principal steps of this confidence game:

> Their MO (method of operation) is to dress in good clothes so as to appear respectable. Passing themselves off as teachers or businessmen, professional men or retirees, they hover near hotels and one approaches an obvious single tourist or couple.
>
> Fluent in English, he asks where they come from. If the reply is the US, UK or Canada he tells them he has been to their country as a tourist himself and was so well treated that he would like to repay that hospitality. "Free, of course. Kindness for kindness."
>
> To recent arrivals who don't know anybody, an offer of friendship from a clean-cut local is difficult to refuse. Even the wary find his earnestness and good manners convincing. With a hint of embarrassment, he admits that not all the denizens of the metropolis are trustworthy.
>
> He warns them about guides only interested in getting kickbacks from establishments they take tourists to. They are informed about false labeling — watches, clothes, tapes, etc. "Stay away from the Patpong area. It's full of clip-joints!"
>
> He appears knowledgeable, intelligent, sincerely concerned about their well-being. "Ah New York/London/Montreal, I remember it well. Of course, there is much to see in Bangkok. I would be honoured to show you around. Have you eaten yet? I know an excellent, inexpensive restaurant."

Sensing that they are hooked, he doesn't object too strenuously when they insist on paying for the meal. In no hurry, he takes them to a temple and for a ride on the river. His anecdotes about old houses along the Chao Phya are informative and interesting. They make an appointment for the following day.

Casually mentioning that he's an amateur gemologist, he wants to introduce them to a jeweller who is above reproach. "Honest as the day is long, as they say." The shop is off the beaten track. "Low rent, low profit."

Brightly lit, everything on display sparkles. The couple are awed. Assured that their credit-card is acceptable, they buy and buy stones. After some bargaining, the bill comes to nearly 100,000 baht. They are told that they would get more than twice if they resold them in their own country.

Their new found friend has his own work to attend to and they part. In time the couple leave for home. And there they have the gems appraised. To their immense disappointment, they are told that in view of the flaws the stones are only worth a fraction of what they paid (Trink, 1989).

Trink's summary is fleshed out by interpretations and case studies from additional sources.

Some reports dwell expressly on the link between a positive image of the Thai people entertained by the tourists, and their willingness to follow a complete stranger who accosts them on the street — while they would deeply suspect anyone who thus approached them in their home environment: "Tourists come to another country and read a brochure telling them how friendly and smiling the Thais are and from that moment they surrender their lives to any punk that comes along" (Davies, 1993: 9)

The conman, indeed, builds upon that image and further enhances his trustworthiness by a carefully constructed front and a credible story. He approaches his victim not as a colorful "professional native" but rather as a cosmopolitan member of the host society, of equal or even higher status than the victims themselves. He presents himself as an English-speaking, "well-dressed Thai gentleman" (Chuensuksawadi and Jinakul, 1990: 1), a government employee, banker, teacher or professor by profession; he usually has a car at his disposal, in which he brings his victims to the store.

Since the tourists are not engaged in a search for gems when the conman approaches them, and may even not be particularly interested in gems, the conman faces the problem of bringing the topic of gems to their attention and arousing their interest. The conman has to choose an indirect approach, touching upon this topic gradually and, as it were, only casually. He may also have to make some investment into the relationship with the tourists, such as taking them for an excursion or inviting them for a meal; this serves to enhance his credibility as well as increases the victims' involvement in the relationship. Indeed, the victims may feel morally obliged to reciprocate by agreeing to accompany the conman to the store.

When he introduces the topic of the gems, the conman tends to play on the tourists' readiness to follow the locals' example, or to exploit an unforeseen opportunity, and on their adventurousness or even greed. He often claims that he himself is going to buy gems at the jewelry store, saying things like: "I am going to buy my mother a beautiful sapphire for her special [Mother's] day" (Kang-Oakins, 1993). To assuage doubts regarding the jewelry store, he points out that he knows the owners well (Weeradet, 1993), or that the store is trustworthy, since it is owned by the government (Jones, 1992, Kang-Oakins, 1993). In order to induce the victims to join him, and to enkindle their interest in making an immediate purchase — a formidable decision, involving relatively large sums of money, which is usually not easily or spontaneously made — the conman uses a ruse; he usually claims that on that very day there is a special occasion for buying cheap gems, such as "[Today] is the only day that you can buy a stone at a 70 per cent discount at this government-sponsored shop" (Kang-Oakins, 1993); or that at a particular store there is a "three day promotional sale that only occurs once a year and is about to finish, when you can buy [gems] wholesale at 25 per cent off" (Jones, 1992). To whet the victims' appetite he also points out that the victims could sell the gems at home at a profit of several hundred per cent (Chuensuksawadi and Jinakul, 1990:4). As a further inducement, he often offers to take the victims to the store in his car (which is in fact rented by the store). While some tourists see through the conman's plot and refuse to go on, others feel that they have chanced upon an unexpected opportunity and consent to visit the store. One of the latter reports: "Vaguely interested in making money and curious to what this store-factory had to offer, I followed my 'Thai friend' into the building. I was escorted to the third floor, given a soft drink, and then I was told about the sapphires, or so I was to think" (Lubke, 1990).

However, though the victims' interest may be aroused at that stage, they are also gripped by a sense of insecurity, since they usually have little knowledge of gems, not to speak of expertise in gemology. However, the conman hastens to reassure them; one of the victims tells his story: "When I told him [the conman] that we know nothing about gems, the man said 'but this is the government, they will explain everything to you — about the method of cutting stones and judging quality'" (Chuensuksawadi and Jinakul, 1990: 1).

Once the victims arrive at the shop, the salespeople, in the appropriately staged, sparkling setting of the stop, take over from the conman to make the kill — inducing the victims to make an expensive purchase. To continue the tale of the foregoing victim: "The saleslady [at the shop] told us the whole story, explained about cutting [the stones] and how you can tell a high quality stone from a low quality one" (Chuensuksawadi and Jinakul, 1990: 4).

Following this explanation, the saleslady "started talking exactly like the man we met in the street — that this was a special day and we can buy at a wholesale price and a discount . . . that the Government allows tourists to buy only a limited amount … on one day in the year." She also explained that the victim and his wife "could make as much as 200 to 300 per cent profit and that they could get their money back because the shop issues certificates and guarantees on each sale" (Chuensuksawadi and Jinakul, 1990: 4).

The explanation by the saleslady, coordinated with the preparation made by the conman, was in this case successful, since the victims eventually bought five "sapphires" to the tune of US$3260, only to find out upon arrival in Tokyo, from the owner of a gem shop there, "that they were worth maybe US$100 each" (Chuensuksawadi and Jinakul, 1990: 4).

One of the last acts of the salesperson, by which the tourists are finally convinced that they are involved in an honest deal, is the apparent authentication of the gems about to be purchased by the victims; in fact, however, this consists merely of "words, promises, personal guarantees, unchecked documents, unauthorized written or verbal statements . . ." which "do not constitute [real] verification" (Weeradet, 1993).

Once the victims make the discovery that the gems they have purchased "are of very low quality and the prices are actually ten times more than they should have paid" (*Bangkok Post*, 1993a) they may seek a refund of their money; however, they "are often at a loss about what to do" and "disadvantaged because their visits are relatively short and they cannot spare the time and expense to seek legal action" (Jinakul, 1990: 3). Moreover, some of the stores' practices, such as their offer to send the gems by mail to the purchasers' home address (Weeradet, 1993), make it impossible for the victims to seek redress while still in Thailand because they will discover that they had been cheated only upon returning home. Once they have left the country, the victims are precluded from seeking redress, except by returning to Thailand.

Even those victims who are able to take steps towards a refund, whether directly at the store, or through intervention of the law-enforcing agencies, are at best only partly successful. The stores usually flatly refuse a refund. Some storekeepers point out that the receipts given to the tourist have been expressly stamped "nonrefundable" (Weeradet, 1993). In case the purchaser did not obtain a receipt for his payment, the storekeepers may claim that the stones had not been purchased in his or her store. In some cases, indeed, the sellers succeed in turning the tables against the victims, as illustrated by the following case: a wealthy Chinese from Hong Kong bought "rubies" in Mae Sai [on the Burmese border] for US$300, only to find out upon returning home, that they were in fact cubic zircons worth US$7.50 each. Since he had been given a written guarantee that he could return the stones, and at the time of the purchase even took a picture with the salesgirl, he used the occasion of another visit to Thailand to seek a refund from the Mae Sai store at which he had bought the stones. Bernard Trink reports his version of what has occurred:

> He took with him the stones, the guarantee, the photo and the written report from the Hong Kong jeweller [on the value of the stones].
> The salesgirl denied that the stones were from her stall. She said the photo was not of her (even though she was wearing the same shirt as in the picture), the guarantee was a forgery, the Chinese jeweller's report was wrong.
> Eventually my friend gave up and moved away to get a drink, but whilst he sat there he noticed some other tourists at the girl's stall. He watched for about five minutes then went over to the haggling tourists and showed them his evidence.
> The salesgirl let out a scream, swore at him and tried to grab the papers which he had. The girl then called over to another stall and the cry went around. A policeman soon appeared on the scene.
> My friend tried to explain, to no avail. The guarantee, the photo and the jeweller's report were taken from him. The stones were forced into his shirt pocket, and the policeman grabbed him by the wrist and dragged him down an alleyway.
> Away from the crowds, the papers were torn up in front of him and thrown on the ground. He was pushed, punched and shouted at, which he didn't understand not being a Thai speaker.
> Again he tried to explain. This was too much for the policeman, who drew his gun, poked it in my friend's chest and then waved the barrel under his nose.
> He was marched out into the main street, down the hill and put on a bus out of town.
> Back in Chiang Mai he went to the police to complain, but as he told his story he could see that it was falling on deaf ears (Trink, 1993).

Similar experiences are reported by the tourist couple who bought the overpriced sapphires; they returned to Bangkok specifically to seek refund of their money; their story, as told by the husband, demonstrates the difficulties and exertions involved in achieving even partial success in that endeavor. Upon arrival at the store from which they had purchased the sapphires, they told the attendants that they wanted to see the manager to file their complaint, but were told that he was not in.

They went outside and waited and noticed a well-dressed man entered the stop with two other tourists. When these tourists came out, the couple asked them if they had bought any gems. The tourists said they had not, but said "this was a special day for gems and that tourists can buy them for a discount."

The tourists [said that] they had been approached by a man who claimed to be a banker and drove them to the shop in a BMW . . . [The husband] started writing down the license plates of the BMW that turned up, but was later approached by a man who came out of the shop who asked what he was doing.

"When I told him he said we were interfering in his business. When we insisted that we could continue to do this he asked us inside and identified himself as the manager. The manager said that he could not give us a refund because only the owner could do so — but the owner was not in" [the husband said].

The couple then went outside, but five minutes later they were told that the owner had arrived and were invited inside again. This time they were escorted into a small room.

"The man started shouting at us, told us he did not have time to waste" [the husband said], adding that the "owner" was accompanied by another man who stood behind them.

"The owner told us that if we were not nice to him the man behind us was his bodyguard. He told us that we could not have a refund and started shouting at us again."

[The husband] said that if he did not get a refund he would go outside the shop and would stop tourists and tell them about his experience.

"The man said that in Bangkok accidents can happen and that he could ensure that he would be off the streets in no time."

[The husband then] went to the Tourist Police to file a complaint. He was asked to write his complaint in English, which he did.

In his complaint [he] identified the shop where he bought the gems twice. But in the official translation the Tourist Police did not mention the name of the shop.

[He] also stated clearly in his English-language complaint that the incident first took place on "July 9th," but in the official Thai version, the tourist police had [him] arriving in Bangkok on August 25 (which he did) but the incident taking place on August 9.

These discrepancies in the official Thai complaint would weaken [his] case if he brought the matter to court.

The Tourist Police then contacted the shop, which at first said they would only refund 60 per cent of the value of the sapphires. [The husband] refused and demanded a 90 per cent refund. They finally agreed on an 80 per cent refund.

The couple were then accompanied by the Tourist Police officer to the shop. On the way the policeman "asked for money for bringing us to the shop."

At the shop, the owner demanded that [he] sign a letter saying that he had come into the shop on July 9 and willingly bought the stones — which legally speaking he did — and that he agreed to sell back the stones on August 17.

The letter also said that he would not cause more "trouble" for the shop. In order to get most of his money back [the husband] agreed and signed.

On the way back [he] asked the police officer for his name. The officer refused to identify himself.

[The husband] decided to return to the Tourist Police to make sure that the shop's name was included in the complaint report, which the Tourist Police later agreed to include.

"The money is not that important because after a couple of months you forget about it. But I hate to be cheated on. And I don't want this to happen to other people. That is my main objective," he said, explaining his insistence. (Chuensuksawadi and Jinakul, 1990: 4).

The reporters on the *Bangkok Post* subsequently approached the store and told the cashier of the couple's complaint. This was her reaction:

> "If you buy a shirt from us for 200 baht and then try to sell it later to another shop they will offer you 150 baht. It is natural they will offer you less than you have paid.
>
> "The receipt given to the tourist clearly states that the goods are nonrefundable. The only exception is that if our purchasing section agrees to buy back the gems. But in this case it is impossible for us to buy back the gems at the original price. At least we have to buy back at less than 10 to 20 per cent of the value.
>
> "When we spoke to him he threatened to cause trouble by going to the press. This is not the way and we spoke to him nicely.
>
> "If they buy the gems, they buy [them] because they are satisfied. We cannot force them to buy the gems. We do not put a gun to their heads.
>
> "Yesterday, he came back and agreed to sell back the gems for 80 per cent of their value. He also signed a letter saying that he agrees to sell back the gems. I don't see why there should be any problem."
>
> Asked about a well-dressed man who approached the tourist and if he was connected with the shop, the woman said:
>
> "I don't know who he met on the street. Most jewellery shops have guides bringing in their customers but the decision to buy or not is up to the tourist. If you buy some jewellery from Pahurat and want to sell it the next day you cannot expect to get the normal price for it. This is the normal price.
>
> "We can't afford to buy back at the original price. We have costs to bear, salaries of staff and the cost of air-conditioning."
>
> "The tourist threatened us," she said.
>
> When asked to comment about what the tourists had told [the husband] outside the shop, the cashier said: "Tourists can make up all sorts of stories" (Chuensuksawadi and Jinakul, 1990: 5).

This account agrees with similar reports of other victims who sought refunds; in no instance did they receive all their money back. The stores usually retain 20−50 per cent of the original purchase price (*Bangkok Post*, 1993a) — which is probably still more than the value of the stones — out of which they pay commission to the touts, while keeping the stones for resale.

Although the conmen are fairly inventive in making their stories convincing, with the proliferation of their occupation, repetitions necessarily occur. Several victims reported being repeatedly approached with similar stories. This, indeed, induced them to doubt the credibility of their original encounter, and hence the value of their purchase (Dodemont, 1990: Jones, 1992).

As more and more people have realized that they have been cheated, complaints to various authorities have accumulated. According to one source, in 1990: "Up to 370 letters complaining about such cases [reached] embassies, the [Thai] Foreign Ministry, and Tourism Authority of Thailand (TAT) offices abroad" (Weeradet, 1993). The TAT consequently sought ways "to get rid of these blood suckers;" however, since the tourist authority lacks "authorization to penalize those involved in dishonest acts to tourists," it "cannot work efficiently to tackle this big problem if it does not get cooperation from related parties" (Weeradet, 1993), which is probably an allusion to the police, and particularly the tourist police.

The TAT, being unable to deal with the problem efficiently, reacted in the manner typical of the Thai bureaucracy; it established a center for tourists with troubles. In 1990, this center received about 300 complaints, in 1992, 375. Gems fraud was one of the principal complaints. The TAT realized that several jewelry shops were involved in a large number of such cases. However, an alleged ambiguity stands in the way of their prosecution: "they cannot be penalized although they are found [informally] guilty," because "there is no standard set to control prices of jewels" (Weeradet, 1993). "Although, according to one source, experts may be able to estimate a price [of a jewel] within 10 per cent of its real value" (Jinakul, 1990), the authorities claim that, in the absence of such a standard, a shopkeeper who sold a stone at ten times its estimated "real" value, does not necessarily commit a crime in the legal sense, even if his action may be considered unethical (Weeradet, 1993). Moreover, even in cases in which recourse to legal action is possible, the process is tedious and expensive, and the outcome uncertain, depending on such legalistic minutiae as the correctness of the translation into Thai of the tourist's complaint to the police (Jinakul, 1990). Since the police, who claim to be helpless against the perpetrators of the gems fraud (*Bangkok Post*, 1993a; Jones, 1992), are often uncooperative, or hostile to the victims, and possibly also in collusion with the shops (Sa-ardsorn, 1994), the victims are discouraged from taking legal action. Virtually the only effective help they receive from the authorities, be it the TAT or the police, is mediation of the conflict which at best eventuates in only a partial refund (*Bangkok Post*, 1993a; Lertikittisuk and Threeranurat, 1990: 3; Weeradet, 1993).

However, the TAT has taken some preventive measures regarding the gem fraud: in particular, it has warned tourists in brochures and posters of the dangers of the con game. Similar warnings were also issued by some gem trading companies (Ferguson, 1990), while the Thai Gem Jewelry Traders Association promised to issue a "special logo to guarantee safe shopping for tourists in addition to the TAT emblem [posted at the gate of TAT approved stores]" (Lertikittisuk and Threeranurat, 1990: 4). By 1993, the promulgation of this logo, however, still remained a promise (Weeradet, 1993). However, judging from experience with the TAT, the credibility of such a logo may be questionable: it emerged that, according to the deputy governor of the TAT, "the [jewelry] shops distinguished with a certification of the TAT . . . [at] the very beginning . . . were doing well in their business. But some of them were later tarnished with bad services and dishonest practices" (Weeradet, 1993). Considering the substantial profits and low risks inherent in the gems fraud, some stores may be tempted to use the logo of the Association, which seemingly enhances their credibility, as a device to mislead and cheat the tourists.

Our case study has an ironic edge. According to the president of the Jewelry Association, the con game is sometimes inverted: "Some *farangs* [foreigners] cooperate with tour guides to buy accessories in a jewellery shop. After the guide gets the commission, the tourist returns with a policeman complaining that the quality was no good and wanting the money back. The *farangs* and the guide, after that, share the commission" (Lertikittisuk and Threeranurat 1990: 4).

Discussion

"Ripoffs" of tourists by locals are a common practice in many countries. In some tourist-oriented professions, such as the antiques business, faking, in the sense of selling new products as antiques, is widespread; shopkeepers have developed a variety of deceptive practices, including the establishment of pseudo-communal relations with the victims, to facilitate the sale of fakes as genuine products (Loeb, 1977). In Thailand, deception has been honed into a "fine art." Whilst in this chapter only one of its most profitable manifestations, the gems fraud, was described, rip-offs and conning of tourists in many other forms are common in Thailand; some of the most blatant examples are the touting of tourists at the Don Muang airport to purchase overpriced tour and shopping packages (*Bangkok Post*, 1991), or the robbing of tourists on the interurban night buses by "friendly" locals who offer them drugged food or drink (eg, Green, 1988).

Various practices of cheating tourists became so widespread in recent years that one tourist sees the emergence of "a Thai culture that says that tourists are free for the taking: the more anyone can squeeze from the *farang* the better" (Okko, 1990).

Even though the authorities are aware of conning and similar practices, condemn them and warn the public about them, and sometimes even identify the perpetrators, most of these practices continue almost undisturbed up to the present: little effective action has been taken to stop them or to bring the perpetrators to justice. The persistence and pervasiveness of such practices indicates that they may be facilitated by some broader characteristics of Thai society. In the introductory section of this chapter I raised several questions regarding the possible relationship between tourist-oriented crime and the structural traits of the host society. Regarding Thailand, three such traits — ambiguity, opacity and duality — have been suggested as possibly related to tourist-oriented crime. I shall now attempt to specify this relationship, on the basis of the case study presented above, in terms of the three questions raised in the introduction.

Crime-facilitating situations

The situations which engender the gems fraud appear spontaneous and occur in public places; the victims are lured from there into jewelry stores, where they are induced to make a purchase of their own free will, rather than by the use of force or threats. The social situations in which the fraud is accomplished clearly reflect the duality of Thai society, of which the tourist is usually unaware. The duality, specifically the split between the pleasant, smiling front presented by the people, and the sometimes devious intentions hiding behind it, facilitate the emergence of friendly, apparently occasional encounters between local conmen and unsuspecting tourists. In such situations, the tourists tend to accept the widely advertised friendliness of the Thai people at its face value and expose themselves thereby to the covert intentions of the conmen.

Prevalent types of crime

The duality of Thai society also facilitates the emergence and prevalence of tourist-oriented criminal activities which involve some kind of deception, in particular, conning. As pointed out above, this duality is expressed, on the personal level, in a marked disjunction between the public "front" and the private "back" in daily contact. Thai people are thus highly adept at role playing in various forms and switch easily from one role to another. Since form is given preference over content, role playing is given preference over role performance. Hence it is easy for some individuals to gain the confidence of unsuspecting foreigners, by convincingly playing roles which they do not in fact possess such as those of a teacher, banker or professor in our case study.

Law-enforcing agencies

The opacity of the Thai institutional processes and the ambiguity and duality permeating most areas of Thai social structure account for the manner in which the gems fraud is dealt with by the authorities, including the law-enforcing agencies.

Even the legal status of the practice is ambiguous: according to the authorities there is no unequivocal way to determine a fair price for gems — and hence it is doubtful whether the conning practice could be legally defined as "crime" and specifically as fraud. Moreover, as we have seen above, shopkeepers are adept at countering the tourists' version of how they have been cheated, by a version of their own, according to which the purchase of the gems began as normal business practice. The ambiguity is also evident in the claim of the tourist police that it cannot prosecute the store keepers, because there are "loopholes in the law" (Jinakul, 1990). Moreover, according to a police general, though a person who receives a commission if he persuades a tourist to make a purchase does in fact transgress a paragraph of the Thai Criminal Code, such cases nevertheless usually end in compromise, owing to the technical difficulties of prosecution (Jinakul, 1990). As we have noted above, compromises are precisely the manner in which conflicts in the "gray zone" between alternative interpretations of social situations are resolved.

Tourists, being temporary strangers, find it hard anywhere to seek redress for injuries and malpractices suffered on their trip (Cohen, 1987: 193−4). In Thailand, the opacity of the institutions and of legal procedures compounds this difficulty. The TAT, the principal "patron" of tourists in Thailand, though trying to protect the tourists' interests and help them when in trouble, lacks authority to prosecute the alleged culprits. In an oft repeated fashion in Thai bureaucracy, the TAT, in response to the spreading malpractice against tourists, established a new unit — a center for lodging complaints. However, beyond trying to intervene and mediate between tourists who claim to have been cheated and the shopkeepers, there is little that TAT can do. Prosecution is up to the police — and the police are often tardy, unresponsive and occasionally hostile to tourist complaints.

The duality characteristic of the mode of operation of many Thai institutions is inaccessible to the tourists — thus, they may be completely unaware of the complex mechanisms of protection and corruption behind the scenes, involving, among others, the police (*The Nation*, 1994). Shopkeepers who deal with tourists are said to receive "protection from high ranking officials [who] have power . . . to pressure the police to turn a blind eye to cases or withdraw their action" (Jinakul, 1990). Moreover, even when legal action is taken, the complexities of Thai legal procedures are beyond the grasp of most tourists, making such action time-consuming and expensive and its outcome highly uncertain.

The legal ambiguities surrounding such tourist-oriented crimes as the gems fraud, and the opacity and duality characteristic of the law-enforcing agencies which are supposed to deal with them, reduce the risks of prosecution for those locals who engage in such practices and facilitate their virtually undisturbed perpetration.

Conclusion

Analyses of tourist-oriented crime, in so far as they went beyond the question of the statistical relationship between crime and tourism, usually approached the problem from the perspective of "touristic victimology" seeking to show why tourists are easy victims of criminal acts in the host country. In this chapter, I sought to invert the perspective: while not denying the significance of the usual perspective, I wanted to examine a possible connection between the structural traits of the host society and tourist-oriented crime. I illustrated my arguments by a single example, the gems fraud in Thailand; it remains to be shown that other types of tourist-oriented crime in Thailand, as well as elsewhere, can be related to some structural characteristics of the host society. A research program is thereby proposed, which may lead to a fruitful comparative analysis of tourist-oriented, and, more broadly, tourism-related crime, which goes beyond mere "touristic victimology."

A final note, regarding the relationship of the present chapter to my earlier work on the topic of tourism and crime: in a previous article (Cohen, 1987), I hypothesized that, while non-conventional tourists will be victimized by law-enforcing agencies, conventional tourists will enjoy their protection. While, on both theoretical and empirical grounds, this hypothesis still appears valid, on the basis of the data presented here, it has to be qualified on one significant point: while it is correct to say that the Thai law-enforcing agencies are officially committed to the protection of tourists, and have even established a special force, the tourist police, for that purpose, the actual functioning of the police, including the tourist police, does not wholly bear out the official stance: lack of cooperation, inefficiency and even animosity against tourists who claim to have been offended is quite common. Moreover, though the law-enforcing agencies may appear to care particularly for the safety of conventional tourists, those tourists, being better off than non-conventional young travelers and drifters — are also the principal mark of the conning game. Hence, in so far as the police colludes with the offenders behind-the-scenes, it denies, at least in some cases, protection to those very tourists whom it is supposed to protect most closely. The same forces which draw the offenders to the conventional tourists — their apparently greater munificence — may thus also induce some policemen to deny them protection and thus participate covertly in the division of the bounty.

References

Anderson, G.R.O'G. (1978). Studies of the Thai State: The state of Thai studies. In Ayal, E.B. (ed.), *The Study of Thailand*. Ohio University Center for International Studies, Papers in International Studies, SEA Series, No. 54: 193−247.

Bangkok Post (1991). The golden harvest at Don Muang . . . *Bangkok Post*, September 22: 8−9.

Bangkok Post (1993a). Police to bust fake jewellery dealers. *Bangkok Post*, March 10: 3.

Bangkok Post (1993b). Absurd claims of Thailand dangers. *Bangkok Post*, July 19: 4.

Chesney-Lind, M. and Lind, I.Y. (1986). Visitors as victims; Crimes against tourists in Hawaii. *Annals of Tourism Research*, **13**: 167−91.

Chuensuksawadi, P. and Jinakul, R. (1990). Gems buy take shine off holiday outing. *Bangkok Post*, August 19: 1, 3−5.

Cohen, E. (1987). The tourist as victim and protégé of law enforcing agencies. *Leisure Studies*, **6**: 181−97.

Cohen, E. (1991). *Thai Society in Comparative Perspective*. Bangkok: White Lotus.

Davies, D. (1993). Never talk to strangers [letter]. *Bangkok Post*, August 30: 5.

Dodemont, I.I. (1990). Another gem story [letter]. *Bangkok Post*, August 19: 3.

Ekachai, S. (1990). *Behind the Smile*, Bangkok: The Post Publishing Company.

Elliot, L. and Ryan, C. (1993). The impact of crime on Corsican tourism, *World Travel and Tourism Review*, **3**: 287−93.

Ferguson, G.W. (1990). Preventing rip-offs [letter]. *Bangkok Post*, March 2: 5.

Goffman, E. (1959). *The Presentation of Self in Everyday Life*. New York: Doubleday.

Green, B.E. (1988). Drugged and robbed on a bus [letter]. *Bangkok Post*, June 16: 4.

Jinakul, R. (1990). Fraud claims mount. *Bangkok Post*, August 19: 3.

Jones, C. (1992). Beware of gem cheats [letter]. *Bangkok Post*, February 26: 4.

Jud, G.D. (1975). Tourism and crime in Mexico. *Social Science Quarterly*, **56**: 324−30.

Kang-Oakins, D. (1993). Wonder what struck you? *Asia Magazine*, **33**(J-3). November 5: 34.

Khanphondee, N. (1994). Con merchants thrive by playing on people's greed. *The Nation* , August 24: A8.

Lertkittisuk, P. and Threeranurat, V. (1990). Tourist body looks at tightening standards. *Bangkok Post*, August 19: 3.

Loeb, L.D. (1977). Creating antiques for fun and profit: encounters between Iranian Jewish merchants and touring coreligionists. In Smith, V.L. (ed.), *Hosts and Guests*, Philadelphia: University of Pennsylvania Press: 185−92.

Lubke, A. (1990). [letter]. *Bangkok Post*, August 19: 3.

Mathieson, A. and Wall, G. (1982). *Tourism: Economic, Physical and Social Impacts*. London: Longman.

McPheters, L.R. and Strange, W.B. (1974). Crime as an environmental externality of tourism: Florida. *Land Economics*, **50**: 288−92.

Meyer, W. (1988). *Beyond the Mask*, Saarbrücken: Breitenbach.

The Nation (1993). British TV programme hurts Thai image anew. *The Nation*, July 16: A1−A2.

The Nation (1994). Dark influence. *The Nation*, September 25: B1−B3.

Nicholls, L.L. (1976). Tourism and crime. *Annals of Tourism Research*, **3**(4): 176−82.

Okko, O. (1990). Not-so-nice Thai ways. *Bangkok Post*, February 3: 5.

Pizam, A. (1978). Tourism's impacts: The social cost of the destination as perceived by its residents. *Journal of Travel Research*, **16**(4): 8−12.

Pizam, A. (1982). Tourism and crime: Is there a relationship? *Journal of Travel Research*, **20** (3): 7−10.

Sa-ardsorm, P. (1994). House committee warns crimes against visitors may hit tourism. *The Nation*, July 27: A10.

Suksawat, S. (1994). Why Thailand is the land of smiles. *Thai Ways*, **11** (4): 58−62.

Trink, B. (1989). A tourist season scam. *Bangkok Post*, December 16: 27.

Trink, B., (1993). A scam in Mae-Sai. *Bangkok Post*, March 27 1993: 27.

Weeradet, T. (1993) Wave of rip-offs of tourists buying gems and jewellery. *Bangkok Post*, January 14: 5.

7 A South African perspective of the effects of crime and violence on the tourism industry

JONATHAN BLOOM

Background

The susceptibility of tourism to instability and negative change is something no stakeholder in the tourism industry can afford to ignore. High levels of crime, violence, political instability and general lawlessness could cause irreparable damage to the image of a given area as a tourist destination.

Until recently South Africa was "black-listed" by many foreign governments and people were discouraged from visiting the country as tourists, or for any other purpose, because of the discriminatory policies pursued by its former government. The transition to a democracy has had certain positive repercussions for the tourism industry, including a more positive international image. Coupled with the increase in long-distance travel, South Africa now appears more competitive as an emerging tourism market within the international community. The transition in South Africa has, however, brought about high levels of crime, non-political violence and general lawlessness. This has led to uncertainty on the part of potential tourists who fear for their safety and general well-being.

This chapter analyzes the extent to which negative aspects may curtail the high market growth rates forecast for the South African tourism industry. The discussion focuses primarily on the issues of violence, crime and political instability as these appear to have the most significant impact on the tourism industry. Several strategic pointers are proposed which may help to alleviate the problems mentioned above, through the adequate and appropriate use of tourism industry resources.

Major South African tourism trends, potential and the historical impact of violence and crime

Tourism world-wide has undergone significant changes over the years. These trend changes include changes in holiday habits, with more emphasis on outdoor recreation, activity-related experiences and the need to experience local cultures and customs (Inskeep, 1991: 13). South Africa, with its diverse population composition, faces

Tourism, Crime and International Security Issues, edited by
A. Pizam and Y. Mansfeld. © 1996 John Wiley & Sons Ltd.

significant challenges in terms of facilitating participation in the tourism industry by all population groups, especially the less privileged, as tourists or as stakeholders in the tourism industry.

Accommodating the diverse needs and interests of all population groups in a burgeoning tourism industry presents a daunting challenge. Efforts may have to be made to adapt to the needs and preferences of all market segments, requiring that consideration be given to factors such as value for money (for example, by providing budget accommodation and transport for low-income tourists), a pleasant climate, the provision of family holidays and courtesy shown by all participants in the tourism industry (Bloom, 1994: 8−9). By attaining goals such as these and given that the political process stabilizes and the safety of tourists can be guaranteed, the future potential of the South African tourism industry appears to be increasingly positive — according to various knowledgeable international and national tourism industry specialists.

In the international tourism context South Africa is a small player with less than 0.25 per cent of the international tourism market (Heath, 1992: 4). However, the South African tourism industry is expected to develop substantially over the next five years (South African Tourism Board and Development Bank of South Africa, 1991).

South African foreign currency earnings from tourism were estimated to be between $1 billion and $1.3 billion in 1992 ($0.843 billion in 1990), with a projected figure of $3.2 billion by 1995 and $8 billion by the year 2000 (Ryan, 1992: 1, 3). The outlook is becoming increasingly positive as forecasts for the year 2000 indicate that taking 1991 (521 257 tourists) as base year, overseas arrivals could virtually double by 1995 (966 000 tourists) and quadruple by the year 2000 (1 750 000 tourists) (Heath, 1992: 13). These figures exclude tourists from Africa, many of whom are over-the-border shoppers. The potential for job creation is substantial if these "scenarios" should develop. It has been suggested that by the turn of the century 40 000 job opportunities could be directly created, while a further 80 000 indirect employment opportunities could be provided (*Rapport*, 1993). These projections, of course, presuppose the creation of a climate or culture conducive to attracting the number of tourists indicated.

Over the years crime and violence and other political factors have often thwarted attempts to establish tourism as an industry which could be classified as a major contributor to the Gross National Product, together with agriculture and mining. Incidents such as the Soweto riots in the mid-1970s (caused by the government's language policy in black schools) and various sporadic outbreaks of violence and crime in the 1980s (perpetrated as a result of the government's policies of racial segregation) caused the tourism industry irreparable harm. There followed an era of increased sanctions and boycotts during which many foreign governments and organizations introduced cultural and tourism boycotts and numerous other measures intended to rally international sentiment against South Africa. The situation altered in 1990 with the advent of significant political change in South Africa, together with the realization that tourism, if approached and managed correctly, could well be a strategic economic force in the country by helping to combat unemployment and providing a socio-economic stimulus for the country as a whole.

Prior to the multi-racial elections in 1994, numerous politically inspired acts of violence negatively affected the anticipated tourism boom in the country. One such incident was the Jan Smuts airport bomb blast on election day, April 27, 1994. While political violence tapered off after the election, there was an apparent increase in non-political violence and crime. During the past five years many attempts have been made to develop the tourism industry and give tourism the priority it deserves in the highest decision making authority. In 1992 for the first time tourism was given full portfolio status with the appointment of a Minister for Tourism. Currently tourism is linked to the portfolio of environmental affairs.

In spite of the very special tourism product that South Africa has to offer and increasing interest and enthusiasm in the international market-place, there are critical factors such as political unrest, violence and crime with the resultant risks to personal safety which could adversely affect the country's tourism potential and thus a major socio-economic lifeline for years to come. Unfortunately many of the initiatives undertaken to promote and attract investment funds for developing the tourism infrastructure, and market South Africa abroad, have been counteracted by these negative occurrences.

Socio-political trends influencing the incidence of crime and violence in South Africa

South Africa is no exception when it comes to the negative effects of crime and violence-related incidents. Many major world cities continually experience high levels of crime and violence, often caused by unfavorable social conditions and political problems. Political intolerance still appears to be prevalent among the various population groups in South Africa. Combined with strong feelings concerning ethnicity, language and religious conviction, this serves to aggravate further an already volatile situation. Among the possible reasons for the increase in crime and violence are a decline in effective law enforcement coupled with the continuing rejection of the police by large sectors of the population, particularly in South Africa. To further compound the problem, a survey conducted by the South African Tourism Board (1992) among the South African population indicates frequent incidents of racial discrimination. The Centre for the Study of Violence and Reconciliation (*Financial Mail*, 1994: 47) believes that the legacy of apartheid lies at the root of the crime rate and that poverty alone does not cause the violence. The proliferation of firearms is another major factor contributing to acts of violence.

In South Africa poverty has been associated historically with an exceptionally high unemployment rate (40 to 50 per cent in some areas), socio-political instability (often experienced at regional and local government level) and a culture of violence (*Financial Mail*, 1994: 47). This has caused dwindling rural populations, a substantial influx of people into urban and metropolitan areas, a proliferation of squatter communities and the resultant breakdown in social structures. Associated with extensive unemployment are the periodic economic downswings, recessionary periods and depression conditions in the economy which serve to aggravate the problem. Tourists unfortunately are not immune to crime and violence. Reports of attacks on tourists and of tourist-related theft, particularly in urban areas, have had negative effects which give cause for grave concern.

Major tourism gateways, attractions and tourism circuits and their susceptibility to crime and violence

Tourist activity is not confined to major urban metropolitan areas. Together with other African destinations, South Africa is well known abroad for its game parks and wonderful scenery. Foreign tourists indicate that the climate (24.4 per cent), scenic beauty (31.2 per cent) and wildlife (15.4 per cent) are major factors that influence the decision to visit South Africa (the percentage for each aspect being shown in parenthesis), (South African Tourism Board, 1993a: 18). A distinction should be made between urban areas, in which crime and violence mostly occur, and established tourist attractions and destinations. Johannesburg, which is often visited by vacation and business tourists, should be distinguished from other attractions such as the Kruger National Park, the Lost City and Sun City resort in the Pilansberg, and from tourist circuits such as the Garden Route in the Southern Cape, the West Coast Route and the various wine routes in the Western Cape. At most these areas may experience isolated occurrences of crime or violence.

A substantial proportion of foreign tourists come to South Africa by air (South African Tourism Board, 1994: 11). The gateways for the majority of foreign tourists (excluding over-the-border traffic from surrounding African countries) entering South Africa include major urban metropolitan areas such as Johannesburg, Cape Town and Durban, which for many of the reasons stated above periodically encounter high levels of crime and violence.

This may well deter tourists who begin their stay in South Africa within the limits of one of these cities or surrounding areas. Research indicates that Johannesburg is the most frequently used destination, with holiday tourists and business tourists spending 9.9 days of their total stay in South Africa in this city, followed by Cape Town with 6.6 days and Durban with 3.9 days (South African Tourism Board, 1993b: 6). Research into the problem of violence and crime mostly focuses on the situation in large urban metropolitan areas.

Primary and secondary research into the effects of crime and violence on tourism in South Africa is limited, and questions posed in country-wide surveys generally do not address the wider consequences of the problem. The perception of personal safety is reflected by surveys among foreign tourists undertaken by the South African Tourism Board (1993b). Figure 7.1 indicates the results for the period from 1988 to 1993. Over the past five years declining standards of personal safety have been experienced. It appears that 70 per cent of tourists rated safety as "good" in 1989 as opposed to 25 per cent in 1992 and 23 per cent in 1993. These perceptions are further enhanced by the comments made by respondents regarding personal safety, 94 per cent of which were negative (South African Tourism Board, 1993b: 35).

A survey conducted in Johannesburg, one of the main industrial and commercial centers of South Africa, reveals the seriousness of the problem of crime and violence (Mynhard, 1992). The research indicates that muggings and robbery are the crimes most often perpetrated against tourists (foreign and domestic), while stone throwing occurs less frequently. It should be mentioned that the situation in Johannesburg is used to provide a worst-case scenario and that other major tourist centers such as Cape Town and Durban may not necessarily experience similar situations. Figures for 1992 indicate that in the Western Cape region only 0.001 per cent of the 437 000 tourists visiting the Cape were victims of crime and violence (Muirhead, 1993: 5). This is particularly significant in light of South Africa's bid to host the Olympic Games in 2004. Table 7.1 shows figures for various categories of crime or violence in which tourists were involved. The statistics shown in Table 7.1 are not comparable with police statistics in many instances. This is significant as many of the crimes associated with tourists are reported directly to their embassies and not necessarily to the police (Fray and Shagowat, 1994: 5).

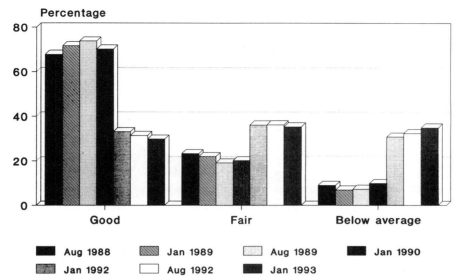

Figure 7.1 Overview of tourist perceptions towards personal safety. Source: South African Tourism Board, 1993b, p. 20 .

Table 7.1 Categories of crime and violence in an urban environment

Incidents	Percentage*
Mugging	52.6
Pickpocketing	37.2
Threatened with a knife	37.2
Threatened at gunpoint	21.8
Stone throwing	3.8
Robbery	52.6
Other	12.8

*Due to respondents being able to indicate more than one possibility the percentages do not add up.

Source: Mynhard, A. (1992: 86).

Besides affecting tourist numbers tourist-related crime and violence also impact on those businesses which rely heavily on tourist expenditure for their survival. Their loss in revenue could be substantial if tourists are unwilling to take risks where they are doubtful about the safety of the inner-city areas. Tourist-related businesses see the crime factor as the main reason for the decline in tourist business activity, accounting for 78 per cent of the decline. The economic and political climate have been found to contribute 58 per cent and 70 per cent respectively to the decline in tourist business (Mynhard, 1992: 63−4). The results are shown in Figure 7.2.

The focus up to now has been on non-political violence, but in many instances the crime and violence result from political actions. In this respect significant but ''expensive''

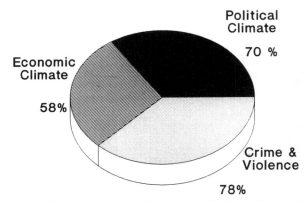

Figure 7.2 Factors which contribute to declining tourist business. Source: Mynhard, 1992, p. 86

lessons concerning the effect these occurrences could have on the tourism industry have been learned from the politically orientated events which led to crime and violence in 1993 such as the Boipatong (township in Johannesburg) shootings and the march on Bisho (capital of the former homeland of the Ciskei). The aftermath of these events caused numerous cancellations, especially by tour groups, and foreign governments warned tourists of the dangers of traveling in or to South Africa.

The cost of violence and loss of tourist revenue for the economy

The impact of crime and violence is often measured in terms of the associated costs to the economy of a country or region. Many other measures could be considered to determine the impact of crime and violence such as the number of man-hours lost or the decrease in productivity. In the Pretoria—Witwatersrand—Vereniging area (now known as Gauteng) estimates indicate that in a matter of six months violence and crime cost the region more than $833 million (*Financial Mail*, 1991: 26).

To illustrate the impact of crime and violence the Western Cape region is selected as an example. In terms of foreign tourist income generation, observers indicate that the Western Cape is the largest region in the country with $500 million in tourist receipts (*Cape Times Supplement*, 1994: 1). The figures used in the example are hypothetical except for actual figures of foreign expenditure, foreign tourist numbers and average duration of stay in the region. In order to include the indirect loss of revenue a conservative tourist expenditure multiplier of 1.6 is used for the region. This implies that the total direct expenditure by tourists can be increased by 60 per cent to indicate the total direct and indirect income from tourism to the region (Western Cape Tourism Plan and Action Programme, 1994: 110). Table 7.2 shows the effects of percentage decreases in foreign tourists numbers and the associated direct and indirect income loss based on a sliding percentage scale.

The damaging effects of slight decreases in tourist numbers on the economy of a country or, as in this example, on the regional economy, could be quite substantial as Table 7.2 indicates. A decline of 2.5 per cent in foreign tourist numbers could cause total (direct and indirect) income losses of $6.9 million. However, with a 15 per cent decrease in numbers the losses could be approximately $42 million. These losses may not appear to

Table 7.2 Effects of decreasing tourist numbers on direct and indirect income from foreign tourists

Foreign Tourist Numbers	Percentage Decrease	Total Estimated Expenditure per Stay** $'000s	Loss of Direct Expenditure $'000s	Indirect Expenditure*** $'000s
480 000*	—	174 720	—	
468 000	2.5	170 352	4368	6989
456 000	5.0	165 984	8736	13 978
444 000	7.5	161 616	13 104	20 966
432 000	10.0	157 248	17 472	27 955
420 000	12.5	152 880	21 840	34 944
408 000	15.0	148 512	26 208	41 933

Notes:

*Figure for 1993 based on an estimated number of foreign tourists which represents a 10% increase over 1992.

**Calculated on an average stay of four days at $91 per day, which gives a total expenditure per stay of $364.

***A multiplier of 1.6 is used in the calculations. An exchange rate of one dollar to three rand sixty cents is used for the conversion.

Source: Compiled from information extracted from a situation analysis of the Western Cape Tourism Region.

be very large in dollar terms, but at an exchange rate of $1 = R3.60 they are quite considerable. Taking into account that these figures are based on a regional "scenario," the effect on the country as a whole could be formidable.

The role of negative media reporting

South Africa has long been the focus of international attention in the media. In most instances the accent has been on negative publicity which has been associated with political instability, violence, and crime before the April 1994 elections, and with non-political violence and general cases of lawlessness after the elections. These incidents tarnished the country's image as an international tourist destination, having received extensive coverage in the international media.

Examples of the negative publicity in the international and local press include banner headlines in local newspapers such as "UK tourists urged to give S.A. a miss" (*The Argus*, September 18, 1990) and "City [Cape Town] risky tourists told" (*The Argus*, July 19, 1991). In the international press headlines such as "Tourism in Florida takes hard jolt in wake of assaults" and "Attacks on visitors spur downturn in Florida tourism: busy season is quiet as foreign travelers turn to other destinations" (*Wall Street Journal*, Eastern Edition, December 28, 1993 and March 7, 1994) brought Florida into disfavor as a popular tourism destination. As an indication of the harmful nature of negative reporting, 800 reports about the incidents in Florida appeared in the media (*The Economist*, 1993: 61−2). Unfortunately, all this negative publicity contributes to the dilemma of reduced sales and income faced by tourism businesses.

Besides having a negative impact on tourism businesses, the unfavorable publicity has a damaging effect on the image of the country as a whole. The perceived risk for tourists

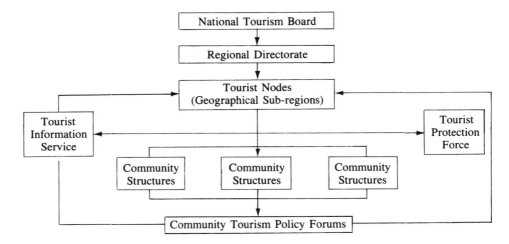

Figure 7.3 Possible avenues for addressing the problem of crime and violence in tourist nodes

and foreign investors if the situation is unstable or insecure becomes too large to risk visiting or investing in South Africa.

The other side of the coin should also be considered, namely that in many instances tourists are uninformed of the situation or are given a distorted view of developments in a given country. Despite occurrences of violence it could still be safe to travel to certain parts of a country, as has been the case in South Africa. To ensure that areas affected do not lose tourist revenue because of problems elsewhere, it is essential to project a realistic image of where it would be safe to travel and what precautions should be taken. A clear distinction should therefore be made between suspect areas and non-suspect areas.

Possible initiatives to combat tourism-related crime and violence

Crime and violence are persistent problems with which many governments have to cope, and each situation requires a different approach. It has been necessary to devise mechanisms for dealing effectively with these situations when they occur. Crime and violence occur mostly in urban areas or in the black townships but seldom in affluent areas or areas frequented by tourists.

To project a favorable image of South Africa internationally the South African Tourism Board is exploring every possible avenue by which the safety and security of tourists to South Africa can be ensured (South African Tourism Board, 1994: 20). Figure 7.3 graphically depicts the measures that are being taken in the various tourist nodes to contend with the problem.

As is illustrated in Figure 7.3 the initiatives to combat violence and crime are focused on tourist nodes (communities with communality in terms of complementary tourism products and geographical togetherness). Well-coordinated and cooperative networking among the national tourism structures, the police, community structures and tourist information agencies and all other industry stakeholders is essential to ensure success.

The objective is to combat crime and violence by creating and operationalizing structures within the tourist nodes. In view of the vastness of the geographical area that has to be covered, the possibility of establishing a tourist protection force or unit in all major tourist nodes, consisting of people specifically trained and identified as tourist police, could be considered. This unit would liaise on a continual basis with the tourist information agencies and community-based tourism policy forums.

Further options in this context include involving the youth in tourist protection initiatives in view of the high levels of crime committed by young persons in the South African situation. Thus a feeling of pride and association could be fostered among the youth within community tourism policing.

The role of tourist information services would be enhanced by providing tourists with information brochures, public signs and a toll-free emergency number on an ongoing basis, while community tourist policy forums could be formed to involve all tourism stakeholders (direct and indirect) in planning activities and decision making in the tourist nodes serviced by the communities. The participants in these forums would include, among others, the police, the public, the business community and vendors. Tourist protection units have been established in several regions with the aim of involving all interested parties, with the purpose of communicating and interacting with tourist areas and generally looking after the well-being of tourists.

To help ensure the success of initiatives undertaken by the tourist police protection units, occasional crime blitzes are conducted, while periodic indemnity is provided to those who hand in to the police any unlicensed or unlawful firearms and other weapons in their possession. Because many of the tourists who visit the major cities and stay in hotels are prime targets for muggers, hotels have also taken the initiative in providing security for business and vacation tourists in an attempt to improve the image of the downtown areas of the major cities in South Africa (Fray and Shagoway, 1994: 5).

Key strategic pointers for combating tourist-related crime in South Africa

Tourism can play a vital role in terms of its employment-generating capacity and as a catalyst to stimulate socio-economic change within communities, particularly in developing African countries. Crime and violence could be addressed effectively through community involvement and upliftment programs to improve social conditions. In this regard the Reconstruction and Development Programme (RDP) is perceived to be a very promising initiative to address backlogs in the various communities and create social and economic upliftment. Pointers focusing on the contribution of tourism to the RDP and several possibilities to support future initiatives aimed at alleviating community violence and crime include the following:

Empowering community role players in regional tourism structures

With the new decentralized government structure in South Africa the role of communities within the regions should become more significant in future. Joint regional tourism decision making may have to address issues such as empowering community role players which could be accomplished by representation of all communities and stakeholders in decision-making forums. Clear demarcation of the roles and functions of tourism bodies at the regional and local level is required to ensure the proper delegation of tasks to community leaders within the tourism structures.

Formulating tourism-linked human resource development objectives, 1995 – 2000

Carefully structured objectives have to be formulated in order to use tourism as a strategic lever in alleviating the problems of crime and violence. These objectives have to include ways and means of meeting basic needs, developing human resources, building the economy and democratizing the state and society. To ensure that the objectives are attained it is necessary to establish priorities and provide a clear indication of the actions needed to minimize the negative impacts on society and the consequent effects on the tourism industry.

Reconstructing sub-sectors of the tourism industry in terms of future challenges and opportunities

Providing tangible benefits to society presents several significant challenges and opportunities. Also important is the trade-off between social and economic uplift on the one hand and tourism development on the other. The challenge manifests itself in the need to promote, invest and restructure tourism industry sub-sectors in terms of the contribution communities themselves could make to their economic development. The emphasis would have to be shifted toward an integrated and coordinated approach in which particular sub-sectors are reorganized to expand their role so as to include previously excluded parties. The restructuring of sub-sectors could provide additional involvement for community members by generating new ideas for the incorporation of local and community cultures and customs in the tourist's experience.

Compiling fast-track programs for capacity-building in human and financial resources

The identification and introduction of specific upliftment programs for the disadvantaged communities in South Africa requires optimalization of the human and financial resources available to the South African tourism industry. A pro-active approach to provide and sustain a practical basis for involving as many people as possible in the tourism industry requires, among other things, extensive training and education programs which focus specifically on the benefits of tourism involvement and the adequate utilization of tourism resources.

Providing guidelines for potential tourism entrepreneurs to become part of the tourism industry

In the restructuring process, medium and small tourism enterprises could serve as an entry point for those people who have not formed part of the traditional mainstream tourist business sector. As the majority of tourism businesses could be regarded as modest in size, there is considerable opportunity for the small business entrepreneur. A particular effort will have to be made to provide guidelines for small businesses in respect of funding possibilities and mechanisms, education and training and business networking opportunities for these people. Initiatives to accommodate less-privileged communities may include the development of tourist attractions, accommodation facilities and tour operations/guiding services in and around townships and rural villages. With the necessary development funds and assistance these projects could be effective in providing opportunities for communities and individuals to become involved as entrepreneurs and hopefully discourage crime and violence while encouraging loyalty and community participation.

Stipulating community responsibilities and self-initiatives

There can be little doubt that full participation of disadvantaged people in local government structures would advance the involvement of the community leaders in the local tourism structures. The outcome should be positive and effective as wide community participation in tourism development and the more equitable distribution of benefits could convince those community members perpetrating crime and violence to direct their efforts at building and securing a positive future though their participation in the tourism industry. In many receiving areas the advantages of tourism could produce tangible benefits in education, farming and local amenities which could help local community developers. This could also make improved recreation, leisure and eating facilities available to the whole community. It then becomes the responsibility of the communities concerned to ensure that these advantages accrue to the local population and that initiatives to attract tourists are launched from within the local areas.

Addressing transparency and control issues

Many of the points or issues raised are implicit in the aim of tourism to be a force which fosters peace and political stability. Tourism could broaden the mind and improve international and community relations by encouraging a culture of openness among all stakeholders. In the present South African situation tourism could play a significant role in bridging the psychological and cultural gaps that separate people of different race, color, religion and stage of social and economic development. As a strategic force, tourism would, therefore, foster the exchange of views and make for greater tolerance in respect of vertical and horizontal differences on a local level as well as on an inter-regional and intra-regional level. The success of any measures taken to enhance the industry will depend on whether the necessary control guidelines are laid down and a culture of frankness encouraged among all tourism industry participants.

Conclusion

Without exception all the pointers mentioned above are aimed at accommodating all interested parties in general formal and informal tourism structures. These structures allow community participation in the industry as well as the formulation of tasks and programs which are coupled with the necessary control and transparency measures. In order to accomplish these goals a major challenge for South African society is to bring about particular value changes within community structures and thus encourage the philosophy of hard work as a virtue, self-expression and acceptance of change. The involvement of community-based organizations in the promotion of tourism-related activities, for example participation by the rural population in eco-tourism projects, could help to foster a feeling of pride and belonging and ultimately help to reduce crime and violence.

References

The Argus (1990). UK tourists urged to give S.A. a miss. September 18: 3.

The Argus (1991). City risky, tourists told. July 19: 5.

Bloom, J.Z. (1994). *National Tourism Market/Industry Trends Relevant to the Western Cape.* Preliminary discussion document complied as part of the Western Cape Tourism Planning Process, Stellenbosch.

Cape Times Supplement (1994). Lucrative prospects for Western Cape tourism. September 24: 1.

Financial Mail (1991). Caught in the crossfire. **120** (11): 26–7.

Financial Mail (1994). Crime, cold comfort. **134** (9): 47.

Fray, P. and Shagowat, C. (1994). Tourist muggings in Central Johannesburg. *The Star*, October 13: 5.

The Economist (1993). Tourists in Florida: hiring and firing. **326** (7802): 35–6.

Heath, E. (1992). *An Overview of the South African Tourism Industry, with Specific Reference to the Strategic Framework for Tourism Development and the Government's White Paper on Tourism.* An address delivered at the AIC conference. Sandton, Johannesburg, August.

Inskeep, E. (1991). *Tourism Planning: An Integrated Sustainable Development Approach.* New York: Van Nostrand Reinhold.

Muirhead, D. (1993). *Opportunities in Western Cape Tourism.* Cape Town: The Association for the Promotion of the Western Cape's Economic Growth, Occasional Report.

Mynhard, A. (1992) An investigation into the scope and nature of crime on tourists and the effect of the phenomenon on the tourism industry in the central business district of Johannesburg. Unpublished report. Johannesburg: Technikon South Africa.

Rapport (1993). Tourism and its potential for South Africa. Appendix on tourism, October 3: 30–6.

Ryan, C. (1992). Tax breaks to boost tourism. *Business Times*, October 22: 1,3.

South African Tourism Board (1991). *Strategic Framework for Tourism Development in Southern Africa.* Pretoria, pp. 1–47.

South African Tourism Board (1992). *The South African Domestic Tourism Market.* Pretoria.

South African Tourism Board (1993a). *Survey of Motivation for International Tourism to South Africa and Evaluation of Facilities by Foreign Tourists.* Pretoria.

South African Tourism Board (1993b). *International Visitors to South Africa.* Executive Summary and Synopsis. Winter, Pretoria.

South African Tourism Board (1994). *A Reconstruction and Development Strategy for the Tourism Industry for the Period 1994–1999.* Consultative Document, Pretoria, pp. 1–23.

Thomas Jr, E. (1993). Attacks on visitors spur downturn in Florida tourism: busy season is quiet as foreign travelers turn to other destinations. *Wall Street Journal* (Eastern Edition), December 28: B6.

Thomas Jr, E. (1994). Tourism in Florida takes hard jolt in wake of assaults. *Wall Street Journal* (Eastern Edition), March 7: B10A.

Western Cape Tourism Plan and Action Programme. (1994). Situation Analysis. Unpublished document (compiled by Taylor and Leibold, consultants for the development of a tourism plan and action program for the Western Cape Regional Services Council), July, Cape Town.

Part 2

Tourism and political instability

8 Tourism, political stability and violence

C. MICHAEL HALL AND VANESSA O'SULLIVAN

> . . .tourism may decline precipitously when political conditions appear unsettled. Tourists simply choose alternative destinations.
>
> Unfortunately, many national leaders and planners either do not understand or will not accept the fact that political serenity, not scenic or cultural attractions, constitute the first and central requirement of tourism (Richter and Waugh, 1986: 231).

Safety is an essential component of the attractiveness of destinations and transport routes to tourists. Safety may be judged by the nature of the physical environment (as in adventure travel, such as white-water rafting or mountain climbing), by the potential for criminal activity (for example, pickpocketing or mugging), the possibility of being caught in a war-zone and/or by the potential for politically motivated attacks on tourists. This chapter is concerned with the last two categories of tourist safety which are intimately related to issues of tourism and political stability.

The political nature of international tourism has received scant attention in the tourism research literature (Hall, 1994a; Matthews, 1978; Richter, 1989). Nevertheless, issues of political stability and political relations within and between states are extremely important in determining the image of destinations in tourist-generating regions and, of course, the real and perceived safety of tourists. As Smyth (1986: 120) noted in the case of the ongoing conflicts between Loyalists and Republicans in Northern Ireland, "as an industry, tourism is particularly susceptible to certain exogenous factors and when civil unrest culminated in violence with subsequent media coverage, visitor numbers and expenditure fell." This chapter is divided into three main sections. The first section provides a framework for understanding the relationship between tourism and political stability, in which the role of the media is highlighted as influencing tourists' perceptions of the relative safety of destinations. This first section also highlights the two different forms which the tourism—political stability relationship takes: political instability which leads to a decline in tourist numbers; and direct attacks on tourists for political purposes. The remaining sections examine these two dimensions of political instability in detail and provide several case studies of the impact of instability on tourist visitation. The chapter concludes by highlighting the role of media and tourist perceptions in determining perceptions of safety and political stability in tourist destinations.

Tourism, Crime and International Security Issues, edited by
A. Pizam and Y. Mansfeld. © 1996 John Wiley & Sons Ltd.

Tourism and political instability

Political instability refers to a situation in which conditions and mechanisms of governance and rule are challenged as to their political legitimacy by elements operating from outside of the normal operations of the political system. When challenge occurs from within a political system and the system is able to adapt and change to meet demands on it, it can be said to be stable. When forces for change are unable to be satisfied from within a political system and then use such non-legitimate activities as protest, violence, or even civil war to seek change, then a political system can be described as being unstable. Clearly, there are degrees of political instability. For example, Italian governments have tended to have a very short life-span due to the nature of the Italian political and electoral system. Nevertheless, the system has generally managed to adapt and change to the demands placed upon it. In contrast, many of the former state socialist countries of Eastern Europe had a highly stable political system for many years which only broke down in the late 1980s as the desire for social, economic and political change overwhelmed the capacity of political systems to adapt and satisfy political demands.

Political stability is therefore not a value judgment as to the democratic nature, or otherwise, of a state. Indeed, it may well be the case that certain authoritarian states which limit formal opposition to government may provide extremely stable political environments in which tourism may flourish. For example, as Hall (1994a: 15) observed, "the perceived nature of a political regime as repressive may not necessarily deter international tourism: both Spain and Portugal developed their very considerable international tourism industries under what many would regard as fascist dictatorships." By their very nature, authoritarian regimes do not have to go through the public consultation measures which are in place in most Western democracies (Hall, 1994a). Therefore, tourism development can be fast-tracked through any local, provincial or national planning system that is in place. In the case of Portugal "the transformation of the . . . tourist industry has been accompanied by major shifts in the priority attached to it in government policy" (Lewis and Williams, 1988: 119), with emphasis being given to tourism in government development plans in the late 1960s and early 1970s in order to attract foreign tourists and up-market tourism. Similarly, in the case of Spain, special laws were passed to facilitate the creation of new tourist settlements in the zones most favored by spontaneous tourism (Valenzuela, 1988).

The role that authoritarian states have played in tourism development highlights the importance of government, media and tourist perceptions of destinations in determining attitudes towards the political characteristics of the destination and the creation of its tourist image. Figure 8.1 provides a model of the factors leading to the creation of images of the political stability of a destination region in tourist-generating regions. Three elements are identified as leading to the creation of destination images: returning tourists through word-of-mouth reporting of their experiences, the media and the government of the tourist-generating region. Governments, through their foreign-policy settings can have a dramatic impact on perceptions of potential destinations. For example, travel was encouraged between the former state socialist nations of Eastern Europe in order to support notions of international communist solidarity (Hall, 1991b). Conversely, travel flows between nations may be suspended it political relations are poor. For example, the prohibition since the early 1960s on Americans wishing to travel direct to Cuba or the dramatic fall in American travel to the Soviet Union following the invasion of

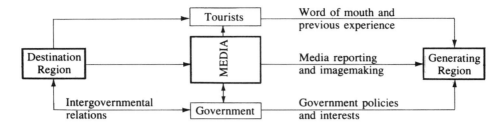

Figure 8.1 Political instability, violence and the imagemaking process

Afghanistan and the shooting down of KAL 007 by Soviet jet fighters (Hall, 1994a). Indeed, international tourism policy is intimately related to foreign-policy objectives. As Richter (1984, p. 614) observed:

> the time is rapidly approaching when travel trade restrictions on the part of one country may in fact constitute an act of war against a small nation heavily dependent on the tourist trade. In some geographic regions, like the Caribbean, this is already the case. Cuba, Jamaica (under Manley), Nicaragua, and even Grenada discovered that the United States as a government has considerable leverage over the tourism industry. Add to that the US travel industry's clout, particularly in terms of airlines and hotels. The result for small destinations is a formidable combination.

Government policy is certainly important in regulating tourist flows and also influencing tourist visitation through the articulation of national government policies towards current or potential tourist destination regions. However, it is the media which will have the greatest influence on the creation of destination images in tourist-generating regions.

Media, through books, magazines and newspapers, have always had a substantial influence on images of destination areas. More recently, the telecommunications revolution of the late 20th century has created a visual immediacy to image creation unmatched in human history. Thanks to satellites and cable links, events in countries and regions far away from the viewer can now be seen as they happen. For example, in June 1989 Americans and other CNN subscribers around the world were able to watch live as tanks rolled into Beijing's Tiananmen Square to quell the student protests. It can be argued that such images were a major influence in changing travel plans to China for many tourists (see below). Similarly, visual images and reporting of political events have greatly affected travel to other destinations such as Egypt, the former Yugoslavia and Sri Lanka.

The critical point, then, is the manner in which the media and, to a lesser extent government, mediate as an image filter between the tourist destination and generating regions. Sometimes the filter will emphasize particular issues or events; other times events may be ignored. Either way, the media will be a major force in creating images of safety and political stability in the destination region. Indeed, it is the very potential for media coverage that provides some political groups with the rationale for attacks on tourists. For example, in the early 1970s the Palestine Liberation Organization (PLO) utilized aircraft hijacking as a means of creating publicity for the plight of the Palestinian people in the Israeli-occupied territories and for promoting the Palestinians' political cause.

Hallmark tourist events also aim to use the media to promote certain images. Hallmark events focus attention on a particular location for a short period of time and can provide a structured set of socio-cultural experiences to both the visitor and the local (Hall, 1992). During such events, the host community and nation are able to highlight certain images, themes and values while, at the same time, protest groups may also attempt to use hallmark events to obtain a profile (Hall, 1989): for example, the PLO attack on the Israeli team at the 1972 Olympic Games in Munich. The "Olympic Games are concerned not only with athletics. They are also about politics, ego, and the compulsion of cities to prove themselves" (Thomas, 1984: 67). Moreover, it has been argued that spectacles, such as the Olympic Games and World Fairs, have come to symbolize the power of commodity relations and the dominance of hegemonic consciousness within modern society (Debord, 1973). For example, the 1984 Los Angeles Olympics were as much a celebration of American capitalism and the processes of capitalist accumulation as the 1980 Moscow Olympics attempted to show the supposed success of state Marxism to the Western world. Similarly, at the micro-political level hallmark events may be used to improved the international and domestic acceptance of unpopular and/or authoritarian regimes. For example, the 1990 Asian Games in Beijing were used by the Chinese to help improve their image in the post-June 4, 1989, Tiananmen Square massacre era (Knipp, 1990). It is a testimony to the power of the media's portrayal of political events that the Square is now a tourist attraction in its own right.

The media are not passive portrayers of events. The media select particular representations and interpretations of places and events amid a plethora of potential representations in terms of time, content and images. Therefore, it is the portrayal of political instability rather than political instability itself which becomes uppermost as a factor in tourist destination choice behavior. Nevertheless, political instability clearly does exist.

Political instability can take a number of forms. A number of different dimensions of political instability can be identified within international tourism: international wars, civil wars, coups, terrorism, riots and political and social unrest, and strikes (after Lea and Small, 1988). Examples of these different types of political instability are illustrated in Table 8.1.

Warfare, whether it be international or civil, is clearly disastrous for tourism. Apart from the dangers which war presents to the individual, military activity can also damage tourist infrastructure. For example, Lebanon's once thriving tourist industry has been devastated by years of civil war and conflict with neighboring Syria and Israel. Much of the former Yugoslavia's tourism infrastructure and attractiveness as a tourist destination has been all but destroyed, particularly in the former Olympic city of Sarajevo and the World Heritage listed city of Dubrovnik (Jordan, 1994). Although substantially shorter than a civil war military coups may also have a major effect on tourist arrivals. For example, following the change of regime in Afghanistan the number of tourists fell by 60 per cent between 1978 and 1979 (Cater, 1987). Nevertheless, military or civilian coups will usually have to be seen as violent or introducing substantial political instability into government before they have a substantial effect on visitor numbers. Similarly, Thailand has been subject to regular changes of government through the intervention of the military. However, such changes have usually been peaceful in nature and external

Table 8.1 Dimensions of political instability

Dimension	Examples
International Wars	Iraqi invasion of Kuwait and consequent invasion of Iraq by multinational force in 1990–1 had massive impact on tourist visitation to the Middle East because of perceived dangers in the region. Also had broader impact on international tourism because of the potential for terrorist attacks.
Civil Wars	The break up of Yugoslavia in 1991 and the ongoing conflict among Bosnia, Croatia and Serbia has devastated tourist visitation in the former federation. Similarly, in the case of Sri Lanka visitor arrivals are only now approaching the record numbers of 1982 following a decade of civil war.
Coups	In the case of an attempted coup in the Gambia in July 1981, the number of visitors dropped from 21 327 in 1980–1 to 16 962 in 1981–2. Similarly, following the May 1987 coup in Fiji, Japanese visitation was halved during June and dropped further during July and August. Tourist arrivals from Australia, New Zealand and the United States were cut by almost 75 per cent. From the 85 000 visitors in April, arrivals fell to 5000 in June. The Australian and New Zealand governments advised their nationals not to travel to Fiji and the occupancy rate in Fiji dropped to approximately 10 per cent.
Terrorism	Muslim extremist attacks on tourists in Egypt in late 1992 and early 1993 seriously damaged the country's US$4 billion tourist industry, cutting the tourism trade by almost half.
Riots/Political Protests/Social Unrest	Following the crushing of the political protests in Tiananmen Square the total number of overseas arrivals in China fell by 22.7 per cent from 31 694 804 international visitors in 1988 to 24 501 394 in 1989. Political and social unrest may also occur in direct response to tourism development: for example, if the local community were opposed to the development of a tourist resort or tourist infrastructure such as an airport.
Strikes	According to the Australian Tourism Industry Association following the 1989 Australian domestic air pilots dispute, an estimated 457 000 people canceled their holidays plans altogether and a further 556 000 had to change their holiday plans.

Sources: Hall, 1994a, b, c.

perceptions of political stability have been maintained. It is only when violence occurs during an attempted coup, such as in 1992, that visitors numbers have been affected (Hall, 1994b).

Warfare may also have long-term impacts on the image of a destination. For example, South Korea's tourism industry has long been harmed by images of the Korean War and conflicts between North and South Korea. A study by Jeong (1988) indicated that the 1988 Summer Olympics in Seoul were perceived as a means to overcome the poor image of Korea in the international tourism market as a "dangerous place to visit" (1988: 176), particularly in the United States because of such factors as MASH (the highly popular television series based on the fictionalized exploits of an American field hospital during the Korean War), the devastation of the country following the Korean War, the shooting down of Korean Airlines flight 007 in the early 1980s, student protests and the ongoing political instability between North and South Korea. Nevertheless, experience from other destinations such as Sri Lanka (Sinclair, 1994) and Zambia (Teye, 1986) indicates that tourism can recover rapidly following cessation of conflict. In the case of Zambia, for example, international tourist arrivals increased threefold after the civil war finished in neighboring Zimbabwe (formerly Rhodesia) and a black majority government came to power (Teye, 1986).

Warfare, coups and political strikes or protests may make tourism development or the attraction of visitation problematic, but they do not by themselves constitute a direct threat to tourists. For example, in the case of Sri Lanka, Sinclair (1994: 13) reported that, "no visitor has ever been involved in the communal strife." However, terrorism constitutes a different nature of threat to tourists because in this instance, tourists may constitute the target for terrorist activity. In highlighting the interrelationship between political stability and tourism it is therefore essential to differentiate between tourists and tourism being the direct or indirect victim of political instability; as our ability to comprehend the nature of risk and threat and, hence, develop the appropriate managerial response will be substantially different. The next two sections illustrate the two different types of threat with references to several case studies of tourism and political instability.

Tourism as the indirect victim of political instability: China and Croatia

As noted above, tourism is extremely vulnerable to perceived political instability and lack of safety. Probably one of the best known examples of the relationship between political instability and tourism was the June 4 1989 crackdown by Chinese authorities on non-violent student protests in Beijing's Tiananmen Square. As Graham (1990: 25) observed:

> The sight of tanks rolling into the Square; the violent battles between students and troops; the steadfastly uncompromising attitude of the Chinese authorities; it was all watched by the world on prime-time television. And most people living in free societies felt revulsion and anger; those planning holidays to China cancelled, while those with a vague notion of visiting the country put it on hold for the distant future — if ever.

The events in Tiananmen Square and throughout many of China's cities at this time dramatically impacted the country's tourism industry. By late 1989 occupancy levels in Beijing's hotels were "below 30 per cent at a time when closer to 90 per cent would have been expected ... 300 tour groups totaling 11,500 people were cancelled in May" (Lavery, 1989: 96). Similarly, Gartner and Shen (1992: 47) noted, "occupancy rates of 15% were considered high in the months shortly after the conflict." In addition to the impact on tourist visitation, business visits were also affected by both perceptions of instability and sanctions that were imposed by many Western governments on their corporations which conducted business in China (Hall, 1994a).

The downturn in tourism following Western and Japanese reactions to the quelling of the pro-democracy movement in China had a substantial impact on China's foreign-exchange earnings. Since the shift by the Chinese government in 1978 to an "open-door

Table 8.2 China's international tourism receipts, 1978–92

Year	Receipts US$ million	% Growth rate
1978	262.90	—
1979	449.27	70.9
1980	616.65	37.3
1981	784.91	27.3
1982	843.17	7.4
1983	941.20	11.6
1984	1131.34	20.2
1985	1250.00	10.5
1986	1530.85	22.5
1987	1861.51	21.6
1988	2246.83	20.7
1989	1860.48	− 17.2
1990	2217.58	19.2
1991	2844.97	28.3
1992	3946.87	38.7

Source: National Tourism Administration of the People's Republic of China, (1993: 122).

policy" in its relations with non-communist countries and the promotion of the doctrine of a "socialist market economy," tourism has been regarded as a key element in the modernization of China and a means to gain important foreign-exchange earnings (Hall, 1994a; Richter, 1989). As Zhao Ziyang stated at the 13th National Congress of the Communist Party of China in 1987:

> Our capacity to earn foreign exchange through export determines, to a great extent, the degree to which we can open to the outside world and affects the scale and pace of domestic economic development. For this reason, bearing in mind the demands of the world market and our own strong points, we should make vigorous efforts to develop export-oriented industries and products that are competitive and can bring quick and high economic returns (quoted in Tisdell and Wen, 1991: 55).

The potential of tourism to net foreign exchange for the Chinese government is substantial. China's accumulated foreign-exchange earnings from international tourism between 1978 and 1988 were estimated to be US$11.65 billion. In 1988 China earned US$2220 million from foreign tourists, but this fell by US$430 million the following year due to the effects of the political unrest during May and June (Tisdell and Wen, 1991). While a substantial loss of foreign exchange was experienced, it was nowhere near as bad as some commentators had forecast (Table 8.2). For example *Travel and Tourism Analyst* estimated that "receipts from foreign tourists will fall by 75 per cent in 1989, reducing earnings to around $550 [million], or, to put it another way, recording a loss of $1.9 [billion] over expected levels" (Lavery, 1989: 96).

Research by Roehl (1990) on American travel agents and Gartner and Shen (1992) on mature travelers, indicated a negative shift in attitudes toward visiting China as a result of the events at Tiananmen Square. However, by 1991 inbound tourism had grown again to exceed pre-Tiananmen levels of visitation (Table 8.3). As Cook (1989: 64) correctly argued, "the massacre of Chinese students and civilians in T'ian-an-men Square put a

Table 8.3 International visitor arrivals to China, 1978–92

Year	Total No. of Visitors	Growth rate %	Foreign visitors No. of visitors	% Growth	Overseas Chinese No. of visitors	% Growth	Compatriots No. of visitors	% Growth	Taiwan No. of visitors	% Growth
1978	1 809 221	—	229 646	—	18 092	—	1 561 483	—		
1979	4 203 901	132.4	362.389	57.8	20 910	15.6	3 820 602	144.7		
1980	5 702 536	35.6	529 124	46.0	34 413	64.6	5 138 999	34.5		
1981	7 767 096	36.2	675 153	27.6	38 853	12.9	7 053 087	37.2		
1982	7 924 261	2.0	764 497	13.2	542 745	10.0	7 117 019	1.0		
1983	9 477 005	19.6	872 511	14.1	40 352	−5.6	8 564 142	20.3		
1984	12 852 185	35.6	1 134 267	30.0	47 498	17.7	11 670 420	36.2		
1985	17 833 097	38.8	1 370 462	20.8	84 827	78.6	16 370 808	40.0		
1986	22 819 450	28.0	1 482 476	8.2	68 133	−19.7	21 269 041	29.9		
1987	26 902 267	17.9	1 727 821	16.6	87 031	27.7	25 087 415	18.0		
1988	31 694 804	17.8	1 842 206	6.6	79 348	−8.8	29 773 250	18.7	437 700	—
1989	24 501 394	−22.7	1 460 970	−20.7	68 556	−13.6	22 971 868	−22.8	541 000	23.6
1990	27 461 821	12.1	1 747 315	19.6	91 090	32.9	25 623 416	11.5	947 600	75.2
1991	33 349 761	21.4	2 710 103	55.1	133 427	46.5	30 506 231	19.8	946 632	−0.1
1992	38 114 945	14.3	4 006 427	47.8	165 077	23.7	33 943 441	11.3	1 317 770	39.2

Overseas Chinese: Refers to Chinese residing in foreign countries who hold a Chinese passport.
Compatriots: Chinese nationals residing in Hong Kong, Macao and Taiwan. Taiwan became a separate category for statistical purposes in 1988.

Source: National Tourism Administration of the People's Republic of China (1992; 1993).

Table 8.4 Overnight stays of foreign visitors in the communes of the Croatian coast, 1987−92

Year	Foreign Visitors ('000s)
1987	4100
1988	4100
1989	3800
1990	3250
1991	3000
1992	500

Source: Jordan (1994).

temporary end to international tourism in China. As history is written in China, however, and as the events of Spring 1989 become back-page news around the world, tourists will return to China. In fact, the number of travelers to China is expected to increase dramatically throughout the 1990s.'' For example, in 1991 and 1992 the number of foreign visitors had grown by 55 and 48 per cent respectively. Nevertheless, Western government and media attitudes towards the Chinese occupation of Tibet (Klieger, 1992) and the transfer of Hong Kong to Chinese sovereignty will have a substantial influence on foreign tourists' perceptions of China as a destination (Hall, 1994a), with the latter being a major issue during the late 1990s.

A major contemporary example of the direct effect that political instability can have on tourist visitation is the impact of the wars in Croatia and Bosnia-Hercegovina in the former Yugoslavia. The coastal area of Croatia has a long history as a tourist destination (Hall, 1991a). In 1989 the last ''normal'' year before the outbreak of hostilities in the coastal area of Croatia, tourism was responsible for 26 per cent of people employed in the public sector and 34 per cent of regional income (Jordan, 1994).

Table 8.4 indicates the overnight stays of foreign visitors in the communes of the Croatian coast from 1987 to 1992. As the table illustrates, the rate of foreign visitation in the late 1980s had already suffered from the general political and economic instability of Yugoslavia and the overall decline of tourism in the northern Mediterranean at that time. However, the outbreak of hostilities in Northern Dalmatia in August 1990 led to a dramatic drop in international tourist arrivals. In 1991, the war in Slovenia and Croatia severely impacted visitor levels with only three million overnight stays being recorded, some 7.8 per cent of the 1989 figures. Figures for 1992 indicated a moderate recovery, but these were isolated to the northern Croatian coast (Jordan, 1994).

In addition to the spatial dimension of recovery, Jordan (1994) also noted that different markets reacted differently to the outbreak and continuation of hostilities in the former Yugoslavia. In the summer of 1992, the British and French continued to avoid the Croatian coast; the Italians, Austrians and the Czechs returned in larger numbers. According to Jordan (1994: 8), ''insofar as it concerns Italians and Austrians this might be explained by a rather intimate knowledge of the situation in Croatia, a high share of longer weekend and [marine] tourism. Insofar as Czechs are concerned the favorable price level on the Croatian coast might have been the strongest impetus.'' In addition, the continued absence of the traditionally strong British and French markets may be related to the presence of peace-keeping forces from those countries in neighboring Bosnia-Hercegovina. Although a substantial distance from the Croatian cost, the presence of the peace-keeping forces means that the hostilities in the former Yugoslavia have a high profile in the British and French media. This may lead to continued perceptions of political instability and an unsafe environment in Croatia.

The legacy of the events in the former Yugoslavia indicates the extent to which political instability can affect regional tourism, as well as the particular destination in which the violence or unrest actually occurs. For example, the actions of Basque separatists have, at times, damaged the tourism industry in northern Spain (Valenzuela, 1988). "Even Switzerland, the pre-eminent symbol of domestic tranquility and political neutrality, has seen tourism drop as a consequence of terrorist attacks in Italy, France, Austria and FR Germany" (Richter and Waugh, 1986: 232). Similarly, in 1985 the South Pacific nation of Vanuatu suffered as a result of the political unrest in neighboring New Caledonia (Hall, 1994d). "Unfortunately, as very little image building had been done there was confusion in many tourism source countries over whether Vanuatu was or was not a part of New Caledonia and Vanuatu's tourism industry suffered accordingly" (National Tourism Office of Vanuatu, 1990: 3). In 1986, arrivals from Australia, the major source of international tourists, were the lowest for nine years. As Lea and Small (1988: 9) commented in relation to the effects of political violence on tourism in the region, "the main lesson for South Pacific destinations is that trouble in one country means trouble for the region."

Although the duration of political violence may be short lived, the longer-term implications for tourism can last for many years, affecting the confidence not only of tourists but also potential investors in the tourism industry (Hall 1994a). Given the increasing potential for destination substitution in the highly competitive global tourism market-place, many destination regions need to pay greater heed to the potential impact of political instability on the image of the destination. For example, attacks on tourists and continued political instability in Jammu and Kashmir, stemming from a dispute between Muslims and non-Muslims concerning the secession of Kashmir from India, has led to a shift in visitor arrivals to other areas of the Himalayan region catering to adventure tourists (Seth, 1990: 65). In 1990, following a period of major political unrest in the region only 1200 visitors entered the Valley of Kashmir in the first eight months compared with 45 000 in the same period in 1988 (Seth, 1990).

Tourism is clearly very susceptible to perceptions of political instability, particularly when such instability is tied to hostilities. In the above cases tourism was an incidental victim of broader political activities. Tourists may sometimes get caught up in a war, coup, or riot, thereby damaging perceptions of the destination and possibly even the overall pattern of tourism development in the longer term, but they are not the direct target of political violence or social unrest. However, in the case of terrorism, which we examine in the next section, tourism is often a direct and deliberate target of political violence.

The tourist as target: tourism as the direct victim of political instability

Most of the evidence on tourist motivations points to fear and insecurity as a major barrier to travel and thus a limitation on the growth of the industry. In addition to the openly stated fear there is often an expression of lack of interest in travel, which can mask an underlying fear. In these circumstances the possibility of terrorism, however remote, will have an effect on the tourist demand of a large number of potential tourists (Buckley and Klemm, 1993: 191).

Travelers have long been subject to banditry. Hence, the word "travail," meaning hard or agonizing labor, from which "travel" derives. However, politically motivated terrorism is a child of the modern era of travel. Images of hijacked aircraft or the taking of tourists as hostages are a common element in television news. The media profile given terrorist activities is probably critical in its occurrence given that "terrorism is a form of communication, of both the threat or reality of violence and the political message" (Richter and Waugh, 1986: 230). Therefore, the media which were identified in Figure 8.1 as being significant in establishing tourist perceptions of political stability in destination regions can also serve the communication needs of political terrorists in highlighting their cause in the tourist-generating regions. Indeed, the internationalization of the media and increased global political and economic interdependence can only serve to lift the profile of terrorist activities.

According to Hall (1994a), tourism is affected by terrorism through two means. First, terrorist activities can damage a destination's or country's tourist industry by creating an image of lack of safety. Second, tourists or tourist facilities, such as airport terminals or aircraft, may themselves be subject to attack. "Tourist facilities are logical targets of terrorist violence because they afford opportunity and relative safety for terrorists to act" (Richter and Waugh, 1986: 233). Although the actual risk of terrorist attack is quite low, it is perceptions that count with the effects of such perceptions on travel decisions usually substantial (Conant et al. 1988). For example, Richter and Waugh (1986: 230) reported "preliminary estimates indicating that 1.8 million Americans changed their plans for foreign travel in 1986, following American raids on Libya and terrorist attacks on several European airports."

According to Hall (1994a), attacks on tourists or tourist facilities can be used by terrorists to achieve a range of tactical, strategic and ideological objectives. One of the most common reasons for terrorist attacks is to gain publicity for the terrorist cause. For example, the hijacking of airliners in the early 1970s by the Palestine Liberation Organization (PLO) was used to gain publicity for the Palestinian cause. In eastern Turkey in 1993, members of the Kurdistan Workers' Party seeking the establishment of a separate Kurdish state, kidnapped a number of tourists. Australian, French and British tourists were abducted and held hostage in order to raise the profile of the Kurdish separatists in the world media. More recently, in August 1994, three tourists, an Australian, British and French citizen traveling on a train between Phnom Penh and Sihanoukville were taken hostage by the Khmer Rouge. They were used as pawns in negotiations with the Cambodian Government over foreign military aid and political recognition of the Khmer Rouge. In this way, terrorist attacks on tourists can also be used to punish nationals of a country which supports the government which the terrorists are trying to overthrow or which is in opposition to their own activities. For example, Richter and Waugh (1986) note that attacks on American tourists may be viewed as a form of punishment of the United States government for its foreign-policy decisions and military actions.

Events which are used by governments to enhance their legitimacy can also be utilized by opposition groups to undermine support for government and to focus attention on government activities. As Richter and Waugh (1986: 238) noted, "uncompromising positions taken by authoritarian leaders in their own states or self-righteous world leaders, often backfire when they cannot enforce their policies and when terrorists view the policies as challenges to be overcome." For example, the 1980 American Society of

Travel Agents (ASTA) Conference in Manila which had over 6000 delegates in attendance was bombed just minutes after President Marcos had given the opening address (Richter, 1989). More recently, in August 1994, the El-Gama'a el-Islamiya (Islamic Group) attacked a tourist mini-bus near Sohag in southern Egypt, killing a 13-year-old Spanish boy, in order to warn foreigners to stay away from the September United Nations World Population Conference to be held in Cairo. According to one newspaper report, "the Egyptian Government hoped that by hosting the conference it could promote the image of a peace-loving, democratic country and a safe destination" (*Canberra Times*, 1994: 12).

The current situation in Egypt with respect to attacks on tourists is an example of how tourists and tourist facilities can be targeted by terrorist organizations in an attempt to achieve ideological objectives and to strengthen their claims to political legitimacy by making the incumbent government appear weak. The deliberate targeting of tourists in Egypt since late 1992 by fundamentalist Muslim militants marked a change in previous political tactics and has seriously damaged the country's US$4 billion tourist industry, cutting the tourism trade by almost half.

Islamic fundamentalists perceive tourism as a soft target on which to wage their mission and are aware of the role tourism plays in the Egyptian economy and in the regional economy of destinations such as Luxor. Such attacks may also gather a degree of sympathy from the general population because many Islamic fundamentalists are also concerned at the contradiction between the values of mass tourism and Islam. Indeed, the El-Gama'a el-Islamiya have been warning foreign tourists to stay away from Cairo and upper Egypt. According to the group: "The Gama'a has carried out about 20 operations targeting the tourist industry and the casualties among the tourists themselves were negligible, in accordance with our policy of 'tourism not tourists'" (Reuter, 1993: 7). In response, the Egyptian government has attempted to imprison many of the leaders of the fundamentalist movement and has used military forces to help protect convoys of tourist buses, particularly in the south of the country. However, the latter action, while helping to ensure tourist safety, does not enhance tourist perceptions of Egypt as a safe destination.

The above examples illustrate the extent to which terrorism can impact tourism. However, as Richter and Waugh (1986: 238) have recognized, "the relationship between terrorism and tourism is important not because the problem is new but because the political and economic ramifications are immense and likely to grow larger." Because of its international visibility tourism is a ready-made target for terrorist groups who are seeking to gain publicity for their objectives. Within this context it becomes imperative for destination areas to understand not only the motivations of terrorist organizations but also the key role that the media play in inadvertently supporting the goals of many terrorist groups. Tourism managers in politically unstable regions and in vulnerable tourist facilities, such as airports, need to develop ways of preventing terrorist attacks against tourists, without giving tourists the impression that a serious threat is present; otherwise there is a likelihood that their behavior in terms of destination and activity choice may well change.

Tourism may also be the object of social and political opposition. Although community-oriented tourism planning is popular in academic circles (Getz, 1991; Hall, 1994a, 1994c; Murphy, 1985, 1988), in many destination areas around the world, local perceptions and opinions regarding tourism development are often ignored by government and tourism developers in their search for profit and foreign exchange. If local people are excluded from planning and decision-making processes and from their lands and resources, then their way of life will undoubtedly change, possibly resulting in resentment and negative social and environmental impacts. For example, following a change of ownership at the Anuha Island Resort in the Solomon Islands and a consequent series of actions which angered the customary land holders, "the angered islanders dug holes in the airstrip, sent painted warriors to force guests off the islands, and closed down the resort in spite of a court ruling against them" (Minerbi, 1992: 19).

The Solomon Islands' situation noted above is not an isolated example of protest concerning tourism development. Throughout the world many people do not want tourism and what it represents, and many people are willing to oppose it from both within and outside of legitimate political structures. Such an observation further reinforces the need for tourism managers and planners to consider non-economic factors such as culture and politics in their assessment of the value of tourism development. As Heenan (1978: 32) recognized:

> In their quest for viability and legitimacy, enlightened investors and community leaders must balance local and outside needs and interests . . . if the constructive impact of tourism is to be realized, collaborate approaches between diverse stakeholder groups will be needed. To survive and prosper in the decades ahead, tourism must develop some multiple constituencies.

Conclusion

> A favourable image is an essential requirement of any tourist destination. The problem with any kind of civil unrest is that unfavourable images are beamed across the world, so that even those who are not afraid of terrorism will be discouraged from taking a holiday there. It is not so much that the area is dangerous; more that it does not look attractive (Buckley and Klemm, 1993: 193–4).

Perceptions of political stability and safety are a prerequisite for tourist visitation. Violent protests, social unrest, civil war, terrorist actions, the perceived violations of human rights, or even the mere threat of these activities can all serve to cause tourists to alter their travel behavior. Tourism managers and planners therefore need to become far more sophisticated in their approach to crisis management and be more aware of the political dimensions of tourism development. At present, "when problems arise, the only response the industry knows is to market more vigorously, regardless of the likelihood of success" (Richter and Waugh, 1986: 232). For example, in response to the May 14 1987 military coup in Fiji, the Fijian tourism industry, aided by the devaluation of the Fiji dollar, slashed holiday prices. By August 1987, there was an increase in Australian and New Zealand arrivals of 9.6 per cent, and by September these markets were up 40 per cent. Then on September 28 a second coup occurred leading to a further 30 per cent drop in arrivals. The Fijian response to the second coup was to launch a promotional campaign with the theme "I wonder whether Fiji is still a paradise?" with the emphasis "that all is normal and 'ordinary Australians' are featured to reassure potential visitors that the destination is safe" (Lea and Small, 1988: 8). However, despite the best efforts of marketers the instability of Fijian politics continued to have an impact on tourist arrivals, with the 1986 visitor arrival total not being reached again until 1990 (Fiji Visitors Bureau,

1992). Indeed, given their substitutability for the Fijian tourism product, both Bali and north Queensland benefited from the coups. "Several destinations used the Fijian coups to highlight the appeal and safety of their own resorts: 'Golden beaches, coconut palms and *no* coups!', was the message used to attract visitors to Magnetic Island [Queensland] in October 1987; and 'War in the Solomons ended in 1945. Why risk Fiji?'" (*Times on Sunday*, May 31, 1987, in Lea and Small, 1988: 9). Cut-price fares and accommodation were only a short-term solution to the problems posed by the coups. Longer-term solutions required a complete reassessment of the way in which consumers perceived Fiji as a tourist destination.

The sheer scope of the implications of political violence for tourism requires a far more sophisticated understanding of the nature of the international traveler's response to political instability and perceived threats to tourist safety than has hitherto been the case. Political threats are often not included in assessments of the external environment within which tourist businesses operate. This chapter has given a brief introduction to the various means by which political instability and political violence can impact tourism. As noted, the effects of political violence can be both direct or incidental and may have repercussions far beyond the immediate location in which violence occurs. Political instability can have major effects on the local tourism economy. For example, the tourist economy of the island of Krk off the Croatian coast has suffered substantially from the effects of the hostilities in that region. Between 1989 and 1993 there has been a decline of persons permanently employed in tourism and catering of 26 per cent, of seasonal workers some 77 per cent and investment in tourism has fallen by 87 per cent (Jordan, 1994). Similarly, the tourist economies of China, the Philippines, Fiji, India, Vanuatu, Egypt, South Africa and Sri Lanka have all been damaged to various degrees by political violence in recent years.

Continuing political instability can have a deterrent effect on tourism at a time when regions are in most need of the foreign- exchange and economic development benefits of tourism, as in the case of the former state socialist countries of Eastern Europe (Hall, 1994a) or in less-developed nations (Hall, 1994b; Harrison, 1992). Currently, there are a number of destinations around the world which may prove potentially dangerous for the traveler and as a result are suffering major impacts on their tourist numbers and on tourism development (Table 8.5).

Attacks on tourists and actual or perceived political instability could create negative tourist images of a destination which may take years to overcome. In some cases, such as China, South Africa and Zimbabwe, changed political conditions and/or favorable media coverage may enable destinations to recover relatively quickly. Indeed, there may even be a "curiosity" factor whereby tourists are interested in seeing a place they may have seen or read about during a period of political instability and which is now safe to visit. However, where political instability and political violence linger, as in the Lebanon, Kashmir or the former Yugoslavia, visitation may take many years to reach the figures of the pre-political instability period. Perceptions of instability can also have consequent long-term effects on tourism development by reducing the likelihood of both foreign and domestic investment in tourist infrastructure, and by increasing the costs of insuring such investments (Hall, 1994a).

Politics has major direct and indirect influences on tourism development and on tourist behavior. The emerging global economy and communications networks, of which the internationalization of tourism is an integral part, make tourism increasingly subject to

Table 8.5 Destinations whose tourism sectors are currently affected by political instability and political violence

Country/Region	Indirect Factors	Direct Factors
Algeria	State of emergency, deteriorating security situation	—
Bosnia-Hercegovina	Continuing political instability and hostilities with Serbia	—
Cambodia	Continuing political instability	Tourists subject to killing and kidnapping and ransom
Croatia	Continuing political instability and hostilities with Serbia. Major damage to tourism infrastructure	—
Cuba	Political instability, ongoing conflict with United States	—
Egypt	—	Tourists subject to direct attack by Muslim fundamentalists
India (Kashmir)	Muslim secessionist movement	Attacks on tourists and tourist infrastructure
Israel	Sporadic violence	—
Lebanon	Aftermath of civil war. Major damage to tourism infrastructure	—
Nepal	Political instability	—
Northern Ireland	Political conflict	Attacks on high-profile tourist infrastructure in the United Kingdom
Palestine	Political instability	—
Papua New Guinea	Political instability	—
Peru	Political instability	Guerilla movement has targeted tourists
Philippines	Political instability	Tourists subject to kidnapping and ransom
Rwanda	Civil war	—
Slovenia	Slowly recovering from breakup of the former Yugoslavia and consequent perceptions of political instability	—
South Africa	Recovering from effects of apartheid	—
South Korea	Political tensions with North Korea	Student riots
Sri Lanka	Continuing political instability	—
Turkey (Kurdistan)	—	Direct attacks on tourists with tourists being hijacked
Wales	—	Damage to second homes owned by English by Welsh nationalist radicals

the effects of political instability and political violence. In a world of increasing interconnection, the severing of touristic relationships through acts of political violence can have repercussions throughout the entire tourist system, dramatically affecting tourist behavior, the destination region, nearby destination regions, transit regions and political relationships. Undoubtedly, it is impossible completely to insulate tourism from the effects of political instability. However, to ignore the political dimensions of tourism may lead not only to an incomplete academic appreciation of tourism but also to an inadequate assessment of the risks associated with tourism development.

Acknowledgements

The authors would like gratefully to acknowledge the assistance of John Jenkins and Dave Crag in the preparation of this chapter.

References

Buckley, P.J. and Klemm, M. (1993). The decline of tourism in Northern Ireland. *Tourism Management*. June: 184−94.

Canberra Times (1994). Muslims misled by Vatican: Egypt. August 19: 12.

Cater, E.A. (1987). Tourism in the least developed countries. *Annals of Tourism Research*. **14**: 202−26.

Conant, J.S., Clarke, T., Burnett, J.J. and Zank, G. (1988). Terrorism and travel: managing the unmanageable. *Journal of Travel Research*. Spring: 16−20.

Cook, D. (1989). China's hotels: still playing catch up. *Cornell Hotel Restaurant and Administration Quarterly*, **30** (3): 64−7.

Debord, G. (1973). *Society of the Spectacle*. Detroit: Black and Red.

Fiji Visitors Bureau. (1992). *A Statistical Report on Visitor Arrivals into Fiji, Calendar Year 1991*. Suva: Fiji Visitors Bureau.

Gartner, W.C. and Shen, J. (1992). The impact of Tiananmen Square on China's tourism image. *Journal of Travel Research*, **30** (4): 47−52.

Getz, D. (1991). *Festivals, Special Events and Tourism*. New York: Van Nostrand Reinhold.

Graham, M. (1990). Culture shock. *Asia Travel Trade*, 22 February: 24−6.

Hall, C.M. (1989). The politics of hallmark events. In Syme, G.J., Shaw, B.J., Fenton, D.M. and Mueller, W.S. (eds), *The Planning and Evaluation of Hallmark Events*. Aldershot: Avebury, pp. 219−41.

Hall, C.M. (1992). *Hallmark Tourist Events: Impacts, Management, and Planning*. London: Belhaven Press.

Hall, C.M. (1994a). *Tourism and Politics: Policy, Power and Place*. Chichester: John Wiley & Sons.

Hall, C.M. (1994b). *Tourism in the Pacific: Development, Impacts and Markets*. South Melbourne: Longman Cheshire.

Hall, C.M. (1994c). *Introduction to Tourism in Australia: Impacts, Planning and Development*. (Second Edition), South Melbourne: Longman Cheshire.

Hall, C.M. (1994d). Tourism in Pacific island microstates: a case study of Vanuatu. *Tourism Recreation Research*, **19**(1).

Hall, D.R. (1991a). Introduction. In Hall, D.R. (ed.), *Tourism and Economic Development in Eastern Europe and the Soviet Union*. London: Belhaven Press, pp. 3−28.

Hall, D.R. (ed.) (1991b). *Tourism and Economic Development in Eastern Europe and the Soviet Union*. London: Belhaven Press.

Harrison, D. (ed.) (1992). *Tourism and the Less Developed Countries*. London: Belhaven Press.

Heenan, D. (1978). Tourism and the community, a drama in three acts. *Journal of Travel Research*, **16** (4): 30—2.

Jeong, G-H. (1988). Tourism expectations on the 1988 Seoul Olympics: A Korean perspective. In *Tourism Research: Expanding Boundaries, Travel and Tourism Research Association, Nineteenth Annual Conference*. Salt Lake City: Bureau of Economic and Business Research, Graduate School of Business, University of Utah, pp. 175—82.

Jordan, P. (1994). *The impact of Wars in Croatia and Bosnia- Hercegovina on the Tourism of the Croatian Coast*. Paper presented at the International Geographical Union Study Group on Sustainable Tourism Symposium on Tourism Geography, Lillehammer, Norway, August.

Klieger, P.C. (1992) Shangri-La and the politicization of tourism in Tibet. *Annals of Tourism Research*, **19** (1): 122—5.

Knipp, S. (1990). A long hard march ahead. *PATA Travel News*, October: 22—3.

Lavery, P. (1989). Tourism in China: the costs of collapse. *EIU Travel & Tourism Analyst*, **4**: 77—97.

Lea, J. and Small, J. (1988). *Cyclones, Riots and Coups: Tourist Industry Responses in the South Pacific*. Paper presented at Frontiers in Australian Tourism Conference, Australian National University, Canberra, Australia, July.

Lewis, J. and Williams, A.M. (1988). Portugal: market segmentation and regional specialisation. In Williams, A.M. and Shaw, G. (eds), *Tourism and Economic Development: Western European Experiences*. London: Belhaven Press, pp. 101—22.

Matthews, H.G. (1978). *International Tourism: a Social and Political Analysis*. Cambridge, MA: Schenkman.

Minerbi, L. (1992). *Impacts of Tourism Development in Pacific Islands*. San Francisco: Greenpeace Pacific Campaign.

Murphy, P. (1985). *Tourism: a Community Approach*. New York: Methuen.

Murphy, P.E. (1988). Community driven tourism planning. *Tourism Management*, **9** (2): 96—104.

National Tourism Administration of the People's Republic of China (1992). *The Yearbook of China Tourism Statistics 1992*. Beijing.

National Tourism Administration of the People's Republic of China (1993). *The Yearbook of China Tourism Statistics 1993*. Beijing.

National Tourism Office of Vanuatu (1990). *A History of Tourism in Vanuatu: a Platform for Future Success*. Port Vila.

Reuter (1993). Cairo bomb a mystery. *New Zealand Herald*, March 1: 7.

Richter, L.K. (1984). A search for missing answers to questions never asked: reply to Kosters. *Annals of Tourism Research*, **11**: 613—15.

Richter, L.K. (1989). *The Politics of Tourism in Asia*. Honolulu: University of Hawaii Press.

Richter, L.K. and Waugh Jr, W.L. (1986). Terrorism and tourism as logical companions. *Tourism Management*, December: 230—8.

Roehl, W.S. (1990). Travel agent attitudes toward China after Tiananmen Square. *Journal of Travel Research*, **29** (2): 16—22.

Seth, P. (1990). Adventurers wary of 'Paradise on Earth'. *Asia Travel Trade*, **22**, November: 65—7, 69.

Sinclair, K. (1994). Colombo's hotels are on the move. *Asian Hotelier*, July: 12—13.

Smyth, R. (1986). Public policy for tourism in Northern Ireland. *Tourism Management*, June: 120—6.

Teye, V.B. (1986). Liberation wars and tourism development in Africa: the case of Zambia. *Annals of Tourism Research*, **13**: 589—608.

Thomas, A. (1984). The spirit of '76?: Calgary, site of the 1988 Winter Games, is showing symptoms of "Montreal disease" — the scandal and debt that followed in the wake of the Montreal Olympics. *Saturday Night*, **99** (3): 67—8.

Tisdell, C. and Wen, J. (1991). Foreign tourism as an element in PR China's economic development strategy. *Tourism Management*, March: 55—68.

Valenzuela, M. (1988). Spain: the phenomenon of mass tourism. In Williams, A.M. and Shaw, G. (eds), *Tourism and Economic Development: Western European Experiences*. London: Belhaven Press, pp. 39—57.

9 Tourism, *realpolitik* and development in the South Pacific

JOHN P. LEA

Since it is desirable for the public health that the sea breeze should circulate freely through the town and not be intercepted by buildings near the water along the shore of the harbour, all persons are hereby warned against erecting or repairing buildings or structures of any kind whatsoever on the north or sea side of the present public road . . . without special permission from the Municipal Board, which permission will only be granted for the erection of boat houses and similar structures near the water. Any violation of this Regulation shall be punished by a fine not exceeding $100 or three months imprisonment with or without hard labour (Apia, Western Samoa, Municipal Regulations, January 30, 1880, cited in Pringle, 1989; Appendix 1).

Whoever got this thing to be built on the waterfront anyway? All it's doing is blocking out the view thus shortening everyone's vision. These games power-hungry men play are maddening, maddening . . . and it has always been the case, it's the ordinary people who end up carrying the burden. This is something everyone should think seriously about (Editorial in *Samoa Observer* March 4, 1992, commenting on the location of a new nine-storey government office building, the largest in Western Samoa, on the Apia foreshore. Cited in Lea and Connell, 1994).

Introduction

Tourism is a key component in the economic prospects of most Pacific island states but, despite this significance, it is only one competing development activity found among many others in a generally poor region of the world. There appears to be a built-in tendency characterizing many feasibility and planning studies that treats tourism as a discrete subject, rather than recognizing its true position as part of a complex development whole. The reasons for this unrealistic and isolated treatment of tourism development in the region are varied, and range from an evident lack of understanding of socio-political structures on the part of tourism advisers to pressures on consultants to come up with tangible and physical proposals when other forms of development may be preferable. Although not an obvious cause of violence, colonial and post-colonial trends in most Pacific states towards private forms of land holding in key urban and coastal locations have led to widespread community unrest. This effect is not confined to tourism

Tourism, Crime and International Security Issues, edited by
A. Pizam and Y. Mansfeld. © 1996 John Wiley & Sons Ltd.

of course and is seen under extreme circumstances in mining development in parts of Papua New Guinea. Particularly problematical has been the question of customary land ownership where land has traditionally been treated as a commodity not capable of alientation to individual ownership and an asset held in the communal realm. Small wonder, then, that some developments in the region have generated widespread community opposition with consequent difficulties being experienced in attracting private capital for tourism and other forms of investment.

This chapter advances the proposition that the *realpolitik* of South Pacific development sets obstacles to growth and change in the regional tourism industry that are not adequately reflected in consultants' planning reports and government policy pronouncements. The long-term antidote to acts of communal violence and the destruction of tourism plant is the promotion of a form of positive development that is sensitive to local custom and priorities. It is argued here that a failure on the part of tourist (and other major land developers in the South Pacific) to design, locate and manage their projects in a way that ensures community support will ultimately lead to community opposition and likely violence. Isolated examples of this in the region already exist, as they do more generally in other Third World locations.

There are certain key factors surrounding contemporary development in the independent South Pacific island states that are central to this discussion. Tourism as a major user of land and a leading consumer of a variety of public services is dependent, among other things, on an orderly and predictable development control system. The opening quotes to this chapter describe developments on the foreshore of the Western Samoan capital of Apia a hundred years apart. Early (and introduced) attempts to impose development control regulations in this town were made under a colonial regime in the 19th century and presupposed a governance regulatory system capable of orderly urban management. More than a century later, Apia possesses a wide range of conventional municipal and building regulations, but it has no municipality, no enforceable town plan and very weak building controls. Many of the trappings of Western urban regulation are in place, but the planning and development process has broken down since Independence. This is not an unusual example in the independent countries of the South Pacific and has led to progressively worsening living conditions, as well as recent attempts by government to arrest the decline. It is an exaggeration, perhaps, to suggest that such circumstances lead necessarily to violence, but badly planned tourism infrastructure (or any other forms, of inappropriate development) exacerbates pressures on the delivery of public services of all kinds and will often be a prime candidate for community opposition in due course (Lea, 1993).

There are more conventional pointers to violence and instability in the tourism market in the Pacific of course, and these are seen mainly in political instability in the newly independent countries of Melanesia (Papua New Guinea, the Solomon Islands, Vanuatu and Fiji) and the remaining French possessions of New Caledonia and French Polynesia. Some analysis of the post-coups situation in Fiji is included in this chapter, but the primary concern here is to examine the issues underlying current problems in establishing new tourism plant and facilities such as the alienation of customary land, the provision and delivery of basic infrastructure and services, pollution of the environment and the need for orderly governance. A recent case study of the violent reaction of villagers on Fiji's Coral Coast to what they perceived as inequitable returns from a major tourism development on their land is also included by way of illustration. It is contended that overcoming these basic barriers and obstacles in the development process will do more to reduce the conflict and tensions in tourism development than most measures directed at improving the operation of the industry itself. The evidence for this approach is seen in the multiplicity of tourism development plans for almost every country in the region. These find it is necessary to recommend widespread changes and reforms in land management, building control and the provision of basic services before tourism can be expected to fulfill a significant and productive national role. Before discussing the contemporary scene it is necessary to revisit the origins of Western interventions in the region.

Settlement in the South Pacific

Much of the history of urban planning world-wide has been concerned first and foremost with physical and technical matters, based on an assumption of legislative controls and sanctions that coerce, persuade, or even force compliance with various regulations. This orderly approach to establishing new settlements was exported to many parts of the world and different cultures by colonizing countries from at least as long ago as Greek and Roman times (and perhaps earlier in Asia) and was certainly present throughout the era of European colonial influence in the Pacific. It is only recently in fact, in the past decade or so, that increasing numbers of Western-educated planners have recognized that creating and maintaining an effective institutional planning process is more of a challenge than solving the technical problems arising out of urban growth. This is seen in the World Bank's contemporary emphasis on "urban management" as a focal point of concern (World Bank, 1991).

As Connell and Lea (1993) have pointed out, urbanization and many of the development problems associated with it is a very recent phenomenon in the Pacific and its origins are tied closely to colonial impacts of various kinds. The most obvious of these are social, political and economic interventions in the 19th century that introduced new ways of exploiting the human, marine and terrestrial environments of the region. Of particular note was the trade in human beings which removed islanders from their homes and subsequently introduced other nationalities to work on the new plantations; the early exploitation of the sea by whaling and fishing which marked the beginning of a domination of the marine environment that has continued unabated; attempts to "capture souls" by rival missionary organizations from several colonial nations; and the outcomes of strategic considerations brought about by great power rivalry in the region at the height of the colonial period. The result was a form of dependent urbanization that owed little to local conditions and life-styles. Major disruptions in both World Wars fast-tracked provision of modern communications and physical infrastructure that might otherwise have taken a further half-century to appear. The scale of urban places that has emerged as a result of these processes over the last century is very small in comparison to cities in most developing countries, but their size is large relative to island populations. It is the capital cities of the South Pacific, however, that are the gateways to a region (Figure 9.1) still generally characterized in literature, film and by the travel industry as an island paradise. There is an image problem and credibility gap here — with few exceptions they are places better described as insecure, where health risks abound, where costs are high

126

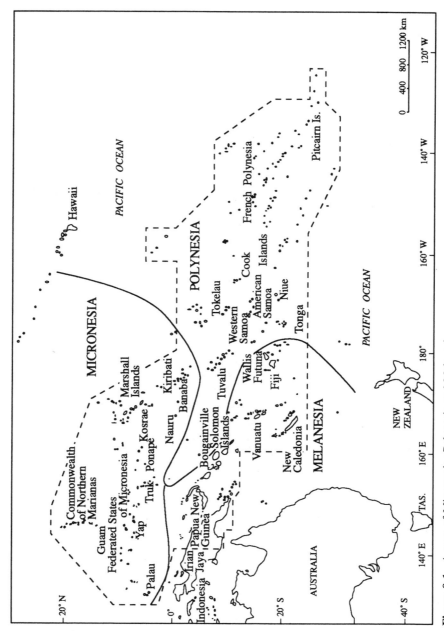

Figure 9.1 A map of Micronesia, Polynesia and Melanesia

and where the poverty of the urban poor is graphically represented by multiplying squatter settlements on the urban fringe.

Small size and recency, however, belie a form of urbanization and the presence of problems that are as severe in local terms as anywhere in the world. Circumstances are not uniform of course across the region and range from difficulties experienced in managing the rapid growth of significant cities such as Port Moresby, capital of Papua New Guinea, with its population of almost 200 000, and greater Suva in Fiji of a very similar size, to the much smaller and newer capitals of Honiara (Solomon Islands), Port Vila (Vanuatu), Apia (Western Samoa) and Nuku'alofa (Tonga), with under 50 000 each. Present also are some of the last remaining colonial outposts in the world, represented by the French cities of Noumea (New Caledonia) and Papeete, the capital of French Polynesia. Included in this group is Pago Pago, the capital of American Samoa, where the direct influence of metropolitan United States is felt in almost every sphere of life. These French and American possessions are not considered in this chapter, but their contemporary circumstances are a better portrayal, perhaps, than anything else of the legacy of the past. There are also important qualitative differences found between and within the three main sub-regions of the South Pacific: in Melanesia (Port Moresby, Honiara, Port Vila and Suva), Polynesia (Apia in Western Samoa and Nuku'alofa in Tonga are the most significant) and Micronesia (Majuro in the Marshall Islands and Bairiki in Kiribati) which illustrate differences in the historical experience and present circumstances.

The colonial period

The experience of individual colonies was dissimilar in many respects, but the overall influence of the colonial period on Pacific urbanization was more significant than any single factor other than World War II. Until recently in this century, for example, there were no towns of any consequence which were not located on the coast. A not unexpected situation in the small Polynesian and Micronesian island countries, perhaps, but of significance in the much larger Melanesian islands, some of which had considerable populations before colonial times. The coastal settlements had various colonial trading, economic and administrative origins and were dominated by external trading links. Some of them, such as Port Moresby (capital of British Papua), were always poorly integrated with nearby regions. The first gold-mining towns were established inland — Wau and Bulolo in Papua New Guinea and Vatukoula in Fiji — before World War II, but it was not until after the war that the first specialized inland towns emerged (Connell and Lea, 1993).

The earlist townships were expatriate centers of a kind familiar all over the colonial world:

> The urban area frequently developed a dual form. A segment was laid out for expatriates, on a regular grid of land holdings and streets, with buildings little different from those of the metropolitan country. In many respects the development of the expatriate segment was a faithful model of the pattern of urban areas in the Western world though industry was usually lacking . . . The nearby indigenous villages coexisted uneasily alongside the expatriate town . . . The dualism which thus developed was paralleled in administrative policy towards urban areas. The town was administered by expatriates, for expatriates and according to expatriate models.

Public health, public order and the maintenance of so called "standards" required, it was thought, an element of insulation from the indigenous population (Ward, 1973: 366−7).

These distinctions, often amounting to a form of urban apartheid, were emphasized through dress codes, and restrictions on access to some public buildings and hotels and other limitations on the urban life-styles of indigenous people (Connell and Curtain, 1982: 463−4). Until 1966 Fijians required administrative permission to leave their villages — the towns were largely places where Europeans could work and enjoy the social amenities. In the 1920s Port Moresby residents of Melanesian origin were regulated by curfew; whistles or bells sounded at eight a.m. and nine p.m. to demarcate periods when they were allowed in town (Connell and Curtain, 1982: 462−5). Under such circumstances the ideology of an elite urban life-style readily became established together with acceptance of the special privileges accruing to government public servants. Across the world in Africa similar sentiments have been expressed:

> The settlers' town is a strongly built town, all made of stone and steel. It is a brightly-lit town with streets covered in asphalt, and the garbage-cans swallow all the leavings . . . The settlers' feet are never visible, except perhaps in the sea, but there you never get close enough to see them . . . The settlers' town is a well-fed town, an easy going town: its belly is always full of good things. The settlers' town is a town of white people, of foreigners (Fanon, 1967: 123).

Life in these towns, however, was scarcely a desirable existence even for most of the privileged colonial elite. As settlements they have been described as seedy and dusty outliers of largely uninterested colonial powers. In the 1920s Port Moresby resembled a "superior mining town" or "a collection of hot tin roofs". Indeed, "it was hard to persuade the residents of Port Moresby to take enough interest in the town to beautify it: nor did the government consider that building beautiful colonial towns in the German manner was the Australian way" (Inglis, 1974: 35, cited in Connell and Lea, 1994). Seventy years later an editorial published in the *Fiji Times* (November 18, 1992) shows that similar attitudes still persist:

> Suva has failed dismally to become an attractive tourist drawcard despite years of trying. It is not for want of assets: it is the national capital and the heart of the country's retail centre, it is surrounded by sea, it has natural beauty and boasts several of our national historical, and architectural heritage [sic]. Yet tourists do not seek out Suva as a holiday destination. Why? . . . the capital city cannot take shelter behind the excuse that it lacks the "surf, sea and sand" attraction. The truth of the matter is that Suva has failed to create a niche for itself in the travel world. It has very little to offer the holiday maker even in the way of shopping . . . Who should take the brunt for such gross neglect? Some of it goes to a shocking lack of civic pride among our people. But most of it lies at the door of our city fathers and city planners . . . There appears to be a lack of commitment, of ideas, and a vision.

Colonial attitudes to things like clothing and housing underlined a fundamental determinant of the colonial way of life: "Both economically and in a larger sense the colonial order depended upon at once creating and excluding its own opposite" (Mitchell, 1988: 164, quoted in Connell and Lea, 1994). When Motu and Koita villagers on the fringes of Port Moresby built houses with iron roofs, the government anthropologist F.E.

Williams wrote: "We like to see the Motu and Koita houses. If you build one like a European copra shed it will not look very pretty" (Inglis, 1974: 7, quoted in Connell and Lea, 1994). Such attitudes persisted well into the years after World War II and shortly before Independence. The most characteristic legacy was of separation. Honiara, capital of Solomon Islands, reflects this in the 1960s:

> . . . there is very sharp segregation. On the flat land by the shore are the port, commercial centre, government offices and other institutional and functional buildings. Further east are a closely built Chinatown and a separate "village" for the Fijian community, then beyond that the main labour barracks, some industry and other institutions, and a shanty settlement euphemistically termed "Fishing Village". In recent years some "low-cost" housing for Melanesians has been built in valleys running inland. Almost the only Europeans living on the flat are single staff, who occupy apartments, and the High Commissioner, who has more palatial quarters: most others live in widely dispersed houses scattered over the pleasant and relatively cool hills behind the town. The contrast between "white highlands" and "black lowlands" — only now beginning to become blurred — is particularly stark, but Honiara is not unrepresentative of post-war towns . . . (Brookfield with Hart, 1971: quoted in Connell and Lea, 1994).

The cities in most of the independent South Pacific, now largely indigenous in ethnic structure, retain their colonial layouts, housing estates and supermarkets. The informal sector so prominent in Asia and Africa is generally absent, a victim of retained colonial legislation (especially against food vendors), a lack of trade skills and small local markets. Inherited Christianity and trading legislation combine to impose peace on Sundays (especially in Polynesia), contrasting dramatically with the life and bustle of the regulated urban weekday markets. Towns are still "foreign" in their appearance and operation, and urban life is mostly a personal phenomenon (Connell and Lea, 1994). It is not unreasonable under these circumstances to expect that maintenance, management and governance should have begun to break down soon after the end of the colonial period.

Tourism industry responses to violence and instability

There have been few regional investigations of effects on the tourist industry of violence and instability in the South Pacific. It is evident that health and safety issues are the major underlying issues affecting would-be travelers, and the most obvious difficulties are experienced as a result of natural disasters such as tropical cyclones, health issues such as the prevalence of malaria in parts of the region, and politically inspired communal violence. The most obvious cause of disruption in recent years was the Fiji military coups of May and September 1987 which resulted in a major though temporary decline in visitor numbers. A couple of years previously there was a huge decline of 84 per cent in Australian tourists to New Caledonia as a result of the riots in January 1985. Although the crude analysis of such effects in terms of visitor decline, unemployment and loss of profits is standard practice in many countries, there is much less understanding of the wide range of factors influencing the would-be traveler in major origin countries (Lea and Small, 1988).

The evidence from the Pacific in the mid-1980s suggests that market responses to disaster, violence and unrest depend on the circumstances of each event. Lea and Small

(1988) show that the 1987 cyclone in Vanuatu caused visitors to cancel completely because much of the tourist plant was put out of action for six months. The riots in New Caledonia and Fiji did not affect the choice of available accommodation, but perceptions about safety led to equally widespread cancellations, even though there were more than 60 killed in the French territory but none in Fiji. Of great importance is the perception gained of the situation by prospective travelers, and it is here that a considerable amount of evidence is available. Australian press reports were accused of sensationalism by the Fiji government, which insisted that street violence was far removed from the chief resorts. Another important influencing factor is the travel advisory issued by some governments following disasters. After the first Fiji coup, several governments issued such warnings but the Australian one was not issued until after demands from the public for travel advice. After the second coup, the advice was issued an hour after the news was received in Australia in spite of assurances from the Fiji Visitors' bureau that all was safe (Lea and Small, 1988).

The effects of official travel warnings can be subject to bureaucratic influences in an apparently random way because of updating policy. According to the Australian Department of Foreign Affairs comments on the Vanuatu riots of 1988, the timing of the advisory resulted in minimal disturbance to the tourist industry:

> Fortunately, the disturbances took place shortly before the bi-monthly review and thus the resulting travel advice soon lapsed. Had they occurred just after such a review, it could have been weeks before the warnings were lifted even though the riots themselves were variously described as nothing more than "a bad Aboriginal land rights demonstration" (Lea and Small, 1988: 311).

Another important influence on visitor traffic after the Fiji coups was the imposition of some airline bans by Australian and New Zealand companies. Here again the response was varied, with Air New Zealand suspending flights because of an attempted hijack at Nadi airport and Qantas labor unions imposing a two-month ban on flights to Fiji in mid-1987. Such actions served to reinforce popular opinion among travelers that it was unsafe to travel to Fiji and raised uncertainty about returning if they did go.

The effect of insurance cover on travelers' perceptions is not well researched. After both the Fijian coups the airlines and most hotels refunded canceled tickets and some insurance companies were accommodating also. This did not extend, however, to granting cover for those who took out a policy after the coup had occurred or for claims directly associated with the disturbances. It appears that Australian-based insurance companies follow the official advice of the Department of Foreign Affairs regarding risk, but in the case of the Fijian coups a state of emergency was still considered to exist even after the Australian government's travel advice had lapsed, thus removing insurance cover from anything relating to that situation (Lea and Small, 1988: 311).

A wider consideration arising out of the tourism downturn in the wake of community unrest in the 1980s is the question of destination substitution. Some evidence exists that Queensland and Bali benefited from the Fiji coups, and a number of rival destinations attempted to capitalize on the misfortunes of others. Among the published advertisements were (cited in Lea and Small, 1988: 313): "Golden Beaches, coconut palms and *no* coups," used in Australia to attract visitors to Magnetic Island near Townsville in North Queensland; and "War in the Solomons ended in 1945. Why risk Fiji?" (*Times on*

Sunday, May 31, 1987). It seems on closer investigation that restricted airline capacity would have minimized the gain to Bali as a destination and that other factors, such as availability and cost, would have been major obstacles to other places. Little is known about substitution for Pacific destinations and clearly demands much more information about visitor characteristics, behavior and the price elasticity of tourism demand in the region.

Although there is probably little that can be done to affect the periodic propensity of some independent Pacific island states to experience various forms of communal violence, there is an obligation on outsiders to understand as best as possible the factors that govern most forms of modern development in the region. As has already been indicated, there are a range of not-so-obvious difficulties and influences confronting would-be providers of tourist facilities in most Pacific island communities that need to be addressed in order to minimize the occurrence of future conflict. Of particular importance here is a good understanding of contemporary urban problems facing many forms of new development, including tourism.

Contemporary urban problems

Difficulties confronted by tourism developers in or close to most Pacific settlements usually originate in underlying problems that are present in the form of urbanization that has already occurred. In their review of Melanesian urbanization, Connell and Lea (1993) drew attention to several key areas where urban problems are now present and which require resolution before meaningful improvement is likely to occur: the alleviation of widespread urban poverty; the resolution of problems with customary land tenure; provision of affordable infrastructure and housing; protection of a deteriorating urban physical environment; strengthening of weak urban management; and making better use of underutilized human resources. These issues are commonplace in the urban areas of most developing countries and in the Pacific, as elsewhere, most of them originate in the manner in which urbanization has occurred. Almost all are underlain by certain far-reaching economic, social and cultural realities found in Pacific towns: the states are poor by world standards and over-dependent on foreign aid for most capital investment (this situation is slowly changing in some of the larger Melanesian countries); ethnic diversity of many kinds is a major issue in Melanesian towns, particularly in Papua New Guinea and Fiji; traditional power structures are paramount over the whole region but especially so in the smaller Polynesian and Micronesian countries; and customary forms of land tenure in rural and urban areas are closely linked to the exercise of power in South Pacific cultures and have determined much of the context for urban development. Interestingly, most of these factors are absent in the metropolitan countries where the urban influences originated, though a customary land-tenure problem has emerged recently in Australia with the passage of the new "Mabo" Land Rights legislation in 1993 favoring indigenous Australians (Lea, 1994).

There is insufficient space here to consider in any detail more than three of the problem areas listed. Those chosen by way of example are first, problems in acquiring land; second, difficulties in providing and delivering certain urban services, particularly water and sewerage; and third, some of the peculiar obstacles which seem to confront urban management and planning throughout the region. These weaknesses in the planning system have resulted in unsatisfactory development controls in much of the South Pacific and prevented anything more than rudimentary urban governance from becoming established.

Land

Throughout the South Pacific urban authorities are experiencing difficulties in resolving problems of land tenure. The presence of large tracts of customary land within and surrounding the towns has made planning, service provision and development control very difficult to manage. In Melanesia, in particular, "the combination of disputed land ownership, increased claims for compensation from [traditional] landowners (who often perceive this to be the most valuable source of income) and mismanagement have slowed the process of urban development and rendered it much more complex than it is in most other countries" (Connell and Lea, 1993: 94). The picture is not uniform and ranges from major constraints in the Papua New Guinea and Vanuatu towns and most of the Polynesian capitals to more orderly institutional arrangements in Fiji. Overall, there is a general problem of "adapting tenures which derive from combined customary and colonial precedents, to serve the needs of non-customary, post-colonial societies" (Crocombe, 1987: 390). But "traditional precedents are of little relevance for modern urban living," as Crocombe (1987: 386) also observes, and it is in the towns where pressures to reform traditional land practices are greatest. The challenge confronting island governments is not found in the welfare of longer-term urban residents, many of whom enjoy the security of a registered title or communal rights, but in satisfying the needs of increasing numbers of new urban migrants drawn from the rural hinterland or outer islands to seek a new life in the city.

There is an extensive specialist literature on land issues because they are so significant in the island states of the Pacific. Urban land for develolpment purposes is scarce in most of the region, even in relatively less-populated Western Samoa, largely because governments are unwilling to exercise their legal rights to acquire additional customary or individually held land for urban purposes. As a result, there is severe pressure on the small amounts of industrial land, almost no opportunity to develop existing residential areas to higher densities and a great incentive to reclaim marine and lagoon areas for various public uses. Effective urban management and planning demands an ability to control land use for priority purposes. The hard reality is not so much a failure to accept this objective but a lack of agreement as to the most appropriate means of achieving it.

For more than two decades now authoritative sources have pointed the way:

> Public authorities must ensure that it [urban land] is made available at reasonable cost to all who need it and must avoid land becoming concentrated in the hands of a few persons who, by the accident that their ancestors held rural land which became urban, or because financial advantage has enabled them to acquire a monopoly position, derive large sums from less fortunate fellow men. This necessitates comprehensive planning and either extensive public ownership of land which is leased to users, or extensive public control over private land. The socially generated surplus in rising land values should be used for the common good (Crocombe, 1987: 387).

Tourism developments are inherently large consumers of land. In October and November 1992 Cuvu landowners in Nadroga (near Sigatoka, Fiji) cut off access to the large Shangri-La Fijian luxury resort on Yanuca Island because of a local dispute about the management of the island's lease money (Connell and Lea, 1993: 62−4). The villagers built a blockade of burning car tires and coconut trunks at the end of the causeway linking the island to the mainland, preventing cars and buses from getting through (Figure 9.2). Some 350 tourists were forced to leave the hotel, and 550 hotel staff were threatened with immediate redundancy. After a disturbance lasting about two weeks, 22 Cuvu villagers were arrested by police and the causeway reopened (The *Fiji Times*, November 5, 9, 10 and 11, 1992). An editorial in the local press came down firmly against the actions of the villagers.

> It's not right. No matter how much the landowners of Cuvu may try to justify their demonstration, it's not right. By their method of demonstration, the landowners have terrorised the tourists who stayed at Shangri-La's Fijian Resort. They have:
> - forced the resort to scale down business so close to a peak season
> - threatened the jobs of hundreds of innocent hotel workers
> - cut telecommunication lines to the resort by melting the cables
> - been lighting fires on private property, and
> - closed access to the resort's private causeway.
> The demonstrators seem to have forgotten one key point: the resort, which attracts mostly family groups, is the goose that lays the golden egg. It is the biggest hotel in the country and it has involved itself and its guests in many [sic] community work in the area (The *Fiji Times*, November 9, 1992).

Of significance in this tourism case study is the fact that the history of land dealing at Yanuca Island dates back to the beginning of the 20th century and illustrates the need to reassess lease and trustee arrangements made in Fiji over the past hundred years. It appears that a 1969 lease agreement between the villagers and Fiji Resorts Limited, the tourism company that held the first lease over Yanuca Island, appointed one of the local chiefs as trustee with the right to negotiate land dealings on behalf of the *tokatoka* (land-owning unit). By 1992, increasing concern had grown among the villagers that they knew nothing about what had happened to the annual lease monies for the past quarter of a century (one per cent of the resort's income in excess of $1.8 million and $20 000 a year rental). They chose to express their frustration with what they perceived as inequity in the leasing arrangements, albeit perfectly legal ones, that had disadvantaged the majority of local residents. This illustration of instability and damage to Fijian tourism had little or nothing to do with current operations of the tourist resort itself but originated in dissatisfaction with development mechanisms that are clearly not serving the majority interests of the local population regardless of what might be said about them by the national government. The same forces that lie behind the actions of the Cuvu villagers on Fiji's Coral Coast are evident in the rebellion of Bougainville Islanders against mining operations on their island province of Papua New Guinea and in the opposition by some urban landowners in Vanuatu to expropriation of their customary rights

Urban services' provision and delivery

As Connell and Lea (1993: 60−1) point out, there is an array of issues which affect the current viability and future growth prospects of the tourist industry. In summary they include the amount and location of investment in transport infrastructure (particularly airports); the extent of health risks; the general safety of travelers; and provision of modern amenities such as clean water and proper sewage treatment. The following editorial from the *Solomons' Voice* (November 11, 1992) vividly describes the situation facing tourists visiting the Solomon Islands capital city of Honiara.

Two weeks ago Henderson Airport was without its fire engine. International flights were informed that they could land but they did so at their own risk. Some planes landed but others refused to come . . . No matter how much Solomon Islanders want tourists to visit the country, enjoy its beauty and meet with its people, certain things have to be in place . . . Honiara could be a first class tourist attraction. Although small by big country standards it boasts hotels, restaurants, stores and shops. The city's communication links — telephone, fax and telex — with the outside world are first class. Our road system, although in poor shape at present, has a $3.2 million road repair plan in place. This should go a long way to correct our poor roads in the next year or so . . . But, as in the case of the missing fire engine, are we killing ourselves and the tourist? A tourist had better not get seriously sick in this country. At present we don't have a hospital. Yes that's right: we don't have a hospital. Until the surgeons come back to work . . . Honiara is now the malaria capital of the world. No other city in the whole wide world has as much malaria as we do. More than 450 people in every

THE FIRST NEWSPAPER PUBLISHED IN THE WORLD TODAY

MONDAY, NOVEMBER 9, 1992   32 PAGES   42¢ inc VAT   123rd YEAR   No.267

Tourists flee Cuvu fire

TOURISTS pack up and leave the Shangri-La's Fijian Resort on Yanuca Island, Nadroga, as landowners continue to keep alight a fire at the resort's causeway. All tourists will leave this week and hundreds have been threatened. More details, photo: Page 3 today. Picture: YAD SINGH

Figure 9.2 Articles from The *Fiji Times*

THE Fiji Times

THE FIRST NEWSPAPER PUBLISHED IN THE WORLD TODAY

THURSDAY, NOVEMBER 5, 1992   32 PAGES + 8-PAGE INSERT   42¢ inc VAT   123rd YEAR   No.264

A car makes its way through flames and the smoke of burning tyres at the entrance of The Fijian Resort on Yanuca Island yesterday. Picture: ASAELI LAV

Cuvu's fires of anger

By WAINIKITI WAQA

THE landowners of Cuvu, in Nadroga, lit two huge fires yesterday and again blocked access to the Shangri-La's Fijian Resort on Yanuca Island.

The fires were the second to be lit in two weeks.

And hotel general manager Radike Qereqeretabua said hotel occupancy had fallen but he could not say whether it was connected with the two demonstrations.

Mr Qereqeretabua sent traditional representation to the landowners yesterday asking them for a meeting which is expected to be held this week.

The group burnt tyres on both sides of the mainland end of the courseway to the hotel which allowed only some vehicles through to the hotel.

Tourists had to walk from the Queens Road to the hotel because drivers refused to drive past the demonstrators who were holding placards near where the fires were burning.

Mr Qereqeretabua said he would not comment on the fires.

"My job is to run the hotel and serve our customers," he said.

Fiji Visitors Bureau chairman Sakeasi Waqanivavalagi is to issue a statement today.

The first demonstration was held on October 23 when the five-star hotel was celebrating its silver jubilee.

The landowners are protesting the management of the island's lease money which is held in a trust fund and managed by Adi Lady Lala Mara, wife of Acting President Ratu Sir Kamisese Mara.

"We're fed up. As Yanuca is our land, we feel it is only right for us to receive its rent money," said the landowners' spokesman, Cuvu village headman Alifereti Uqeuqe.

Mr Uqeuqe said they wanted an account of how the lease money was being spent.

Mr Uqeuqe, a barman at The Fijian, has been suspended for having been present at the first demonstration while he was on sick leave on a doctor's orders.

A staff notice put up at the hotel by Mr Qereqeretabua said: "This is to advice you that he was suspended because he was found in a public place, which is not a hospital or health institution, whilst on sick leave and not for being at the demonstration.

"This was made clear to him by me at the time of suspension."

Yesterday's demonstration was held soon after the poeple of Nakuruvakarua had celebrated the fourth anniversary of the rule of Bulou Eta Vosailagi as Ka Levu, the paramount chief of Nadroga.

Adi Lady Lala's mother is Bulou Eta's niece and comes from the same chiefly Nadroga clan.

Adi Ladi Lala is the Roko Tui Dreketi, the paramount chief of Burebasaga, a Fijian confederacy which covers Nadroga.

Figure 9.2 Continued

1000 are sickened with malaria in Honiara each year. Tourists like to take back small gifts and carvings in their bags when they return from the Solomons. Unfortunately our mosquitos are filling their bodies with malaria . . . Honiara is once again falling back to its dirty ways . . . Plastics, paper and just plain dirt remain . . . Creating a strong tourist industry could be a great tool to make our lives better, cleaner and healthier. Investing funds in cleaner water, a functioning hospital, reducing malaria and keeping the city clean and attractive helps, first and foremost the Honiara citizen. But once these things are in place we can count on visitors coming to enjoy them as well.

As this Solomon Islands example illustrates, an inability to manage the growth pressures of modern development has led to a breakdown in urban services' delivery since colonial times in many parts of the region. Tourism is an important casualty of this situation but it is only one of them, the chief sufferers being members of the local population.

A characteristic of colonial urban development was the strong correlation between formal housing and good access to urban services. In most developing countries the best water supply and sewerage/sanitation services were commonly provided in the most affluent parts of cities, even though such areas, often located on slopes and hilltops, were more expensive to service (Ludwig and Browder, 1992). By 1977, for example, in Port Moresby only 24 per cent of households in unplanned settlements had an adequate water supply compared to 95 per cent of those in formal housing (Papua New Guinea Bureau of Statistics, 1980: 18). This distinction, far from declining, has become more marked in the two decades since independence (Connell and Lea, 1993). A pattern of urban development had been created which perpetuated inherited spatial and other distinctions in service standards. The Executive Chairman (Finance) of the National Capital Development Commission of Papua New Guinea spoke recently at the Pacific Asia Congress of Municipalities in Port Moresby about the Commission's plans to overcome this problem:

For the next financial year, he said, it plans to receive some K13 million from sales and services taxes so that it can address, in a positive manner, the city's residue of inherited problems through poor long term planning by the colonial administration, ineffective management of the city's affairs by the former Port Moresby City Council and starvation of funds for two decades (*Times of Papua New Guinea* October 14, 1993).

In Vanuatu the inability of government to provide satisfactorily for water supplies in Port Vila has led to firm plans to privatize the service. Urban water supply has been managed on an *ad hoc* basis and governmental responsibilities shared among Public Works, the Department of Geology, Mines and Rural Water Supply, the Environmental Health Unit in the Department of Health and an inter-departmental Water and Sanitation Advisory Group, set up in 1984. A new Water Resources Bill will establish a National Water Authority and expedite, it is hoped, the modernization of the system. The problems are urgent, with supplies in Port Vila coming from a spring and three bores and thought to be close to extraction limits. A study has been underway for some time to establish water catchment boundaries and capacity, and a provincial protection zone has been delineated (which has no legal effect). Urban squatters have moved into this area and enforcement notices for their removal have not been acted upon. The piped distribution system is inefficient, with up to 35 per cent of water in 1988 wasted due to leakage (Halliburton,

1992). Although the majority of households in the designated urban area have a piped supply (84 per cent in 1989), this is not the case in the large and expanding peri-urban settlements located on customary land. The Service de l'eau, a state enterprise since independence in 1980, was privatized in 1993 and will be managed for 40 years by the Société Unelco-Vanuatu Ltd. (a branch of the French company Lyonnaise des Eaux-Dumez) which had previously run the system in colonial times (Lea and Connell, 1995).

Privatization (and corporatization) of public utilities is gaining in popularity across the developing world (Roth, 1987) in recognition of the difficulties experienced by governments in coping with infrastructure, service provision and delivery, using public resources. The trend is not without its critics, however, as argued by Gilbert (1992: 436):

> My pessimistic prediction is that by about 1995, government regulations will have been cut back a great deal and people will have been left even more to their own devices. No doubt this will have brought some benefits, especially for the affluent minority who can afford to pay for quality services. But the majority will have discovered how exploitative most illegal subdividers are, about the dangerous state in which most private companies run their buses, and how few private entrepreneurs are prepared to provide services to the unprofitable poor.

Further moves towards corporatization of water and sewerage are being considered in Fiji and have now also occurred in Polynesia. In Western Samoa recent changes have seen the Water Division of the Public Works Department transformed into an autonomous Water Authority responsible for efficient cost recovery in water and sewerage services. The old Water Division had a poor cost recovery record (of less than 10 per cent) and no means of managing water consumption efficiently. The advent of metering is problematic in a city like Apia where no such control has been present before and it is thought may lead to an inequitable service. One review has suggested the likely emergence of a "two-speed" water supply with a relatively expensive clean supply of potable water available to those who can pay and a free, erratic and dirty supply for the majority (Robert, 1993).

There is no public sewerage in Western Samoa at present and no requirement for large establishments, like hotels and factories, to provide their own mechanical treatment of effluent. Although such plants are notoriously unreliable in such settings, it is clear that pollution of the Apia waterfront from domestic and commercial sources and in other parts of the city has reached unacceptable levels. One large Japanese-owned factory in Apia employing 1500 people operates on a septic system which is continually overflowing and causing pollution in the adjoining residential neighborhood (*Samoa Observer*, November 17, 1993). Appropriate modernization to provide Apia with a sewerage system is expensive, costing sums beyond the reach of a small island state, and demands reasonable cost recovery. Such a system would entail conventional sewer reticulation covering the central town, a sewage treatment plant (screening) and an ocean outfall costing WS$42 million (1992 estimate by Robert, 1993): a feasible objective, perhaps, with the help of foreign aid but also an extremely problematical one when it is realized that no effective urban planning, urban governance or development control mechanisms exist in Western Samoa. Decisions on major national infrastructure investment of this kind can be taken at present without any serious planning inputs at all. This reality prevails over much of the Pacific region and results in a sort of *ad hoc realpolitik* that determines much of the current debate on urban affairs.

Urban management in the region

All capital cities in Melanesia have formal and elected urban governments responsible for planning and management. These are direct legacies from colonial times, apart from the new National Capital Development Commission in Port Moresby, but even here a close parallel with nearby Australian urban institutional origins is obvious. Experience of post-independence urban administration differs in the four Melanesian states in recognition of their historical, human and geographic distinctions. Each country, however, is characterized by the presence of similar factors relating to difficulties in creating robust local government and coping with competing claims over urban and peri-urban land. The exercise of development control and provision and maintenance of urban services in this situation raises overwhelming difficulties. Some of these problems are common to both Melanesia and Polynesia and are examined here first, before considering a more detailed example of problematic tourism planning from Tonga.

Among the more obvious general difficulties in urban management is the problem of sustaining two levels of government in the primate city of a small developing country where skills, both technical and political, are in short supply. The inherited system of elected adversarial local government has run into problems in many former colonial territories (Lea, 1980) where effective control over urban affairs in the capital city rests with national government. Robust urban government on the Western model assumes a largely unpaid and elected council, considerable popular participation, a sufficient tax base and the presence of enough technical skills to administer a range of modern urban services. None of these attributes are present in adequate amounts in the composition of national government in most of the South Pacific, let alone in the cities. In Western countries election to a local government council assumes possession of considerable technical abilities on the part of councilors and access to skilled advice where needed. Though the situation differs between the larger and older cities like Suva and Port Moresby when compared to Honiara, Port Vila and the Polynesian capitals, most of the basic assumptions are missing. This has led to the curious situation, so common in the region, where highly technical and expensive reports on the upgrading of urban facilities are commissioned in the absence of any realistic ability to implement them. This is the *realpolitik* of urban decision-making in the Pacific that has given rise to frustration and disillusionment on the part of government, people and donor countries.

The question of land tenure in the region is equally complex, as we have seen, and differentiated, but here too the problem is sufficiently common to make possible some generalizations about effects on urban management. The presence of an extensive proportion of urban or peri-urban land held under customary tenure applies to every Pacific capital. Custom and tradition (even in colonial times) removed such land from the day-to-day provisions of urban administration in many key respects. These are many, and range from the difficulty in acquiring finance to develop such areas when tenurial status does not provide conventional collateral to the calculation of appropriate compensation due to customary owners who will not otherwise allow the installation of urban services on their land. In Port Moresby, future planning of the urban area must contend with the strategic location of customary Motu and Koita urban villages throughout the expanding urban area (Lea, 1983). Even in Suva, where customary land is managed much more predictably through the operations of the Native Land Trust Board, there are urban villages which are not subject to normal planning and development control. In Polynesia, the capitals, like Apia in Western Samoa and Nuku'alofa in Tonga, are scarcely more than collections of urban villages and the acquisition of further alienated land for urban purposes may only be possible through lagoon reclamation. In other places, like Honiara and Port Vila, the chief problem lies on the urban fringe where old colonial boundaries represent artificial areas of municipal control, now outdated by the large and rapidly growing peri-urban settlements. The existence of sophisticated urban-planning legislation seems pointless if most of the growing city cannot be controlled through its use.

The isolation of tourism planning: an example from Tonga

The relevance of a larger and more important tourism industry in any of the Pacific countries depends to a significant extent on the national characteristics of development and the place of tourism within them. The industry does not exist in a vacuum and it will be rare that justification can be made to spend large amounts of the national infrastructure budget to accommodate tourism priorities alone. Separate tourism plans, in these circumstances, can act as mischievous documents holding out unreal prospects for national economic advancement. One recent example of this pseudo-planning is found in the South Pacific Kingdom of Tonga where a newly commissioned national tourism plan has recommended that the central Ha'apai island group be designated for World Heritage listing (Nicholas Clark and Associates, 1993). The idea is justified in the plan on both economic and environmental grounds, with the possible location of a World Heritage Research Centre in Ha'apai, a marine tourism resort and an international standard hotel complex costing some US$15 million. The cost would be justified, according to the plan, by increased tourism revenue and access to international funds to manage the natural resources of the area. But what of the impact of such a development on the 9000 people living in the 17 inhabited islands of the Ha'apai group?

The tourism plan justifies the promotion of the marine environment of Tonga in order "to establish an international image and icon for tourism . . . and the establishment of a centre for international marine research as a means of attracting . . . high expenditure and long stay tourists who will utilize facilities at other tourism developments" (Nicholas Clark and Associates, 1993, Volume 1: 30). The effects of this proposal on the people of Ha'apai is quite another matter. This ancient "heartland" of the country has been losing population steadily for many years, and among the region's few commercial attributes are modest prospects for an export fishing industry. Many of the islands exist in a semi-subsistence state and depend through artisanal fishing on the exploitation of the rich marine environment. World Heritage listing would introduce severe limitations on this life-style, as well as offering most of the few new jobs to outsiders. Infrastructure would be improved in some respects, but it can be argued that local development priorities (already investigated in a government regional plan in 1988) would be at odds with the Heritage listing. This example is a not uncommon attempt to treat tourism development needs in isolation of priorities that affect the whole community. World Heritage listing sounds impressive, but the responsibility of offering it as a regional development solution, without serious economic and social impact analysis of a kind that would be demanded in most developed countries, must be questioned.

Conclusions

Neither tourism itself nor violence has figured prominently in this review of the development picture in the South Pacific in the 1990s. There have been serious outbreaks of violence in the region in the past decade, but few of them are directly attributable to tourism. Indeed, tourism has suffered as a result of disasters and disturbances but has recovered when the immediate threat has passed. The issues raised in this chapter, however, point to underlying factors that may contribute to considerable community unrest in the years to come. Evidence for this comes from the experience of places like the state of Goa, on India's west coast, where local frustration with perceived levels of "overdevelopment" by the tourism industry has led to outright opposition and direct action (Lea, 1993). Few would anticipate such an occurrence in the South Pacific today, but then few would have foreseen the bloodshed that still characterizes events in Bougainville (Papua New Guinea's North Solomons Province) that amounts almost to civil war. The causes and effects that exist between poor development planning, the alienation of customary land, the "capturing" of good locations for tourism development and community disturbances have not been clearly established here and demand further investigation.

Tourism can contribute to positive forms of development but to do so requires a careful analysis of the industry's place in the society concerned. Among the more obvious lessons from the South Pacific is that trouble in one country can adversely impact on the region as a whole. There is some evidence, for example, that Australia and New Zealand lost international visitors in 1987 who had planned holidays that included Fiji. It is also evident that in a region where tourism and foreign aid are such important economic features, any significant downturn in an island economy as a result of visitor decline can lead to demands for increased foreign aid to compensate for the loss. Indeed, the whole question of aid is complicated by the fact that donor countries can actually withhold aid flows as a means of securing their own objectives in the case of violence and political unrest. This occurred in 1987 when Australia suspended aid to Fiji for several months (Lea and Small, 1988).

It is not the function of this chapter, however, to identify gratuitous solutions that are the responsibility of individual governments in the Pacific and the urban populations concerned. It may be appropriate, however, to re-emphasize the fact that the present pattern and functioning of the development process is peculiarly influenced by a foreign past which extends far beyond the physical trappings of built form. Much emphasis has been placed hitherto on the concrete evidence of colonial urban form, when it is the unseen influences resulting in changes to custom and economy that have resulted in the most intractable difficulties: such as changes leading to increased population mobility, displacement, urban poverty and a legacy of administrative structures that do not work well in a Pacific setting.

A new form of urbanization is emerging in the South Pacific which reflects the special mix of regional circumstances (Connell and Lea, 1994). Some of the solutions to current tourism development problems, like acquisition of suitable building land in the urban areas and efforts being made to provide modern services, will follow developments in nearby industrialized countries on the Pacific Rim, but answers to other more social and administrative difficulties are not so clear cut. The *realpolitik* of development in island communities is probably nowhere more important than in the management of the tourism industry. In some countries there appears to be a "tourism-led" attempt to modernize and transform old practices. The list of necessary improvements seems endless and stretches from attempts to improve public health in the Solomon Islands to calls for better urban design in Fiji. The key to it all is the ability of Pacific Island communities to manage the course of development themselves and in the generality of cases this has not yet occurred in the tourism industry.

References

Brookfield, H.C. with Hart, D. (1971). *Melanesia: a Geographical Interpretation of an Island World*. London: Methuen.

Connell, J. and Curtain, R. (1982). Urbanisation and inequality in Melanesia. In May, R.J. and Nelson, H. (eds), *Melanesia Beyond Diversity*. Canberra: Australian National University: 461−500.

Connell, J. and Lea, J.P. (1993). *Planning the Future: Melanesian Cities in 2010*. Canberra: National Centre for Development Studies, Australian National University.

Connell, J. and Lea, J.P. (1994). Cities of parts, cities apart? changing places in modern Melanesia. *The Contemporary Pacific*, **6**(2): 267−309.

Crocombe, R.G. (ed.) (1987). *Land Tenure in the Pacific*, 3rd edition, Suva: University of the South Pacific.

Fanon, F. (1967). *The Wretched of the Earth*. Harmondsworth: Penguin.

Gilbert, A. (1992). Third world cities: housing, infrastructure and servicing. *Urban Studies*, **29**(3/4): 435−60.

Halliburton, T.W. (1992). *Urban Policy in Vanuatu: a Review*. Port Vila: United Nations Economic and Social Council for Asia and the Pacific.

Inglis, A. (1974). *Not a White Woman Safe. Sexual Anxiety and Politics in Port Moresby, 1920−1934*. Canberra: ANU Press.

Lea, J.P. (1980). Swaziland: local government subjugation in the post-colonial state. *Review of African Political Economy*, 15/16: 146−7.

Lea, J.P. (1983). Customary land tenure and urban housing land: partnership and participation in developing societies. In Angel, S. et al. (eds), *Land for Housing the Poor*. Singapore: Select Books: 154−72.

Lea, J.P. (1993). Tourism development ethics in the Third World. *Annals of Tourism Research*, **20**(4): 701−15.

Lea, J.P. (1994). Regional development planning in the Torres Strait: New directions in Melanesian Australia. *Third World Planning Review*, **16**(4): 375−94.

Lea, J.P. and Connell, J.H. (1994). Urban management in Polynesia. *Development Bulletin*, **31**: 15−18.

Lea, J.P. and Connell, J.H. (1995). Managing urban environmental sanitation services in selected Pacific island countries. *Annotated Bibliography of Regional Literature and Data Sources*. Washington DC: The World Bank.

Lea, J.P. and Small, J.J. (1988). Cyclones, riots and coups: Tourist industry responses in the South Pacific. In Faulkner, B. and Fagence, M. (eds), *Frontiers in Australian Tourism*, Canberra: Bureau of Tourism Research: 305−15.

Ludwig, H.F. and Browder, G. (1992). Appropriate water supply and sanitation technology for developing countries in tropical monsoon climates. *The Environmentalist*, **12**(2): 131−9.

Mitchell, T. (1988). *Colonizing Egypt*. Cambridge: Cambridge University Press.

Nicholas Clark and Associates (1993). *Tonga National Tourism Plan Draft Final Report*, 3 vols, Nuku'alofa: Government of Tonga and Asian Development Bank.

Papua New Guinea Bureau of Statistics (1980). *Urban Population Survey 1977. Housing, Population, Education, Training, Economic Activity and Migration*. Bulletin No. 8, Port Moresby.

Pringle, G. (1989). *Heritage Assessment Apia, Western Samoa*, Master of Science (Arch/Cons) thesis, University of Sydney.

Robert, D. (1993). *Water Authority Organization and Tariff Study, Draft Report*. Suva: Government of Western Samoa and Commission of the European Community.

Roth, G. (1987). *The Private Provision of Public Services in Developing Countries*, New York: The World Bank and Oxford University Press.

Ward, R.G. (1973). Urbanisation in the Pacific: facts and policies. In May, R.J. (ed.), *Priorities in Melanesian Development*, 6th Waigani Seminar, Research School of Pacific Studies, Australian National University, Canberra and University of Papua New Guinea, Port Moresby: 362—72.

World Bank (1991). *Urban Policy and Economic Development: An Agenda for the 1990s*. Washington DC: World Bank.

10 Terrorism and tourism: an overview and an Irish example

GEOFFREY WALL

Introduction

In recent years, terrorism has had a substantial impact upon international tourism. At the time of writing in 1994, the frequency of terrorist acts appears to have subsided somewhat. For example, there are signs of reduced hostilities and a movement towards peace in Ireland. On the other hand, there are countries, such as Egypt, whose tourist industries continue to be hampered by terrorist activities. At the same time, the air traveler cannot avoid repeated searches and baggage checks and the considerable associated expense and inconvenience, even on domestic flights, which can be viewed as a legacy of terrorism. Thus, the impacts of terrorism are still very much with us.

The vulnerability of tourism to extreme events has been demonstrated numerous times in many parts of the world. For example, the Jamaican tourism industry suffered a rash of holiday cancellations based upon a political analyst's forecast (which did not come true) that the island would erupt in electoral violence, as had occurred in the 1970s (Norton, 1987). In other instances, countries have found that their tourism has been adversely affected by regional political events. For example, the political instability of Sri Lanka has affected tourism in India and the Maldives. Similarly, political violence in Zimbabwe has hampered the Zambian tourism industry (Richter and Waugh, 1986; Teye, 1986).

An unpublished review of academic research on tourism and terrorism indicates that research on the topic was practically non-existent until 1986 (T. Walker, personal communication), a year in which Greece, Italy and Egypt lost a combined total of approximately US$1.4 billion in tourism expenditures because of the threat of terrorism (Iglarsh, 1987). However, as described by D'Amore and Anunza (1986: 21):

> In a nine-day period that month (June, 1985), the world witnessed the crash of an Air India jumbo jet, in which 329 people were killed, believed to be caused by a bomb; the hijacking of a TWA flight from Athens; an explosion in baggage taken from a CP Air Boeing 747 in Tokyo: a bombing at the Frankfurt airport; and the hijacking of a Norwegian airliner.

According to D'Amore and Anunza (1986), terrorism increased from 206 major events in 1972 to 3010 in 1985: since then it has tended to decline. Both media and academic

Tourism, Crime and International Security Issues, edited by
A. Pizam and Y. Mansfeld. © 1996 John Wiley & Sons Ltd.

interest escalated, peaking in 1986. Since then it has subsided but not to pre-1986 levels, waxing and waning with the rise and fall of terrorist activities. A useful overview of this literature has been produced by Ryan (1991).

Although terrorism receives a great deal of media coverage, and attempts to thwart the activities of terrorists should be obvious even to the casual air traveler, terrorism is, in fact, difficult to define. This is because, depending upon one's political persuasion, activities may be regarded as legitimate or illegitimate and their perpetrators may be regarded as fighting for a just cause at great personal risk or attempting to impose the views of a minority on a majority by force. In fact, terrorists may be viewed as villains by some and heroes by others, as freedom-fighters by supporters and as destroyers of freedom by their antagonists. In this chapter, no attempt will be made to evaluate the legitimacy of the perspectives or activities of groups which are often accorded terrorist status.

Terrorism may be defined very broadly as the systematic use of terror as a means of coercion. The motives of terrorists are usually political: to draw attention, usually international attention, to the political causes which they support. However, there is a fine line between crime and terrorism, and it is not always easy to draw a sharp distinction between the two. Thus, terrorists are often viewed and prosecuted as criminals when apprehended, whereas their supporters often regard them as pursuing a legitimate cause.

The attraction of tourism to terrorists

A successful action from a terrorist perspective is one that generates a great deal of international publicity, clearly demonstrates the resourcefulness of the terrorist group, emphasizes the determination of the group and affords a direct strike against the enemy and its symbols. Indeed, Norton (1987) has suggested that a pistol pointed at a hostage is equivalent to a pistol pointed at a country's heart.

Terrorists are attracted to tourists and tourism infrastructure because they provide targets which enable them to meet their goals. As has already been indicated, terrorists are usually seeking international publicity for the causes which they espouse. International travelers, by definition, have links to other places and when they are harmed or inconvenienced in a massive way publicity is immediately generated in the areas of their origin. Terrorist events, accidents and natural disasters receive great media publicity with indications of losses of life and, usually, special emphasis on those affected from the nation to which the media are reporting. The opportunity to impact individuals from a diversity of origins thus increases the likelihood of acquiring widespread publicity. The seizure of the cruise ship, the *Achille Lauro*, in October 1985 and the Rome and Vienna airport attacks in December of the same year are examples of ways in which terrorists may target the tourist industry.

At the same time, tourists constitute relatively easy, often unsuspecting targets. They are usually unarmed and they may already be somewhat disoriented as they may be in an unaccustomed environment. They are easy prey. Furthermore, many tourism plants, such as airlines, major hotels and cruise ships or major tourism events, such as world fairs or Olympic games, involve national or multi-national corporations. Thus, a strike against such places or events can be viewed as direct impact upon the property and activities of the oppressors. In so far as the terrorist activities negatively influence the image of the locations in which they occur, they may discourage future travelers from visiting, thereby harming the tourism industry and the economy of the target areas.

Methods of terrorism

A wide variety of methods are used by terrorists. However, hijacking and skyjacking of cruise ships and planes have been popular methods of terrorism, as well as the destruction of such transportation systems by bombs or missiles. The link with tourism is obvious.

The planting of bombs in crowded places, such as airport hotels, central business districts, shopping areas and at special events, is another type of terrorist action. Although not necessarily directed specifically at tourists, these are places in which a large number of tourists may be found, and so tourists and the tourism industry are directly affected.

Some terrorist organizations make a speciality of using "signature" methods. For example, the Irish Republican Army has used tar and feathering, and knee-cap shooting. Such methods are seldom employed against tourists but, because they increase tension and lead to the raising of questions concerning safety, they influence the image of the locations in which they occur.

Public relations

The immediate reaction of the international public to a terrorist event is usually one of horror, although one suspects that it may gain less attention if it is distant, particularly if no nationals are involved and if it is one among a long series of such events. The media usually cover such events, often with graphic pictures and film, and this may lead to the creation of a distorted perception of risk. In fact, the risk of being involved in a car accident is probably greater than being involved in a terrorist event, but that is not appreciated by most of the traveling public.

Regardless of the degree of risk involved, international tourism is a highly competitive business and potential travelers have many potential destinations from which to choose. Although safety may be only one among many factors influencing destination selection, and its relative importance appears not to have been studied in depth, particularly in the context of terrorism, and is likely to vary from place to place, at different times, and among varied types of travelers, it is apparent that it is likely to be an important factor influencing the decisions to visit specific places.

Consequences

The consequences of terrorism for tourism are wideranging. They are both short term and long term. They affect tourists and tourism plant and destination areas. They have implications for profitability and for the economies of destination areas and even for entire countries when their economies depend heavily upon international tourism.

Reduced tourism activity

The immediate effect of a terrorism event is likely to be cancellation of bookings to the location in which the event took place. At the same time, those scheduled to pass through the destination may try to re-route. There is also likely to be a reduction in new bookings. The effect may extend well beyond the specific location in which the event occurred because, as in the case of the Gulf War which had global implications, the situation may be generalized to a larger area in the minds of potential visitors. Although it is uncertain how long the effect of a terrorist event is likely to last, the immediate result is likely to be a reduction in the number of visitors. The corollary of this situation is that for those who persist in visiting the area, there may be bargains, cheap flights, reduced accommodation rates and lack of crowding. However, a survey of Americans found that less than half would be enticed to travel overseas by airline promotions following a terrorist event (Feiler, 1986).

The magnitude of these effects can be seen in figures reported to the 1986 hearing on International Terrorism and its Effects on Travel and Tourism of the House of Representatives of the US Congress. There was a dramatic drop in the number of people traveling to Europe and also in the number of people willing to take international flights. In June 1985, 1.2 million Americans (19 per cent of all American travelers that month) either canceled or changed bookings after the TWA hijacking in June 1985. After the *Achille Lauro* piracy incident and the December 1985 attacks on airports in Rome and Vienna, 35 per cent (1.8 million) of all American international travelers canceled or changed reservations. In 1986, American visitation to Rome dropped by 59.3 per cent (1 034 190) (Hurley, 1988). In the same year, US travel to France and Greece fell by 60 per cent (Lewis, 1986). While it would be wrong to attribute all of this to terrorism, it was clearly a major factor.

For those who do travel, however, there may be changes in the quality of the experiences obtained, as they are exposed to searches, delays and increased military presence. At the same time, they may be particularly welcomed by residents of destination areas as providing support in time of need; in contrast those who canceled or chose not to come may be resented as capitulating to the desires of the terrorists. Sylvester Stallone's decision to cancel a visit to the Cannes film festival for fear of a terrorist attack was viewed in Europe as being particularly at odds with the image of Rambo (Hobbs, 1986; Rowe, 1986).

Costs of operation are likely to increase as security is strengthened and increased expenditures are made on publicity and advertising to counteract the unfavorable image created by the terrorist event. At the same time, in an attempt to maintain occupancy rates, prices for transportation to and accommodation in the destination area are likely to be cut. Promotion campaigns have included seat sales, two-for-one ticket offers, surprise mystery trips and trip giveaways. For example, British Airways reportedly spent between $6 and $8 million on its promotion campaign in 1986, a year of many terrorist events. More than 5000 of the airline's seats on flights from the United States to London were given away in a sweepstakes draw. Some of the winners received additional prizes such as a Rolls Royce, a portfolio of stocks and bonds, a five-year lease on a luxury apartment and an opportunity to meet Margaret Thatcher (D'Amore and Anunza, 1986). Thus, industry profitability falls as both numbers of visitors and prices decline while the costs of operation increase. If the situation is sufficiently severe, staff may be laid off and bankruptcies and closures may result.

Relocation of tourism

It is likely that some tourists may postpone their visit until the situation appears to have calmed down but, more likely, activity will be redirected to destinations which appear to be more safe. The extent to which this occurs is likely to vary with the market segment. Thus, for business travelers or those visiting friends and relatives in a specific place, the ability to relocate is likely to be less than for those who are on vacation and are traveling for pleasure.

There is also considerable variation in the ability to relocate between tourists, mobile plants and fixed plants. Potential tourists have the greatest flexibility and they can often substitute locations with minimal adverse consequences for their experiences, subject to time and cost constraints. Mobile tourism plants, such as airlines and cruise ships, have less flexibility than potential tourists but they may be able to adjust their activities to avoid locations which appear to be threatened by terrorist activities. The more flexible sectors of the tourism industry, especially airlines and tour operators, try to reposition themselves in the market (D'Amore and Anunza, 1986; Lewis, 1986). For example, following the *Achille Lauro* incident in 1985, many cruise ships were moved from the Mediterranean to the Pacific which was seen to be a safer area of operations. Airlines and cruise ship operators may reduce the number of services to perceived "hot spots" and increase the number of runs to safer destinations such as Hawaii and Alaska. Tour operators may remove risky destinations from their brochures and packaged tour offerings.

Owners of fixed plants, such as hotels and tourist attractions, have fewer options. They seldom have the opportunity to relocate and have little option in the short term but to find ways to weather the storm.

Long-term investments

The implications of a single terrorist event may be substantial in the short term but relatively short-lived. Potential tourists appear to have quite short memories and it appears that, after a single event, things may approach normalcy again in a matter of weeks. However, the same may not be true for investors, who are likely to be reluctant to invest in a new plant or up-grade existing infrastructure in locations where the business climate appears to be unreliable as a result of terrorist threats.

Terrorist events as externalities

While it is possible for individual travelers to reduce their likelihood of being caught in a terrorist action and guides have been written with suggestions as to how this might be done, and the tourism industry may reduce the likelihood of being impacted by a terrorist event by increasing security, terrorist events are like natural hazards in that, ultimately, they are outside the control of the tourist industry. Like natural hazards, terrorist events are seldom planned for by individual tourist establishments until after the damage has been done (Drabek, 1994). They may be insured against, but the cost may be prohibitive in locations where the threat is perceived to be the greatest.

Teye (1988), in an investigation of the implications of *coups d'état* for tourism, drew attention to the large number of consequences of such events for international tourism. Although all of the outcomes of a *coup d'état* which he identified are unlikely to occur in association with all such events or with all terrorist activities, there is sufficient overlap to make it worth reporting his findings. The effects which he identified included the following: airport and transportation systems are occupied and disrupted, information systems such as radio and television stations are occupied, both incoming and outgoing tourists are impacted, key installations such as airports and hotels are occupied, border crossings may be difficult to accomplish, currency may be devalued and there may be a currency black market, projects in progress may be curtailed, investments in new projects may be reduced, bad publicity and an image of instability may influence future tourists and investors and night life may be adversely affected because of reduced willingness or ability of individuals (in the case of curfews) to go out at night.

The above discussion has examined the implications of terrorism for tourism in general terms with the aid of a few very brief examples. It has been demonstrated that the nature of international tourism makes it particularly vulnerable to terrorist activities, and the consequences may be far-reaching, particularly in the short term but also in the long term. All airline travelers now pay the costs of past and potential terrorism in increased security and extended check-in times for both domestic and international departures.

The remainder of this chapter will discuss a case study of the implications of terrorism for tourism in Ireland, with particular emphasis on the behaviors of different market segments. Ireland is an appropriate location in which to investigate the implications of terrorism because of the long history of violent events. Also, it is a particularly interesting place to investigate the impacts of terrorism on tourism, for it is comprised of two political jurisdictions: the Republic of Ireland or Eire, and Northern Ireland or Ulster.

Tourism in the Republic of Ireland and Northern Ireland

Background

Ireland has much to offer tourists including a beautiful, rugged coastline, green rural landscapes, excellent golf and fishing, and ancient buildings and monuments. In addition, many Britons and North Americans have family ties or trace their roots to the island; thus, there is a strong resource base for tourism, and tourism is important to the economies of both the Republic of Ireland and Northern Ireland. Space does not permit a detailed discussion of tourism in the Republic of Ireland or Northern Ireland and, in addition to the references which will be cited below, the interested reader is referred to the writings of O'Hagen (1973) and O'Connor and Cronin (1993), Smyth (1986), and Buckley and Klemm (1993). However, there is a long history of unrest which has hampered the achievement of the region's full tourism potential, particularly in Northern

Ireland. A chronology of such events is presented in Appendix A and Wilson (1993) has described the consequences of such events and their media reporting for the image of Northern Ireland.

It is clear that political violence has affected tourism in Northern Ireland. For example, in 1967, a peak year for tourism in Northern Ireland, 1 080 000 tourists visited Northern Ireland (Northern Ireland Tourist Board, 1987). Nine years later in 1976, after a spate of violent events, the number of tourists plummeted to only 321 000 visitors (Northern Ireland Tourist Board, 1987). Tourist numbers have been slow to recover to mid-1960s levels.

Some believe that an inaccurate perception of violent events does more harm to the tourist industry than the events themselves. For example, Richter and Waugh (1986) stated that "terrorist violence has become a familiar phenomenon of modern times. That familiarity is largely due to the mass media rather than to the nature of the violent acts themselves or the numbers of casualties and actual property losses." Lewis (1986) places the blame squarely on the shoulders of the media:

> News coverage of terrorism and other dire events over the past eighteen months left the holiday industry wondering whether it didn't have more to fear from media hyperbole than from the crises themselves. Yet the experience, however bitter, taught the industry that the media in today's global village may come to play an even greater part in leading people to decide where they would — or rather wouldn't — spend their holidays.

As for the case of Northern Ireland, Griffith-Jones (1984) affirmed that three times as many people were killed annually in car accidents than through terrorist acts. However, he also acknowledged the power of the media in forming images of an area. He indicated that changing the perceptions of the United Kingdom market would be most difficult because they had daily news coverage of political unrest whereas the rest of the world only heard about the most dramatic events.

Regardless of whether visitor numbers are influenced predominantly by actual terrorist events or inaccurate perceptions of terrorist activities, it is clear that terrorism has affected tourism in Northern Ireland.

Comparing the Republic of Ireland and Northern Ireland

Ireland is currently divided into two political jurisdictions. It is suggested that it will be helpful to examine and compare tourism in Northern Ireland and the Republic of Ireland for several reasons:

1. they are in close proximity to each other and share an island in the Atlantic Ocean on the western periphery of Europe;
2. they share a similar climate, topography and scenery and, therefore, offer similar tourist attractions;
3. Northern Ireland and the Republic of Ireland shared a common history until the 1920s and even today they are bound together in many ways. Thus there is sufficient similarity to make a comparison worthwhile.

At the same time, of course, they also exhibit many differences. The most significant difference for present purposes is that Northern Ireland has suffered from severe internal political violence which has often given rise to terrorist acts, whereas the Republic of Ireland has experienced comparatively little terrorist activity. Because the two places share many characteristics yet only Northern Ireland has experienced a large number of terrorist events, it is possible to compare the two countries and to draw conclusions concerning the implications of terrorism for tourism in Northern Ireland.

Comparisons of visitor numbers

Table 10.1 provides a historical overview of tourist numbers in Northern Ireland and the Republic of Ireland for the period 1959 to 1992. The table reveals immediately that fewer tourists have visited Northern Ireland than the Republic, although, of course, the former is much smaller in size. Additionally, tourist traffic to Northern Ireland has undergone great fluctuations since the late 1960s when there was an escalation in political violence. It appears that travel flows to the Republic, although fluctuating, have been substantially more stable than those to Northern Ireland.

Northern Ireland relied very heavily on tourist traffic from Britain and from the Republic (Table 10.2): from 1978 to 1986, visitors from these two places comprised over 85 per cent of all visitors. The Republic of Ireland depended on tourists from Britain and its neighbor, Northern Ireland, but to a lesser extent (Table 10.3). During the same period they constituted approximately 70 per cent of the Republic's visitors.

North Americans accounted for approximately 6 per cent of visitors to Northern Ireland from 1978 to 1986. More than twice the proportion of North Americans visited the Republic in the same period, with even greater differences in the absolute numbers of visitors (compare Tables 10.2 and 10.3). Less than one-sixth as many North Americans visited Northern Ireland each year as visited the Republic.

Europeans comprised about 4 per cent of all visitors to Northern Ireland from 1978 to 1986 as compared to 14 per cent for the Republic. This constituted a difference of almost twelve times in the absolute numbers of visitors from Europe. Although the proportion of visitors from other overseas countries was similar at 3 per cent, approximately three times as many such travelers visited the Republic as visited Northern Ireland.

Comparisons of visitor expenditures

As would be expected from the number of visitors, those from Britain and the Republic collectively spent the most money in Northern Ireland (Table 10.4). From 1982 to 1984, visitors from these places supplied an average of 77 per cent of Northern Ireland's non-resident tourist expenditures. Somewhat similarly, visitors from Britain and Northern Ireland provided a large proportion (an average of 45 per cent) of visitor expenditures in the Republic (Table 10.5). However, in contrast, from 1982 to 1986 North American visitors to the Republic contributed a much larger proportion of tourism revenues than in the case of Northern Ireland (33 compared to 14 per cent). Similar findings exist for European visitors who are much more significant financially to the Republic than to Northern Ireland.

Table 10.1 Number of tourists visiting Northern Ireland and the Republic of Ireland, 1959—92

Year	Northern Ireland	Republic of Ireland
1959	633 000	na
1960	na	1 373 000
1961	na	1 449 000
1962	na	1 459 000
1963	704 600	1 508 000
1964	na	1 687 000
1965	na	1 733 000
1966	na	1 696 000
1967	1 080 000	1 812 000
1968	1 139 000	1 917 000
1969	1 066 000	1 942 000
1970	977 000	1 758 000
1971	670 000	1 692 000
1972	435 000	1 458 000
1973	486 800	1 614 000
1974	486 000	1 628 000
1975	529 600	1 688 000
1976	423 000	1 720 000
1977	503 200	1 953 000
1978	628 100	2 299 000
1979	728 000	2 360 000
1980	710 000	2 258 000
1981	588 000	2 188 000
1982	712 000	2 250 000
1983	865 000	2 257 000
1984	908 000	2 579 000
1985	863 000	2 536 000
1986	824 000	2 467 000
1987	943 000	2 664 000
1988	930 000	3 007 000
1989	1 090 600	3 484 000
1990	1 152 000	3 666 000
1991	1 186 000	3 535 000
1992	1 254 000	3 666 000

na = not available

Sources: Statistics for Northern Ireland obtained from the Northern Ireland Tourist Board. Statistics for the Republic of Ireland obtained from Borde Failte; Plettner, (1979); *The Economist* Intelligence Unit (1983).

Comparisons of numbers and expenditures

A comparison of the proportion of revenue derived from each country of origin with the proportion of tourists which they supply reveals an interesting fact: while Britain and Northern Ireland/Republic of Ireland supply a large proportion of the visitors, they tend to spend less per head than those from further afield.

An examination of 1986 statistics reveals that most tourists to Northern Ireland visit friends and relatives (Table 10.6). The proportion of such visitors from North America and countries other than Europe was particularly high. It is largely only the Europeans who come to Northern Ireland for a holiday. Data gathered by Borde Failte (Irish Tourist Board) for the same year, although reported in slightly different categories, show that

Table 10.2   Origin of tourists visiting Northern Ireland, 1978–86

	Great Britain		Irish Republic		North America		Europe		Other Overseas		Total Tourists	
	'000s	%	'000s	%	'000s	%	'000s	%	'000s	%	'000s	%
1978	349	55.6	194	30.9	45	7.2	26	4.1	14	2.2	628	100.0
1979	397	54.5	227	31.2	48	6.6	32	4.4	24	3.3	728	100.0
1980	403	56.8	217	30.6	44	6.2	27	3.8	19	2.6	710	100.0
1981	343	58.3	167	28.4	33	5.6	24	4.1	21	3.6	588	100.0
1982	352	49.4	277	38.9	40	5.6	28	3.9	15	2.2	712	100.0
1983	377	43.6	390	45.1	52	6.0	29	3.3	17	2.0	865	100.0
1984	405	44.6	412	45.4	43	4.7	30	3.3	18	2.0	908	100.0
1985	419	48.6	331	38.3	63	7.3	28	3.2	22	2.6	863	100.0
1986	453	55.0	262	31.8	47	5.7	35	4.2	27	3.3	824	100.0

* Tourism statistics obtained from Northern Ireland Tourist Board.

Table 10.3   Origin of tourists visiting the Republic of Ireland, 1978–86

	Great Britain		Northern Ireland		North America		Europe		Other Overseas		Total Tourists	
	'000s	%	'000s	%	'000s	%	'000s	%	'000s	%	'000s	%
1978	1 055	46.0	544	23.7	309	13.5	317	13.8	71	3.0	2 296	100.0
1979	1 077	45.6	566	24.0	293	12.4	358	15.2	66	2.8	2 360	100.0
1980	1 068	47.3	527	23.3	260	11.5	336	14.9	67	3.0	2 258	100.0
1981	1 008	46.1	508	23.2	278	12.7	319	14.6	75	3.4	2 188	100.0
1982	1 031	45.8	531	23.6	315	14.0	313	13.9	60	2.7	2 250	100.0
1983	1 049	46.5	543	24.1	310	13.7	295	13.1	60	2.6	2 257	100.0
1984	1 120	44.6	676	26.9	344	13.7	305	12.1	69	2.7	2 514	100.0
1985	1 119	44.3	585	23.1	422	16.7	334	13.2	69	2.7	2 529	100.0
1986	1 127	45.7	586	23.8	343	13.9	337	13.7	71	2.9	2 464	100.0

* Tourism statistics obtained from the Borde Failte and *The Economist* Intelligence Unit.

most people traveled to the Republic of Ireland to take a holiday (Table 10.7). This is especially true of visitors from North America. Most of those visiting friends and relatives, on business or visiting for "other" reasons, were from Britain. Thus it is evident that many more people were on holiday in the Republic of Ireland than in Northern Ireland. Alternatively, visiting friends and relatives plays a more significant role in the tourist trade of the latter than the former.

Summary

The analysis of tourist statistics for Northern Ireland and the Republic of Ireland leads to the following observations:

1. The Republic of Ireland attracted more visitors than Northern Ireland from all major countries.

Table 10.4 Revenue from tourism in Northern Ireland by country of origin, 1982–6

	£m	Cdn$m	%	£m	Cdn$m	%	£m	Cdn$m	%	£m	Cdn$m	%	£m	Cdn$m	%
Great Britain	23.1	54.4	48.1	30.6	72.1	42.4	34.3	80.0	44.1	34.3	80.8	43.7	43.8	103.2	53.5
Irish Republic	12.5	29.4	26.0	27.5	64.8	38.1	27.4	64.5	35.2	23.0	54.2	29.3	19.2	45.2	23.4
North America	6.6	15.5	13.7	9.3	21.9	12.9	9.9	23.3	12.7	14.2	33.4	18.1	10.4	24.5	12.7
Europe	2.4	5.7	5.1	3.7	8.7	5.1	3.7	8.7	4.8	3.3	7.8	4.2	4.3	10.1	5.3
Other Overseas	3.4	8.0	7.1	1.1	2.6	1.5	2.5	5.9	3.2	3.7	8.7	4.7	4.2	9.9	5.1
Total International Tourism Revenue	48.0	113.0	100.0	72.2	170.1	100.0	77.8	183.2	100.0	78.5	184.9	100.0	81.9	192.9	100.0

* Revenue figures from the Northern Ireland Tourist Board.
Canadian exchange rate (April 15, 1988) = 2.355

Table 10.5 Revenue from tourism in the Republic of Ireland by country of origin, 1982–6

	IR£m	Cdn$m	%	IR£m	Cdn$m	%	IR£m	Cdn$m	%	IR£m	Cdn$m	%	IR£m	Cdn$m	%
Great Britain	123.4	250.5	36.8	128.4	260.7	34.4	154.1	312.8	36.0	172.1	349.4	34.2	171.1	347.3	36.0
Northern Ireland	34.0	69.0	10.1	37.5	76.1	10.1	45.3	92.0	10.6	41.6	84.5	8.3	39.7	80.6	8.4
North America	97.3	197.5	29.0	125.4	254.6	33.6	140.0	284.2	32.7	190.2	386.1	37.7	151.0	306.4	31.7
Europe	64.2	130.3	19.1	62.0	125.9	16.6	66.5	135.0	15.5	80.3	163.0	15.9	87.7	178.0	18.4
Other Overseas	16.5	33.5	5.0	19.5	39.6	5.3	22.4	45.5	5.2	19.6	39.8	3.9	26.2	53.2	5.5
Total International Tourism Revenue	335.4	680.8	100.0	372.8	756.9	100.0	428.3	869.5	100.0	503.8	1022.8	100.0	475.7	965.6	100.0

* Revenue figures from the Northern Ireland Tourist Board.
Canadian exchange rate (April 15, 1988) = 2.355

Table 10.6 Main purpose of visit to Northern Ireland by main market areas, 1986 (%)

	Visiting Friends and Relatives	Holiday and Shopping	Business	Other
England	54	5	38	3
Scotland	61	5	25	9
North America	64	26	6	4
Europe	27	48	18	7
Other Overseas	66	19	6	9

* Tourism statistics obtained from the Northern Ireland Tourist Board.

2. The number of visitors to Northern Ireland fluctuated more than the number going to the Republic.
3. Northern Ireland relied particularly heavily on Britain and the Republic for tourist traffic and expenditures.
4. More tourists from North America and Europe visited the Republic than Northern Ireland, a fact more significant to the Republic in terms of expenditure.
5. Most tourists to Northern Ireland visited friends and relatives. Most going to the Republic are on holiday.

Discussion

Now that selected visitor statistics have been compared, it is possible to discuss their likely significance in terms of terrorism in Northern Ireland.

The number of visitors to Northern Ireland was much smaller than to the Republic. Although there may have been additional reasons for this, it is likely that the fear of terrorism was a strong contributing factor. Faced with media reports of extreme events in Northern Ireland, it is likely that many potential visitors elected to travel elsewhere.

Large fluctuations in visitor numbers in Northern Ireland are likely following terrorist events. It appears that the impacts on tourism numbers of specific events may be large but shortlived, but the cumulative impact of numerous events may be substantial. It is not possible to demonstrate this conclusively through analysis of annual statistics.

The fact that the majority of tourists to Northern Ireland go there to visit family and friends, whereas the majority visiting the Republic are on holiday, may also be partially

Table 10.7 Purposes of visits to Irish Republic by main market areas, 1986 (%)

	Visiting Friends and Relatives	Holiday and Shopping	Business	Other
Britain	57	51	23	21
North America	32	83	13	9
Europe	17	71	22	12
Other Overseas	34	72	14	14

* Percentages total more than 100 since some tourists visit the Irish Republic for more than one reason. Tourism statistics obtained from the Borde Failte.

attributable to terrorism. Holidays are usually thought of as times of enjoyment and relaxation: very few would choose to visit places where they feel they may be uncomfortable. Without the pull of family, many people may not be attracted to an area where, rightly or wrongly, they believe that their lives may be endangered. Those with family links have a concrete reason to visit Northern Ireland and they also may be more aware of the reality of the terrorist situation and feel less threatened by it.

Differences in the relative importance of various market segments may also be partially attributed to perceptions of terrorism. The Republic receives proportionately more tourists from North America and Europe who are on holiday. At home they are far removed from the reality of the situation and they may play safe and avoid Northern Ireland. Prospective travelers from Britain and the Irish Republic receive more details concerning terrorist events in Northern Ireland and probably have access to a greater variety of sources of information. In consequence, they may have more realistic perceptions of the terrorist threat. In addition, they may have more binding reasons for visiting, such as to see relatives or friends or for business purposes, than those from North America and Europe.

Unfortunately, especially from the perspective of Northern Ireland, the most reliable, the friends and relatives market segment, spend the least money per visit whereas the more high-spending and more distant vacation markets are more likely to be deterred by actual or threatened terrorist events.

Overview

This chapter has discussed the relationships of terrorism and tourism through an overview and an example. The difficulty of defining terrorism was addressed and reasons for the attraction of tourism targets to terrorists were presented. Following a brief discussion of the methods employed by terrorists, public reactions to terrorism were examined. The consequences of terrorism for tourism were outlined under the headings of reduced tourist activity, relocation of tourist plant and long-term investments, and the similarities between terrorist events and coups were pointed out. The chapter concludes with a discussion of tourism in Northern Ireland and the Republic of Ireland which emphasizes the differential impact of terrorism on different market segments and associated economic implications.

Acknowledgements

The author has benefited greatly in the preparation of this chapter from the input and insights of a number of students and wishes to acknowledge the input of Barbara Henderson, Kim Langille, Ian Martin, Michelle Ryan and Tim Walker.

References

Borde Failte (1987). *Tourism Facts 1986*. Dublin: Borde Failte.
Buckley, P.J. and Klemm, M. (1993). The decline of tourism in Northern Ireland: The causes. *Tourism Management*, **14**(2): 184–94.

D'Amore, L.J. and Anunza, T.E. (1986). International terrorism: Implications and challenge for global tourism. *Business Quarterly*, November: 20−9.

Drabek, T.E. (1994). *Disaster Evacuation and the Tourist Industry*. Program on Environment and Behavior Monograph No. 57. Boulder: Institute of Behavioral Science, University of Colorado.

The Economist Intelligence Unit (1983). *International Tourism Reports*. Republic of Ireland. National Report No. 86. London: *The Economist* Intelligence Unit.

Feiler, S.I. (1986). Terrorism: Countering the crisis. *Hotels and Restaurants International*, **20**(11): 87−90.

Griffith-Jones, R.G. (1984). Northern Ireland — Putting the record straight. *Tourism Management*, **5**(2): 138−41.

Henderson, I.G. and Mullaghan, C. (1983). The effects of violence on the tourism potential of Northern Ireland as measured by market research. *Seminar on the Importance of Research in the Tourism Industry*. Helsinki: Esomar: 233−53.

Hobbs, P. (1986). Business as usual in Britain. *The Globe and Mail*. 7 June: E9.

Hurley, J.A. (1988). The hotels of Rome: Meeting the marketing challenge of terrorism. *The Cornell Hotel and Recreation Administration Quarterly*, **20**(1): 71−9.

Iglarsh, H.J. (1987). Fear of flying: Its economic costs. *Terrorism*, **10**: 45−50.

Lewis, P. (1986). Tourism and terrorism. *Report on Business Magazine*, **3**(5): 102−8.

Northern Ireland Tourist Board (1987). *Tourism Facts 1986*. Belfast: Northern Ireland Tourist Board.

Norton, G. (1987). Tourism and international terrorism. *The World Today*, **43**(2): 30−3.

O'Connor, B. and Cronin, M. (eds) (1993). *Tourism in Ireland: A critical analysis*. Cork: Cork University Press.

O'Hagen, J. (1973). Export and import visitor trends and determinants in Ireland. *Journal of the Statistical and Social Inquiry Society of Ireland*, **22**(5): 1−31.

Plettner, H.J. (1979). *Geographical Aspects of Tourism in the Republic of Ireland*. Galway: Social Sciences Research Centre, University College.

Richter, L.K. and Waugh Jr, W.L. (1986). Terrorism and tourism as logical companions. *Tourism Management*, **7**(4): 230−8.

Rowe, P. (1986). Brits sneer at Yank fears. *The Toronto Sun*, May 28: 74.

Ryan, C. (1991). Tourism, terrorism and violence: The risks of wider world travel. *Conflict Studies 244*. London: Research Institute for the Study of Conflict and Terrorism.

Smyth, R. (1986). Public policy for tourism in Northern Ireland. *Tourism Management*, **7**(2): 120−6.

Teye, V.B. (1986). Liberation wars and tourism development in Africa: The case of Zambia. *Annals of Tourism Research*, **13**(4): 589−608.

Teye, V.B. (1988). Coups d'état and African tourism: A study of Ghana. *Annals of Tourism Research*, **15**(3): 329−56.

Wilson, D. (1993). Tourism, public policy and the image of Northern Ireland since the troubles. In O'Connor, B. and Cronin, M. (eds), *Tourism in Ireland: A critical analysis*. Cork: Cork University Press: 138−61.

Appendix A: Violence related to terrorism in Northern Ireland, 1972−91

1972   Jan. 30, "Bloody Sunday", British army killed 13 Catholics in Londonderry.
Feb. 22, official Irish Republican Army (IRA) bomb killed seven in Aldershot, England.
July 21, "Bloody Friday", Provisional Irish Republican Army (PIRA) bombs in Belfast killed 9 and injured 130.
Dec. 1, bombs in Dublin killed two and injured 80.

1973   March 8, bombs in Belfast, Londonderry and London.

1974   May 17, car bombs killed 22 in Dublin and five in Monaghan.
Nov. 21, "Birmingham Pubs bombing", 19 killed and 182 injured.

1975   No major incidents.

1976   Jan. 4, five Catholics killed.

Jan. 5, 10 Protestants killed.

1977 No major incidents.

1978 Feb. 17, PIRA fire bomb killed 12 and injured 23 in County Down.
Oct. – Nov., rioting and PIRA bomb attacks.

1979 Aug. 27, PIRA blew up Lord Mountbatten in Eire and 18 soldiers in County Down.

1980 No major incidents.

1981 May 5, riots in Belfast, Londonderry and Dublin when PIRA member Bobby Sands died as the result of a hunger strike.

1982 April 20, PIRA bombs exploded in Armagh, Ballymena, Belfast, Bessbrook, Londonderry, Magherafelt and Strabane.
July 20, PIRA bombs killed 11 of the Queen's troopers, many horses and injured 51 people in London.
Dec. 6, bomb killed 17 at a Ballykelly pub.

1983 Jan. 16, PIRA murdered a Catholic judge in Belfast.
July 13, PIRA land mine killed four Ulster Defence Regiment (UDR) soldiers in County Tyrone.
Nov. 4, PIRA bomb killed three policemen and injured 33 at Ulster Polytechnic.
Nov. 21, three killed in machine gun attack on a Pentecostal church in Armagh.
Dec. 17, PIRA bomb killed five and injured 80 at Harrods in London.

1984 March 6, PIRA assassinated the Assistant Governor of the Maze prison.
May 18, PIRA bomb killed two British soldiers in Fermanagh.
Oct. 12, PIRA bomb killed five in Brighton during the Conservative Party conference.

1985 Feb. 28, PIRA mortar attack killed nine Royal Ulster Constabulary (RUC) officers in Newry.
Aug. 20, PIRA assassinated a Catholic businessman for dealing with security forces.

1986 Jan. 1, PIRA bomb killed two RUC officers in Armagh.

1987 April 25, Lord Justice Gibson and his wife killed by PIRA bomb.
May 8, RUC killed eight IRA men.
Nov. 8, PIRA bomb at Enniskillen killed 11 and injured 63.

1988 March 6, three PIRA members shot in Gibraltar.
March 16, three killed at PIRA funeral.
March 19, two soldiers killed at IRA funeral.
May 1, PIRA killed two British airmen, one in West Germany and one in the Netherlands.
May 15, Ulster Volunteer Force killed three Catholics in Belfast.
June 15, PIRA killed six soldiers in Lisburn.
Aug. 1, PIRA blast killed one and wounded nine in London.
Aug. 20, eight soldiers killed and 28 injured by PIRA bomb.
Aug. 30, three PIRA killed by British army.

1989 Feb. 20, four PIRA bombs hit British army barracks in Shrewsbury, one soldier injured.
Sept. 22, PIRA bombed the Royal Marines School of Music, nine killed and 22 injured.
Oct. 25, soldier and six-year-old daughter shot and killed by PIRA in West Germany.

1990 May 14, PIRA bomb wounded seven in London.
May 16, PIRA bomb killed soldier in London.
June 1, PIRA shot three soldiers at Lichfield, England; 1 died.
June 1, PIRA shot and killed soldier in West Germany.
June 25, PIRA bomb injured eight in London.
July 30, PIRA bomb killed a member of Parliament near London.

1991 Feb. 7, PIRA fired three mortar rounds at 10 Downing Street (residence of Prime Minister); three injured.
Feb. 18, PIRA bomb killed one and injured 41 at railway station.
Dec. 1, PIRA fire bombed five London stores.
Dec. 12, PIRA bombs in Armagh injured 70.
Dec. 1 – 16, 25 PIRA bombs caused $70 million in lost business.

Source: T. Walker, personal communication.

11 Measuring the effects on tourism of violence and of promotion following violent acts

RAPHAEL RAYMOND BAR-ON

Violence is a feature of today's world, highlighted by instant news and pictures from most parts of the world. It may be directed specifically against tourists from abroad, since this will gain maximum publicity for politically minded terrorists and/or for those who want to harm a country by reducing its income from tourism (eg the fundamentalists' attacks in Egypt from 1990 and the rebel attacks in Turkey from 1991). Stealing from tourists may be more profitable for thieves and easier than mugging or robbing local residents — as occurred in Miami (*Time*, September 1993) — and may be rationalized as taking money from rich exploiters. Acts of violence may affect tourism in several ways:

1. Tourists may fear being killed or injured (Demos, 1992; Echtner and Ritchie, 1993; Livingstone and Halevy, 1989; Pinhey and Iverson, 1994; Roehl and Fesenmaier, 1992).
2. Tourists may fear being involved in an unpleasant experience, eg a riot, or in police or army action against terrorists, possibly injured themselves.
3. Tourists may not be able to keep to their plans and visit all the places that they want to see at the dates and times they choose.
4. Security checks, especially at airports, may take a long time and even be unpleasant for some tourists.
5. There may be some sympathy with the terrorists, if regarded as "freedom fighters," and antagonism towards the government of the country, especially if it takes repressive measures, eg China (Gartner and Shen, 1992).
6. National governments may issue Travel Advisories or embargoes regarding trips to specific regions. The US State Department has issued advisories on many occasions, and forbidden US travel to some destinations (eg to Israel after the Suez campaign, 1956: Bar-On, 1963).
7. Tour operators, travel agents and airlines may not want to risk organizing trips to a region, fearing damage to their reputation, insufficient bookings and/or extra costs.

Tourism, Crime and International Security Issues, edited by
A. Pizam and Y. Mansfeld. © 1996 John Wiley & Sons Ltd.

8. Conferences, business meetings, incentive tours etc. may be canceled, postponed or diverted to another destination: future events (with a lead time of up to five years) may not be scheduled at this destination until the situation improves.

9. Travel insurance of tourists and airlines may be difficult, limited or expensive.

10. Journalists may flock to the area involved, also adventurous tourists (especially if cheap: *Time*, August 1993).

11. The effects of violence on tourists may be highlighted by the media, especially if one or more from their country of residence has been killed. A successful rescue may add to a country's image (eg Israel from Entebbe, Germany from Mogadishu).

12. Friends or relatives at the destination may advise against the proposed trip.

13. Violence in one country or region may affect tourism to countries not directly involved: eg the terrorist attacks on international travelers from June 1985 to September 1986 which were targeted especially against US tourists; the Gulf War. The terrorist attacks in Egypt and Turkey may have postponed the visits of those who wanted to visit Israel or made them decide to visit only Israel.

14. Expectations of violence from a specific date may cause some advancing of trips, eg before the UN ultimatum of November 1990 to Iraq (effective January 15, 1991).

Domestic tourism may be affected too, to alternative destinations in the country or to those which had experienced violence — especially if there is increased promotion and/or price cuts to compensate for loss of inbound tourists. Residents in a violent area may take more trips abroad. Tourists may substitute more peaceful destinations, abroad or domestic.

Economic factors, political events, tourism development and attractions, promotion, new routes (air, sea and land), prices of the many components of the travel and tourism industry, environmental and other factors also contribute to changes in international and domestic tourism, and it is not always easy to distinguish between the causes of changes. There are many *Diaries of Events* (eg *Keesings*), and *Time* magazine publishes a weekly *Traveler's Advisory* on some of the new and exotic attractions.

Some of the above also applies to other disasters and emergencies, eg earthquakes, epidemics etc. (ULA, 1994). Even if a tourist is not affected personally by the above, the attitude of his/her family, friends and colleagues may be negative enough to postpone a trip or participation in a conference.

WTO (the World Tourism Organization) has devoted considerable attention to this subject (Pahr, 1987; Handszuh, 1990: see also Richter and Waugh, 1986). Efforts are made to promote tourism to countries and areas affected by violence or by natural and accidental disasters (Pottorf and Neal, 1994, ULA, 1994).

Monitoring the effects of violence

Tourism to and in Israel has been affected by violence since the establishment of the State in 1948. The War of Independence lasted until 1949, and Israel has been involved in six wars and many conflicts since then. Table 11.1 and Figure 11.1 show the annual visitor arrivals and tourist arrivals by air (the main component) from 1970 to 1994 (updating Bar-On, 1993d) with the main events. Nine of these 25 years show a decrease from the previous year, mainly due to violence. Other events also contributed to changes in international tourism and in travel to Israel over some of these periods, including the progress towards Arab—Israel peace (flagged **P** in the table and chart).

> 1970—1: The **War of Attrition** (along the Suez Canal, from November 1969 to November 1970), together with the destruction of a Swissair plane to Israel, an explosion on an Austrian airline plane, the hijacking of six planes (in the Middle East and Greece) and terrorist attacks at Munich airport and in Israel.
>
> 1973—5: The **Yom Kippur War** (October 1973) and terrorism at airports and in Israel: the Oil Crisis raised travel and tourism costs in most countries.
>
> 1981—2: Rockets on Galilee and Israel's **War in Lebanon** (June 1982 to June 1985): the economic crisis in Europe and America in 1980 also affected tourism to Israel.
>
> 1985—6: **International terrorism against travelers** (from June 1985 to September 1986): arrivals in 1985 were higher than in 1984, during which there had been attacks on Israel embassies in Cairo and Nicosia.
>
> 1988 to date: The *Intifada* (Palestinian uprising) started December 1987: a bus was attacked in March 1988.
>
> 1990 and 1991: **Gulf crisis** — Iraq invaded Kuwait in August 1990 but had made threats on Israel from April 1990. The **Gulf War** (January—February 1991) brought missiles on Israel from Iraq. The crisis and war also affected tourism to other countries (see Figures 11.7 and 11.8).

Despite these unfavorable events, visitor arrivals totaled 2.17 million in 1994, five times their number in 1970, ie an average growth rate of nearly 7 per cent per annum. The agreements with the Palestinians (from September 1993) aided growth and the peace agreement with Jordan (October 1994) will also be of help. The massacre in Hebron of Moslems by a Jewish settler (February 1994) and the suicidal blowing-up of two buses in Dizengoff Street, Tel Aviv-Yafo (October 1994) may have reduced arrivals from March 1994 and reservations for 1995, also conferences for the next few years.

Analysis of monthly series

The effects of a major violent act (or a series of related acts) are different if it occurs: early in the year, off-season (Gulf War, for example), before the main tourist season (eg Six Day War, June 1967) or during the high season, when it may be difficult for tourists to change their plans, reserve at another destination or postpone their trips (Gulf Crisis, from August 2, 1990). The loss of visitors may be spread over many months. The recovery may be rapid or slow and uneven; demand may include trips which had been postponed as well as restored current demand (which may be lower for several years than before the violence).

The *annual data* and changes from year to year in the annual totals (illustrated in Table 11.1 and Figure 11.1) provide only a partial picture of the changes in tourism series. *Monthly data* are available for hundreds of travel, tourism and accommodation series for most tourist countries, including distinct series by market segments and by region and city (or major resort: Bar-On, 1994) and some series on domestic and outbound tourism. Most of these series show *seasonality*, which may improve or worsen over the years, changes in the underlying *trends* and possibly *multi-annual cycles*. Comparisons of the monthly

Table 11.1 Israel: visitor arrivals and tourists by air, 1970–94

Year	Visitor Arrivals ('000)	Change on Previous Year (%)	Tourists by Air ('000)	Principal Events (month)	Type
1970	441	8	382	Swissair plane to Israel blown up; hijacking of six aircraft in Middle East (July–Sept.); terror in Israel and at Munich airport; War of Attrition (Suez Canal; Nov. 1969–Nov. 1970)	– – WA
1971 1972	657 H 728	49 11	566 627	Sabena hijack; El Al operates first jumbo (June) Terror at Tel Aviv airport (May, Aug.) and against Israelis at Munich Olympics (Sept.)	– + –
1973	662	–9	562	Yom Kippur War (Oct. 6–24); World Oil Crisis; Lufthansa hijack; terror at Rome airport (Dec.)	WY –
1974 1975	625 620	–6 –1	526 508	Terror attacks in Israel and at Rome airport Terror in Israel, including at hotel, Tel Aviv (March) and at Orly airport (Jan.); charters to Eilat (Nov. +)	– – +
1976	797	29	672	Entebbe hijack (June) and rescue; terror in Israel and at Istanbul airport (Aug.); charters to Tel Aviv airport (from Oct.)	– +
1977	987	24	820	Mogadishu hijack (Oct.) and rescue; terror in Israel, President Sadat visited Israel (Sept.)	PE
1978	1071	9	871	Iran: revolution ended tourism to Israel; terror attacks in Israel, at Orly airport (May) and in London (Aug.); Litani Campaign (in Lebanon, May); Egypt–Israel Agreement (Camp David, Sept.)	– – – PE
1979 1980	1139 H 1176	6 3	925 956	Accord with Egypt (Washington, March); terror in Israel Economic crisis, USA and Europe; anti-Jewish terror, Paris (Oct); direct flights Tel Aviv airport–Egypt (Feb.)	+ – – – PE
1981 1982	1137 998	–3 –12	922 788	Israel bombed Iraq's atomic pile (June); rockets on Galilee Return of Sinai to Egypt (Apr.); Israel Ambassador in London attacked (June); War in Lebanon (from June to June 1985); Sabra and Shatila massacre (Lebanese)	– PE – WL WL
1983	1167	17	852	France restricted travel allowance; US Embassy in Beirut blown up (Apr.)	– WL
1984	1259	8	936	Attacks on Israel Embassies, Cairo and Nicosia (June, Oct.)	–

Table 11.1 Continued

Year	Visitor Arrivals ('000)	Change on Previous Year (%)	Tourists by Air ('000)	Principal Events (month)	Type*
1985	H 1436	14	1079	International terror, especially against aircraft, airports and US travelers (June to Sept. 1986) and Israelis (Cyprus, Sept.); Eilat Free Trade Area (from Nov.)	XA +
1986	1196	−17	930	Continued international terror (Feb.−Sept.) and in Israel; USA bombed Tripoli (terror headquarters, Apr.)	XA −
1987	H 1518	27	1151	Stock Exchange Crisis, USA + (Oct.); *Intifada* (Palestinian uprising: from Dec.)	− IN
1988	1299	−14	979	Terror, Nicosia (May) and on bus near Dimona (March); Pan Am airliner destroyed, Lockerbie (Dec.)	− −
1989	1425	10	1033	Eastern Europe liberalization, including tourism to Israel; return of Taba to Egypt (March)	+ −
1990	1342	−6	933	Iraqi threats to Israel; Kuwait invasion, Gulf Crisis (Aug.); terror in Israel (Apr.−July); Moslems killed on Temple Mount (Oct.)	WK −
1991	1118	−17	806	Gulf War, Iraqi missiles on Israel (Jan.−Feb.)	WG −
1992	1805	61	1257	Attacks on Israel Embassy, Argentina and on diplomat, Ankara (March); start of Arab−Israel Peace Process (Madrid, Oct.); expulsion of Hamas activists to Lebanon (Dec.)	P − −
1993	1945	8	1378	Terror in New York (Feb.) and Egypt; US attacks on Iraq (Jan.); agreement with PLO (Sept.); peace negotiations	− PP
1994	H 2170	12	1503	Transfer of Gaza and Jericho to Palestinian Authority; peace with Jordan (Oct.); massacre of Arabs, Hebron (Feb.); bus bombed in Tel Aviv (Oct.)	PJ −

H Highest year to date (both series)

+ Positive effects (other)
− Negative effects (other)

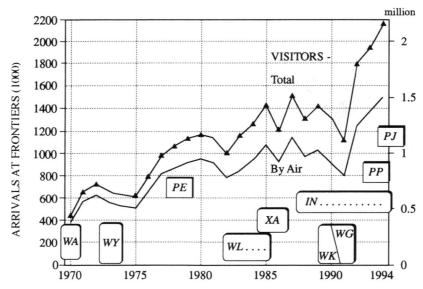

Figure 11.1   Israel: visitor arrivals and tourists by air, annual data 1970 to 1994. Major events see Table 11.1

original data with the corresponding month in the previous year (or years) and of the cumulative data (from January or from the start of the season) are widely used but do not give a full understanding of the effects of events and of promotion policies (Bar-On, 1975, 1989, 1993a, b).

Monthly series can be regarded as the result of the combined operation of systematic, periodic and other components in the "time domain." The Multiplicative Model assumes that for each month:

> Original datum M = Trend-Cycle C × Seasonal factor S × Irregularities I, where M and C are in the same units (eg thousand visitors per month) and S and I in per cent, with average S in each year 100 per cent and I measured around 100 per cent.

Day-of-the-week factors D and Festival-date effects F (especially Easter, falling from March 20 to April 23) may also be taken into account. This model is suitable for most travel and tourism series with significant seasonality and strong trends, where the magnitude of the seasonal effects varies with the level of the Trend-Cycle C. The X11 ARIMA/88 Program uses Auto-Regressive Integrated Moving Averages, identifies outliers (data unusually high or low, often as a result of Unusual Events U) and imputes more regular data for such months. It then calculates Seasonal factors S for each month and year.

Historic data are then seasonally adjusted, printed by X11 on a monthly basis as $Z = M/S$, dividing also by D and/or F if significant (Dagum, 1988).

We prefer

> Annualized Levels $A = 12 \times M/S = 12 \times C \times I$, the annualized Trend-Cycle perturbed by Irregularities: or $12 \times M/(S \times D \times F)$ if D and/or F are significant.

For many purposes the Short-term Trend is useful, calculated by smoothing Z (or A) with a three-term weighted annualized moving average $B = 3 \times [1, 2, 1]Z$ for each month (double weight for that month, single weight for the previous month and for the following month). This shows most of the effects of Unusual Events, smoothing an unusually high or low month with its adjacent months. For the last month available $B' = 4 \times [1, 2]Z$ (double weight for that month, single weight for the previous month).

The Projected Growth can be calculated from any base period, eg before violent events, using a rate of growth as in "normal periods," or using the ARIMA extrapolations (printed for the following 12 months, if an ARIMA model can be fitted for the series up to these events: Bar-On, 1989, 1993a, b, c).

Trends in tourism and the effects of violence

Monthly Visitor Arrivals in Israel have been analyzed from 1949 and Tourist Arrivals by Air from 1952 (Bar-On, 1963), with the analysis of the sub-series by 12 countries or regions of residence from 1960. Hotel Nights of Tourists and of Israelis have been analyzed from 1961 (Bar-On, 1969, 1973) and by cities in Israel from 1985 (IMT/CBS, B, Q).

A detailed analysis of the seasonally adjusted data of Tourist Arrivals by Air in Israel from January 1956 to December 1976 was prepared, indicating 11 unusual periods totaling 121 months in these 21 years (Bar-On, 1978).

The trends of tourism to Israel, to Cyprus, Egypt, and to nine other countries were studied from January 1964 to 1974, including the Cyprus conflicts and the Yom Kippur War, also North Atlantic Air Travel (Bar-On, 1975). The Oil Crisis following this war makes it difficult to separate the direct effects of the war from the economic effects of increased prices of travel etc.

International terrorism, 1985–6

Figure 11.2 shows the Short-term Trend B for tourist arrivals in Israel from the USA by air from January 1984 to December 1987 together with the annual data Y (dotted horizontal lines, with each year's total underlined) and per cent changes from year to year y (revised from Bar-On, 1990). The 1984 total was 283 000 tourists, and the trend level increased to 361 000 annualized in January–May 1985, the Basic Pre-violence Level (flagged **BB**): the highest month's level (seasonally adjusted) A was 377 000 per annum in February 1985. There were many terrorist attacks by air and sea from June 1985 to September 1986, aimed principally at American tourists, and the trend to Israel in this series dropped 56 per cent from **BB** to the lowest level, 159 000 per annum in April–May 1986 (flagged **LB**). Total arrivals in the year 1985 (321 000) were, however, 13 per cent above total 1984.

The trend recovered slowly, rising to 220 000 per annum end 1986; the total for 1986 (193 000) was 40 per cent below total 1985. The trend continued to rise to 288 000 per annum in July–August 1987 (flagged **RB**), 81 per cent above **LB** but still 20 per cent below the pre-violence level **BB**. The trend declined from September 1987, apparently because of the Stock Exchange Crisis (October 1987) and the *Intifada* from December 1987; there were also changes in exchange rates, in fares and in US travel to Europe and

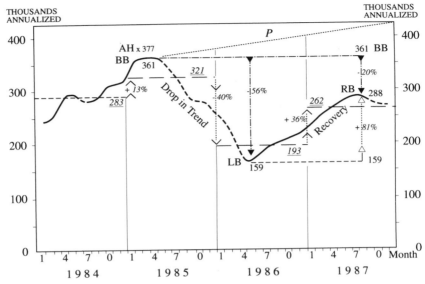

Figure 11.2 Tourism by air from USA to Israel, Jan 1984−Dec 1987. Short-term trend B and annual totals Y.
BB basic level of B (before main effects of terrorism) 361 000 per annum (Jan−May 1985); AH highest level of seasonally adjusted monthly data A 377 000 per annum (Feb 1985); LB lowest level of B 159 000 per annum (Apr−May 1986); RB recovery of B to highest level in 1987, 288 000 per annum (July−Aug 1987); P projected growth but for terrorism, at 6 per cent per annum from BB. The months are indicated: 1 = Jan, 4 = Apr, 7 = Jul, 0 = Oct

the Mediterranean. The destruction of the Pan-Am plane at Lockerbie in December 1988 also affected US travel to Israel and other countries. The trend in this series regained the level of early 1985 only in November 1992, ie after six and a half years, but then declined before surpassing this level from January 1994 (IMT/CBS, Q).

Tourist Arrivals in Israel from Canada by air were less affected, dropping 37 per cent from the high of 37 000 per annum in April−July 1985 to 23 000 in May−June 1986. We estimated that Israel lost about 332 000 visitors from North America from Spring 1985 to end 1987, mainly due to these terrorist attacks, compared with projected arrivals (a growth of 6 per cent per annum from the pre-violence level **BB** of 361 000 per annum, the dotted line P). This caused a loss of about 3.8m hotel nights and 4.4m nights in other means of accommodation (eg VFR, with friends or relatives) and the loss of about US$540m in receipts from tourism from North America in Israel. There were also losses in tourism from most other countries to Israel over this period. Israel's international carriers (mainly El-Al) showed increased receipts in 1986 and in 1987, due to increased fares (in US$) and because there was some transfer of tourists to them from foreign carriers (because of El-Al's high security reputation).

The annual data on US and Canadian tourism to Europe and the Mediterranean from 1985 to 1987 were analyzed for 34 countries and the series for their nights at hotels in 27 countries (Bar-On, 1990). We estimated that the total loss of tourism receipts from North America to Europe and the Mediterranean over 1985 to 1987 was between four and seven billion dollars (including losses of the international carriers); some other destinations benefited from switching of travel (Brady and Widdows, 1988; Conant et al., 1988).

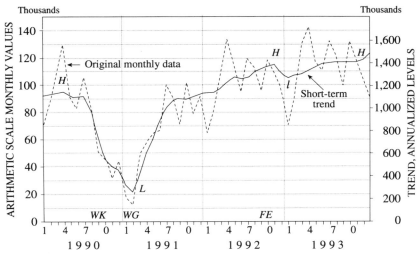

Figure 11.3 Israel: tourist arrivals by air, Jan 1990−Dec 1993. Original monthly data M and short-term trend B.
WK, WG, as in Figure 11.1; FE exchange rates crisis (Sept−Nov 1992); the *Intifada* started in Dec 1987; trend: *H* high *L* low *l* secondary low; The months are indicated: 1 = Jan, 4 = Apr, 7 = July, 0 = Oct; based on IMT/CBS, Q

The Gulf Crisis and Gulf War

Iraq invaded Kuwait in August 1990, leading to a period of tension in the Middle East (Desert Shield, flagged **WK** in the charts) and reduced tourism from and to many countries. US Travel Advisories against tourism to the region were published from October 1990, and the UN set an ultimatum on November 29, 1990 announcing the deadline of January 15 (leading to advancing of some travel). The war (Desert Storm, flagged **WG**) lasted from January 16 to February 28, 1991. Israel was affected from May 1990, because of Saddam Hussein's threats of biological and chemical warfare, and by the 40 Scud missiles rained on Tel Aviv and other parts of Israel from January 17 to February 25, 1991. Iraqi missiles were also launched on Saudi Arabia.

The trend of tourist arrivals by air in Israel from January 1990 to December 1993 is shown in Figure 11.3, with the original monthly data (dashes show the combined effects of seasonality, trend and events and other irregularities). The trends from the UK, the Nordic Countries and South Africa to Israel by air from January 1987 to December 1992 are presented on a logarithmic scale in Figure 11.4 (to stress relative changes, Fisher and Bar-On, 1993); trends from nine other countries are tabulated in IMT/CBS, Q and shown in IMT/CBS, B. Figure 11.4 also shows the effects of the *Intifada* from December 1987. Analyses have also been made of daily arrivals at Tel Aviv airport (Bar-On, 1989, 1993a) and arrivals by age group and by US State.

The trends of nights in tourist hotels in Israel of tourists and of Israelis from 1987 to 1993 were also studied. Figure 11.5 shows the original monthly data M (dashes) and trends B for total Israel from January 1990 to December 1993 (repeating the monthly tourists' nights as boxes, together with the Israelis' original data), while Figure 11.6

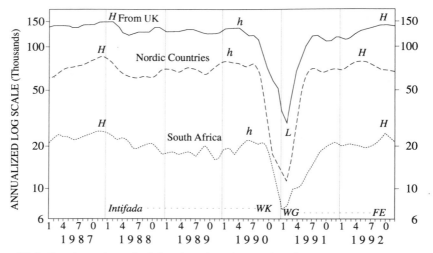

Figure 11.4 Israel: tourist arrivals by air: selected countries of residence. Short-term trends B, Jan 1987—Dec 1992.
WK, WG, as in Figure 11.1; FE Exchange rates crisis (Sept—Nov 1992); the *Intifada* started in Dec 1987; The months are indicated: 1 = Jan, 4 = Apr, 7 = July, 0 = Oct; trend: *H* high *L* low *h* secondary high *l* secondary low; based on IMT/CBS, B, which also presents nine other countries/ regions of residence (a monthly scale is also shown there)

shows logarithmic trends of hotel nights in Jerusalem, Tel Aviv-Yafo and Eilat from January 1987 to December 1993, distinguishing tourists' and Israelis' nights and showing total nights in both charts. Tourists' nights in Jerusalem were most affected by the *Intifada*, while in Tel Aviv-Yafo and Eilat their nights were reduced because of the decrease in tourism to Israel, with some tourists switching their main destination from Jerusalem to Tel Aviv-Yafo (or spending more nights outside Jerusalem). Israelis' hotel nights in Jerusalem also dropped sharply from March 1988, improving at the end of 1989, while their nights in Eilat increased in 1988 and early 1989.

Iraq's threats, the Gulf Crisis and increased terrorism in Israel reduced the trends of tourists' nights in these three cities from July 1990, with sharp drops during the Gulf War months; Eilat was also affected by the cancellation of foreign charter flights from October 1990. Regarding Israelis' nights — the trend in Tel Aviv rose in February 1991, due to several hotels housing people whose homes had been destroyed or severely damaged, while there were sharp increases in Jerusalem and Eilat in January 1991 (since many Israelis preferred the safety of these cities: Bar-On, 1994; Bar-On and Paztal, 1994). Similar data and charts are presented in IMT/CBS, B and Q; also for the Dead Sea, Netanya and Tiberias.

Terrorism in Spain

Terrorist attacks by Basques and others have occurred frequently in Madrid and other parts of Spain from 1989, extending even into France and the Netherlands. These have been aimed at Spanish officials rather than at tourists and have received some publicity in

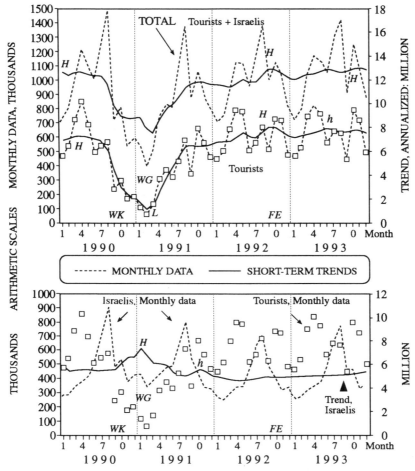

Figure 11.5 Nights in tourist hotels: Israel (total) Jan 1990 – Dec 1993.
See Figure 11.4 for key

the countries of residence of potential tourists. Visits to Spain reached 54.2m in 1988 (including Spaniards resident abroad), decreased by 0.2 per cent in 1989 and by a further 4 per cent in 1990 (annual total, compared to 1989). Figure 11.7 (with a truncated arithmetic scale) shows that the trend reached its highest value of 56.6m (annualized) in February 1990, decreasing rapidly from Spring 1990 (before the Gulf Crisis, WK). The trend dropped further during the Gulf War (WG) to 50.2m per annum, January 1991). It recovered unevenly during 1991, went up to 56.6m by April 1992, increasing during the Expo (April – October) and the Olympics (July – September), though low in June – July. There have also been considerable changes in tourist costs in Spain, in fares to Spain and in exchange rates. The annual data are also shown in Figure 11.7 (horizontal lines) and in Figure 11.8 together with the trends in Spain and in Turkey (to similar logarithmic scales). It is difficult to separate the effects of the terrorist attacks.

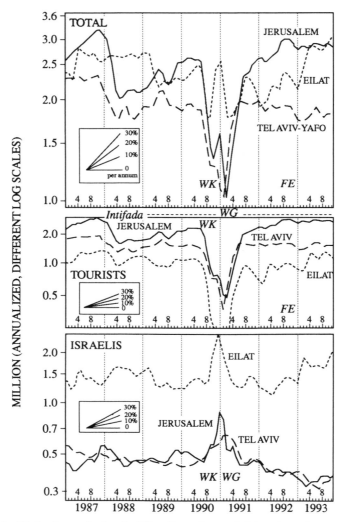

Figure 11.6 Nights in tourist hotels: Eilat, Jerusalem and Tel Aviv-Yafo. Short-term trends B, Jan 1987–Dec 1993.
See Figure 11.4 for key

Terrorism against tourists in Egypt and Turkey

Visitor arrivals in Egypt from the USA dropped 62 per cent in 1986 and by 14 per cent in total (compared with 1985), mainly because of the terrorist attacks aimed at American tourists (described above; Bar-On, 1990). Total visitors grew to 2.6m in 1990, then dropped 15 per cent in 1991 (in comparison to 1990), mainly because of the Gulf War. From February 1990 there have been Moslem fundamentalist attacks on tourists in Egypt — in Cairo, on Nile floating hotels and at other tourist destinations or highways. Visitor arrivals in Egypt dropped 22 per cent from 3.2m in 1992 to 2.5m in 1993, with decreases of 74 per cent from Spain and of 45 per cent from France (for example).

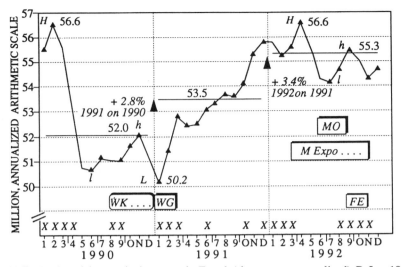

Figure 11.7 Spain: visitor arrivals — total. Trend (short-term, annualized) B Jan 1990 — Dec 1992, annual totals Y and % change from year to year y.
WK, WG, FE, H, h, L as in Figure 11.7. MExpo Sevilla (April 20 — Oct 12, 1992), MO Olympics Barcelona (Jul 25 — Sept 8, 1992), X terrorist attacks in Spain or affecting Spain

In Turkey visitor arrivals from the USA dropped 59 per cent in 1986 (compared with 1985) and in total by 9 per cent. In 1990 they increased by 21 per cent (compared to 1989) and in 1991 by 2 per cent to 5.52m (despite the Gulf War: Turkey assisted the alliance against Iraq). The trend from January 1990 to December 1992 is shown in Figure 11.8 on a logarithmic scale (to stress relative changes). The pre-crisis high h (June — July 1990) was 5.48m annualized, decreasing in July — September 1990, then increasing to a high H of 6.3m in December 1990, followed by a drop of 22 per cent to 4.9m in June 1991 (following the Gulf War). The trend recovered to the high H of 7.6m per annum in January 1992. It dropped in the following two months, recovered partially up to July, then decreased rapidly to about 6.5m per annum (end 1992).

Turkey has suffered from anti-government violence, which from March 1991 was aimed mainly at tourists. In 1992 visitor arrivals totaled 7.08m, dropping 8 per cent in 1993 (from Sweden −28 per cent and from Italy −15 per cent). These losses stimulated Turkey to promote tourism from Israel, price-elastic and only slightly affected by the terrorist attacks (none of which were aimed at Israeli tourists): 101 000 Israelis visited in 1993, more than double the 1992 figure, with a similar increase in 1994.

The above is part of a study of trends in origin-destination tourism up to the end of 1992, including tourism to Greece and tourism to and from the UK (by major regions overseas), from Canada overseas and from Israel by air (Bar-On, 1993b).

The EIU (1994) analyzed tourism to countries which had security concerns in 1983 — 93, including India, Jamaica, Kenya, Peru and the Philippines as well as Egypt, Israel and Turkey (analyzed above), but excluding Spain, and those with long-term war or terrorism (Northern Ireland, Sri Lanka, Uganda and former Yugoslavia).

Mansfeld (1994) presents a further picture of the Middle East Conflict and its effects on tourism. The 60 Euro-terrorist attacks in 1984 — 5 are discussed by Kurtz (1990). Hawkins (1993) surveyed experts regarding tourism policies: escalation of terrorism and

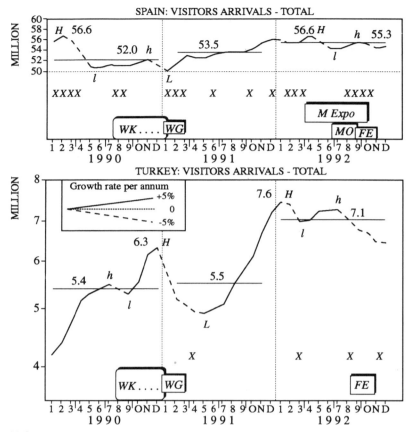

Figure 11.8 Tracking trends in travel and tourism — Spain and Turkey. Trend (short term, annualized) B, Jan 1990 – Dec 1992 and annual totals Y: similar logarithmic scales. See Figure 11.7 for key

of regional conflicts was ranked as the second most important event expected. Surveys of tourists visiting a country and of potential tourists may reveal attitudes to violent acts and fear of further violence.

National and local crisis planning and management should include the tourism industry. Many tourists may not speak the local language or understand news and instructions — unless in English or another language they speak. Special care is needed to inform the tourists, travel agents, tourists' families etc. of the effects of major violence and the steps taken to care for them — accommodation, evacuation etc. (ULA, 1994).

Summary

Terrorism and other violent events or series of crimes against tourists are notable in many tourist destinations, highlighted by instant news world-wide. They affect tourism in many ways: tourists may cancel or postpone trips to such destinations, often switching to alternative destinations. Their effects and the recovery from them and of promotion campaigns following them can best be studied by seasonal adjustment of monthly data and monitoring the smoothed short-term trends, by market segments and by tourist cities or regions (where possible). Examples have been presented of tourism to Israel (from 1970) including the 1985−6 wave of terrorism against international travelers (especially US travelers and carriers) and the effects on arrivals by air from USA in Israel. Inbound and domestic tourists' nights in tourist hotels in Jerusalem, Tel Aviv-Yafo and Eilat have been analyzed, including the effects of the *Intifada* and the Gulf Crisis and War (1990−1), also on tourist arrivals by air in Israel — in total and from three markets. The effects of the Gulf Crisis and War and terrorist attacks on tourism to Egypt, Spain and Turkey were also presented. Market surveys may reveal attitudes to violent acts and fear of further violence.

The author would be glad to receive similar data for other countries and air routes.

References

Bar-On, R.R. (1963). *Seasonality in Israel: Seasonal Analysis and Adjustment of Selected Time Series*. Jerusalem: Central Bureau of Statistics.

Bar-On, R.R. (1969). *Seasonality and Trends in Israel Tourism*. Jerusalem: Central Bureau of Statistics.

Bar-On, R.R. (1973). *Analysis of Seasonality and Trends in Statistical Series — Methodology and Applications in Israel*. Jerusalem: Central Bureau of Statistics.

Bar-On, R.R. (1975). *Seasonality in Tourism — A guide to the Analysis of Seasonality and Trends for Policy Making*. London: *The Economist* Intelligence Unit.

Bar-On, R.R. (1978). The Analysis of Single and Related Time Series into Components — Proposals for Improving X-11. In NBER (National Bureau of Economic Research)/US Bureau of the Census Conference, held in Arlington, September 1976, *Seasonal Analysis of Economic Time Series*. Washington DC: Bureau of the Census: 107−58.

Bar-On, R.R. (1989). *Travel and Tourism Data — A Comprehensive Research Handbook on the World Travel Industry*. London: Euromonitor; Phoenix and Toronto: Oryx.

Bar-On, R.R. (1990). The Effects of Terrorism on International Tourism. In Lewis A. and Kaplan, M. (eds), *Terror in the Skies — Aviation Security*: 83−103. The Proceedings of The First International Seminar on Aviation Security, held in Herzliya (February 5−9, 1989). Jerusalem: ISAS, POB 574.

Bar-On, R.R. (1993a). Seasonality. In Khan, M., Olsen, M., Var, T. (eds), *VNR's Encyclopedia of Hospitality and Tourism*. New York: Van Nostrand Reinhold: 705−34.

Bar-On, R.R. (1993b). Tracking of Travel & Tourism Trends (Example, Six Countries — Inbound by Country of Origin, Residents' Travel Abroad). Jerusalem: Praedicta (mimeo).

Bar-On, R.R. (1993c). A User's Guide to Analysis of Seasonality and Trends by X11 ARIMA/88, Together with the Conventional Comparisons. Jerusalem: Praedicta (mimeo).

Bar-On, R.R. (1993d). The Development of Tourism and Tourism Investments in Israel. Paper presented at *IFTI* — The First International Conference on Investments and Financing in the Tourism Industry, Jerusalem (May 16−21, 1993). In Bar-On, R. and Even-Zahav, M. (eds), *Investments and Financing in the Tourism Industry*. Jerusalem: Ministry of Tourism (1995). Also as Desarrola del Turismo y de las Inversiones Turisticas en Israel. *Estudios y Perspectivas en Turismo* 4(2), 1995.

Bar-On, R.R. (1994). Statistics of Travel and Tourism — Local Needs and Possibilities. In *Recent Developments in Regional and Urban Statistics*: (405−14). *SCORUS* (Standing Committee on Regional and Urban Statistics) 19th Conference, Helsinki (August 30−September 1) with *ISI* (International Statistical Institute) and *IAOS* (International Association for Official Statistics).

Bar-On, R.R. and Paztal, G. (1994). *Minimising and Measuring the Effects of Disasters on Tourism*. Paper presented at Local Authorities — Confronting Disasters and Emergencies, 1st International Conference, Tel Aviv (October 16−19).

Bar-On, R.R. and Even-Zahav, M. (eds) (1995). *Investments and Financing in the Tourism Industry*. Jerusalem: Ministry of Tourism in association with WTO.

Brady, J. and Widdows, R. (1988). The Impact of World Events on Travel to Europe during the Summer of 1986. *Journal of Travel Research* **26**(3): 8–10.

Conant, J.S., Clark, T., Burnett, J.J. and Zank, G. (1988). Terrorism and Travel: Managing the Unmanageable. *Journal of Travel Research* **26**(4): 16–20.

Dagum, E.B. (1988). *The X11 ARIMA/88 Seasonal Adjustment Method — Foundations and User's Manual*. Ottawa: Statistics Canada.

Demos, Epaminondas (1992). Concern for Safety: A Potential Problem in the Tourist Industry. *Journal of Travel and Tourism Marketing* **1**(1): 81–8.

Echtner, Charlotte M. and Ritchie, J.R.B. (1993). The Measurement of Destination Image: An Empirical Assessment. *Journal of Travel Research*, Spring: 3–13.

EIU (1994). The Impact of Political Unrest and Security Concerns on International Tourism. *Travel & Tourism Analyst* **2**: 69–82.

Fisher, J. and Bar-On, R.R. (1993). Information and Forecasting Systems to Aid Investors in Tourism. Paper presented at *IFTI* — The First International Conference on Investments and Financing in the Tourism Industry, Jerusalem (May 16–21, 1993). In Bar-On, R.R. and Even-Zahav, M. (eds.), *Investments and Financing in the Tourism Industry*. Jerusalem: Ministry of Tourism (1995).

Gartner, William C. and Shen, Jingqin (1992). The Impact of Tiananmen Square on China's Tourism Image. *Journal of Travel Research* **30**(2): 47–52.

Handszuh, Henryk (1990). Terrorism and Tourism. In Lewis, A. and Kaplan, M. (eds), *Terror in the Skies — Aviation Security*: 69–77. The Proceedings of The First International Seminar on Aviation Security, held in Herzliya (February 5–9, 1989). Jerusalem: ISAS, POB 574.

Hawkins, Donald E. (1993). Global Assessment of Tourism Policy — A Process Model. In Pearce, D.G. and Butler, R.W. (eds), *Tourism Research — Critiques and Challenges*. London and New York: Routledge: 175–200.

IMT/CBS (B) Biennial tourism statistics (detailed). Jerusalem: Israel Ministry of Tourism with Central Bureau of Statistics. Latest, *Tourism 1991–1992*: with Annual Summaries.

IMT/CBS (Q) *Tourism and Hotel Statistics Quarterly*, Jerusalem: Israel Ministry of Tourism with Central Bureau of Statistics (with monthly updates).

Kurtz, Anat (1990). Terrorism and Tourism. In Lewis, A., and Kaplan, M. (eds), *Terror in the Skies — Aviation Security*: 69–77. The Proceedings of The First International Seminar on Aviation Security, held in Herzliya (February 5–9, 1989). Jerusalem: ISAS, POB 574.

Livingstone, Neil and Halevy, D. (1989). Is it Really Safe to Fly? *Washingtonian Magazine* (May 1989): also in *Terror in the Skies — Aviation Security*: 221–36.

Mansfeld, Yoel (1994). The Middle East Conflict and Tourism to Israel. *Middle Eastern Studies* **30**(3): 646–67.

Pahr, W.P. (1987). The Economic Impact of Terrorism upon Tourism. Paper presented at the International Conference on Terrorism in a Technological World, Washington DC, January 20–2.

Pinhey, Thomas K. and Iverson, Thomas J. (1994). Safety Concerns of Japanese Visitors to Guam. *Journal of Travel and Tourism Marketing* **3**(2): 87–94.

Pottorf, Susan M. and Neal, David M. (1994). Marketing Implications for Post-Disaster Tourism Destinations. *Journal of Travel and Tourism Marketing* **3**(1): 115–22.

Richter, K.R. and Waugh, W.L. (1986). Terrorism and Tourism as Logical Companions. *Tourism Management* **7**(4): 230–8.

Roehl, Wesley S. and Fesenmaier, Daniel R. (1992). Risk Perceptions and Pleasure Travel: An Explanatory Analysis. *Journal of Travel Research* **30**(2): 17–26.

Time (1993). Holidays in Hell. August 23.

Time (1993). Miami Violence. September 6.

ULA (1994). Local Authorities — Confronting Disasters and Emergencies, 1st International Conference, Tel Aviv, October 16–19, *Abstracts*: Tel Aviv-Yafo, Union of Local Authorities.

12 Tourism and terrorism: synthesis of the problem with emphasis on Egypt

SALAH WAHAB

Introductory background

The various existing patterns and newly emerging typologies of tourism, the positive factors that are likely to foster its expansion in any destination, the new trend in recreational activities already manifesting itself and the constraints that negatively affect tourism growth all have to be carefully studied before embarking on setting up a tourism development strategy. However, destination-tourist-products development and marketing in the nineties are witnessing profound changes due to alterations in expectations, habits, attitudes and motivations of tourists. These changes should be considered in adopting unconventional strategies and innovative measures. Moreover, special circumstances are involved where terrorism, political instability or uncertainty impose themselves upon destinations and threaten their tourism future (Lea, 1988: 23).

Regardless of the various constraints that hinder tourism expansion internationally as well as in various destinations, reliable statistics show that tourism has achieved unprecedented ratios. International tourism reaching 500 million visits in 1993 with a direct tourist spending of US$304 billion, is only one-tenth of what domestic tourism has recorded. Latest estimates show that world tourism encompassing both types has already become the world's largest productive sector signaling US$3.4 trillion dollars in 1993.

While the economic impact of tourism is rewarding, being a creator of employment even in slack periods, a source of foreign exchange earnings and a stimulator of various industries, tourism is a sensitive industry. It has demonstrated susceptibility to political upheavals, instability and risks to personal safety while at the same time being a world movement that fosters peace and promotes understanding between peoples of various nations.

The contribution of tourism to the economies of such destinations varies according to its volume, growth of disposable income and the aggregate size of the national economy itself. A striking example of a major tourist industry with a relatively minor economic contribution to the Gross National Product (GNP) is the United States (0.9 per cent in 1992). Conversely, Bermuda and Barbados would be two examples of a tourist destination in which tourism yields a high percentage of the GNP (Bermuda 27 per cent and Barbados 27.3 per cent in 1992). Egypt, as a tourist destination, falls in between as international tourist receipts constitute 7.95 per cent of its GNP (WTO, 1994).

Tourism, Crime and International Security Issues, edited by
A. Pizam and Y. Mansfeld. © 1996 John Wiley & Sons Ltd.

When some chain of events deters tourists from visiting a certain destination, other destinations, whether proximate or faraway, will benefit. Thus, the total volume of international tourism would probably increase, remain intact or be negatively affected but may continue within reasonable limits. As an illustration, when former Yugoslavia was dismantled and the Bosnian War broke out, all tourist attractions in this region lost their attractiveness to international tourists. Greece, Cyprus, Turkey, Italy, Spain and Portugal benefited from this Yugoslav tourist decline. Similarly, when the tourist traffic to Egypt dropped in 1993, Israel, Cyprus, Turkey and Jordan gained through an increased tourist flow.

Terrorism as a real threat to tourism expansion

Such a vital and effective force for world peace is presently seriously threatened by the outbreak of terrorism which started more than a decade ago. Almost all sectors of the travel industry in many countries have been affected by terrorist attacks: airlines, hotels, travel agencies, tour operators, restaurants, nightclubs etc. Such attacks have been particularly effective since the early 1980s in Europe and the Middle East. Airport attacks in Rome and Vienna in 1985 resulted in North American tourists changing their travel plans from the Mediterranean to Northern Europe and the UK. They even began to avoid Europe altogether especially after the Chernobyl incident on April 25, 1986. Thus, Europe and the Mediterranean suffered touristically because of terrorist activities to an extent that a crisis strategy was developed by some destinations and airlines to mitigate, if not overcome, the negative effect of terrorism (D'Amore, 1986).

Terrorism, as such, may be directed toward the state or its institutions with repercussions upon tourism that differ according to the extent of its damaging nature to tourists and tourist facilities. Sometimes, terrorism is explicitly orientated against tourism itself, considered as a movement of "alien" visitors representing a form of neo-colonialism or a threat to well-established societal norms, traditions, value systems and religious convictions.

It is a well-established fact that terrorism exists in many countries and cities around the world. The Red Brigade in Italy, the IRA in Northern Ireland and Britain, Basque separatists in Spain, the Neo-Nazis in Germany, the Fundi in Algeria and the Sikh sect in India are only a few examples. While these terrorist factions have different aims, and their actions are of varied nature and frequency with diverse effects on tourism, it could be safely said that they are of special importance in some of these countries. Conversely, as illustrated by Edgell (1993: 30) "media coverage and global attention to politically motivated terrorist activities can have severe effects on international travel." Linda Richter and William Waugh Jr were clear in stating that "terrorism is a form of communication, of both the threat or reality of violence and the political message. To some extent the mass media are responsible for that communication" (Richter and Waugh, 1991: 318).

As rightly put by Peter Buckley and Mary Klemm (1993: 184): "Terrorism is a political weapon which can be used to greater effect in the postwar world because of the mass media, whose coverage gives to the terrorist organization an illusion of power and efficiency which is out of proportion to its real zeal."

Tourism, when affected by terrorism, turns into a sector of political significance and public concern because of the political implications of terrorism upon state security, and as it causes heated discussions between proponents and opponents of tourism development on the effectiveness of tourism as a contributor to the destination's economic, social and environmental progress. Moreover, because of low-profile involvement of state police in the tourism environment, it is readily accessible to transgressors, felons and criminals and therefore, the security of foreign tourists and safety of tourist facilities needs tailor-made and well-planned strategy.

An example of tourism becoming a direct target for tourist campaigns would be Peru, where the activities of Sendero Luminoso (Terrorist Group) in 1989 to 1991 caused a drastic decline in the foreign tourist movement to Peru (from 350 000 overseas visitors in 1989 to 33 000 overseas visitors in 1991). Terrorist action against tourism was justified by Abumael Guzman, the founder of Sendero Luminoso on the following grounds:

1. Tourism is a symbol of capitalism;
2. Tourists generally come from wealthy countries and thus represent capitalist and oppressive regimes;
3. Tourism is a government-assisted industry and therefore an attack on tourism is an attack on the government (Ryan, 1993: 180).

In such cases, when international publicity is generated, it is only logical that tourists cancel their bookings and change their destination to a more peaceful one.

In a resolution at WTO's General Assembly in Bali, Indonesia (1993) the organization's member countries condemned all violence, threats of violence and all criminal acts against travelers, tourists and tourism facilities. The resolution also urged countries to take all appropriate measures against those who perpetrate such criminal acts to safeguard travelers, tourists and tourist facilities.

Terrorism identified and distinguished from other similar events

Terrorism should not be confused with crime, nor should it be considered a synonym of political violence. It is a systematic and persistent strategy practiced by a state or political group against another state, political or social group through a campaign of acts of violence, such as assassinations, hijacking, use of explosives, sabotage, murder and the like, with the intent of creating a state of terror and public intimidation to achieve political, social or religious ends (Ezzedin, 1987: 39 — 40).

Terrorism, therefore, should be distinguished from various other forms of violence, namely, guerrilla warfare, state dictatorship, political crime and organized crime. While those engaged in guerrilla warfare and terrorism both use systematic violence to achieve their ends, terrorism usually occurs in cities, involving small groups, and seeks to destroy the enemy's morale. Guerrilla warfare is a clear and definite pattern of war acts which are mainly practiced in woods, mountains and rural areas. While guerrillas do not normally use terrorist actions, they may resort to them with reservation to help achieve their political aims, particularly in the case of national liberation movements and popular resistance against colonialists, as was recently the case in Afghanistan.

State dictatorship, on the other hand, may use violence to influence political decisions and eradicate opposition. It strives to achieve social and political change by superimposition. Its scope of activities is usually extensive, overwhelming and includes all the population. This particular aspect makes it more comprehensive than terrorism which, no matter how strong it may be, is limited in its scope. Dictatorships may use methods similar to those used by terrorism such as assassinations, kidnapping and bombing. But terrorism differs from state dictatorship in motives and the social, economic, ideological and political considerations which drive its activities.

Terrorism is also different from political crime, which is subject to controversial opinion among jurists; it is usually considered a crime connected to the basis of social order like anarchy and communism. The Sixth International Conference for Standardizing Criminal Laws held in Copenhagen in 1935 was clear in defining political crimes as "crimes committed against the regime of the state and its proceedings as well as against its citizens rights." This definition does not apply to terrorism.

Organized crime is also different from terrorism in that its main aim is to work outside the government and the people's framework to achieve financial benefit through illegal means. It embraces hundreds or thousands of criminals performing according to very strict and intricate rules that exceed by far the rules governing legitimate societies. While the terrorist believes in the nobility and honesty of his motives and sacrifices himself to that end, the only objective of criminal organizations is to obtain financial gain regardless of its sources and notwithstanding its means (Ezzedin, 1987: 41−62).

Concluding remarks on terrorism

1. While terrorism is an international contemporary phenomenon, it absorbs the characteristics of the society in which it appears and thus reflects some aspects of its problems. It is an unsigned message of violence without content and sent to a person with an unknown address.
2. Moreover, terrorism represents an opinion that is not endorsed by the population majority; otherwise, it would not choose violence as its way of expression. It is therefore much closer to crime than to resistance, and its relationship with political life is confined to its impact upon state security and internal stability. Thus, terrorism is an aggressive movement that lies outside the constitutional and legal framework of the state.
3. Terrorism, as such, is a temporary phenomenon that appears in relation to some specific circumstances prevailing at a given time in certain societies. It is an expression of minority dictatorship and thus does not signify a trend that could be labeled as national resistance.
4. Terrorism has not succeeded throughout history in overthrowing political regimes or introducing a real substitute for an existing political system. It may succeed in creating chaos through challenging the established socio-political and economic norms. Therefore, its impact on the tourist industry in any destination would be noticeable given that tourism by its very nature is a sensitive industry.

Egyptian tourism and terrorism

International tourism in its modern sense in Egypt is more than a century old. It dates back to the first organized group tour by Thomas Cook in 1863. Since then, Egypt has been an attractive destination for elite tourism of the 19th and early 20th centuries. This period was characterized by a limited number of visitors (thousands), long periods of stay and high spending power. In 1950, 65 000 visited Egypt, while in 1952 the number of tourists rose to 75 000, representing 0.3 per cent of the total international tourist traffic in that year. The revolutionary government in Egypt became interested in tourism promotion as early as 1953 when it created the Supreme Council for Tourism. The wars of 1956, 1967 and 1973 exerted a profound impact on tourism represented by the ups and downs in the volume of the tourist traffic.

The average rate of increase was exceptionally high in the sixties (25 per cent yearly), then it dropped to the international average rate of increase in the seventies. In the eighties, after the implementation of the open-door policy, the average rate of growth of the tourist traffic ranged between 15 and 20 per cent except in the years when some eruptive events emerged (eg the *Achille Lauro* incident in 1985, the central security forces revolt in 1986 and the Gulf War of 1990).

The year 1992 was the apex year of Egyptian tourism. Statistics show that 3.2 million tourists visited Egypt recording 22.5 million tourist nights. The total tourist expenditure in Egypt in 1992 reached US$2.4 billion, irrespective of the fact that systematic terrorist attacks actually started in September 1992. As a result of these terrorist attacks, tourism traffic to Egypt in 1993 dropped by 22 per cent in tourist numbers and 30 per cent in volume of tourist nights.

The setback in tourism receipts was much more profound as statistics show a decrease of over 42 per cent to about US$1.380 million. In January/June 1994 the total number of tourist arrivals was 1 049 040, 12.4 per cent less than the tourist arrivals recorded in the similar period of 1993. Tourist nights in the first half of 1994 reached 5.7 million nights in contrast to 7.1 million in the same period of 1993, registering a decline of 19.6 per cent.

While the aforementioned percentages are sufficiently high, terrorist impacts on the Egyptian tourist business were felt far beyond this, as it almost came to a standstill and consequently the national economy was affected.

The history of terrorism in Egypt is rather recent. Although individual criminal acts occurred occasionally even before the assassination of President Sadat in 1981, terrorist attacks in the true sense started only in September 1992.

It is generally claimed in the international media that these terrorist attacks are led by Moslem Fundamentalists and particularly directed against tourists. While fundamentalist movements are prevalent in most parts of the world (the subject of a comprehensive research project leading to a six-volume publication edited by Martin E. Marty and R. Scott Appleby and sponsored by the American Arts and Science Academy), not all these fundamentalist movements adopt terrorism as their strategy.

The case of terrorism in Egypt is rather unique. Egypt was always known to be a country of peace and stability. Its population was ethnically homogeneous, although 90 per cent are Moslems and 10 per cent Christians. History tells us that Egyptians were of moderate temperament, endured and survived many outside attacks, fought three wars since 1952 and were generally tolerant toward their rulers. This did not prevent them from revolting against colonial powers several times which rendered the continuation of foreign occupation extremely difficult. These liberation movements cannot be labeled as terrorism nor could it mean that the Egyptian people have coarse and intolerant natures. At the same time Egyptians are quite religious but not over-zealous or fanatical. This, however, did not prevent some Egyptians from forming groups aimed at the revival of classic Islamic rules of societal behavior to combat the ills of distorted modern ways of life which they consider as a deviation from Islam. This was not in itself the reason for terrorist attacks. It was, however, the fertile soil that enabled some fanatics, with personal political ambitions coinciding with certain foreign political objectives, to take advantage of the religious revival and incite some poorly educated or half-educated young people in the name of Islam to serve their political purpose. With the relatively difficult times, underemployment and the diverse political and economic understandings, terrorism infiltrated particularly into the remote areas of Upper-Egypt. It was mainly directed towards the government's political and economic policy, aiming at the government's embarrassment and pushing it until it became unable to solve its problems, thereby reaching a standstill. This could, in their minds, facilitate their seizure of power. They found out that the shortest way to achieve this end was to attack some tourist buses and a few Nile cruisers. Over a period of 22 months in 1992–4 some 127 terrorist attacks resulted in the killing of nine tourists and injury to about 60. This is much less than incidents in other tourist destinations in the USA, Europe and elsewhere.

International media, however, were overenthusiastic about terrorism in Egypt, resulting in the governments of some tourist-generating countries issuing statements to the effect that travel to Egypt is considered unsafe. This resulted in the aforementioned decline of international tourist traffic to Egypt. Recently, most of these statements were rescinded, but tourism, until the date of writing this chapter, is not yet back to normal although good signs of improvement are already evident. In July and August 1994 over 100 000 Arab tourists arrived and caused a noticeable upswing in the tourist and commercial centers.

It is good to be able to say that no terrorist attacks have occurred since February 1994, since the State Security Police started to take the initiative and lead in counteracting and arresting groups of terrorists. Courts in Egypt were keen to accelerate trials and render quick but just decisions in terrorist crimes. Also, due to the earnest efforts exerted by the Islamic high institution, Al-Azhar, many former terrorists have declared their rehabilitation from their false religious convictions and publicly admitted that they were misled by their leaders and some foreign sources.

The Sixth Conference of the Supreme Council for Islamic Affairs that convened in Alexandria, Egypt on August 16, 1994, attended by over 1200 delegates, as well as the UN Conference on Population and Development that was held September 5–12, 1994, attended by over 16 000 participants including 16 presidents and about 3000 international journalists, are conclusive evidence that Egypt is again a safe and stable country.

Counteracting terrorism in Egypt

Although the state police in any given country is usually the defense front line against terrorism, counteracting this danger should not be confined only to the state police. All government departments have to share the responsibility of fighting against terrorism, each in its own jurisdiction. Moreover, unless the majority of the population condemns terrorism and resists its destructive activities, there can be no complete and fast relief from it.

The Egyptian government's initial response was to stress the fact that terrorist activities were of restrained scope and low-risk level. At the same time, the Egyptian media made it clear that Egypt's terrorist attacks are far less effective and dangerous than terrorist attacks in many other countries. In contrast, the international media treated the news about terrorist attacks in Egypt in a forceful way that left very little room for counter-arguments. The messages were quite frequent and so persuasive to the public that travel to Egypt was deemed unsafe. This induced most, if not all, tour operators in the USA and Europe to take Egyptian tourist programs off their sales catalogs, an act which inflicted much harm on Egypt's tourist industry for almost two years.

The Egyptian police force adopted a series of counter-measures against terrorism that were heavily based upon tight anti-criminal actions aiming at protecting the country at large and the vulnerable tourist industry in particular. Every bus, train and Nile cruiser transporting tourists has a "discreet" police guard (*Travel & Tourism Analyst*, 1994: 75).

Later the Egyptian police moved from defensive measures to preventive actions or from a reaction position to an action-led and oriented position. This change of strategy resulted in the success of the government in confining terrorism after its main leaders were found and arrested. The terrorist movement has become paralyzed, particularly after the non-Egyptian sources of funding and planning were discovered and unveiled. At the same time, the 1000-year-old Islamic institution Al-Azhar embarked on an exhaustive national educational campaign based on lectures by a number of its able professors and panel discussions with the youth in all Egyptian governorates, cities and villages. Egyptian television and radio broadcasting successfully participated in this informative campaign against terrorism and helped disseminate news of the dangers of terrorist groups through the falsification of their erroneous religious claims that contemporary society is disbelieving and should be boycotted and fought against.

By the same token, the Egyptian government intensified and accelerated its policy to help raise the standard of living in certain remote areas, the cradle of terrorism in Egypt. It embarked, in the remote hilly areas of the governorates of Assiute and Quena, upon an ambitious program in the areas of global economic and social development, thus creating thousands of new jobs with an effective policy of eliminating some of the government red tape in these areas. An investment program of multimillions of Egyptian pounds was launched in these areas to eradicate illiteracy, help expand the agricultural belt in the area and assist the young people in creating cooperatives and small enterprises under the auspices of the Social Fund for Development, an agency reporting to the Council of Ministers of Egypt.

The role of the Ministry of Tourism

With the negative impact of terrorists upon tourism, the tourist image of Egypt became drastically hampered as an unsafe destination. Table 12.1 shows the decline of Egypt's tourist traffic because of terrorism. The Ministry of Tourism started out by organizing road shows to various generating markets in Europe and Arab countries headed by the former Minister Fouad Sultan. Two expeditions to eight European countries were organized in late 1992 and early 1993.

With the advent of the new cabinet in October 1993 and the appointment of Dr Mahmoud el-Beltagui as Minister of Tourism, a new policy document was laid down in

Table 12.1 Decline in tourist arrivals and tourist nights, 1992–4

Years	No. of tourists	Change	No. of tourist nights	Change
1992	3 206 940	44.8%	21 836 705	34.5%
1993	2 507 762	−21.8%	15 089 017	−30.9%
1994	1 049 040	−12.4%	5 693 957	−19.8%
(6 months)				
1993	1 197 753		7 095 644	
(6 months)				

December 1993 to combat the ills of tourism. This policy document analyzed the situation and concluded that the existing tourism crisis in Egypt was multi-dimensional going back to the Gulf War (1990–1) and to terrorist events which started in the fall of 1992. The same document referred to the fact that regardless of these two impediments Egypt's share of the international tourist traffic is rather modest because even in Egypt's tourism climax year of 1992, its share did not exceed 0.80 per cent. The reasons for this, the policy document claimed, are structural rather than financial. From a structural viewpoint, while Egypt has 16 overseas tourist offices, this in itself is not sufficient to achieve the objectives of tourism expansion. These overseas offices lack the capabilities and contemporary technical and technological tools necessary for the fruition of their ambitions. The Ministry, thereafter, would need to engage in a comprehensive assessment of these offices and to reach a more effective utilization of their resources in view of the new international changes. Another very important structural shortcoming is the lack of an effective marketing system that could successfully promote Egypt on the national level according to economic criteria prevailing in the open market of tourism. Egypt's tourist promotion, based for so long on the association with the tourism distribution channels, has proved insufficient. Therefore its marketing efforts should be additionally directed to the tourist himself, as consumer, through the mass media and in particular television networks.

From a financial viewpoint, Egypt's marketing and tourist promotion budget is insufficient to produce the desired results, especially because of the hampered image due to terrorism. Spending Eg£10.2 million in 1992 was not competitive in the world tourist market. As a destination's tourist budget should not be less than 1 per cent to 3 per cent of the tourist receipts (Ministry of Tourism of Egypt, 1994), Egypt should not have spent less than US$20–40 million in 1992 and US$14–30 million in 1993. The present crisis, indicated the Ministry's policy document, caused many tourist establishments to sell their services for reduced tourist income for Egypt and to a lower category of tourists. All the above stressed the need to formulate a new tourist promotion plan for Egypt within an estimated budget of US$30 million for 1994.

The tourist promotion plan of 1994

Scientific and objective assessment of Egypt's overseas tourist promotion unveils some weaknesses that may be summarized in conventionalism, absence of a scientifically based marketing policy at the national level, as well as lack of homogeneity between components of promotion campaigns, absence of a scientific plan for the allocation of tourist promotion funds among various generating markets and lack of variation in promotion strategies in different markets according to differences in their characteristics and traveler behavioral patterns.

This is why the drafters of the tourist promotion plan of 1994 were keen to reshape Egypt's tourism promotion, in order to avoid previous weaknesses and redesign its objectives to remedy the distorted tourist image of the country to the level achieved in 1992.

The Egyptian third five-year plan for economic and social development (1993 – 7) determined the objectives of the tourism sector in reaching four million tourist arrivals, 39 million tourist nights and US$3.5 billion as tourist receipts in 1997. The new tourist promotion plan, adopting that objective as its overall objective for 1997, expressly stipulated that its specific target for 1994 would be to restore Egypt's international tourist traffic to what it was in 1992, surmounting the difficulties imposed on Egypt's tourism by terrorism.

Other secondary targets of the plan were: (1) to raise the level of promotion tools presently used and create additional tools; (2) to create an audio-visual library to serve tourist promotion purposes: (3) to draw a framework for a coordinated overseas effort by public and private sectors to serve the Egyptian tourism industry: (4) to originate an agenda for cultural, musical and sportive events and festivals to be used as an additional tourist attraction; (5) to open up new and alternative tourist-generating markets for Egyptian tourism; (6) to activate the investment climate for Arab and foreign investors to encourage them to invest in the new tourist regions.

The various strategic tourist promotion tools of the Ministry (MOT) were elaborated upon in the following manner:

1. Addressing the ultimate consumer (the tourist) directly through mass media (general and specialized newspapers, and magazines, television networks, etc.) in addition to working closely in tourist promotion with conventional and unconventional distribution channels;
2. Raising the standard of promotion publications in so far as language, technical content and presentation are concerned in order to be competitive on the world market;
3. Using the road-show tools, which should encompass press conferences, touring archaeological replicas, musical and folkloric shows and promotion film projections;
4. Activating and intensifying participation in international conferences, tourist trade shows and international mega events;
5. Expanding the invitation program of famous tourist and media personalities to visit Egypt in order to make sure that it is a safe and stable country (Wahab, 1975: 118, 119).

The plan concentrated on six primary tourist-generating markets for Egypt, namely USA, UK, Germany, France, Italy and Japan. Criteria for choosing these countries are the number of tourist visits, types of tourists, average length of stay, average daily expenditure, the potential market growth rate and condition of Egypt's image in each market. Moreover, it was found that the implementation of the plan should not be left exclusively to the Tourist Promotion Authority (which is a subsidiary of the MOT) but that there should be coordinated participation by field-specialized advertising agencies.

An action program was included in the plan. It was divided among publications, promotion films, press, trade shows, conferences, tourist agendas, overseas visits and familiarization tours, road shows and contents.

Various government agencies which would be involved in executing the plan are: the Ministry of Tourism through the Tourist Promoting Authority; the Ministry of Culture; the Ministry of Information through its information service; the Ministry of Economy through its Exhibitions Authority; the Ministry of Foreign Affairs through the various embassies and EgyptAir as the national flag carrier.

In addition to these government agencies, the participation of the tourist private sector is represented by the National Federation of Tourist Chambers, the Egyptian–American Chamber of Commerce and various friendship societies created to promote good relations between Egypt and many countries in the world.

The plan also emphasized the importance of control of the results achieved. Thus, monitoring and evaluating were entrusted to a permanent committee composed of representatives of the Ministry of Tourism, other aforementioned ministries, the Treasury and the private sector.

The committee is headed by the Minister of Tourism and meets on a regular basis once every three months. It has the power to review and amend the promotion plan in the light of actual application and results achieved.

The budget is allocated as follows:	US dollars
1. Advertising campaigns in the general and specialized press in the six chosen markets plus a contingency sum for international magazines	7 million
2. Television ads (about 1120 ads total in the six countries × average US$20 000 per ad)	22.4 million
3. Conventional promotional efforts in the other tourist markets	2.6 million
4. Trade shows, conferences, and Egyptian nights and receptions	3 million
5. Road shows (six)	1.2 million
Total	36.2 million

Conclusion and recommendations

Tourism-generating markets are usually segmented by demographic factors such as gender, age, social and cultural groups and income groups as well as by psychographic characteristics based on motivations for travel, need for escape and adventure, fear of air travel, and fear of the unfamiliar and need for security and safety (Plog, 1974). Terrorism, therefore, proved to be a main barrier to travel, and consequently an impediment to tourism industry development, because the general traveling public anywhere naturally fears to travel to a destination plagued with terrorist attacks. Tour operators, as architects of group travel, would not be interested in promoting program sales to that destination. Media coverage of terrorism in various tourist destinations varies depending on many factors. For destinations like the USA, France and the UK, while terrorism has exerted an impact on tourism, it has not substantially decreased. In Egypt, terrorism's effect on tourism demand was quite marked.

It is a proven fact that sustained terrorism almost immediately projects an adverse image on the destination, caused by large media coverage affecting both potential tourists and travel distribution channels. The only way to overcome such poor image projection is by vigorous and professionally guided promotions that can provide wide exposure sufficient to capture the international media's attention. This could be achieved through the help of unusual events that capture the eyes of the world and undoubtedly needs creative thinking and innovative action.

Maintaining good contacts with the international media to ensure that reports about Egypt are balanced and accurate is another important element in managing the present tourism crisis. Providing detailed briefing to international tour operators, travel agents and the press that would put the risks in their proper context is a further positive step. This is practiced in Florida, Kenya and China where tourists are reassured about their own safety by being guided away from potential trouble spots.

Tourism itself has little influence on the management of terrorism. However, effective planning and management, sound educational training and personal strategies, responsible environmental policies, well-guided integration within the national economic and social development, the raising of popular awareness about the benefits of tourism and cautious integration between guests and hosts all will actively contribute to achieve sustainable economic and social benefits to the destination through tourism and emphasize its importance to the country and the economy.

Finally, one may recommend some additional unconventional promotional steps that would foster catching the attention of international media, namely:

1. Declaring *1996* the *"Tourism Year of Egypt"* in agreement with the World Tourism Organization which would include festivals, operas, folkloric shows, sportive activities, conferences and trade shows in Egypt as well as friendship weeks to be held in many European, American and Asian tourist-generating countries.
2. Convening and organizing a major world conference to be held in Egypt in 1997 such as a Middle East Peace Conference, North—South Dialog Conference or a World Tourism for Peace Conference.
3. Taking advantage of the WTO General Assembly meeting scheduled to be held in Cairo 1995 to publicize internationally that Egypt, the storehouse of history, is one of the major tourism destinations of the world where the ancient and the modern coexist.
4. Researching the world niche tourist markets by professional research institutions and putting up a tourism marketing plan that is compatible with the latest developments on the world scene, especially in the light of territorial integrations and the GATT treaty of 1994.
5. Boosting world interest in Egypt through holding monthly dinners in various large capitals of the world where an international dignitary would be invited as a keynote speaker and attended by leading politicians, movie stars, public opinion leaders, world-reputed university professors, famous businessmen etc. These dinner topics would always center around Egypt.
6. Fixing an annual Egyptian celebration date (September 27 being the World Tourism day) to hold an international festival including musical and folkloric shows in all Egyptian cities, food festivals in all hotels and restaurants, trade shows, free visits to all museums that would open for 24 hours etc.

7. Holding an annual contest for journalists and television presenters in various tourist-generating countries such as the USA, the UK, France, Switzerland, Italy, the Netherlands, Germany, Austria, Sweden, Denmark, Spain, Japan, Australia, etc. where articles as well as television programs would feature Egypt. Large awards for the best article (writer of the year) and program (TV presenter of the year) to be distributed in Cairo in a world-wide celebration.

8. Hosting an internationally famous personality, such as a leading Hollywood movie star, to speak about Egypt in the introduction of a promotional film about Egypt or in a TV promotional ad about Egypt.

9. Restructuring the Egyptian Tourist Promotion Authority to function as a systems marketing-oriented organization which can succeed in implementing the 1994 promotion plan backed by creative thinking and innovative action, thus positively helping the Ministry of Tourism in its difficult task.

References

Buckley, P. and Klemm, M. (1993). The decline of tourism in northern Ireland. *Tourism Management*, **14**(2), 184−94.

D'Amore, L. (1986). International terrorism; implications and challenge for global tourism, *Business Quarterly*.

The Economist Intelligence Unit (1994). *Travel and Tourism Analyst*, 2: 75.

Edgell, D. (1993). *World Tourism at the Millennium*, US Department of Commerce, US Travel and Tourist Administration.

Ezzedin, A. (1987). *Terrorism and Political Violence*, Urbana: Office of International Criminal Justice at the University of Illinois.

Lea, J. (1988). *Tourism and Development in the Third World*. Routledge.

Ministry of Tourism of Egypt (1994). *General Policy and Action Plans, December 1993. Tourist promotion plan*.

Plog, S.C. (1974). Why destination areas arise and fall in popularity. *The Cornell Hotel and Restaurant Administration Quarterly*, **14** (4).

Richter, L. and Waugh, W. (1991). Terrorism and tourism as logical companions. In Medlik, S. (ed.), *Managing Tourism*, Butterworth Heinemann: 318−27.

Ryan, C. (1993). Crime, violence, terrorism and tourism. *Tourism Management*, **14** (3) June: 173−83.

Wahab, S. (1975). *Tourism Management*. London: Tourism Int. Press.

World Tourism Organization (WTO) (1994). *Compendium of Tourism Statistics*.

13 The tourism industry in the partitioned island of Cyprus

YOEL MANSFELD AND NURIT KLIOT

Introduction

The long-lasting dispute between Greek and Turkish Cypriots has been well documented in the literature (see, for example, Attalides, 1977 and Dodd, 1993). Since the mid-1950s, this island's struggles for ethno-political independence have changed its economic landscape. One of the leading sectors which has evolved into a dual economic landscape in the partitioned island of Cyprus is tourism. Modern tourism in Cyprus has developed in two stages. The first began in the mid-1960s as part of overall rapid growth in the demand for sea and sun tourism and attracted to the Mediterranean basin people from western and north-western European countries. The second stage occurred after the 1974 partition of the island due to Turkey's occupation of North Cyprus (Kammas, 1991). This military action resulted in two entirely separate political entities: the Republic of Cyprus that lost about a third of its territory as a result of the Turkish invasion and the Turkish occupied territory (the so-called Turkish Republic of Northern Cyprus — TRNC), which is internationally recognized only by Turkey and has been facing both political and economic embargoes, imposed by the United Nations after the invasion.

The literature on political unrest and its impact on tourism development in island countries is relatively limited (Butler, 1993; Lockhart, 1993; Hall, 1994). Since 1974, Cyprus has presented a unique example of an island country specializing in tourism as an economic activity, having to deal with a political, socio-cultural and economic partition, and a tourism industry evolving in two parallel yet different ways (Lockhart and Ashton 1990; Witt, 1991; Kammas, 1992; Ioannides, 1992; Wilson, 1992; Martin, 1993; Lockhart 1993).

The aim of this chapter is to characterize and analyze the evolving tourist landscape of post-1974 Cyprus. The analysis will demonstrate how the eruption of a long-lasting dispute between a Greek majority and a Turkish minority into a full-scale war on this island has managed to cause a dramatic change in the functioning tourist industry and hence on the entire economic and social texture of this island. The discussion will concentrate on three main issues: (a) the rearrangement of the tourism sector as a result of the change in size and spatial distribution of tourism resources; (b) the contribution of the tourism sector to the reactivation of the island's economy after its partition in 1974; and

Tourism, Crime and International Security Issues, edited by
A. Pizam and Y. Mansfeld. © 1996 John Wiley & Sons Ltd.

(c) the impact of the tourism development process on the environmental qualities which partially form the tourist attraction of Cyprus.

Cyprus's tourism in the pre-partition period

Since its independence in 1960 and until its partition in 1974, unlike many other island and micro-state countries, the Cyprus government regarded tourism as a means of economic diversification and not just as a sole solution for its poor foreign-revenue situation (Government of Cyprus, 1961; Andronicou, 1979).

Thus, two types of tourism facilities have emerged. The first was the development of sun and sea resorts in two locations: the modern southern suburb of Famagusta — Varosha located on the finest sandy beaches of the island on the eastern coast — and Kyrenia, an old port town on the north coast. In 1973 these two resorts concentrated 65 per cent of the island's hotel bed capacity and have managed to capture 63 per cent of the year's inbound tourist flow (Andronicou, 1979; Witt, 1991; Burton, 1991). The second type was mountain tourism located mainly in the village of Platres on the peaks of the Trodos mountains (see Figure 13.1). Since 1960 and until 1974, the year the Turkish Army invaded the island, the average growth rate of tourist arrivals was 19 per cent, excursionists' arrivals growth rate was 8 per cent and foreign-exchange earnings were growing by an average of 19 per cent (Cyprus Tourism Organization, 1977). In other words, relative to the overall growth of world tourism Cyprus was in a very dynamic development situation (Witt, 1991; Ioannides, 1992).

This pre-partition period was characterized by occasional terror attacks and social unrest as a result of each community's efforts to ensure its interests within the newly established Republic (Kitromilides, 1977; Witt, 1991). Despite the general upward trend in the 1960s and until 1974, tourists' demand for both sun and sea, and mountain tourism, was occasionally hampered by unrest situations. In fact, in terms of yearly figures of tourist arrivals, since its independence in 1960 and until 1974, only once (in 1964) did the island suffer a major drop in tourist arrivals (Figure 13.2). This was a result of the severe political crisis, where Turkish ministers had to leave their positions in the bi-communal government and intercommunal violence erupted between Turkish and Greek Cypriots. This confrontation led to the partition of the capital Nicosia and the start of an on-going process of ethnic cleansing against the Turkish minority and its consequent geographical relocation in Turkish enclaves.

Two major reasons can be attributed to the fact that during 1960–74 tourism in the island was only marginally affected by the political and inter-communal unrest. The first is that the actual violence took place in remote areas not specializing in tourism and in any case far from the major tourist centers of Varosha, Kyrenia and the Trodos mountains (Lockhart, 1993). The second is the overall weak effect of the media on tourists' propensity to travel. The British market forms the largest market segment in Cyprus. Good prior knowledge of the island and its problems meant that British tourists have not had to rely on the media in order to assess the risks involved in visiting this country.

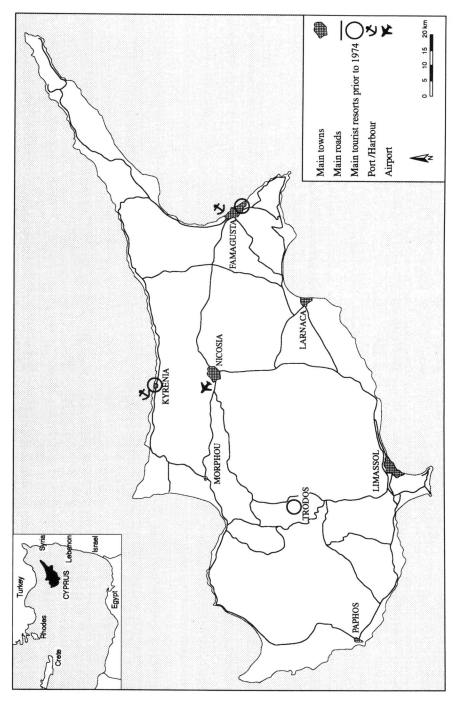

Figure 13.1 Areas of tourism development prior to the 1974 partition

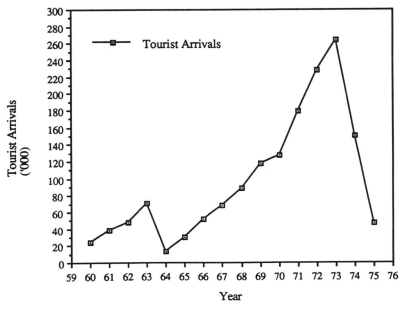

Figure 13.2   Tourist arrivals in the Republic of Cyprus, 1960—74

1974 onwards: the emergence of a dual tourist landscape

The partition of Cyprus and the size—space aspects

The most distinctive impact of the 1974 civil war following the invasion of the Turkish army was a loss of just over a third of the area by the government-controlled Greek part. This was not just a matter of losing land. It meant also forfeiting the two highly developed resorts of Famagusta on the eastern coast and Kyrenia on the northern coast (Wilson, 1992). Consequently, the government had to redistribute its tourism infrastructure in order to reactivate this sector as soon as possible. In many parts of the Greek side this involved a landscape transformation, from agriculture and residential land uses into tourism land uses. However, landscape transformation as a result of competition between agriculture and tourism land uses, as often suggested in the literature (Gunn, 1988), has not occurred in the Republic of Cyprus. In this case it was a matter of rationalizing resources. After 1974, the government-controlled area lost most of its fertile land and hence agriculture as an exportable sector ceased to exist. Alternatively, tourism could be used to fill this gap (Andronicou, 1979; Katsouris interview, 1992). Thus, villages such as Ayia Napa were turned rapidly from rural communities into saturated ''Tourist Ghettos'' (to use Krippendorf's 1987 term).

However, tourism in the South started to develop not just in rural areas but also in urban settings in Limassol, Paphos and Larnaca (see Figure 13.3). Also, in urban areas the penetration of tourism should not be regarded as competition between land uses, but redistribution and enlargement of the town's built-up area in order to take advantage of the economic and social benefits of the tourism sector (Katsouris interview, 1992). One of the major social benefits was the ability of the emerging tourist sector to absorb

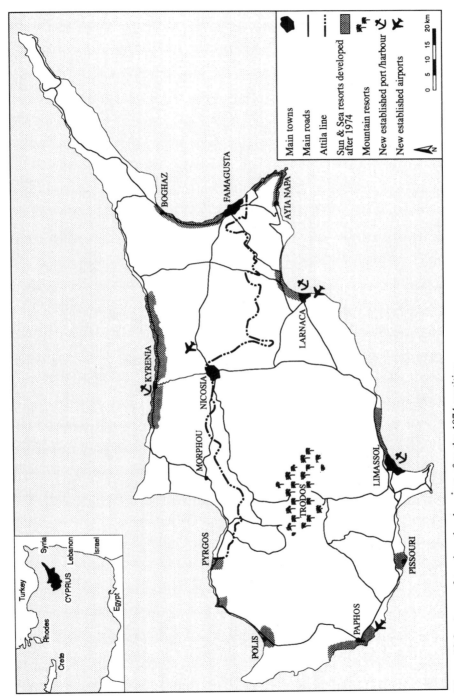

Figure 13.3 Areas of tourism development after the 1974 partition

substantial numbers of refugees who were employed in the tourism and hospitality industry and lost their jobs as a result of the war. Indeed, people who used to live in the Varosha and Kyrenia areas managed to rehabilitate themselves by working in the relocated tourism sector (Kliot and Mansfield, 1995).

However, in the south, these benefits did not fully materialize as a result of a rapidly emerging high level of locals/tourists ratio. In 1990 this ratio already stood at 2.83 tourists to one local (Republic of Cyprus, 1991). The government had to produce solutions to negative repercussions arising as a result of this high ratio. For example, in the summer of 1992 the tourism sector had to import up to 30 000 temporary workers from other countries to fill vacancies in the hotel industry (Demetriadou, interview 1992).

As a result of the 1974 partition, the Turkish-occupied north gained a relatively smaller area, yet one which already contained well-developed tourism infrastructure in two resorts — Famagusta and Kyrenia. However, as decision making was not accomplished by local leaders but by the Turkish Army and the mainland Turkish government, reactivating these facilities was limited only to the Kyrenia resort. The whole tourist area of Famagusta (Varosha) was declared by the Turkish Army as a no-go zone, leaving over 31 hotels obsolete (CTO, 1980). In fact this whole area is still inaccessible to anyone except the Turkish Army (Lockhart and Ashton, 1990; field survey, 1992). Nevertheless, the existing infrastructure in Kyrenia did somewhat compensate for the smaller area resulting from this Turkish policy.

The country's limited geographical scale as a result of the 1974 civil war did not result in a land use competition between tourism and other sectors in the Turkish-occupied north. The first reason for the lack of such competition was the small size of the tourist market attracted to the Turkish part. It was only in the late 1980s that inbound tourist flows both from Turkey and Europe began to grow enough to require further infrastructure and superstructure tourism development (Lockhart and Ashton, 1990). The areas chosen were the beach strip north of Famagusta (the Salamis area) and those east and west of Kyrenia (see Figure 13.3). Only recently, in the Kyrenia region, are tourism land uses tending to replace agricultural land. However, this process is not characterized by competition but rather by a replacement of land uses, as agricultural land in many areas was not utilized at all after the partition (Sadi, interview 1992; field survey, 1992). The landscape transformation process evolving from this land use shift has recently gained momentum, as more expatriates and foreigners invest in the island (in hotel apartments and villas) before the economic boom expected to occur as a result of the peace negotiations between the two sides (Sadi, interview 1992).

There is perhaps only one other competing factor between tourism and other land uses as a result of the size and space changes after 1974. This is the Turkish Army which, accidentally or not, deployed its troops in some of the best tourist attractions along the coast (eg west of Kyrenia) and also in mountain and forest areas (eg near St. Hilarion on the Kyrenia Mountains: field survey, 1992).

Despite the small size of the Turkish-occupied north, this part of the island does not face any locals/tourists ratio problems. The redistribution of population after 1974 had marginal effects on the Turkish side as its overall population size has been relatively small (estimated today at 180 000 people). The locals/tourists ratio in the case of the north has until 1987 been less than one (fewer tourists than locals). In 1987 for the first time these figures broke even, with the ratio exceeding one after 1989 (Turkish Republic of Northern Cyprus, 1992). However, such a small ratio, the fact that the majority of tourists visiting this part of the island are mainland Turkish and the way tourism infrastructure is geographically distributed do not provide a basis for the development of any kind of friction between hosts and guests as has occurred in the south.

The above review of the size–space aspects of tourism development in Cyprus since 1974 proves that, with regard to potential, the main loser in the partition is the government-controlled south. Its ability to reactivate its tourism infrastructure more rapidly than the north brought it more quickly into conflict situations typical of small island countries that suffer on the one hand from a size constraint and on the other from a growing and inflexible demand for tourism services. The north, despite its relatively smaller area, has not encountered major size–space constraints as yet. This is due to the low number of inhabitants, the lack of strong tourism demand, the relatively small number of tourists compared to those visiting the Greek side and the fact that established and comprehensive tourism infrastructure remained in its control as a result of the Turkish occupation.

The economic consequences of the partition and their impact on the "tourist map"

The Turkish invasion in 1974 has effectively partitioned the island's economy causing obvious damage to almost all sectors. The disturbed balance of the economy has resulted primarily because the area occupied produced 70 per cent of the gross output, accounted for 50 per cent of the exports and attracted 70 per cent of inbound tourist flows (Republic of Cyprus, 1976; Symeonides, 1977; King, 1984). Thus, the copper-mining region in the Morphou bay area came under Turkish Cypriot control. The same thing happened with the whole agricultural plain of Morphou, which was the main source for citrus exports on the island. All of the springs in the Kyrenia mountains remained under Turkish control, and the highly developed tourist resorts of Varosha and Kyrenia including the port of Famagusta were all lost to the Republic of Cyprus (Government of Cyprus, 1988).

Both parts of the island had to reactivate their economies in order to overcome the damage caused by the war, the loss or gain of economic resources and the displacement and unemployment of refugees. In the south the unemployment rate reached 29.1 per cent at the end of 1975 (Republic of Cyprus, 1976). The displacement of both Greek and Turkish Cypriots as a result of the partition necessitated a huge capital investment both for resettlement schemes and for the reintegration of these refugees into the segregated evolving economies (Kliot and Mansfeld, 1995). In planning new economic systems the two political entities had to look upon refugees as a positive factor for economic rehabilitation and a resource for further growth (Zetter, 1992). Unless such an approach could be considered, refugees, who constitute a direct human, social but also economic problem, would become a burden rather than positive contributors to the economy.

The fact that only the Greek refugees were perceived as a resource for economic rehabilitation through the reactivation of the tourism sector contributed enormously to the different emerging economies of the two parts of the island. In fact, tourism was the most suitable economic sector to be developed in the south, as it fitted in extremely well with the strategic planning for reactivation of the south's economy. Thus, it utilized the natural resources still available for sun and sea tourism and for mountain tourism; it is a labor-intensive activity and, hence, apposite in overcoming the unemployment problem

Table 13.1 Development of the south's tourism sector: selected indicators

Indicator	1975	1990	Overall Growth (%)
No. of tourist arrivals	47 084	1 561 479	3216
Gross tourist earnings[1]	5.4	573	10 511
No. of star beds	4682	59 956	1180
Employed in the hotel sector	1070	10 000	843

[1] Cyp £ million
Source: Republic of Cyprus (1976); Republic of Cyprus (1991); CTO (1991).

mentioned above. Moreover, being an export-oriented industry it is capable of both earning large amounts of hard currency and of mobilizing the necessary financial resources, particularly from abroad, that are needed to establish both an efficient and positive business climate (Government of Cyprus, 1988). It is the high level of overlap between tourism as an economic sector, the economic needs following the partition and the available resources, which have enabled the rapid growth of this sector since the partition in 1974.

On the way towards a successful tourism development process, the government of the south managed to overcome two potential problems that cause a dependency syndrome and a loss of hard currency revenues from tourism (Pearce, 1987; Butler, 1993). Since tourism was reactivated into the south's economy, both the Republic's government and the south's Cyprus Tourism Organization, which was responsible for the implementation of tourism development plans, officially obstructed the penetration of transnational corporations into the Cypriot tourist system (*The Economist* Intelligence Unit, 1992; Ioannides, 1992). The south could afford such a policy, as millions of dollars have been pouring into this part of the island in the form of foreign aid (Katsouris, interview 1991; Inskeep, 1991). The government used part of this money as incentives (government loans and grants) for the local private sector (many of whom were Greek refugees who had been engaged in tourism in the north before the partition). Thus, tourism contributed to the reactivation of the economy while generating many jobs and at the same time ensuring that profits were not leaked out of the country as a result of transnational corporation investment in the south (Wilson, 1992).

Leakage effect was also successfully minimized for other reasons such as the ability of the hotel industry to use only local construction companies; the production of most of the degradable and non-degradable items needed for the hotel industry; the availability of a wide selection of local foods and beverages and because it was unnecessary (until recently) to import a trained work force during the tourist season. This minimized leakage effect boosted the multiplier effect and the diversification of the south's economy (Wilson, 1992).

In retrospect, the contribution of the tourism sector on the reactivation of the Republic of Cyprus's economy after the partition has been remarkable. Using various indicators, Table 13.1 illustrates these achievements in terms of annual growth rate.

It is evident from Table 13.1 that despite the short time period the south has managed not only to recover from the territorial and resource loss but to enter into an accelerated tourism development process and has eventually become one of the leading tourist resorts in the Mediterranean basin.

One would have expected the Turkish-occupied north, smaller in size and population than the south, and with excellent tourism resources, to concentrate only on tourism development. However, this has not been the case. In fact, from the early days of the newly established Turkish Cypriot territorial entity it was obvious both to locals and to the Turkish government in Ankara that North Cyprus would have to rely quite heavily on Turkish government financial support even if a new economic system were to develop. This was due to the decision by the international community to impose an economic embargo on the north because of what was considered an illegal occupation of part of the island by the Turkish Army. This economic boycott has not yet been lifted and the north became economically reliant on the mainland Turkish government. However, because of the weakness of the Turkish economy, mainland Turkey put pressure on the north to start reactivating the economy on the basis of its newly "acquired" resources (Atün interview, 1992; Örek interview, 1992).

As most of the Turkish Cypriot community in the north were farmers, the initial aim of the local authorities was to reactivate agriculture, food processing and textile manufacture. The tourism sector, meanwhile, was neglected and no breakthrough in tourism occurred until the mid-1980s (TRNC 1977, 1992; Cemal interview, 1992). Since 1977 agriculture has maintained its position as the leading economic activity, contributing one-third of the available jobs compared with 10 per cent in manufacturing, 25 per cent in public administration and less than 10 per cent in tourism and trade (TRNC, 1992).

Tourism in the north did not attain the achievements of its equivalent sector in the south, mainly due to the inability of the government to act as a real stimulus for private-sector investments; the level of tourism infrastructure is still behind European standards in most tourist facilities (Inskeep, 1991); since the international boycott on the north is strictly adhered to, foreign investors have taken hardly any risks. The international boycott means also that the north is disconnected from the international air transport system (Dilsen interview, 1992; Martin, 1993); all flights to and from the north have to stop over in Turkey. Thus, the north still attracts mostly Turkish tourists (see Figure 13.4) (Inskeep, 1991; TRNC, 1992). The economic impact of these tourists has been very limited as they do not bring hard currency into the island (the Turkish Lira is also the official currency in the North).

However, positive results of the tourism incentive law (introduced in the mid-1980s) can already be seen (Table 13.2). This comprehensive package of incentives for foreign investors attracted a number of expatriates to take the risk and invest in the north (Cemal interview, 1992). The result was a substantial rise in hard-currency revenues, and since 1986 tourism has become the dominant exporting economic sector. In fact, in US dollars the North saw a sharp rise from 1987 to 1990 as receipts from tourism more than doubled (Table 13.2).

The problem is that one of the most attractive items in the incentive package offered by the government was the opportunity to remit profits from tourism to Turkey or other countries (TRNC, 1985). Consequently, achievements in hard-currency yield from tourism are actually not as impressive as initially envisioned (Cemal interview, 1992). It looks as if until the international boycott on the north is lifted all the consequent constraints involved will result in a restrained tourism development process — far from the model characterizing similar small island countries.

Unlike the south, the incentive package offered by the north reflected its struggle to attract transnational corporations, as it was reluctant to receive any official foreign aid,

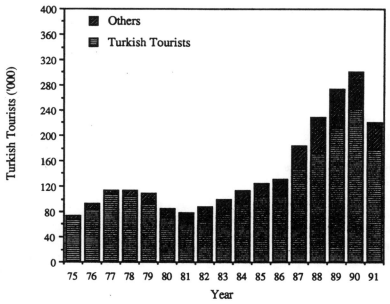

Figure 13.4 Turkish market share in total international tourist arrivals to the north, 1975–91

Table 13.2 Development of the north's tourism sector: selected indicators

Indicator	1975	1990	Overall Growth (%)
No. of tourist arrivals	74 171	300 810	305
Gross tourist earnings[1]	24.0[2]	224.8	836
No. of star beds	2952	6125	107
Employed in the hotel sector	1302[2]	3900	199

[1] US$ million, constant at 1977 prices
[2] 1980 figure; 1975 figure is not available
Source: TRNC. (1985), (1992).

either from various countries (except Turkey) or from international financial organizations (Atün, interview 1992). There were two main reasons for this situation: first, the international economic embargo imposed on the north following the Turkish occupation. With only a few exceptions, this embargo has been very well maintained by both the international community and transnational corporations. Second, the north's currency system is still totally linked to Turkey, which until the mid-1980s did not allow the conversion of Turkish Lira into hard currency in order to permit repatriation of revenues. Under these circumstances foreign investors felt reluctant to invest in an unstable country, with no independent currency system, and using continually depreciating Turkish money due to the high inflation rate in mainland Turkey. The economic hardship of the mainland Turkish government, and negative Turkish public opinion regarding

Turkey's economic aid to the occupied north, prevented its government from financing the reactivation of tourism and transforming it into the leading exporting industry (Atün interview, 1992).

Tourism — environment relations as a result of the partition

Rapid and uncontrolled tourism development in small island countries causes severe damage to such a fragile environment. This damage is further intensified if the development process is a result of reactivation of a given economy hit by war and/or terror events. It is the urgent need to rehabilitate and stabilize such an economy which leads decision makers to turn a blind eye to environmental damage emerging in the wake of tourism development (Dolman, 1985; Christodoulou, 1992; Sutton et al., 1993). The consequences of the partition of Cyprus resulted in environmental problems through the uncontrolled rapid development of the tourism sectors. Thus, the problems of water scarcity, sewage disposal, congested tourist attractions which result in air and noise pollution and landscape and architectural pollution have all been intensified since the civil war in 1974.

Having hardly any aquifers, Cyprus has always faced a major water problem. However, the partition of the island has left the government-controlled south with an even greater problem, as it lost the Morphou area which is one of the richest water sources in the island. The rapid expansion of the tourist industry in the south has increased the demand for water resources especially in tourist destinations such as Ayia Napa, Protaras and Paralimni, where water scarcity and shortage were a problem even before the massive development had begun (Matsis interview, 1992). Consequently, the government of the south constructed a water conveyor, pumping water from Paphos and the south-eastern slopes of the Trodos mountains and conveying it to Limassol and the arid East. However in 1991, after three consecutive drought years, the hotel industry found itself in a situation where the water supply to the tourist resorts in the east had to be interrupted occasionally. In other words, the severe scarcity of water due to a loss of water resources to the North should have acted as a severe constraint on tourism development. However, the urgent need to reactivate the economy caused the government of the south to ignore the water scarcity situation, thus causing an even more severe shortage of water. This shortage affected not only private consumers but also farmers and hotel owners, who faced cuts in the regular water supply with subsequent aggravation to their guests (Demetriadou interview, 1992).

Rapid tourism development aimed at rehabilitating the ruins of the south has another negative impact. Air and noise pollution caused by congestion of tourism activities have become a major problem. Cities such as Limassol and Larnaca and the compact, yet highly developed, resort of Ayia Napa face severe problems of congestion during peak tourist seasons. This is clearly a result of over development and saturation where, according to Butler (1980) and Krippendorf (1987), tourists feel threatened and squeezed into a "sardine box." When encountering such a development stage they will most probably never return to the resort, leaving the space for low-spending tourist masses whose impact on the multiplier affect is minimal yet whose contribution to further congestion is higher. If such a scenario materializes, the south will achieve the opposite of what it is aiming at, ie an upper-market clientele with a strong spending potential. Being aware of the possible negative consequences, the Cyprus Tourism Organization has launched various activities to reduce pollution in general and air and noise pollution in particular (Cyprus Tourism Organization, 1990b, 1992b). Thus, it set up a Central Coordinating Committee and Regional Tourism Coordinating Committees to promote awareness and action against environmental problems resulting from tourism activities, among them the issues of noise and air pollution. However, because of the rapid geographical expansion of the tourist sector and the area lost to the north, congestion and noise resulting from the after-effects of the war will become more and more evident.

The need to reactivate the south's economy within a very short period of time has resulted in another environmental damage — "architectural pollution" and/or "landscape pollution" as has happened in Limassol and Ayia Napa. In Limassol the whole shoreline is blocked by high-rise hotels and hotel apartments designed in a pronounced sterile international rather than local style (Christodoulou, 1992; field survey, 1992). A similar situation can also be seen in Larnaca, Paphos and Ayia Napa where many hotels sprawl along the shore obstructing the view and sea breezes (field survey, 1992). This landscape pollution has emerged despite the country's planning laws and zoning regulations which say that buildings should be erected more than 100 meters from the sea (Demetriadou interview, 1992). Only in recent years has the government managed to impose the 100-meter regulation in newly built beach resorts such as Polis in the north-west and in Pissouri, 40 kilometers west of Limassol.

Despite its poorer economic situation as a result of the civil war, the Turkish-occupied north has not yet reached such a level of environmental pressure. Water availability, for example, has not acted as a constraint to further tourism development (Sadi interview, 1992). This is mainly because of a decline in agricultural activities as compared to the pre-1974 period and the relatively low demand for tourism as compared to the south. Thus, the Kyrenia region gets its water from several mountain springs which can ensure a steady supply, even if further tourism development takes place. However, in the Famagusta — Bohgaz region the situation is more complicated as the availability of good quality water is more scarce. Although in the north water is still not a major problem, it is interesting to note that planning decisions on where to locate new tourist facilities (mainly hotels), and on their size, do not take into account the future demand for water by the tourist sector versus the water capacity of the available reservoirs (Cemal interview, 1992).

While in the south air and noise pollution resulting from the intense concentration of tourism activities are already a major problem, this is not the case in the north, due to the low level of tourism activities (Burton, 1991). The only congested place in the north is the capital Lefkosa (the northern part of old Nicosia); however this town is never overcrowded with tourists, who only travel through it as part of their regular tour of the north and usually do not stay overnight (TRNC, 1992; field survey, 1992).

With regard to landscape pollution, it appears that the north is less strict about planning regulations which are aimed at preserving the view and the landscape. Thus, although zoning regulations exist also in the north (where the planning regulation system which existed before the partition has been maintained), on this side of the island the minimum required distance for location of hotels and other tourism accommodation facilities is only 50 meters from the shoreline. Hoteliers are also not allowed to build more than 300 rooms per hotel (Kuchuk interview, 1992), but these regulations are not strictly adhered to (field survey, 1992). At the present time, conflicting land uses have not been observed.

However, when the new power plant 40 kilometers east of Kyrenia begins operating, there will be problems of air and sea pollution which will affect tourists in neighboring resorts (field survey, 1992). Kyrenia has already faced much criticism, by environmentalists and tourists alike, who claim it will grow into the same "tourist monster," called Ayia Napa, in the south. Therefore, northern administration is seriously considering stopping any further tourism development along the Kyrenia shore (Cemal interview, 1992). Whether this policy will be maintained when and if international money pours into the economically boycotted north remains to be seen.

To summarize the environmental issue, it would appear, in both parts of the island, that given the need to reactivate and develop the economy on the one hand, and by ignoring the fact that the environment is a major tourist resource on the other, environmental degradation has been the ultimate result. However, the current imprint of this degradation differs between the two parts as a result of their different tourism development stage. In the south, environmental damage is already evident and in many cases is irreversible. In the north, because of its low level of development as a result of the international economic embargo, environmental damage is not yet causing problems. However, the government of the north prefers to turn a blind eye as the south did during the boom years of its tourism development. This is due to the lack of financial resources to monitor and maintain the environment. Such a policy is typical of small island countries which are desperate to generate hard-currency receipts but, at the same time, more distinct in countries which desperately need this money to overcome the economic impacts of civil war and international boycott.

Summary and conclusions

This chapter analyzed the evolving tourist landscape of Cyprus since its partition in 1974. The impact of the civil war between Turkish and Greek Cypriots has left a different imprint on the tourism industry of the government-controlled south versus the Turkish-occupied north. It is well documented in the literature that tourism systems in small island countries are subject to a combination of constraints which shape a unique model of tourism development. The case of Cyprus represents a combination of these constraints and the impacts of the civil war. Thus, different war impacts yielded a different tourism landscape in each part of the island.

The current chapter examined the impact of the war and the consequent partition of Cyprus on its tourism landscape using three different issues: the effect of size changes on the tourism system; the effect of economic reactivation and rehabilitation on the tourist landscape; and the environmental consequences of a rapid and uncontrolled tourism development while seeking economic balances. The analysis of the issue of size effects shows that in the south a territorial loss combined with loss of existing tourist resources led to rapid redevelopment of the tourist sector relocated in coastal and mountain areas. The north, on the other hand, gained new territory and highly developed resorts but these did not lead to economic success due to the characteristics of the local population, the closure of the resort of Varosha by the Turkish Army and the economic boycott by the international community which deterred tourists other than Turks from visiting this part of the island until the mid-1980s.

International economic aid, poured into the government-controlled south in the first decade after the partition, enabled a rapid economic recovery. Apparently the unique characteristics of tourism have turned it into one of the leading economic activities which helped Cyprus in its urgent search for economic recovery. On the other hand, the north's economy has been reluctant to use tourism as a major catalyst of economic recovery because of the international boycott and its over-dependency on the economically fragile Turkish market. Thanks to the peace talks between the two communities in recent years, the north has managed to attract tourists from Europe and not just from mainland Turkey. This has boosted a tourism development process which is, to a large extent, still constrained by the economic outcome of the 1974 war. However, in the north, one can already detect signs of a tourism development process which will imitate the model observed in the south. In other words, instead of avoiding the mistakes of uncontrolled tourism development while in search of economic rehabilitation, the Turks are adopting a short-sighted development policy. Such a policy ignores the "boomerang" economic effect of uncontrolled development as well as the irreversible damage to the physical environment while seeking economic independence.

One aspect of the impact of war on the tourist landscape which has not been discussed here with respect to Cyprus is the "military landscape" and the way it is perceived by tourists. Our initial observation of this aspect in Cyprus shows that in the south the military landscape resulting from the conflict, and particularly the Attila line and its military installations in Nicosia, has become a tourist attraction. By exposing tourists to the physical dimension of this conflict, the Greek Cypriots hope to gain more political sympathy with their struggle for reunification of the island. Our observation of the north is totally different. The Turkish Cypriots want to veil the military landscape and to promote a "business as usual" atmosphere in the tourists resorts. However, this is not easily achieved as the Turkish army has been deployed over the years all over the Turkish part, with no consideration to the negative impression this might convey to potential tourists from Europe. Our personal feelings were that this part of the island is a danger rather than a pleasure zone. Therefore, it is suggested that further research attention should be given to the way evolving tourist landscapes in attractions hit by war are perceived by tourists. Such research is extremely important as an input for marketing policies aimed at selling tourist attractions located in conflict areas.

References

Andronicou, A. (1979). Tourism in Cyprus. In De Kadt, E. (ed.), *Tourism Passport to Development*. London: Oxford University Press, 237–64.

Andronicou, A., (1987). *Development of Tourism in Cyprus: Harmonisation of Tourism with the Environment*. Nicosia: Cosmos.

Attalides, M.A. (ed.) (1977). *Cyprus Reviewed*. Nicosia: The Jus Cypri Association.

Bryant, R.L. (1992). Political ecology — an emerging research agenda in third-world studies. *Political Geography*, **11**: 12–36.

Burton, R. (1991). *Travel Geography*, London: Pitman.

Butler, R.W. (1980). The concept of tourist area cycle evolution: Implications for management of resources. *Canadian Geographer*, **14**: 5–12.

Butler, R.W. (1993). Tourism development in small islands — past influences and future directions. In: Lockhart, D.G., Drakakis-Smith, D. and Schembri, J. (eds), *The Development Process in Small Island States*. London and New York: Routledge, 71–91.

Christodoulou, D. (1992). *Inside the Cyprus Miracle — The Labors of an Embattled Economy*. Minnesota Mediterranean and East European Monographs. Minneapolis: University of Minnesota.

Cyprus Tourism Organization (1977). *Annual Report 1976*. Nicosia: CTO.

Cyprus Tourism Organization (CTO) (1980). *Annual Report 1979*. Nicosia: CTO.

Cyprus Tourism Organization (1990a). *Annual Report 1989*. Nicosia: CTO.

Cyprus Tourism Organization (1990b). *Tourism in Cyprus 1990*. Nicosia: CTO.

Cyprus Tourism Organization (1991). *Tourism in Cyprus 1991*. Nicosia: CTO.

Cyprus Tourism Organization (1992a). *Tourist Survey*. Planning and Organization Department. Nicosia: CTO.

Cyprus Tourism Organization (1992b). *Annual Report 1991*. Nicosia: CTO.

Dodd, C.H. (1993). Historical introduction. In Dodd, C.H. (ed.), *The Political, Social and Economic Development of Northern Cyprus*. Huntingdon: The Eothen Press, 1–14.

Dolman, A.J. (1985). Paradise lost. In Dommen, E. and Hein, P. (eds), *States, Microstates and Islands*. London: Croom Helm.

The Economist Intelligence Unit (1992). *International Tourism Report — Cyprus*. London: EIU.

Government of Cyprus (1961). *Five Year Plan for Economic and Social Development — 1961–1966*. Nicosia: State Planning Bureau.

Government of Cyprus (1988). *Financing and Development: a Case Study of the Republic of Cyprus*. Paper presented at the meeting of Commonwealth Finance Ministers, Cyprus, September 20–2, 1988.

Gunn, C.A. (1988). *Tourism Planning*. Second Edition. New York: Taylor & Francis.

Hall, C.M. (1994). *Tourism and Politics: Policy, Power and Place*. Chichester: John Wiley & Sons.

Inskeep, E. (1991). *Tourism Planning — An Integrated and Sustainable Development Approach*. New York: Van Nostrand Reinhold.

Ioannides, D. (1992). Tourism development agents: the Cypriot resort cycle. *Annals of Tourism Research*. **19**: 711–31.

Kammas, M. (1991). Tourism development in Cyprus. *The Cyprus Review*. **3**(2): 7–26.

Kammas, M. (1992). Smallness, Economic development and Cyprus. *The Cyprus Review*. **4**(1): 65–76.

King, J.M.C. (1984). The air traffic market and tourism: Some thoughts on the South Pacific. In Kissling, C. (ed.), *Transport and Communications for Pacific Microstates*. Western Samoa: Institute of Pacific Studies, University of South Pacific, 113–23.

Kitromilides, P.M. (1977). From coexistence to confrontation: the dynamics of ethnic conflict in Cyprus. In Attalides, M.A. (ed.), *Cyprus Reviewed*. Nicosia: The Jus Cypri Association.

Kliot, N. and Mansfeld, Y. (1995). Resettling displaced people in North and South Cyprus: a comparison. *Journal of Refugee Studies*. (Forthcoming).

Krippendorf, J. (1987). *The Holiday Makers*. London: Heinemann.

Lockhart, D.G. (1993). Tourism and politics — The example of Cyprus. In Lockhart, D.G., Drakakis-Smith, D. and Schembri, J. (eds), *The Development Process in Small Island States*. London and New York: Routledge, 228–246.

Lockhart, D.G. and Ashton, S. (1990). Tourism to Northern Cyprus. *Geography*. **75**: 163–7.

Martin, J. (1993). The history and development of tourism. In Dodd, C.H. (ed.), *The Political, Social and Economic Development of Northern Cyprus*. Huntingdon: The Eothen Press, 335–72.

Pearce, D. (1978). Form and function in French resorts. *Annals of Tourism Research*. **15**: 142–56.

Pearce, D. (1987). *Tourism Today: A Geographical Analysis*. New York: Longman.

Pearce, D. (1989). *Tourist Development*. Second Edition. Harlow: Longman.

Poon, M. (1988). The future of Caribbean tourism: A matter of innovation. *Tourism Management*. **9**: 213–20.

Republic of Cyprus (1976). *Second Emergency Economic Action Plan 1977–1978*. Nicosia: Planning Bureau, Planning Commission.

Republic of Cyprus (1991). *Statistical Abstract 1989 & 1990*. Nicosia: Department of Statistics and Research, Ministry of Finance.

Republic of Cyprus (1992). *Statistical Abstract 1990 & 1991*. Nicosia: Department of Statistics and Research, Ministry of Finance.

Sutton, S.T., Delvin, P.J. and Simmons, D.G. (1993). Kapati Island, a natural area in demand: Assessing social impacts. *Geojournal*. **29**: 253−62.

Symeonides, N.S. (1977). The unity of the economy and the economics of separation. In Attalides, M.A. (ed.), *Cyprus Reviewed*. Nicosia: The Jus Cypri Association.

Tinsley, J.F. (1979). Tourism in the Virgin Islands. In Holder, J.S. (ed.), *Caribbean Tourism: Policies and Impacts*. Christ Church, Barbados: Caribbean Tourism Research and Development Centre, 295−316.

Turkish Republic of Northern Cyprus (TRNC) (1977). *The Five Year Development Plan (1978−1982)*. Lefkosa: TRNC, Prime Ministry, State Planning Organization.

Turkish Republic of Northern Cyprus (1985). *A Brief Outline of the Tourism Sector in the Turkish Republic of Northern Cyprus*. Lefkosa: Ministry of Communications, Public Works and Tourism.

Turkish Republic of Northern Cyprus (1991). *Economic Development in the Turkish Republic of Northern Cyprus (1986−1990)*. Lefkosa: Prime Ministry, State Planning Organization.

Turkish Republic of Northern Cyprus (1992). *Tourism Statistics*. Lefkosa: Tourism Planning Office.

Wilkinson, P.F. (1988). *Tourism in Island Microstates: Bibliography*, Monticello, Illinois: Public Administration Series, Bibliography P2504, Vance Bibliographies.

Wilkinson, P.F. (1989). Strategies for tourism in island microstates. *Annals of Tourism Research*. **16**: 153−77.

Wilson, R. (1992). *Cyprus and the International Economy*. New York: St. Martin's Press.

Winpenney, J.T. (1982). Issues in the identification and appraisal of tourism projects in developing countries. *Tourism Management*. 3: 218−21.

Witt, S.F. (1991). Tourism in Cyprus: Balancing the benefits and costs. *Tourism Management*. 12: 37−46.

Zetter, R. (1992). Refugees and forced migrants as development resources: The Greek Cypriot refugees from 1974. *Cyprus Review*. 3(2): 7−39.

14 Does tourism promote peace and understanding between unfriendly nations?

ABRAHAM PIZAM

The following chapter reports on a set of four empirical studies intended to evaluate the contribution of tourism to better understanding among unfriendly nations. The impetus for these studies was the organization of an international conference on "Tourism — A Vital Force for Peace," held in Vancouver, Canada, in October 1988 (D'Amore, 1988a; 1988b). This conference advanced the idea that tourism results in positive changes in the attitudes of tourists towards their hosts and ultimately contributes to world peace (D'Amore, 1987−8; D'Amore and Jafari, 1989). The popular proposition was that there "is no better bridge between people, ideas, ideologies and culture than travel" and that "tourism in its broadest sense, can do a lot to develop understanding among people" (quoted in Brayley and Var, 1989: 578). The authors of the above four studies recognized that tourism *may* lead to positive change in attitudes and ultimately improve understanding among unfriendly nations. But based on the results of a limited number of existing empirical studies, they acknowledged that tourism could also cause a negative change in attitudes and consequently result in worsening relationships (Bystrzanowski, 1989; Dogan, 1989; Evans-Prichard, 1989). Therefore they decided to test this proposition empirically and under strict experimental conditions.

The four studies reported here evaluated the role of tourism as an agent of change between pairs of countries that have been traditionally unfriendly or hostile to each other and analyzed tourism's potential contribution to the reduction of negative ethnic attitudes. These studies analyzed the effect of tourism on the change in attitudes of American tourists visiting the USSR (Pizam et al. 1991), Israeli tourists visiting Egypt (Milman et al. 1990), Greek tourists visiting Turkey (Anastasopoulos, 1992) and Turkish tourists visiting Greece (Anastasopoulos et al. 1994). The common research question for all the above studies called for investigating whether the tourist experience, and consequently the contact between citizens of unfriendly nations, reduced intergroup prejudice, conflict, and tension.

The studies hypothesized that:

1. The tourist experience will improve the ethnic negative attitudes that tourists have of their hosts.

Tourism, Crime and International Security Issues, edited by
A. Pizam and Y. Mansfeld. © 1996 John Wiley & Sons Ltd.

2. The tourist experience will lead to a reduction in the perceived differences between tourists and hosts, people who have been traditionally hostile to each other.

These hypotheses were derived from the "contact model" of the social psychology of intergroup conflict. The contact model is based on the belief that:

> intergroup contact will lead to a change in mutual attitudes and relations of the interacting members. Underlying this belief is the assumption that contact among individuals from diverse groups creates an opportunity for mutual acquaintance, enhances understanding and acceptance among the interaction group members, and consequently reduces intergroup prejudice, conflict, and tension (Amir and Ben Ari, 1988; Allport, 1954; Cook, 1962).

The application of the contact model to tourism situations contends that during contact between tourists and hosts of diverse or conflicting groups, members of one group may discover new positive information about the members of the other group and therefore change their perceptions of them.

Attitude change through tourism

The question of attitude change and intercultural understanding through tourism has been investigated in the past. Several studies have examined the influence of travel or sojourn on students (Pearce, 1982b: 209; Weiler, 1989). Carlson and Widaman (1988), for example, explored potential shifts in international understanding of American students studying for their junior college year in another country. Their study revealed that the sample and control groups had:

> essentially identical attitudes on all of the attitudinal dimensions assessed prior to their trip . . . the only major difference in attitudes arose after the students' junior year . . . the study abroad group showing higher level of international political concern, cross cultural interest, and cultural cosmopolitanism than the comparison group. In addition, students who studied abroad reported significantly more positive, yet also more critical attitudes toward their own country than did the control group (1988: 13).

Welds and Dukes studied influence of a "Semester at Sea" program on the student participants. They surveyed the participants' attitudes before and after the trip and compared the data with those collected from a control group who did not take the trip. The comparison revealed that participants had been positively influenced, with more accommodating attitudes towards the host they had visited. It is, however, important to note that the student travel programs differed from those for tourists: activities included cultural events, home visits, sightseeing and other opportunities for face-to-face interaction with people who live in the countries visited (Welds and Dukes, 1985: 114). Such programs normally prepare the participants for the trip. Further, during the stay, they are carefully guided through the exposure and encounters and are often asked to contemplate or discuss their experience.

H. Smith (1957) studied the effects of intercultural contact on young Americans who spent a summer in Europe. In like manner, this study included pre- and post-trip questionnaires. Similar to Welds and Dukes' (1985) study, Smith's comparison of the data again revealed some attitudinal change in the response supplied by the participants.

Weiler (1989) studied groups of Japanese summer students in Canada whose sojourns were "for the combined purposes of English learning, cross-cultural experience, and pleasure travel." Although the study featured methodological considerations of this type of touristic cross-cultural contact, the focus was "on changes in belief and attitude with respect to the destination," finally suggesting that the Japanese participants' perception had somewhat changed (1989: 304, 307). Still another study dealt with "how a sample of Argentinian university students perceived the socioeconomic and environmental impacts of tourism and whether or not these students shared the sentiments that tourism enhanced world peace and international understanding." The study found that the participants viewed tourism favorably and were "aware of its potential for fostering international understanding and world peace" (Var et al. 1989: 431−43).

Adult tourists have also been studied for their attitude change. Grothe's (1970) study involved investigating attitude change of Americans visiting the Soviet Union. His survey of the tourists, which included both pre- and post-travel questionnaires, shows that most of the respondents went to the USSR with an attitude somewhat positive towards the host but negative towards the Soviet government and system. They returned home even more positive about the host and more negative about the government (on the latter, see Wattenberg, 1987). In other words, the "people-good, government-bad" dichotomy was greater after than before the trip. People, far more than any other aspects of the Soviet Union, were liked most by the respondents. Pearce's (1982a) research was on small samples of tourists visiting Greece and Morocco. His purpose was to investigate whether their post-travel image of the countries visited differed from their pre-trip image. He found that tourists can "modify their perceptions of their hosts" (1982b: 215).

Social contact as a means of changing negative ethnic attitudes was studied extensively by Y. Amir and colleagues, both within Israel (Amir and Garti, 1977; Amir and Ben-Ari, 1988; Ben-Ari and Amir, 1988b) and between Israel and Egypt (Amir and Ben-Ari, 1985; Ben-Ari and Amir, 1988a). In a series of studies on Israeli tourists visiting Egypt, the authors attempted to evaluate cognitive interventions aimed at improving relations between Israelis and Egyptians. Their findings indicate that contact provided by tourism alone did not produce a positive attitudinal change.

In order to grasp the positive and negative aspects of the host and guest interaction, it is important that the subject of attitude change is viewed both in respect to specific questions and general context. For example, attitude change becomes more meaningful if examined as to its *type* and *degree*, that is, what type of attitudes are changed and to what degree. To enlarge on this point, both type and degree of change are rooted in the initial attitudes held prior to the exposure (M. Smith, 1947−8; Walsh, 1944−5). Grothe's (1970) research reveals that the tourist finds what he expects to see. For example, if the tourist expects a friendly host, he will in fact return home considerably more positive than the one who expected an indifferent or even hostile host. Pearce's findings also support the position that "travelers' initial confidence in their beliefs influenced the changes which occurred, since the beliefs which were mostly likely changed were those which were held less confidently" (1982b: 212−13). In the same manner, "deeply rooted attitudes were not affected by travel experience" (H. Smith, 1957).

Methodology

Sampling

Each of the four studies was composed of an experimental group — first-time tourists visiting one of the four destinations, and a control group, residents of the origin country who did not visit the destinations.

In the case of Israelis visiting Egypt the experimental group consisted of a sample of 82 Jewish—Israeli tourists who traveled to Egypt during the months of March—May 1988. Subjects were sampled at random on escorted bus tours to Egypt that lasted one week. The control group consisted of 41 Jewish—Israeli citizens who did not travel to Egypt. These individuals were randomly selected subjects residing in the cities of Tel-Aviv and Beer-Sheva.

The experimental sample for the American students who traveled to the Soviet Union consisted of 24 University of Wisconsin students who traveled to the Soviet Union for the first time. The control group was composed of 38 University of Wisconsin students, taking a section of the "Introduction to Tourism" course at the University of Wisconsin-Stout. Since little information was available on the exact profile of the experimental group, the University of Wisconsin system tour coordinator's remarks (personal communication) were considered when selecting the control group. The instructor of the course (one of the authors of the study) told the students about the research project and its purpose in very general terms but without going into details.

The study of Greek tourists traveling to Turkey consisted of 97 first-time Greek travelers visiting Turkey (experimental group) and 82 Greek citizens who remained in Greece (control group). The one-week escorted bus tour originated in Athens and the final destination was Istanbul and its surrounding vicinity. The survey was conducted during the months of December 1990 to May 1991.

In the case of Turkish tourists visiting Greece, the experimental group consisted of 56 first-time travelers on escorted bus tours to Greece, and the control group consisted of 42 Turkish citizens who remained in Turkey. The survey was conducted during the months of February 1991 to May 1992 and the trip was of one week's duration.

Method of administration

Each experimental and control group was surveyed twice, once before the experimental group left for the destination (pre-test) and again upon the group's return home (post-test). A coordinated effort was made so that the pre-test and post-test were distributed to both the experimental and control groups at approximately the same period of time. The rationale of involving a control group was for the purpose of detecting factors which, although unrelated to the trip, may have influenced public opinion and, consequently, the attitudes of the traveling group.

Research instrument

Subjects in both the experimental and control groups were asked to complete a structured questionnaire that measured attitudes towards the people of the destination countries,

Table 14.1 Opinions about (Egyptian, Soviet, Turkish, Greek) people

[1]	Coldhearted	[7]	Warmhearted
[1]	Awful	[7]	Nice
[1]	War loving	[7]	Peace loving
[1]	Old fashioned	[7]	Modern
[1]	Cruel	[7]	Kind
[1]	Bad	[7]	Good
[1]	Boastful	[7]	Modest
[1]	Tense	[7]	Relaxed
[1]	Dishonest	[7]	Honest
[1]	Unfriendly	[7]	Friendly
[1]	Weak	[7]	Powerful
[1]	Aggressive	[7]	Submissive
[1]	Unreliable	[7]	Reliable
[1]	Rigid	[7]	Flexible
[1]	Stupid	[7]	Intelligent
[1]	Lazy	[7]	Hard working
[1]	Not at all me	[7]	Like myself
[1]	Illiterate	[7]	Educated
[1]	Dirty	[7]	Clean
[1]	Slow	[7]	Fast
[1]	Discriminate against women	[7]	Egalitarian

Key: 1 to 7 scale; 1 = negative, 7 = positive

Table 14.2 Opinions on (Egyptian, Soviet, Turkish, Greek) political beliefs

1. Egyptians believe that the establishment of the Jewish State violates the right of the Palestinian Arabs to self-determination.
2. Egyptians/Soviets/Turks/Greeks believe that Israel/USA/Greece/Turkey has no right to exist.
3. Egyptians believe that the peace treaty is just a scrap of paper.
4. Egyptians/Soviets/Turks/Greeks hate Israelis/Americans/Greeks/Turks.
5. Soviets love their country and its political system.
6. Soviets believe that the USA wants to dominate the world.
7. The Turks/Greeks believe the Greeks/Turks want to dominate the entire Aegean Sea.

Key: 1 = Strongly disagree; 2 = Disagree; 3 = Neither agree nor disagree; 4 = Agree; 5 = Strongly agree

their political beliefs and their institutions. The majority of the items in the questionnaire were designed by using a series of adjectives listed in Semantic Differential form (see Table 14.1) and the remaining were statements formulated in Likert format (Tables 14.2–14.4). The Semantic Differential is a well-accepted and reliable method of measuring attitudes (Osgood et al. 1954; Snider and Osgood, 1969). In this technique each concept is measured on a bipolar adjectival scale, usually with seven points. Factor-analytic studies over many pairs of bipolar adjectives and using subjects from several countries have shown that the scales in the Semantic Differential rather consistently reflect three major underlying dimensions. An evaluative dimension (ie, good−bad; clean−dirty), an activity dimension (ie, fast−slow; active−passive) and potency (ie,

Table 14.3 Opinions about life in (Egypt, USSR, Turkey, Greece) compared to life in (Israel, USA, Greece, Turkey)

---

1. Overall rating of Egypt/USSR/Turkey/Greece[a]
2. Compared to Israel/USA/Greece/Turkey, Egypt/USSR/Turkey/Greece[b]
   a. Life in general
   b. Level of education
   c. Quality of arts, letters and music
   d. Quality of life
   e. Standard of living

Key: [a] 1 to 7 scale, 1 = very negative, 7 = very positive
[b] 1 to 7 scale, 1 = very inferior, 7 = very superior

Table 14.4 Opinions on (Egyptian, Soviet, Turkish, Greek) institutions

---

1. Egypt/USSR/Turkey/Greece is a modern country in terms of research and science.
2. The Egyptian/Soviet/Turkish/Greek government takes care of the economic welfare of its residents.
3. The Egyptian/Soviet/Turkish/Greek government system is not democratic.
4. Egyptian/Soviet/Turkish/Greek government officials are corrupt.
5. The Egyptian/Soviet/Turkish/Greek economy is very healthy and stable.
6. Egyptians are anti-Jewish.
7. In the USSR there is no freedom of speech.
8. Gorbachev's policy of *Glasnost* (openness) is 'just a public relations trick for Western consumption.'
9. The Soviet governmental system is bureaucratic and inefficient.
10. The USSR's major goal is to spread world communism.
11. The Soviet people have freedom of religion.

Key: 1 = Strongly disagree; 2 = Disagree; 3 = Neither agree nor disagree; 4 = Agree; 5 = Strongly agree

strong—weak; hard—soft) (Rossi et al. 1983). With few exceptions, the attitudinal dimensions for all four studies were identical and were selected on the basis of previous research conducted in this field by Grothe (1970) and Amir and Ben-Ari (1985).

Results

The Impact of the tourist experience on the trip takers

In order to test the hypotheses previously stated, it was necessary to examine whether the opinions of the trip takers about their hosts, their political beliefs and their institutions changed significantly as a result of the tourist experience. To confirm that these changes were attributed to the tourist experience and not to other exogenous events (such as a deterioration in the relations between the two countries that occurred between the administration of the first questionnaire and the second one), a series of t-tests were conducted between the pre-test and post-test of the control groups. The results showed no statistically significant differences between the pre-test and post-test opinions of any of the control groups. Therefore it was valid to assume that any significant difference found between the pre-test and post-test of the experimental groups (the trip takers) could be attributed to their tourist experience.

Israelis visiting Egypt   First, the experiences that the Israeli tourists encountered did not change their opinions and attitudes towards the Egyptian people and their institutions, in a positive direction. Overall, out of 33 attitudinal statements only six (18 per cent) show a change as a result of the tourist experience. Of those, only one changed in a positive direction while the remaining five changed in a negative direction. Israeli tourists who returned from Egypt thought that Egyptians were more relaxed than they had believed before their journey. However, Egyptians were perceived to be slower than before the encounter with them. The tourist experience worsened the perception of Israeli tourists of Egyptian political beliefs and institutions. Israelis who came back from Egypt had a more negative opinion of the role of the Egyptian government in caring for its residents' welfare, the stability and health of the Egyptian economy and Egypt's level of modernization.

Second, the tourist experience did not lead to any statistically significant reduction of perceived differences between Israelis and Egyptians. Third, Israelis who returned from Egypt perceived Egypt to be even more inferior to Israel than they perceived before leaving for Egypt.

Americans visiting the USSR   The hypothesis that "the Soviet tourist experience will change the ethnic negative attitudes of American tourists who visit the USSR" was not confirmed. This conclusion was reached because in the majority of the items (36 out of 41) no changes in opinions and attitudes occurred as a result of the tourist experience. Furthermore, out of the five items that had an opinion change only two were positive changes and the remaining three were negative changes.

American students who returned from the Soviet Union changed their opinions in a positive direction in two dimensions. They thought that the Soviets were more reliable and agreed less with the statement that "the Soviets believe that the US wants to dominate the world" than they thought before they went to the USSR.

In addition, three negative changes occurred as a result of the trip. Students who returned from the Soviet Union thought that the Soviets were less clean than they thought before the trip, and agreed less with the statement that "the Soviet government takes care of the economic welfare of its residents." Furthermore, at the conclusion of the trip students thought that "life in general in the Soviet Union was more inferior to the US than they thought before going on the trip."

Greeks traveling to Turkey   The major conclusion of this study was that travel to Turkey had affected the Greek travelers' attitudes towards the Turkish people, their country and its institutions. The Greek travelers changed their attitudes and opinions relating to the Turkish people and their institutions in 33 out of 36 (92 per cent) variables. Out of these 33 changes only one was in the positive direction while the remaining 32 were in the negative direction.

The only positive change that occurred as a result of the trip was that the Greek tourists disagreed with the statement suggesting that the Turks believe that the "Greeks want to dominate the entire Aegean Sea.'' This was in contrast to their pre-trip opinion which appeared undecided on this same issue.

Turks traveling to Greece   A comparison between the mean scores of the pre-trip and post-trip opinions and attitudes of Turkish people towards Greece and its people indicated only a negligible attitude change as a result of the trip. In 33 out of the 36 opinions and attitudes, there were no significant changes resulting from the trip. The only three notable changes — two positive and one negative — were that after the trip, the Turkish travelers found the Greek people to be more relaxed, less hard working and have a higher quality of arts and letters than they thought before the trip.

Cumulative results   When combining the results of the four studies it becomes obvious that for the most part, the tourist experience had only a minor effect on the perceptions, attitudes and opinions of the travelers. Out of the total of 141 opinions, only 47 (33.3 per cent) changed as a result of the trip experience. Of these, 37 (78.7 per cent) changed in a negative direction and the remaining 10 (21.3 per cent) in a positive direction.

Discussion and conclusions

The cumulative findings of the four studies showed only a relatively small number of changes in the opinions and attitudes of travelers resulting from their tourist experience. More importantly they showed that the majority of changes occurred in a negative direction. *Does this mean that tourism does not influence people's opinions of each other, nor does it bring them closer to each other?*

Following the results of these studies our speculation is that by itself, tourism does not automatically contribute to positive attitudinal changes nor to the reduction of perceived ethnic and nationality differences. It is obvious that some tourist experiences may not affect attitudinal changes at all, others may affect them in a positive direction, while a third type may reinforce existing negative opinions or even change positive ones to negative.

Going back to the literature on intergroup relations in general and tourist—host relations in particular, it is obvious that contact does not always result in positive change in ethnic attitudes and relations. Brewer (1984) in an article describing the results of American tourism to a Mexican town came to the conclusion that:

> Of most importance, this study indicates that not only is communication between native and tourist small, but also that native—tourist interactions themselves generate distortions of understanding ... Contrary to the travel literature promoting international tourism (Turner and Ash, 1975), tourism may well lead to greater rather than lesser problems of understanding between people (Brewer, 1984: 501).

Amir (1969, 1976) and Cook (1970) summarized the research results in this area and came to the conclusion that in order to achieve positive changes in ethnic relations certain conditions must be present in contact situations; other conditions may lead to negative results. The most important conditions for positive changes were suggested to be:

1. Equal-status contact between the members of the interacting group.
2. Intergroup cooperation in the pursuit of common goals; this creates an interdependence between the groups and discourages competition between them.
3. Contact of intimate rather than casual nature which allows the interacting members to get to know each other beyond the superficial level.
4. An 'authority' and/or social climate approving of and supporting the intergroup contact.
5. The initial intergroup attitudes are not extremely negative. (Amir and Ben-Ari, 1988).

It is maintained here that for the experiences described, in all four cases conditions 1−4 were not present. By definition, the contact between tourists and hosts on escorted bus tours is not perceived to be between people of an equal status; on these tours the contact with the host population is limited to tourism occupations. For most tourists on such tours the only local people they meet are tour guides, bus drivers, shop-keepers, waiters, hotel employees etc., all "living off" the tourist trade and interested in "good tips." This stimulates the sensation that the locals are "servers" and therefore of lower status.

Second, the contact and the type of tourist experience on escorted tours is limited to casual rather than intimate interaction between tourists and hosts. In all four cases the escorted tours did not provide real opportunities to interact with the local people for any length of time, and form significant opinions about their feelings, wants and needs, satisfactions and dissatisfactions, political beliefs etc. Third, in the cases of Israel−Egypt and Greece−Turkey the political climate was not very favorable (because of previous incidents). None of the four governments showed signs of encouraging or promoting social contact at grassroots level. Last, but not least, two of the escorted bus tours (Egypt and Turkey) emphasized the ancient and Middle-Eastern aspects of the destinations. The trip included visits to bazaars, peddlers' shops, crowded and unclean streets inhabited by beggars and other attractions typical of a "non-modern" society. Under such conditions it is little wonder that these tourists came to the conclusion that Egypt and Turkey are not modern countries, their economies not very healthy and their governments do not take care of the welfare of their people.

In conclusion, the four studies found that escorted bus tours cannot be considered a means for changing people's negative attitudes towards each other and therefore indirectly promoting peace among hostile or unfriendly nations. As previously indicated, only when certain conditions are met, such as a balanced tourist experience including opportunities to come into close and intimate contact with the destination's residents, can this occur. Unfortunately these conditions cannot be met by typical escorted bus tours.

The author is in agreement with all those who suggest that tourism in general *may* have the potential for becoming an instrument for the promotion of cultural understanding, leading ultimately to harmony among people. Furthermore, he supports the third paragraph of the Shannon Declaration which states that "international tourism is a particularly appropriate instrument for the development of peace building programs designed to reduce conflict." However, the premise that tourism in all its forms and manifestations will necessarily cause "good will and understanding" among people is unacceptable. For this to occur, careful planning and programming with regard to both the generating and the destination countries is required. "Tourism, by itself, neither leads to automatic prejudice reduction nor facilitates improvements in social relationships.

Tourism simply provides the opportunity for the social contact to occur" (Anastasopou-los, 1992).

References

Allport, G.W. (1954). *The Nature of Prejudice*. Cambridge MA: Addison-Wesley.

Amir, Y. (1969). Contact hypothesis in ethnic relations. *Psychological Bulletin*, **71**, 319−42.

Amir, Y. (1976). The role of intergroup contact in change of prejudice and ethnic relations. In P.A. Katz (ed.), *Towards the Elimination of Racism*. New York: Pergamon Press.

Amir, Y. and Garti, C. (1977). Situational and personal influences on attitude change. *International Journal of Intercultural Relations*, **1**: 58−75.

Amir, Y. and Ben-Ari, R. (1985). International tourism, ethnic contact, and attitude change. *Journal of Social Issues*, **41** (34): 105−15.

Amir, Y. and Ben-Ari, R. (1988). Enhancing intergroup relations in Israel: A differential approach. In D. Barkai et al. (eds), *Stereotyping and Prejudice: Changing Perceptions*. Berlin: Springer-Verlag.

Anastasopoulos, P.G. (1992). Tourism and attitude change: Greek tourists visiting Turkey. *Annals of Tourism Research*, **19** (4): 629−42.

Anastasopoulos, P.G., Korzay, M., Pizam, A. and Var, T. (1994). *Influence of Tourism on Attitude Change: Turkish Tourists Visiting Greece*. Paper presented at the 1994 CHRIE conference, Palm Springs, CA, July 27−30.

Ben-Ari, R. and Amir, Y. (1988a). Intergroup contact, cultural information, and change in ethnic attitudes. In W. Stroebe, A.W. Kruglanski, D. Bar-Tal and M. Hewston (eds), *The Social Psychology of Intergroup Conflict: Theory, Research and Application*. Berlin: Springer-Verlag.

Ben-Ari, R. and Amir, Y. (1988b). Promoting relations between Arab and Jewish Youth. In J.E. Hoffman et al. (eds), *Arab-Jewish Relations in Israel: A Quest in Human Understanding*. New York: Wyndham Hall Press.

Brayley, Russ, and Var, Turgut (1989). Canadian perceptions of tourism's influence on economic and social conditions. *Annals of Tourism Research*, **16** (4): 578−82.

Brewer, Jeffrey D. (1984). Tourism and ethnic stereotypes: Variations in a Mexican town. *Annals of Tourism Research*, **13**: 487−501.

Bystrzanowski, Julian (ed.) (1989). *Tourism as a Factor of Change: A Sociocultural Study*. Vienna: European Coordination Centre for Research and Documentation in Social Sciences.

Carlson, Jerry and Widaman, Keith (1988). The effects of study abroad during college on attitudes toward other cultures. *International Journal of Intercultural Relations* **12** (1): 1−127.

Cook, S.W. (1962). The systematic analysis of socially significant events: A strategy for social research. *Journal of Social Issues*, **18**: 66−84.

Cook, S.W. (1970). Motives in a conceptual analysis of attitude-related behavior. In W.J. Arnold and D. Levine (eds), *Nebraska Symposium on Motivation — 1969*. Lincoln: University of Nebraska Press.

D'Amore, Louis. (1987−8). Tourism — The world's peace industry. *Business Quarterly*, **52** (3): 78−85.

D'Amore, Louis. (1988a). Tourism — The world's peace industry. *Journal of Travel Research*, **27** (1): 35−40.

D'Amore, Louis. (1988b). Tourism — A vital force for peace. *Annals of Tourism Research*, **15** (2): 269−71.

D'Amore, Louis, and Jafari, Jafar (eds) (1988). *Tourism — A vital force for peace* (A pre-conference publication) Montreal: L.J. D'Amore and Associates.

Dogan, Hasan Zafer (1989). Forms of adjustment: Sociocultural impacts of Tourism. *Annals of Tourism Research*, **16** (2): 216−36.

Evans-Prichard, Deidre (1989). How "they" see "Us," Native American images of tourists. *Annals of Tourism Research*, **16** (1): 89−105.

Grothe, John (1970). *Attitude change of American tourists in the Soviet Union*. Ph.D. Dissertation, Washington, DC: The George Washington University.

Milman, Ady, Reichel, Arie and Pizam, Abraham (1990). The impact of tourism on ethnic attitudes: The Israeli−Egyptian case. *Journal of Travel Research*, **29** (2): 45−9.

Osgood, Charles Egerton, Succi, G.J. and Tannenbaum, P.H. (1954). *The Measurement of Meaning*. Urbana: University of Illinois Press.

Pearce, Phillip L. (1982a). Perceived changes in holiday destination. *Annals of Tourism Research*, **9** (12): 145−64.

Pearce, Phillip L. (1982b). Tourists and their hosts: Some social and psychological effects of inter-cultural contacts. In Stephen Bochner (ed.), *Cultures in Contact: Studies in Cross-cultural Interaction*. New York: Pergamon Press, 192−221.

Pizam, Abraham, Milman, Ady and Jafari, Jafar (1991). Influence of tourism on attitudes: US students visiting USSR. *Tourism Management*, **12** (1): 47−54.

Rossi, Peter H., Wright, J.D. and Anderson, A.B. (1983). *Handbook of Survey Research*. New York: Academic Press.

Smith, H.P. (1957). The effects of intercultural experiences: A follow-up investigation. *Journal of Abnormal and Social Psychology*, **54**: 266−9.

Smith, M. Brewster (1947−8). The personal settings of public opinions: A study of attitudes toward Russia. *Public Opinion Quarterly*, **12** (4): 507−23.

Snider, James G. and Osgood, C.E. (eds) (1969). *Semantic Differential Technique: A Source Book*. Chicago: Aldine Publications.

Turner, L. and Ash, J. (1975). *The Golden Hordes: International Tourism and the Pleasure Periphery*. London: Constable Press.

Var, T., Schlutter, R. Ankomah, P. and Lee, T.H. (1989). Tourism and world peace: The case of Argentina. *Annals of Tourism Research*, **16** (3): 431−43.

Walsh, Warren (1944−5). What the American people think of Russia. *Public Opinion Quarterly*, **8** (4): 513−22.

Wattenberg, A. (1987). 'Bad Marx': How the world sees the Soviets. *Public Opinion Quarterly*, **59** (3): 9−11.

Weiler, Betty (1989). The effects of international travel on the tourists: Seeing and clearing methodological roadblocks. *GeoJournal* **19** (3): 303−7.

Welds, Kathryne and Dukes, Richard (1985). Dimensions of cultural change, coping styles, and self-actualization in a shipboard university. *Annals of Tourism Research*, **12**: 113−19.

15 Uprising in Chiapas, Mexico: Zapata lives — tourism falters

WAYNE J. PITTS

The event

> We are a product of 500 years of struggle: first against slavery, then during the War of Independence against Spain led by the insurgents, then to avoid being absorbed by North American imperialism, then to promulgate our constitution and expel the French empire from our soil, and later the dictatorship of Porfirio Diaz . . .
>
> They don't care that we have nothing, absolutely nothing, not even a roof over our heads, no land, no work, no health care, no food, nor education. Nor are we able to freely and democratically elect our political representatives, nor is there independence from foreigners, nor is there peace nor justice for ourselves and our children (Communiqué and Declaration of War released by the Ejército Zapatista de Liberación Nacional (EZLN): January 1994).

On January 1st, the day the North American Free Trade Agreement (NAFTA) between Mexico, Canada and the United States went into effect, a previously unknown guerrilla group launched an offensive against the Mexican government capturing several towns in the southernmost Mexican state of Chiapas (Figure 15.1). For the next ten days, intermittent skirmishes between the Mexican Army and the EZLN were furiously reported by a third army of international journalists.

A unilateral cease fire was declared on January 12, but not until the EZLN and other groups expressing solidarity with the movement of the EZLN, such as the *Partido Revolucionario Obrero Clandestino Union del Pacifico*, (PROCUP), made good on threats to widen the uprising outside of Chiapas. EZLN supporters made several strikes throughout the country including: detonating a car bomb in Mexico City; tearing down electrical towers in Puebla and Michoacan; setting off explosions near a military base in Mexico State; and launching a grenade attack on an empty federal government building in Acapulco (SourceMex, 1994: 1).

Although the rebels were only able to defend their positions in Chiapas for a few days, and in some cases only a few hours, the offensive seriously affected Mexico's political, economic and social stability. All in all, the Mexican government reported that 145 people lost their lives during the first twelve days of the uprising. However, the diocese in Chiapas and other unofficial sources suggested that as many as 500 or more may have been killed. In the months that followed there were numerous and persistent claims of human rights abuses and suspected assassinations.

Tourism, Crime and International Security Issues, edited by
A. Pizam and Y. Mansfeld. © 1996 John Wiley & Sons Ltd.

Figure 15.1   State of Chiapas and Southeastern Mexico

The immediate response by the Mexican government to the uprising in Chiapas following the declaration of a cease fire was to appoint a governmental negotiator to head up talks with the rebels. The two sides agreed to meet in San Cristóbal de las Casas, the third largest city in Chiapas. Both sides agreed to have Archbishop Samuel Ruíz act as a mediator. Throughout January and February, the two sides met and discussed the positions of the EZLN and the government. Tensions often ran high as it seemed on several occasions that talks might be abandoned. By March, no real progress had been made and the talks were beginning to stalemate.

Also during this time the military continued to reinforce their positions by bringing in more troops and continuing to increase armaments. Throughout the state, military checkpoints became routine along all the main routes. These roadblocks would usually entail an entourage of well-armed soldiers verifying proof of identification of all persons who wished to pass. Personal vehicles were almost always searched, and occasionally bus passengers would also have their belongings searched.

On March 23, the international media eye refocused its attention on the controversy surrounding the assassination of Luis Donaldo Colosio, the heavily favored presidential candidate of the ruling *Partido Revolucionario Institucional* (PRI). While various conspiracy theories surfaced about the Tijuana assassination, the leading consensus was that the PRI had been involved in ordering the shooting. In the meantime, the peace talks in Chiapas had been abandoned.

All of these factors seriously affected the tourist economy: (1) the armed rebellion, (2) the widespread perception that the Mexican government was committing rampant human rights abuses, (3) rumors of continued violence in some remote and not so remote areas, (4) heightened security as evidenced by frequent roadblocks and military envoys, (5) intense domestic and international media attention, (6) generally unstable political situations in other parts of Mexico and (7) various well-attended exposé tours and presentations given by Chiapans in several host countries (the United States and Canada particularly). This chapter will outline the immediate effects of the uprising and the avalanche of other issues that arose around the rebellion on arguably the most important sector of the economy in Chiapas — tourism. After a brief review of some of the other areas of the world that have been affected by political violence, wars, terrorism etc, data will be presented that will show the impact of the rebellion on tourism. A discussion follows explaining what the drop in tourist trade in Chiapas has meant to the state in the short run. In the concluding sections, the future ramifications on tourism will be discussed. Finally, several points will address ways that Chiapas and other areas in similar situations may be able to redirect some of the negative impacts on the tourist economy and how the immediate effects and long-term effects may be lessened.

Political violence and tourism

In the past quarter-century, there have been numerous studies which have considered the effects of political violence and crime on tourism. In Africa, countries which have suffered declines in tourism during this period include Zimbabwe, Zambia, Egypt, Senegal, Morocco and others (Ryan, 1991: 13; Teye, 1986: 598). Certain Asian countries, such as Vietnam, Cambodia and Indonesia (Bali), have only recently begun to see dramatic increases in tourism in their countries following periods of political violence. The conflict in Bosnia-Hercegovina has contributed to significantly lower tourist dollars in neighboring Greece, Austria, Bulgaria and Romania. Latin America has not been spared either by this phenomenon of political violence coupled with far-reaching drops in tourism. Costa Rica, Peru, Nicaragua and El Salvador are just a few of the more dramatic examples from the eighties that attest to this recurrent situation (Ryan, 1991: 129).

Surprisingly, however, there have been relatively few scholarly works which have focused specifically on the topic of the effect of political violence (wars, rebellions, revolutions, riots etc) on the tourist economy. Most research in this area has tended to deal more with terrorism and crime, particularly terrorism and crime directed at tourists (Chesney-Lind and Lind, 1986; Conant, et al., 1988; Pizam, 1982; and Ryan, 1991). Victor Teye (1986) did however contribute a particularly useful article concerning "liberation wars and tourism development in Zambia and Zimbabwe." It is hoped that the following case study and discussion will shed some light on general trends that characterize the inter-relationship between tourism and political violence.

Methodology

The data reported in the following pages was collected during two separate research visits to Chiapas. The first excursion took place from February 27 to March 17, 1994. A return, follow-up visit was made between July 19 and August 9, 1994.

During these two visits, 27 interviews of varying degrees of formality were conducted with certain "participants" in the tourism industry. Participants ranged from wealthy hotel owners to governmental agency officials, to vendors in the informal economy. The majority of the interviews were conducted in Spanish with a few exceptions where English was spoken.

During the initial trip, access to key figures (the Ministry of Tourism in Tuxtla-Gutiérrez and certain members of the Hotel and Motel Association) was facilitated by Frederico Salazar, a Business/Finance Professor at the *Instituto Superiores de Chiapas* located in Tuxtla-Gutiérrez. In other parts of the state (Palenque, Ocosingo, San Cristóbal de las Casas, Chiapa de Corzo and Comitán) contacts were approached informally. In some cases, the researcher gained access through prior acquaintances and second-hand referrals.

The initial research visit was undertaken with the main objective of making contacts and solidifying the research design in preparation for the second occasion. In general, the strategy was very effective, although it would have been preferable to have interviewed more "owners" of tourism production. Furthermore, survey questionnaires were sent to several hotel and motel owners once the researcher returned from the field, in an attempt to solicit more information. The response rate to these questionnaires was extremely low.

Finally, a considerable amount of data was collected at the State Offices of Tourism in Tuxtla-Gutiérrez and San Cristóbal. Statistics from 1983 to 1993 were supplied by the Tuxtla-Gutiérrez office in compiled form. All 1994 data for the first six months of the year was collected by hand from hard-copy data lists in both offices. Access was gained to two tourism-dependent businesses in San Cristóbal. This data was also collected by hand from unrefined hard-copy data sources.

The structure of tourism in Chiapas

International tourism has experienced tremendous relative growth in the state of Chiapas during the past ten years. This growth has occurred both in the amount of money exchanged and the number of tourists. In contrast, domestic tourism has remained relatively stable, although there has been some growth in the industry. The following section will present data that was supplied by the Tuxtla-Gutiérrez Office for Tourism Development, the district office of tourism in San Cristóbal and one independent business located in San Cristóbal.

The statistics included in this section are provided to the Office of Tourism Development by each of the five main "sectors" or "departments" of tourism in Chiapas. They are, specifically, Tuxtla-Gutiérrez, San Cristóbal, Palenque, Tapachula, and Comitán (see Figure 15.1). Each of these sectors collects and records data from all hotels, motels and guest houses. According to the newly appointed Minister of Tourism and the Statistical Records Office of the Office of Tourism Development, the basic data reported is reliable. Basic data would include numbers of tourists and nationality of tourist (foreign or domestic). Other data that is typically less reliable would include self-reported estimates of daily expenditures and estimated length of stay in the state.

In all cases, the Office of Tourism Development data is based on tourists who spend at least one night in a hotel, motel, campground or guest house. Clearly, the data presented here does not include accounts of tourists (primarily domestic) who stay with friends or relatives, nor does it include tourists (primarily international) who pass through the state without spending the night. When asked about this missing data, the minister explained that these people are an important factor, though it is suspected that they do not contribute a significant amount of capital in comparison with other visitors to the state.

Trends in the tourist trade, 1990–4

As mentioned above, the five sectors or divisions of tourism in Chiapas are based around the cities of Palenque, San Cristóbal, Tuxtla-Gutiérrez, Tapachula, and Comitán. One of the main factors behind this delineation was simply the geographic placement of these cities. Tuxtla-Gutiérrez, besides being the capital of the state, is the largest city. Tapachula is the second-largest city, followed in size by San Cristóbal. Within these five sectors, there are differences in "who" they attract and "why." Each area has a unique history which also contributes to this formation, but it is beyond the scope of this work to present that information here. Each regional area will be addressed before an account of the entire state is presented.

Tuxtla-Gutiérrez

Tuxtla-Gutiérrez has a population of 289 626 (Estados Unidos Mexicanos, 1991). Due to its importance as the capital city of Chiapas, it attracts a large number of domestic tourists (presumably business and government associates). There are also some major tourist attractions in the immediate vicinity including numerous monuments and official structures, Sumidero Canyon, Chiapa de Corzo, a Museum of Anthropology and a large Zoological Park. The largest airport in the state is also located in Tuxtla-Gutiérrez. Although no direct international airport is available in Chiapas, it is possible to connect to the airport in Tuxtla-Gutiérrez by Mexicana Airlines.

According to the data, the total volume of tourists to the city has not been greatly affected by the January 1st uprising. Tuxtla-Gutiérrez normally draws significantly more domestic than international tourists. Although the estimates for 1994 show domestic tourism remaining relatively stable, it is likely that this total appears inflated. Throughout the first six months of 1994, the main plaza in the capital attracted huge crowds (sometimes in the thousands) of protesters and other demonstrators. Many demonstrators who stayed several days slept on the ground outside or hung hammocks in the plaza. A few of the demonstrators stayed in local economy hotels and motels. Generally, these demonstrators did not purchase rooms in more expensive hotels such as El Safari and the Posado del Rey, which are very close to the plaza. While these demonstrators made small contributions to the local tourist economy, most had very little money and their inputs were inconsequential. Restated, the domestic tourist population did not decrease significantly, but the domestic tourist expenditures were far less. See Figure 15.2.

Tapachula

The second largest city in Chiapas with a population of 138 858, Tapachula is heavily influenced by the economy of Guatemala (Estados Unidos Mexicanos, 1991). Its geographical location makes it especially attractive to international and domestic travelers

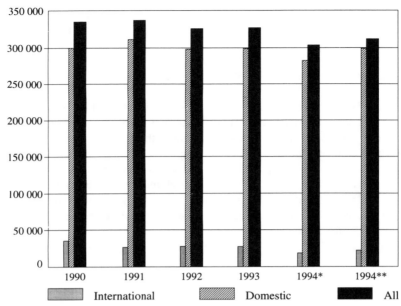

Figure 15.2 International and domestic visitors to Tuxtla-Gutiérrez, 1990−4

alike. Tourists can purchase Guatemalan textiles inexpensively without crossing the border. Besides the markets, local beaches are also a major attraction for visitors.

Tapachula saw significant drops in its international tourism during the first six months following the uprising. Most likely, this occurred for a number of reasons. First, the uprising occurred in the highlands and thus, any journalists or war tourists probably didn't reach the Soconusco, as they did other areas. Another likely factor was the number of roadblocks and military checkpoints that had to be endured in a trek to the far south of Chiapas. Only the most intense and rugged tourists were likely to go through all that trouble to get to Tapachula. Finally, numbers of tourists *en route* to Guatemala were down as a result of US State Department warnings concerning some violent incidents there against tourists. This had a direct effect on tourists to Tapachula since the town is located near a major border crossing. See Figure 15.3.

San Cristóbal de las Casas

Pierre van den Berghe (1994) has documented the ethnic tourism appeal of this colonial city of 73 388 (Estados Unidos Mexicanos, 1991). San Cristóbal has many attractions for both domestic and international tourists. Many people visit the town because of its reputation as a center of modern Mayan life. The ethnic markets in San Cristóbal are some of the most colorful in Mexico. The nearby Mayan villages such as San Juan Chamula offer visitors a unique experience of seeing Indian life first hand. Other attractions near the town include several colonial architecture structures and the caves of Rancho Nuevo.

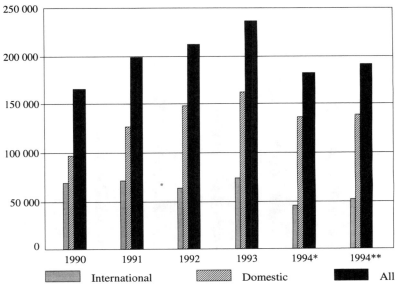

Figure 15.3 International and domestic visitors to Tapachula, 1990−4

San Cristóbal experienced the most dramatic drops in both domestic and international tourism during the first six months of 1991. In many ways, the uprising in Chiapas was centered in San Cristóbal: it was the largest town held by the Zapatistas and the location of the subsequent mediations. Van den Berghe (1995) suggests that tourism in San Cristóbal was reduced by at least 90 per cent during January and February (van den Berghe, 1995). This estimate seems to be overly severe. According to records kept by one San Cristóbal business, the total number of tourists served dropped nearly 70 per cent in January and almost that much in February (compared to 1993).

Some entrepreneurs took advantage of the excitement and sold guided tours of the "Zapatista homelands" for around US$500. War souvenirs also became popular among both journalists and war tourists. Zapatista dolls, Mexican Army dolls, black ski masks, T-shirts, lighters, pens and other conflict ephemera could be purchased at often exorbitant amounts. The sale of such items was particularly meaningful to local market and street vendors. As alluded to earlier, not only were there huge drops in tourist numbers, but the composition of visitors also changed dramatically. Because of its "ethnic ambience," and the perception that the Zapatistas represented a much larger dissatisfied Indian population, journalists from around the world flocked to the city. In addition to the journalists, "conflict" or "war tourists" also abounded. Just like drivers on the interstate stretching their necks trying to get a glimpse of "what happened" at a wreck scene, these individuals wanted to be a part of the action. In any case, 1994 tourists were very different from the tourists to San Cristóbal in recent years. Generally, they tended to be less interested in the "usual" attractions and their travel patterns were more sporadic. Some shop owners also suggested that tourists tended to spend less money on more expensive craft items in favor of cheaper souvenirs. So, while the official data sources suggests sharp drops in tourism, the impacts of those decreases and the composition of the tourists who replaced the former are significantly more important. See Figure 15.4.

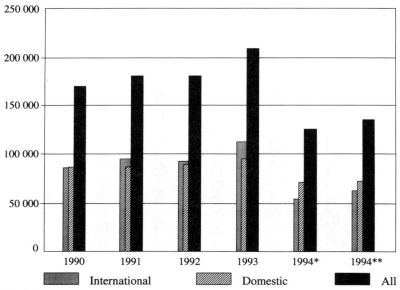

Figure 15.4 International and domestic visitors to San Cristóbal, 1990−4

Palenque

Palenque has a population of 17 061 (Estados Unidos Mexicanos, 1991). The economy of Palenque and its immediate surroundings tends to operate more under the influence of the state of Tabasco than Chiapas. What this means in real terms is that most workers in Palenque can earn wages up to two times more than similar workers in other parts of Chiapas performing similar tasks. Palenque has a relatively small population and one possible explanation for the fairly severe drop in domestic tourism would be that this site, more than all the others, represents a more leisurely vacation as opposed to a more varied agenda in a visit to the capital city (business, visit relatives etc).

The main attractions in Palenque are the magnificent Mayan ruins located just outside of the modern city. As the most important archaeological attraction in Chiapas, Palenque has begun to attract more international tourists than domestic tourists since 1990. This trend probably reflects increased advertising and marketing campaigns and the growth of international tourism in the Yucatan Peninsula. Because of its geographic location and accessibility by the main road connecting the Yucatan Peninsula with the rest of the country, international tourists can visit Palenque with a relatively small temporal and economic investment. See Figure 15.5.

Comitán

According to the 1990 Mexican census, Comitán had a population of 48 299 (Estados Unidos Mexicanos, 1991). Comitán is located in the Chiapan highlands and like San Cristóbal it experienced relatively slow population growth until the 1970s. Comitán is a colonial city, with some interesting architectural scenes to be viewed. There are several

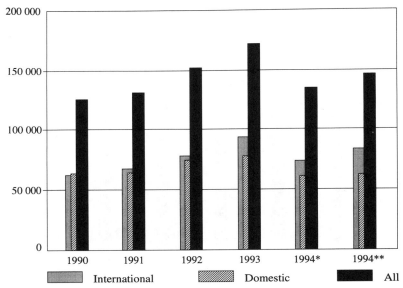

Figure 15.5   International and domestic visitors to Palenque, 1990−4

museums including the Rosario Castellanos Museum, the Comitán Valley Archaeological Museum and the former home of Dr Belisario Dominguez. Comitán also offers interested tourists some minor Mayan ruins (Tenam Puente and Chincultic) in the general vicinity. The attraction which offers the greatest allure to tourists must certainly be the magnificent *El Parque Nacional de los Lagos de Montebello* (Montebello Lakes National Park) located just east of Comitán. Although transportation to the lakes may be a bit treacherous for most tourists, those who persevere are well rewarded.

Probably due to the difficulty in accessibility and its relatively fewer attractions (than San Cristóbal), Comitán has been unable to attract international tourists in large numbers. Domestic visitors are the most important to the tourist trade. The drop in domestic tourism in Comitán can probably be attributed to the higher visibility of military personnel. According to an army sergeant interviewed near Ocosingo in March, Comitán, Las Margaritas and Altamirano were considered to be the most "at risk" sites for future conflicts. See Figure 15.6.

Tourism in 1994

The uprising in Chiapas had far-reaching implications for the tourist economy. Some areas were affected more than others due to the composition of the tourist populations, the types of attractions and the hardships involved in reaching a potential tourist destination. In the case of Chiapas, all sectors evaluated show evidence of serious tourism declines. Clearly international tourism was the most affected, but in Tuxtla-Gutiérrez and Comitán domestic tourism also suffered severely. It should be noted once again that the data presented here may be deceptive. At first glance, it may appear that although there are significant drops in the total number of domestic and international tourists, they are not as

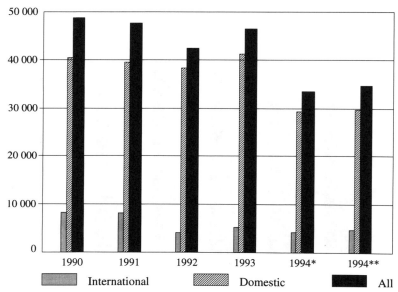

Figure 15.6 International and domestic visitors to Comitán, 1990–4

severe as one might think. This is extremely misleading. As mentioned above, in some cases the data did not show massive drops in tourism numbers, but business owners reported that sales were extremely low. Furthermore, the Minister of Tourism for Chiapas explained that the average length of stay was down an average of two to three days during the first six months of 1994. These points will be expounded on further in the concluding sections.

The composition of the tourists also changed. Historically, much of Chiapas has been an attraction because of ethnic tourism (van den Berghe, 1994: 76–7). However, when the rebellion in Chiapas occurred, many would-be ethnic tourists to Chiapas refrained from visiting because of fear. On the other hand, a number of the tourists recorded in the data were in Chiapas precisely because of the conflict. This number would include journalists, researchers, human rights activists and more generally "war tourists" — persons who were in Chiapas to experience the thrill of political violence. One magazine reported a Canadian woman as saying her reasons for visiting Chiapas in June were "journalism, a tan and revolution," (Caragata, 1994: 28).

Future implications

The 1994 tourism trends and calculated variances for 1993–4 are listed in Tables 15.1–15.3. The weighted estimates for the last six months of 1994 are optimistic. Notice that the estimates for domestic tourists (102 per cent) were weighted lower than international tourists (115 per cent). The rationale behind this difference is that it is predicted that domestic travel will remain relatively stable. International tourism will probably begin to see signs of recovery given the peaceful and uncontested PRI victory in the August 1994 elections.

Table 15.1 International Visitors to Chiapas 1994

	January	February	March	April	May	June	Jan−June Total
Tuxtla	1347	1079	3576	2727	1160	728	10 617
Tapachula	5175	3043	5249	2593	4598	2329	22 987
San Cristóbal	1528	3322	5761	7537	4599	2888	25 635
Palenque	4740	5018	8344	6404	3834	2751	31 091
Comitán	217	172	841	543	224	140	2137
Other	725	484	1444	1360	864	372	5249
Total	13 732	13 118	25 215	21 164	15 279	9208	97 716

Source: Tuxtla−Gutiérrez Office of Tourism Development.

Table 15.2 Domestic Visitors to Chiapas, 1994

	January	February	March	April	May	June	Jan−June Total
Tuxtla	26 435	21 822	30 145	27 847	18 177	17 468	141 894
Tapachula	8812	7099	14 192	14 693	10 730	13 196	68 722
San Cristóbal	4834	4030	4379	6074	6333	5509	31 159
Palenque	2945	1166	4901	6016	5295	5111	25 434
Comitán	2878	1551	1961	3633	2574	2186	14 783
Other	13 766	12 461	16 600	13 746	11 474	12 042	80 044
Total	59 670	48 084	72 178	72 009	54 583	55 512	362 036

Source: Tuxtla−Gutiérrez Office of Tourism Development.

Table 15.3 International and Domestic Tourism Variance, 1993−4

	International Visitors*			Domestic Visitors**			All Visitors***		
	Foreign Visitors 1993	1994* Total	Foreign Variance (%)	Domestic Visitors 1993	1994** Total	Domestic Variance (%)	All Visitors	1994*** Total	All Visitors Variance (%)
Tuxtla	28 988	24 419	−15.76	299 039	289 463	−3.2	328 027	313 882	−4.31
Tapachula	74 307	52 870	−28.84	162 935	140 193	−13.96	237 242	193 063	−18.62
San Cristóbal	113 573	58 961	−48.08	95 833	63 564	−33.67	209 406	122 525	−41.49
Palenque	93 850	71 509	−23.81	78 224	51 885	−33.67	172 074	123 394	−28.29
Comitán	5155	4915	−4.66	41 363	30 147	−27.12	46 518	35 062	−26.32
Rest of State	20 367	12 073	−40.7	204 310	163 290	−20.08	224 677	175 363	−21.95
Total	336 240	224 747	−33.16	889 704	738 542	−16.99	1 217 944	963 289	−20.91

 * Estimate based on the following equation:
   First six months total $\times$ 2 $\times$ 115% = Estimated 1994 International Tourism Total
 ** Estimate based on the following equation:
   First six months total $\times$ 2 $\times$ 102% = Estimated 1994 Domestic Tourism Total
*** Estimate based on the sum of International and Domestic Tourism Estimates.

Strategies towards recovery

One of the first steps taken by the Mexican government following the uprising in Chiapas was to appoint an official spokesperson for the government. In a similar move, the state government of Chiapas appointed a new Minister of Tourism for Chiapas within the first month and a half following the uprising. The first objective of Minister Francisco Pedrero Pastraña was to cut their state's losses by encouraging domestic tourism. The State Office of Tourism Development sent out one million letters to businesses throughout Mexico urging business leaders to consider holding conferences or other meetings in Chiapas. Pedrero hoped to be able to entice business persons to make use of the recently completed convention center in Tuxtla-Gutiérrez that remained unopened due to lack of bookings. Another area that Pedrero was working on was to lower accommodations pricings in order to be more competitive with neighboring states. In fact, he was lobbying the government to allow tax breaks to businesses who used Chiapan accommodations. There was also a push for certain tourism subsidies. Probably the minister's greatest challenge for the future will be to re-establish the confidence of tourists to the area.

Lessons to be learned

Given the events in Chiapas during 1994, is there anything that could have been done differently to help deter the negative effects on tourism? Can other areas in similar circumstances implement some form of crisis management to deal with the issues? These are literally "million dollar questions." Certainly, there are some instances where crisis management may help.

One of the first issues that must be addressed by tourism planners in situations similar to the case of Chiapas is the personal safety of the tourists. Safety for their belongings is also essential. In general, most tourists do not want to risk life and limb during their vacations. Although there has only been one reported case of a tourist (a magazine journalist) being killed in Chiapas since the uprising, the safety of tourists in the area cannot be assured. The government did try to limit the contact of the public with the military, and soldiers for the most part were polite. During the first six months after the uprising in Chiapas, many travelers were more afraid of the Mexican military and their checkpoints than they were of Zapatista insurgents. One of Pedrero's concerns was that tourists were being unduly harassed at road blocks. In most cases, the military were extremely cordial during their ID checks. Other times, soldiers were unnecessarily intimidating to both domestic and international travelers. Internal image maintenance is an important point for recovering economies to focus on.

Tourism markets in decline due to political violence can foster recovery through external means as well — primarily marketing. According to the Minister of Tourism, their long-range marketing goals were to create and distribute videos showing a peaceful and enticing Chiapas. The main purpose of these promotional videos would be to interest international tourists. Such marketing activities can be very effective. In July, several campaigns were already under way to persuade potential customers that officials in Chiapas wanted peace. Several slogans emerged, but among the most prominent was ChiaPAZ (*paz* means peace). Other campaigns included solidarity strikes and primary school promotions. Ryan discusses the importance of advertising and marketing in shaping the perception of place (Ryan, 1991: 174). He goes on to suggest a model of image perception in marketing that is directly relevant to this discussion. Potential tourists make decisions to travel based on a wide variety of perceived attributes of a destination. Heading the list of priorities are the value of the vacation experience, cleanliness and hygiene and personal safety. Other attributes that are considered less important would include mode of transport at destination, luxury hotels and nightlife (Ryan, 1991: 180).

Unstable events continue to hold the tourist economy in Chiapas under siege. The efforts of the state government to help tourism recover will be unsuccessful until the perception of safety is once again assured to potential tourists. It is expected that there will be a rise in war tourists visiting the state in the near future. However, once the political unrest begins to stabilize, Chiapas will no longer be attractive to those tourists either. Most likely, Chiapas will begin to appeal once again to ethnic tourists while becoming less attractive to war tourists. There is no immediate solution in Chiapas. Economic recovery from the uprising in Chiapas will no doubt take many years.

References

Benjamin, T. (1989). *A Rich Land a Poor People: Politics and Society in Modern Chiapas*. Albuquerque, NM: University of New Mexico.

Caragata, W. (1994). Down and out in Mexico: Poverty stalks a southern state. *Maclean's* **107** (June 13): 28—29.

Chesney-Lind, M. and Lind, I. (1986). Visitors as victims: Crimes against tourists in Hawaii. *Annals of Tourism Research*, **13** (2): 167—92.

Communiqués released by the EZLN (1994). All communiqués prior to June 10, 1994, translated into English and available in the *Anderson Valley Advertiser*. Mendocino County, CA, **42** (31), August 3.

Conant, J.S., Clark, T., Burnett, J. and Zank, G. (1988). Terrorism and travel: Managing the unmanageable. *Journal of Travel Research*, **26** (4): 16—20.

Estados Unidos Mexicanos (1991). Resultados definitives datos por localidad (Integracion territorial) Tomo 1. *XI Censo General de Poblacion y Vivienda, 1990*. Aguascalientes, AGS, Instituto Nacional de Estadistica.

Fox, J. (1994). The challenge of democracy: rebellion as catalyst. *Akwe:kon: A Journal of Indigenous Issues*, **XI** (2): 13—19.

Pitts, W. (1994). *Summary of Events Surrounding Rebellion in Chiapas*. SourceMex. Latin American Data Base: University of New Mexico (ID# 020908), January 12.

Pizam, A. (1982). Tourism and crime: Is there a relationship? *Journal of Tourism Research*, **20** (3): 7—10.

Ryan, C. (1991). *Tourism, Terrorism and Violence: The Risks of Wider World Travel*. London: Research Institute for the Study of Conflict and Terrorism.

Teye, V. (1986). Liberation wars and tourism development in Africa: The case of Zambia. *Annals of Tourism Research*, **13** (4): 589—608.

van den Berghe, P. (1994). *The Quest for the Other: Ethnic Tourism in San Cristóbal, Mexico*. Seattle, WA: University of Washington Press.

van den Berghe, P. (1995). Marketing Mayas: Ethnic tourism promotion in Mexico. *Annals of Tourism Research*, **22**(3): 568—88.

Part 3

Tourism and war

16 Tourism and warfare — the case of Slovenia

TANJA MIHALIČ

The purpose of this chapter is to analyze the consequences of the war in Slovenia and of the war in other former Yugoslav republics on tourism in Slovenia. To this end, we have analyzed trends of tourism demand before and after the war. We have also added an analysis of the impact of war on the tourist industry. In order to illustrate more clearly the complex relationship between war and tourism, we have initially put forward some theoretical findings and examples of how various factors influence the development of tourism.

Factors in tourism development

Various explanations have been put forward in the relevant literature for the prosperity in tourism evident today all over the world. General demand factors known from economic demand theory — needs, income and prices — are also important in the sphere of tourism. However, in tourist demand, an additional factor has to be taken into account — that of leisure time (Socher, 1985). The prerequisite or the basis for the occurrence of tourist demand is in most cases the natural, cultural and social attractions of tourist resorts. Since tourism implies leaving the residence area, one of the factors of its development is also transport (development, routes, prices). Some analysts highlight urbanization as another factor, as well as irrational factors like fashion and exclusiveness. Tourist literature contains various models of this type (Cicvarić 1980; Krippendorf, 1984; Kaspar, 1991; Vanhove, 1991).

Tourism development forecasts are good, and could only be seriously hindered by a third world war. Other limits to growth mentioned recently are based on social, environmental (sustainable tourism) reasons and health problems (Gajraj, 1989; Petty, 1989). There are many studies in which tourism demand functions are estimated. They are used in various forms to explain either the number of tourist visits or tourist nights and tourist receipts/expenditure related to selected factors.

Income is, undoubtedly, the most important factor with respect to demand. Hunziker and Krapf (1942) stated as early as the forties that income determines the quantity of tourist demand. Econometrically, the impact of income on tourism demand, calculated through income elasticity of tourism demand in Europe, was first studied by Menges (1957) in the case of Germany and Switzerland. In the literature, there are some other

Tourism, Crime and International Security Issues, edited by
A. Pizam and Y. Mansfeld. © 1996 John Wiley & Sons Ltd.

examples of quantifying the impact of various factors. Crouch and Shaw (1992) made a list for the period after 1960 showing 64 studies of this type. They found that the majority of the models quantify the impact of income, relative prices, costs of transport, exchange rates and trends. Quite a few models (45 per cent) include disturbance factors which were included in analyses by using dummy variables. These were included in order to explain tourism demand, allowing for the impact of disturbance factors.

While it is sensible to study the factors of tourism demand (eg impact of income growth and transport development on world tourism development) on a global basis, it is also useful to look regionally or at specific destinations (eg influence of recession in certain states, influence of exchange-rate changes etc).

It often happens that, all factors of tourism demand seem to be developing well, but suddenly a new factor appears which turns all previous expectations upside down. Such was the case of the Chernobyl catastrophe and also the oil crises in 1973 and 1979 which had a detrimental influence on tourism demand (Martin and Witt, 1989). Another example might also be the algae blooming of the Adriatic which affected destinations along its coast. Thus, the number of tourist nights in Rimini (Italy) was, due to sea blooming, reduced by almost 50 per cent in 1989, and by an additional 11 per cent in 1990 (Becheri, 1990). Such may also be the case with war. Vukonić (1993) assumes that war, though unjustly neglected in tourism theory, is an extremely important factor in negative influence on tourism demand.

Tourism and war

The relationship between tourism and peace has two dimensions. On the one hand, tourism "can be a vital force for world peace" (WTO, 1980) and on the other, tourism needs peace for its development and prosperity. The nature of the concept of peace is very diverse. One definition says that within the context of tourism, peace applies to the concept of harmonious relations (Var et al., 1994). War is defined as "the clash of arms among countries" (Lexicon CZ, 1987: 1038).

Since the tourist product is connected to destination, some of its basic components are the attractions of the destination such as natural and socio-cultural factors (Kaspar, 1991). According to Burkart and Medlik (1974: 193) "attractions . . . may be defined as those elements in the tourist product which determine the choice of the tourist to visit one destination rather than another." In the case of war, the war itself with all its dimensions becomes part of the tourist product. Normally the state of war means a "dis"-attractiveness — in some cases tourist demand drops, in extreme situations, to zero.

Impact of war on tourism development was noted by Teye (1988). The war affects both sides of tourism, supply and demand. On the side of demand, he describes the following impacts of war:

1. Borders are closed for land, air and sea transport;
2. Foreign authorities recommend that their citizens do not travel to war-stricken states;
3. Maltreatment of tourists traveling to a state involved in war;
4. Adverse publicity in international media;
5. "Blacklisting" by tour operators and travel agents.

On the side of tourist supply there are two types of impact: the one influencing tourism development and the other influencing the existing tourist supply. The related consequences are:

1. Development plans are reduced or cancelled;
2. Loss of investment capital from abroad;
3. Tourist infrastructure is occupied (airports, hotels);
4. Destruction of game parks due to excessive poaching;
5. Consequences on night life (due to curfews);
6. Military blackmail (towards passengers in airports and elsewhere);
7. Emergence of a foreign-currency black market.

Vukonić (1993) also describes the problem of war refugees which can destroy the demand for a certain destination. In war conditions, the population flees from the conflicts. Some tourist facilities are suitable for refugees, but this has several consequences for tourism:

1. Letting rooms for refugees precludes letting them to tourists;
2. Long-term accommodation of refugees in hotels results in damaged hotel equipment;
3. After the hotels are emptied, they have to be refurbished which prevents their use for a further period;
4. The presence of refugees in tourist destinations has a negative impact, as tourists try to avoid them (Vukonić, 1993).

Recent history has shown several factors which hindered tourism demand in Europe. For the year 1986, the OECD (1987) states three factors which had a negative influence on the growth of European incoming tourism, although it is not possible to assess their individual impact. These factors were fears for personal safety aroused by terrorism, the consequences of the Chernobyl accident and the continuing fall of the dollar against European currencies. Witt (1994: 517) states that "the tourism flows to Greece were lower than expected in 1974 because of the heightened threat of war between Greece and Turkey as a result of the Turkish invasion on Cyprus." Mavris (1993) states that the Turkish invasion had a significant negative effect on the tourist industry in 1974 and 1975. The Lebanese conflict (1976−92) had both a positive and a negative effect on tourism in Cyprus: positive because tourist flows were redirected towards Cyprus and away from Lebanon; and negative because of the potential for trouble in the region, such as terrorism. The Gulf War influenced tourism flows from abroad to Europe.

The Gulf War was the first limited war — that is, a war which did not involve the whole world (Vukonić, 1993) — which had a strong negative effect on the development of international tourism (Impact of the Gulf Crisis on International Tourism, 1991). According to the World Tourism Organization (WTO), the number of tourists fell by 1.4 per cent for the first time after a nine-year period of constant growth, and international traffic from Japan and the United States was reduced by 2 per cent. At the same time, the development of tourism was influenced by another factor, economic recession in most tourist-generating countries. Archer (1994) assumes that this other factor was even more significant.

Not only were the tourist flows to the Mediterranean, Europe and the Middle East reduced, but the influence of the Gulf War was even felt by the Australian tourist industry (Rowe, 1993), and even American domestic tourism (eg in Hawaii and Florida) was affected (Goeldner, 1992; Anderson and Anderson, 1992). The Gulf War kept Americans from taking holidays. It affected both leisure and business travel (Jusko, 1991), but the war itself had only a short-term effect on international travel. During 1990 the threat of war and international terrorism caused a substantial decline in international tourism. However, when the war ended, the tourists did not return immediately because they had already booked their holidays elsewhere.

The war in the Balkans — the war in Slovenia and later in Croatia and Bosnia Hercegovina has not had such catastrophic effects on international tourism as the Gulf War, although it has practically destroyed tourism in this part of the Mediterranean Adriatic zone. Yugotours, a specialized tour operator for Yugoslavia, lost more than one million booked tourists in 1991. A similar thing happened to Bemextours, another large tour operator for the Yugoslav tourist territory (Vukonić, 1993).

Vukonić (1993) states that the war in Yugoslavia clearly reveals the actual consequences of war on tourism development. Losses have not only affected Yugoslav destinations, but, indirectly, due to lower transit tourism, they have affected neighboring countries, too. At the same time, tourist flows inside the region have been redirected from affected countries toward other competing countries. Thus, some of the tourists who traditionally spent their holidays on the Adriatic coast, spent their 1991 holidays in neighboring Austria and Italy.

Due to the reasons mentioned by Teye of fears for personal safety, destinations involved in war become unattractive for potential tourists. However, there are reports of cases where "war horrors" are sold as a tourist attraction. Wilkson (1994) states that a current tourist brochure for Mexico City promises that, "if you are lucky, you may be able to see the rebels" (Zapatistas) for the price of $533. Tourists traveling to Dubrovnik or Split (Croatia) wish to see the consequences of war. This was also the case for Sarajevo.

When the war is over, it becomes part of the historical memory of a certain destination and this memory becomes a tourist attraction. The tourist literature cites the case of Thomas Cook who in 1866 took British tourists on a journey to Richmond and to the famous Potomac battlefield using the recent civil war in the USA as a motive for traveling. Well known also are tourist journeys to the World War II battlefields, travels of war captives to places of their deportation and the Vietnam War nostalgia in several Vietnamese cities including Hanoi, Da Nang and Ho Chi Minh City (Vietnam, 1994). Goodrich (1991) states that travel agents even offer special travel discounts to soldiers who fought in the Persian Gulf War in order to stimulate this tourist segment demand.

In order to understand the relationship between war and tourism better another dimension has to be included. Very often, famous tourist attractions are destroyed during the war; this is emphasized strongly in the media. Attacks on tourists are also featured. It is well known that terrorist attacks on tourists in Egypt greatly diminished tourist circulation (Gubernick, 1993). In former Yugoslavia, the first armed conflicts between Croats and Serbs had started before the war in Slovenia, during the Easter holiday in 1991 in the Plitvice National Park. The Plitvice lakes are a famous tourist destination and are listed by UNESCO as a world heritage site. The reaction of tourism demand on the territory of the entire republic was instantaneous. In April, Croatia registered only 30 per

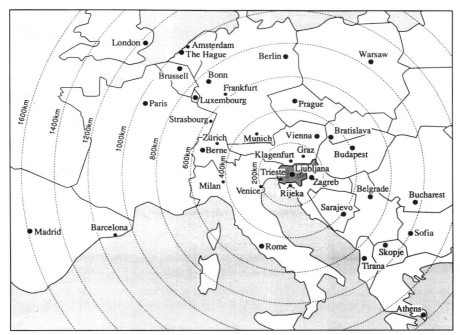

Figure 16.1 Slovenia's location in Europe. Surface area 20 256 square km (7820 sq. miles), no. of inhabitants: 1 966 000 (1991), gross national income per capita: US$6334 (1991), state borders: Italy: 235 km, Austria 324 km, Hungary 102 km, Croatia 546 km, and the Adriatic coast 46 km, no. of tourist beds (all means of accommodation): 71 761 (1992). Source: ZRSS (1993)

cent of the expected scope of tourist nights (Vukonić, 1993). The later shooting on Dubrovnik — one of the best-known tourist destinations of the former Yugoslavia — also falls into the same category of destroying tourist attractions. Reports on military attacks on this world cultural heritage and pearl of tourism were published worldwide.

Case study — War impact on Slovenian incoming tourism

Slovenia is a new country in Central Europe, established on 25 June 1991 by the proclamation of independence and by breaking connections with former Yugoslavia, to which it had been attached as a constituent republic. Today Slovenia is an internationally recognized country; in May 1992 it became a permanent member of the United Nations.

Slovenia is a small country, half the size of Switzerland, with a population one-third that of Switzerland (see Figure 16.1). Two days after independence was officially declared, the Yugoslav Army attacked Slovenia on June 27, 1991. The Yugoslav army besieged border passes, occupied several road links and attacked the Slovenian airport at Brnik, blocking its operation. Ten days later by signing the Brioni Declaration, the Yugoslav Army terminated its military involvement in Slovenia. The war in Slovenia was over, the army forces moved to Croatia, where war began the same year. In 1992 military fighting expanded to Bosnia-Hercegovina, where it still continues.

Table 16.1 Number of foreign and domestic tourists and tourist nights in Slovenia for the period 1985–93 and indexes 1991/2, 1993/90, 1993/91

in 1000 tourists/nights

Year/Index	TOURISTS Total	Foreign*		Domestic	NIGHTS Total	Foreign*		Domestic**
		Classic Abroad	Former Yugoslavia			Classic Abroad	Former Yugoslavia	
1980	2378	869	851	658	7772	2795	2593	2384
1985	2753	1056	948	749	8823	3729	2434	2660
1988	2724	1117	900	707	8808	3874	2248	2686
1989	2664	1137	833	694	8509	3887	1952	2670
1990	2536	1095	790	651	7956	3673	1672	2611
1991	1426	299	440	687	4886	970	1207	2709
1992	1368	423	194	751	5098	1356	659	3083
1993	1451	505	120	826	5384	1656	356	3372
$I_{1991/90}$	0.56	0.27	0.60	1.06	0.61	0.26	0.72	1.04
$I_{1993/90}$	0.57	0.46	0.16	1.26	0.68	0.45	0.21	1.29
$I_{1993/91}$	1.02	1.69	0.27	1.20	1.10	1.71	0.29	1.24

 * Refers to: (1) number of foreign tourists (nights spent by foreign tourists) from the republics of former Yugoslavia (without Slovenia) and (2) number of other foreign tourists (nights spent by other foreign tourists) from other countries (Classic Abroad).
** Refers to number of tourists (nights) from the Republic of Slovenia.
Source: ZRSS (1993 and 1994a).

In the past Slovenia used to be a tourist transit country for the European tourist stream towards the Adriatic (Croatian coast). It had in 1990 an index value of foreign tourist nights per inhabitant of 1.8 compared to 5.5 for Switzerland and 12.4 for Austria (OECD, 1992; WTO, 1990).

Slovenia's income from international tourism for the same year was only $420 per inhabitant, total earnings from tourism were 857 million dollars. In the same year the income from international tourism per capita in Switzerland was $1033, in Austria $1550 (OECD 1992; WTO, 1990).

It can be seen from Table 16.1 that tourism in Slovenia grew steadily until 1988, declined slightly in the years 1989 and 1990, partly as a result of political instability (in summer of 1988 the military trial of a journalist and an army officer led to calls for an independent Slovenia) and partly as a result of the deteriorating competitiveness of Slovenian tourism supply.

The number of foreign tourists from so-called "classic abroad" (ie, the number of foreign tourists from outside the former Yugoslav republics) contributed 43 per cent to the total number of tourist nights; the number of tourists from former Yugoslav republics 31 per cent. The share of domestic tourism was only 26 per cent. The number of tourists dropped substantially in 1991, resulting in an overall decrease of 44 per cent due to the ongoing war in Slovenia and Croatia. Nights spent by tourists in Slovenia declined by 39 per cent. Domestic tourism increased but did not replace the decline in foreign tourism. The number of domestic nights increased by 4 per cent, as a result of the increased efforts of the Slovenian tourism supply to attract domestic tourists. Additionally, many Slovenian tourists, who were used to spending holidays in the neighboring Croatian coastal areas, stayed in the home country as a result of the war in Croatia.

In 1993, two years after the ten-day war, the figures for Slovenian tourism were still far behind the pre-war figures. The number of total nights in 1993 was 32 per cent lower than in 1990. Foreign tourism development has been hindered particularly by the following factors:

1. a new, young state is not very well known,
2. actual political circumstances are not very well known either,
3. mistaking the name Slovenia for Slavonia (region in Croatia),
4. vicinity of war in former Yugoslavia (the distance between Ljubljana, the capital of Slovenia, and Sarajevo is ca. 500 km).

The short war in Slovenia and the still ongoing war in the former Yugoslavia have very dramatically influenced the development of tourism in Slovenia. This is best illustrated by the comparison between tourism demand trends before and after the war. This trend can help us analyze a change in the popularity of Slovenia as a tourist destination over a period of time. The impact of the war factor was quantified by using the war as a dummy variable.

Model

In analyzing the trend "number of tourist nights," we have used the mathematical function where the linear relationship between dependent and independent variables is postulated:

$$Y = \beta_0 + \beta_1 X_1 + \beta_2 X_2 + \ldots + \beta_n X_n + u$$

where

Y	is the tourism demand,
$X_1, X_2, \ldots X_n$	are the influencing variables,
$\beta_0, \beta_1, \beta_2 \ldots \beta_n$	are parameters,
u	is a random error term.

The most commonly used mathematical functions for tourism demand functions are log-linear (multiplicative) and linear (additive) (Crouch and Shaw, 1992). In this case we have used the linear function which allows us, through its enlargement, to estimate two different trends with one function: the one before and the one after the war.

The basic linear model we are deriving from is the following:

$$Y_{ij} = \beta_0 + \beta_1 t + u$$

where

Y_{ij}	number of tourist nights from origin i to destination j in year t,
t	technical time, $t = 1, 2 \ldots 14$ ($1 = 1980, \ldots 14 = 1993$)
β_0, β_1	estimated parameters,
u	a random error term.

To the basic model we added war as the variable and obtained the following model:

$$Y_{ij} = \beta0 + \beta1t + \beta2D + u$$

where

D   dummy variable which picks up the effects of war in Slovenia and former
           Yugoslavia:
           D = 1 if war (if 5 = 12, 13, 14) and
           D = 0 otherwise.

In addition to trend and war components, a product between trend and the dummy variable is incorporated into the model:

$$Y_{ij} = \beta0 + \beta1t + \beta2D + \beta3tD + u$$

where

Dt   product between dummy variable D and time t (D * t).

Incorporating the product between the dummy and the technical time enables us to calculate two different trend functions (pre- and after-war function) with different parameters:

if D = 0 ⇒ Ypre-war   = $\beta0 + \beta1t + u$,
if D = 1 ⇒ Yafter-war = $\beta0 + \beta1t + \beta3 + \beta4t + u =$
                      = $\beta0 + \beta3 + (\beta1 + \beta4)t + u$.

The obtained results allow us to analyze trends before and after the war in Slovenia in 1991. Since the war on the territory of the former Yugoslavia has been going on since that same year, dummy variables also measure the influence of this war on tourism demand in Slovenia.

Pre- and post-war trends for tourism demand in Slovenia by country of origin

The number of tourist nights has decreased in Slovenia after the war in 1991 by 49 per cent. For a short period of time, the army besieged the border passes and blocked the airport. Publicity in the mass media was negative, while even worse and longer lasting were the consequences of the fact that Slovenia as a tourist destination was put on the black list of tour operators.

Table 16.2 shows that the post-war demand trend has a positive side from most countries except from the former Yugoslavia and the UK. However, not all estimated trend functions are statistically significant. The results are significant at the 5 per cent level for the Croatian, Slovenian and Austrian models.

Table 16.2   Pre- and post-war trends for tourism demand in Slovenia for the periods 1980−90 and 1991−3

General estimation function: $Y_{ij} = \beta 0 + \beta 1t + \beta 2D + \beta 3tD + u$

Tourism Demand	Trend 1980−1991	Trend 1991−1993	Adjusted R squared
Total	7524.44 + 119.11t (2.30*)	1840.67 + 249.00t (−1.13, 0.34)	0.86
Domestic	2343.89 + 43.75t (2.89*)	−1245.83 + 331.50t (−2.46*, 2.54*)	0.72
Foreign			
Former Yugoslavia	2531.18 − 45.00t (−1.83)	6272.16 − 425.50t (1.58, −2.07*)	0.87
— from Croatia	1095.95 − 35.63t (−3.13*)	3904.50 − 269.50t (2.54*, −2.75*)	0.81
Classic abroad	2980.53 + 127.73t (5.58*)	1268.23 + 343.00t (−2.58*, 1.26)	0.94
— from Germany	1013.00 − 9.89t (−1.22)	−474.86 + 54.00t (−1.90, 1.95)	0.93
— from United Kingdom	88.36 + 57.14t (7.39*)	654.66 − 44.00t (0.76, −1.75)	0.67
— from Austria	291.98 + 10.11t (2.47*)	−1423.66 + 132.00t (−4.33*, 3.98*)	0.67
— from Netherlands	281.44 + 7.34t (1.47)	−124.83 + 12.50t (−0.84, 0.14)	0.84
— from Sweden	6.22 + 12.51t (7.19*)	−4.33 + 1.00t (−0.06, −0.88)	0.87
— from United States	46.69 + 2.54t (3.08*)	−71.67 + 7.00t (−1.49, 0.73)	0.83

The figure in brackets is t value for the regression coefficient for TREND. The figures in brackets are t values for the regression coefficient for the DUMMY variable (war) and for the product TREND*DUMMY.
* indicates significant at 5 per cent level.

Domestic tourism demand has increased during the war and the post-war period. The reasons have already been explained (more aggressive marketing to attract domestic tourists, fewer travels to the Croatian coast).

The estimated results for foreign tourism are basically worse after the war, although the pre-war growing trend does continue more steeply. However, starting values in 1991 and 1992 are lower, the result of lesser tourism demand during the war year. It can be said that the war in Slovenia and the beginning of the war in former Yugoslavia had a negative impact on foreign tourism demand in Slovenia.

This analysis does not confirm the thesis that the common trend for foreign tourism after 1991 is turning more steeply upwards because tourists from different states have reacted in different ways.

The average annual growth of tourist nights from Austria is 13 times larger since the war. These are tourists from states near Slovenia. The fall of tourism demand has pushed

Table 16.3 Nights spent by foreign tourists in Slovenia in different types of tourism destinations for the period 1985—93 and indexes 1990/91, 1993/90, 1993/91 (in '000 nights)

Year	Total	Health Resorts	Sea Resorts	Mountain Resorts	Cities and others
1989	8509	1747	2291	2245	2226
1990	7956	1823	2102	2118	1913
1991	4885	1481	1000	1352	1052
1992	5098	1675	1266	1133	1024
1993	5384	1820	1454	1260	850
I1991/90	0.61	0.81	0.48	0.64	0.55
I1993/90	0.68	1.00	0.69	0.59	0.44
I1993/91	1.10	1.23	1.45	0.93	0.81

Source: ZRSS (1993) and (1994b).

the Slovenian receptive tourism close to the beginning of the typical "S" curve which describes the demand development. Since at the beginning of the "S" development the growth rates are higher than later when a more advanced phase occurs, such a development is theoretically sensible, too. The results of tourism demand from the United Kingdom, Sweden and the United States do not reach the 5 per cent significance level. These are more distant markets where the image of Slovenia is still negative and where the demand for Slovenia is influenced by the war in nearby Bosnia-Hercegovina. The actual reaction of the British tourists was stronger also because most of them visit Slovenia by charter flights organized by tour operators. The loss of charter flights thus naturally destroyed this type of tourism. After the airport was re-opened in 1992, charter flights were not re-established, foreign-tour operators reacted slowly, the process of booking in foreign markets was very slow — all this had even more negative consequences on 1992 booking. Some tourists from Germany and Italy do come to Slovenia individually, by cars. They reacted much more quickly to the war in 1991 and returned after the war sooner than the others. Since tourists from different states reacted differently, we will return to this question in analyzing the demand according to destinations.

Pre- and post-war trends for tourism demand for different destinations in Slovenia

Not all types of tourist destinations suffered equally from the decline in tourist demand. From the index 1991/90 in Table 16.3 the following declines in tourist nights, as the result of the war in 1991, can be seen: decline in total tourist nights in Slovenia was 49 per cent; nights in health resorts declined only by 19 per cent; nights in sea resorts by 52 per cent; nights in mountain resorts by 36 per cent and nights in other tourist destinations by 45 per cent. The strongest negative reaction was by "the sun and beach" oriented tourists and the weakest by the "health" oriented tourists.

Table 16.4 only shows the aggregate movement of trend according to different destinations. It does not include domestic tourism demand since we have already found out that under war conditions these reacted with fewer travels abroad, particularly to the traditional Croatian coast (due to the war and political tensions), and by consequence, with an increased number of nights in their homeland. The one-day domestic tourism also increased in these destinations (not covered by this analysis) since Slovenians compensated for the loss of (cheaper) holidays in Croatia with one-day trips in their own country (swimming in the lakes, the sea and spa pools).

Table 16.4 also shows that incorporation of independent variables of trend and war for mountain destinations was statistically significant. B3 is the only statistically insignificant parameter which corrects the estimation for the after war average growth rate.

The trend of tourism development in mountain destinations was negative even before the war. The reasons can be the discrepancy between the tourism offer and the modern tourist demand, and the discrepancy between the price and the value of the service. The post-war trend is positive, but the estimated starting value in 1991 is almost four times lower than it was in 1980. These destinations had a large share of tourists from distant countries. A lot of them spent their holidays in the former Yugoslavia. Typical travel included several Yugoslav destinations such as Dubrovnik, Plitvice (Croatia) and Bled (Slovenia). These tourists were linked to charters (Adria Airways, Aviogenex, JAT) and to the cooperation with British outgoing tour operators (Yugotours). When the Yugoslav army attacked the Slovenian airport Brnik and took most of the equipment, Adria Airways planes were evacuated to Austria and the company lost its flying license. For the same reasons charter flights of the Croatian Aviogenex and JAT were cut. Slovenia as a destination was removed from the British tour operators' catalogs. It turned out that it was extremely difficult to make a comeback. At the same time, in 1992 and 1993, the British tourist market showed no interest in Slovenian arrangements. At that time, the British BBC network was constantly reporting on the war in Sarajevo in Bosnia-Hercegovina.

For similar reasons American charter tourism stopped. There was a more positive reaction from Italians and Germans, but only for a short time. The number of tourist nights from the German-speaking countries (Germany, Austria) greatly increased. The reasons are many: Germany was the first state to acknowledge Slovenia, holidays in Austria and Switzerland became expensive, Slovenia is relatively close to these states and easy to reach by car or bus and there was an aggressive tourist promotion in these countries.

As regards mountain destinations, war caused a shift from package tourism organized by tour operators to a non-packaged type which was more advantageous for hotel owners since they could raise prices. German tourists are, in terms of expenditure, more profitable than the British. Therefore the forecasts for tourism earnings are, in spite of the war going on in Bosnia-Hercegovina, optimistic.

In the case of sea resorts, the statistical results are not so significant except for the factor trend before war. After the war in 1991, tourism demand was probably influenced also by other factors, not only the end of the war in Slovenia.

Like the mountain tourist destinations, the seaside tourist destinations before the war existed through unorganized tourism. German but also British and Scandinavian tourists were coming to Slovenia under the auspices of large tour operators (TUI, Neckermann, Star Tour, BTTC, Thompson, Yugotours etc). Only some 30 per cent of guests were non-inclusive (individual) guests. The latter were mainly Italians, due to the nearby Italian border and because historically Italians are familiar with and attached to Slovenia. When, after the war, tour operators turned down contracts, the season was partly saved by individual Italian and domestic tourists.

Table 16.4 Pre- and post-war trends for tourism demand for different destinations in Slovenia for the periods 1980−90 and 1991−3.
General estimation function: $Y_{ij} = \beta0 + \beta1t + \beta2D + \beta3tD + u$

Tourism demand	Trend 1980−1991	1991−1993	Adjusted R squared
1. Health resorts	151.87 + 29.08t (11.95*)	−798.67 + 81.00t (−4.03*, 2.85)	0.93
2. Sea resorts	739.25 + 80.25t (4.17*)	−1005.50 + 107.50t (−0.94, 0.19)	0.81
3. Mountain resorts	1317.13 − 20.49t (−3.45*)	−184.66 + 42.00t (−2.61*, 1.41)	0.97
4. Cities and others	414.93 + 33.16t (1.82)	−1142.83 + 112.50t (−0.88, 0.58)	0.33

The figure in brackets is the t value for the regression coefficient for TREND. The figures in brackets are t values for the regression coefficient for the DUMMY variable (war) and for the product TREND*DUMMY
* indicates significant at the 5 per cent level.

After the war seaside tourism was restructured toward individual tourism, which today represents over 60 per cent. The loss of income in tourist companies was therefore not as great as the loss in physical flows, since individual guests bring more profit. In 1994 the tourist industry reached the same magnitude of circulation as before the war, with a more profitable guest structure financially.

As regards spa tourism the case is slightly different. The model of tourism demand is statistically significant. The war has basically changed the trend of tourism demand, and also its starting value in 1991.

The majority of guests in health resorts were Austrians, Italians, Germans and guests from neighboring Croatia. The latter, who in the past had their holidays paid for on the basis of contracts for medically approved holidays, did not return after the war. The first to come back were Italians, somewhat later also Austrians and Germans. Spas were not particularly linked to large tour operators, unlike the case with the mountain and seaside destinations. They cooperated with smaller Italian and German travel agencies (Aurora, Etli, Union Reisen) with whom they renewed the allotment contracts very quickly and by 1994, the spas were again included in their catalogs. Furthermore, they did not depend on air charter links but on bus charters. One difference between spa and other destinations is also that health resorts have a large share of regular guests who are acquainted with conditions in Slovenia and remained loyal to a country that had experienced war. When the first guests started to return after the war, word-of-mouth publicity spread very fast and this increased the demand from their friends and relatives. In order to normalize their relationship with their (former) regular guests, the spas increased their marketing efforts (direct mailing).

Statistical parameters of variables for towns and other tourist resorts have too low t-test values to allow us to say that the analysis included adequate factors of tourism demand. The reason is that it is a very heterogeneous group. This group also includes the capital of the new state — Ljubljana. After gaining independence the capital has become a business, exhibition and congress center, and the number of tourist nights is constantly increasing.

Another factor is the large number of diplomatic representatives, journalists during and after the war and guests from former Yugoslav states.

Although the number of tourist nights basically decreased in Slovenia after the war, the economic consequences were not that drastic. Since tourist complexes were in state ownership there were no bankruptcies. The private sector (rooms to let and apartments) was much more afflicted by a lower demand, but its losses have not been evaluated.

The consequences of war on large enterprises were partly alleviated by the state, which granted funds to the hotels. Hotels raised loans from banks but these were regularly paid out. Before the war Slovenian hotels had no liabilities because they could easily pay back investment loans taken for construction under conditions of inflation. The exceptions were hotels constructed with foreign loans. Some tourist companies even invested in infrastructure in order to improve quality and for reorientation to convention tourism. Some hotels which were, during and after the war, conducting very heavy investment projects, are nowadays indebted to banks and affluent companies. During the privatization of state ownership which has only now been initiated in the tourism industry, these debts will probably be transformed into ownership shares for creditors.

The number of employees in the tourism industry has been reduced by about 30–40 per cent, mainly due to natural turnover and because seasonal workers are no longer employed. Very few employees were dismissed. Some hotel managers estimate that the number of employees is still too high and will additionally decrease when the privatization procedure is over.

The entire income loss was in most cases lower than the loss in tourist arrivals because of a more convenient structure of guests (more individual guests who bring more money). In 1991 foreign-currency income from tourism was one-third ($122 million) lower than expected. In 1994, according to the Bank of Slovenia, Slovenia had earned $1 billion from foreign tourism, which is more than in the record pre-war year, when it earned $857 million. The major reason was the restructuring of tourism demand (towards non-inclusive tourism) and offer (towards higher quality).

Influence of war on tourism in neighboring Austria

The model of tourism demand with two independent variables was tested also on the example of the Austrian incoming tourism. After 1985, Austrian tourism was in constant growth which globally continued even after 1991 when neighboring Slovenia was at war. The growth is above all due to German tourist nights, which represent about 70 per cent of the total foreign guest nights. German tourists were reported, in the case of Slovenia, to have reacted quickly to the war but for a short period of time. The loss of tourism demand in Austria due to the war in the neighboring state probably alleviated the counter effect: tourism demand in Austria increased due to the loss of the Yugoslav and Slovenian tourist market and reorientation of tourist trends to the benefit of Austria. Slovenian outgoing tourism turned to Austria instead of Croatia. Statistically significant is the impact of war in former Yugoslavia on tourism demand of Austria from Switzerland, Italy and France. In all the three cases the trend shifted from positive into negative with a substantial decrease. Probably the war also influenced the demand of British tourists, but we could not prove this with this model.

Table 16.5 Pre- and post-war trend for tourism demand in Austria from different countries of origin for the periods 1980−90 and 1991−3

Tourism demand	Trend		Adjusted R squared
	1980−1991	1991−1993	
1. Foreign total	88 799.09 − 372.18t (−0.36)	117 093.83 − 1407.50t (0.28, −0.14)	0.02
— from Germany	64 697.89 − 913.44t (−3.61*)	60 155.50 + 346.40t (−1.19, 0.67)	0.61
— from Netherlands	9830.96 − 63.60t (−2.04*)	14 033.50 − 395.50t (1.39, −1.42)	0.46
— from United Kingdom	2640.96 + 218.81t (5.71*)	7396.83 − 262.50t (1.28, −1.78)	0.70
— from Switzerland	924.96 + 182.76t (12.20*)	5129.83 − 156.60t (2.90*, −3.03*)	0.95
— from Belgium/ Luxembourg	2939.33 − 18.37t (0.75)	3460.50 + 18.50t (0.22, −0.00*)	0.19
— from Italy	211.02 +225.48t	6645.84 − 262.50t (2.35*, −2.31*)	0.91
— from France	1591.07 + 134.06t (9.97*)	6354.66 − 267.00t (3.66*, 3.99*)	0.91
— from United States	1396.64 + 52.41t (1.57)	192.67 + 90.00t (−0.37, 0.15)	0.13

The figure in brackets is the t value for the regression coefficient for TREND. The figures in brackets are t values for the regression coefficient for the DUMMY variable (war) and for the product TREND*DUMMY.
* indicates significant at 5 per cent level.

Conclusion

War is undoubtedly one of the factors of tourism demand with a negative effect. In most cases it causes reorientation of tourist flows.

In 1991, Slovenia was placed on the black list of war destinations so it is only to be expected that the tourist flows dropped. When the war ended, tourism was not quickly restored. Slovenia was still partly burdened with a war image, especially in more distant outgoing tourist markets (the United Kingdom, the United States, Scandinavian states); other factors were severed charter links and lack of cooperation from large tour operators. At the same time, Slovenian tourism experienced restructuring from inclusive to the more profitable (in terms of prices) individual tourism. Therefore financial losses are not as dramatic as the physical loss of number of tourist nights. At the same time, hotels have also rationalized their business. The tourist nights in the year 1994 are close to those in the year 1990; tourism income is much higher (ZRSS, 1994b).

Ongoing war in former Yugoslavia (Croatia, Bosnia-Hercegovina) does not have as negative an impact on Slovenian tourism development as the war in Slovenia or the beginning of the war in former Yugoslavia. Tourism demand trends after the war in

Slovenia are positive, the pre-war growing trends continue even more steeply. However, the drop in the year 1991 was substantial. Tourists from different countries reacted in different ways. This is also the case with package-tour and individual guests. The result was a shift from tour operators to self-organized travel that is more financially advantageous for the hospitality industry.

The comparison between trends before and post-war (calculated from a common linear function) showed the negative war impact on the tourism demand in Slovenia (a drop in 1991) and different reactions from tourists from different countries after the war. Some statistical results are significant at the 5 per cent level, but for future research the Slovenian tourism demand model should take into account (besides the war) other factors many of which were mentioned above.

References

Archer, B.H. (1994). Trends in International Tourism. In *Tourism Marketing and Management Handbook*, L. Moutinho and S.F. Witt (eds), 93—8. Cambridge: Cambridge University Press.

Anderson, B. and Anderson, H. (1992). Site Selection — Hawaii: Oahu & the Big Island. *Successful Meetings* **41**(10): 222—9.

Becheri, E. (1990). Rimini and Co. — the end of the legend? Dealing with the algae effect. *Tourism Management,* **11**(3): 229—35.

Burkart, A.J. and Medlik, S. (1974). *The Management of Tourism.* London: Heinemann.

Cicvarić, A. (1990). *Ekonomika turizma.* Zagreb: Zagreb.

Crouch, G.I. and Shaw, R.N. (1992). International Tourism Demand: A Meta-Analytical Integration of Research Findings. In P. Johnson and B. Thomas (eds), *Choice and Demand in Tourism,* 175—207.

Economist (1994). *Vietnam — the Profit Hunters,* **331**(7867): 31—2.

Gajraj, M. (1989). Warning signs. *Tourism Management,* **10**(3): 202—3.

Goeldner, C.R. (1992). The outlook for Travel in 1992. *Journal of Travel Research,* **30**(3): 52—4.

Goodrich, J.N. (1991). An American Study of Tourism Marketing: Impact of the Persian Gulf War. *Journal of Travel Research,* **30**(2): 37—41.

Gubernick, L. (1993). Damage Control. *Forbes,* **152**(2): 196—7.

Hunziker, W. and Krapf, K. (1942). *Grundriss der allgemeinen Fremdenverkehrslehre.* Zurich: Polygraphischer Verlag.

Impact of the Gulf Crisis on International Tourism (1991). *Journal of Travel Research,* **30**(2): 34—6.

Jusko, J. (1991). Forum Indicates Industry Recovery Will Take Awhile. *Hotel & Motel Management,* **206**(21): 2, 44.

Kaspar, C. (1991). *Die Tourismuslehre im Grundriss.* Bern: Paul Haupt Verlag.

Krippendorf, J. (1984). *Die Ferienmenschen.* Zurich: Orell Fuesli Verlag.

Leksikon CZ (1987). *Ljubljana: Cankarjeva zalo ba.*

Martin, C.A. and Witt, S.F. (1989). Tourism demand elasticities. In L. Moutinho and S.F. Witt (eds), *Tourism Marketing and Management Handbook,* Cambridge: Cambridge University Press: 477—85.

Mavris, C. (1993). The Effects of Political Instabilities in Cyprus and Neighbouring Countries on the Tourist Industry. *Proceedings of International Conference on Sustainable Tourism in Islands and Small States.* Malta, 18—20 November 1—19.

Menges, G. (1957). Die Einkomenselastizitaet des Fremdenverkehrs. *Revue de Tourisme,* **12**(2): 46—51.

OECD (Organization for Economic Cooperation and Development) (1987). *Tourism Policy and International Tourism in OECD Member Countries,* Paris: OECD.

OECD (1992). *Tourism Policy and International Tourism in OECD Member Countries.*

Petty, R. (1989). Health limits to tourism development. *Tourism Management,* **10**(3): 209—121.

Rowe, M. (1993). Looking up down under. *Lodging Hospitality,* **49**(8): 52–3.

Socher, K. (1985). Fremdenverkehr in der oekonomischen Theorie. *Wirtschaftspolitische Blaeter* (5): 398–406.

Teye, B.V. (1988). Coup d'Etat and African Tourism: A Study of Ghana. *Annals of Tourism Research* **15**(3).

Vanhove, N. (1991). Research and Education in Tourism. *Proceedings of the 50 Jahre touristische und verkehrswirtschaftliche Forschung an der Hochschule St. Gallen,* St. Gallen, 24–5 October: 129–148.

Var, T., Ap, J. and Van Doren, C. (1994). *Tourism and World Peace.* In W.F. Theobald (ed.), *Global Tourism.* Oxford: Butterworth Heinemann Ltd: 27–39.

Vukonić, B. (1993). *Turizam u vihoru rata.* Zagreb: MATE d.o.o.

Wilkson, P. (1994). Mexico City, *TRINET, 4* February.

Witt, S.F. (1994). Econometric demand forecasting. In L. Moutinho and S.F. Witt (eds), *Tourism Marketing and Management Handbook.* Cambridge: Cambridge University Press: 516–20.

WTO (World Tourism Organization) (1980). *Manila Declaration on World Tourism.*

WTO (1990). Compendium of Tourism Statistics.

ZRSS (Zavod za statistiko Republike Slovenije) (1993). *Statistič ni letopis Republike Slovenije 1993.* Ljubljana: ZRSS.

ZRSS (1994a). *Statistič ne informacije 27.* Ljubljana: ZRSS.

ZRSS (1994b). *Statistič ne informacije 318.* Ljubljana: ZRSS.

17 War and its tourist attractions

VALENE L. SMITH

War: an armed contest between two independent political units, by means of organized military force, in the pursuit of a tribal or national policy (Malinowski, 1941: 523).

War, associated with bloody battlefields, cemeteries filled with grim white crosses and Holocaust museums, seems an unlikely candidate for popularity with tourists. However, visitor attendance at the leading tourist attractions in Hawaii, two of which are war memorials, for five consecutive years (1989–93) suggested otherwise (Table 17.1). This data stimulated a study of the relations between warfare and tourism, and this chapter is the first published account. When this research began in 1992, it seemed incongruous in the vacation islands so well described in *Hawaii: The Legend that Sells* (Farrell, 1982), that for three consecutive years (1988 through 1991) the National Cemetery of the Pacific received more visitors than the other five leading attractions combined. In 1991, National Cemetery Park administrators monitored the continuous traffic flow and realized the cemetery was being visited by virtually every tourist sightseeing bus, not as a memorial

Table 17.1 Attendance at museums and other cultural attractions

	1989	1990	1991	1992	1993
National Cemetery of the Pacific	5 343 974	6 281 431	5 522 948	N/A	N/A
USS Arizona Memorial	1 845 557	1 870 805	1 501 607	1 535 591	1 460 149
Jagger Monument/ Kilauea Volcanic National Park	1 373 000	2 368 219	2 675 460	2 493 363	2 494 908
Polynesian Cultural Center	1 001 708	844 043	814 832	838 000	871 643
Honolulu Zoo	758 485	652 228	600 726	704 424	742 000
Dole Plantation	N/A	1 029 000	895 000	893 000	803 000

Source: Hawaii Visitors' Bureau (1994).

Tourism, Crime and International Security Issues, edited by
A. Pizam and Y. Mansfeld. © 1996 John Wiley & Sons Ltd.

but because the site afforded the best photographic view of Waikiki Beach and Honolulu. The Park Service decried this heavy daily traffic, noting that sound pollution was destroying the appropriate quietude for those who Rest in Peace. In 1992, the memorial was closed to tour buses.

The consistent second in popularity among tourist destinations in the island state is also war-related (Table 17.1). The Arizona Memorial floats in Honolulu's Pearl Harbor anchored to the rusting hull of the *USS Arizona*. The battleship sank during the Japanese attack on December 7, 1941 which precipitated the Pacific phase of World War II. This leaking vessel, with air bubbles still rising to the surface, serves as a tomb for some 1400 sailors killed aboard. The adjoining museum combines continuous videos and inter-active displays with restaurants and souvenir stores, and visitors are of many nationalities including Japanese. For many Hawaii tourists, this military park is a full-day attraction despite long waiting lines for the US Navy excursion boats that provide free tours to the memorial itself.

The Hawaii data may be unique in numbers but probably not in principle. The research undertaken for this chapter strongly supports the statement that despite the horrors of death and destruction (and also because of them), the memorabilia of warfare and allied products (such as the houses where "George Washington slept here") probably constitutes the largest single category of tourist attractions in the world. The list is almost endless and includes battlefields and cemeteries; victory monuments to the heroes and flames for the fallen; museums dedicated to medals, armaments and little tin soldiers; and historical re-enactments that attract thousands of participants and far greater throngs of observers. The booty of war decorates homes as stylistically different as a Borneo Dyak Longhouse with its strings of dust-covered human skulls suspended from the rafters or as opulent as the czar's Winter Palace in St. Petersburg, now alleged to house booty of World War II origin (*Time*, 17 October 1994: 35). Many forms of entertainment use war as their theme: the stirring marches of John Phillips Souza, played by military bands, numerous operas, of which *Aida* with its dramatic Triumphal March is a prime example; and countless novels, to say nothing of motion pictures which date as early as *Ben Hur*. Because war tourism is both geographically and temporally extensive, it also contributes significantly to growing travel industry receipts. The world in general views warfare with distaste for the carnage is disruptive, costly and lethal, and only munitions manufacturers and power hungry politicians such as Hitler or Saddam Hussein seem to benefit. Political instability and the threat of war is an immediate deterrent to tourism. Therefore why make of its memories important tourist attractions? This chapter examines the anthropological literature pertaining to warfare, and discusses some of the types of tourism attractions associated with military conflicts.

An analysis of war

The French anthropologist Balandier introduces a lengthy essay on war with:

> In the beginning was violence, and all history can be seen as an unending effort to control it. Violence is always present in society and takes the form of war in relations between societies when competition can no longer be contained by trade and market.

> Violence has been a major theme throughout the development of political thought in the West and elsewhere (Balandier, 1986: 499).

The study of violence has long engaged scholars in many disciplines, especially political science, history and psychology. Cross-cultural studies, the hallmark of anthropology, that focus on conflict are few in number and of comparatively recent origin. To name a few key scholars from this discipline, Turney-High (1949) pioneered the analysis of warfare through his fieldwork with Native Americans, especially the Flathead and Kutenai tribes of Montana. He defined warfare as essentially a matter of social organization rather than economics or as an extension of diplomacy. His "Afterword" to the second edition of *Primitive War* (1971) is recommended as a still instructive essay for evaluating wars of the 1990s. Hoebel (1954), another noted ethnographer of the Plains Indians (in this case the Cheyenne), expanded the research to link warfare and formal legal systems as an outgrowth of primitive social organization. To illustrate, the Plains Indians regularly engaged in territorial wars, developed strong hierarchical military societies that conferred rank upon successful warriors and in wars against the Europeans created national battlefields such as the Little Bighorn.

Pospisil (1958) added the blood-feuds of the Kapauku Papuans (New Guinea) to a widening interest in conflict. Then scientific fashion changed and anthropologists of the 1960s devoted more attention to the Flower Children, drug culture and urbanization except for a 1967 symposium on war held in conjunction with the annual meetings of the American Anthopological Association (Fried et al, 1968). Haas (1990) revived scholarly interest in the study of warfare and organized a Guggenheim Foundation symposium to analyze the origins of, for example, the maintenance of warfare in prestate societies. Tourism is not mentioned in any of the above-cited works, nor is warfare indexed in the *VNRS Encyclopedia of Hospitality and Tourism* (Khan et al., 1993).

The first serious effort to link war with the pleasure periphery appears in *Back to the Front: Tourisms of War* (Diller and Scofidio, 1994), ostensibly a catalog created to accompany the French exhibition, *The Production of National Past*, held in the Abbaye-aux-Dames, Caen, January 14–March 27 1994. However, in reality the book includes several profound philosophical statements by two very observant American architects on aspects of tourism. A notable opening quotation sets the theme,

> Tourism and war appear to be polar extremes of cultural activity — the paradigm of international accord at one end and discord at the other. The two practices, however, often intersect: tourism of war, war on tourism, tourism as war, war targeting tourism, tourism under war, war as tourism are but a few of their intersecting couplings (Diller and Scofidio, 1994: 19).

These authors also call attention to the symbiosis of modern war, as in Israel, where "war is fueled by tourism within war." They correctly note that Israel lives in a state of permanent war, and it is tourist receipts on which their national defense budget depends. When tourist income disappeared during the 1991 Gulf War, Israel billed the United States for direct damages from Iraqi Scud missiles in the amount of US$200 million and an additional US$400 million for lost revenues from tourism (Ibid: 20). Thus Diller and Scofidio (1994) make an important contribution at this early stage of warfare—tourism studies, although they tend to follow the materialist economic lead of Balandier quoted above and focus on the geography of tourism, its landmarks, heritage and authenticity.

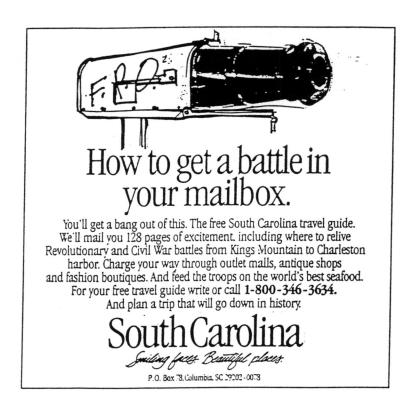

Figure 17.1 The advertisement, "How to get a battle in your mailbox," linking war themes with domestic tourism, was sponsored by the South Carolina State Office of Tourism.

These tangible remnants of war can be described in tourist brochures and serve as incentives for tourism (Figure 17.1), but that alone is not sufficient motivation to attract large numbers of pleasure-seekers to sites of carnage.

Following the lead of Turney-High, tourism and warfare can both be identified as social processes that are inseparable from the underlying and diverse cultural threads of group values, sanctions, beliefs and behaviors. Warfare and tourism are sometimes cojoined and intertwined as in the Israeli example cited above. Under different circumstances, the two powerful themes seem discrete even though still linked, as when war rages and tourism simply disappears — to return with peace. For example, in 1944 – 5, Americans were prideful of their active role in the war fought to "make the world safe for democracy," and ticker-tape parades heralded the heroes home. Anthropologist Margaret Mead captured that spirit in her "national character study" of American wartime culture, *And Keep Your Powder Dry* (1965). In gratitude for their liberation the French deeded land to the Allied forces to ensure their war dead were buried on "American," "British" or "Canadian" soil.

Fifty years later, these Allies staged a world class event on June 6, 1994 to commemorate D-Day at Normandy, complete with a parade of ships and attendance by heads of state. Defeat creates few such celebrations. The Germans in an effort to seek a sentiment of "forgive and forget" (and because they also suffered many casualties in Normandy during the same battle) asked to participate in the June 6th events. The requests were denied. The French, however, did extend a token of reconciliation, inviting a small German presence to the 1994 Bastille Day parade in Paris. Throughout 1994 new museums were opened and large, impressive statues and memorials erected to publicly document forever the positive aspects of that war. In this instance, war and tourism coalesce on a grand and positive scale. The final tally for revenues generated by the 50th anniversary victory festivities may never be known but it is certainly substantial.

By contrast, the 1975 US troop withdrawal from Vietnam (essentially a defeat in battle) brought little hero recognition to returning soldiers; many veterans faced difficulties finding employment. In 1993, at the time of the author's visit to Saigon, the war museums were pointedly anti-American, and reflected existent government policy; their exhibit captions described the USA invaders as aggressors with oppressive intents. The American war dead had been relocated to cemeteries away from Vietnam, and the US government was still negotiating for the return of POW bodies. Vietnam, however, intends to develop international tourism for its economic benefits, and in 1994 construction was underway on several major resort properties along its coast. The beaches are unquestionably some of the world's most beautiful and unspoiled, and the nation hopes to be a center for international tourism and especially to attract the huge potential Asian vacation market (Jansen-Verbecke and Go, 1994). Beginning in 1993, some American cruise operators featured Vietnam as an itinerary stop, to attract veterans as passengers but the response has not been great. Perhaps time will overcome latent prejudice to foster American tourism, but the question remains: in defeat, will there be major commemorative events in 2025 AD to honor these veterans and mark the 50th anniversary of this war?

The violence of warfare differs from that of crime and terrorism because of its penetrating societal involvement. Crime is usually one-on-one or an interpersonal interaction; terrorism is a politically motivated small-group activity directed toward individuals to "strike terror" into their midst and thereby defeat or control the opposition. In both instances, the activity is local and of short duration. Crime and terrorism leave little or no heritage to become permanent tourist markers. Although the site itself may remain of interest to families and close friends of the victims, the curiosity-seekers who swarm to such scenes are but transients soon on the move to the next event locale.

As other authors in this volume have shown, crime against tourists breeds in areas of economic deprivation and primarily against "foreigners" who commonly do not return to the area to prosecute even if the perpetrator is found and detained. Therefore crimes against tourists often "pay" or are worth the risk (Cohen, 1987). Terrorism may be deliberately tourist-oriented, to shatter a local economy that is heavily dependent on tourism revenues. Loss of their employment (and livelihood), coupled with fear of reprisals if they resist, frequently turns marginal employees toward the political cause of the terrorists, thereby fostering broader support for their aspirations.

However, the *violence and events of crime and terrorism* are quickly forgotten by most of a public now conditioned to "updated" news flashes on CNN. How many tourists who will eventually visit Sarajevo after conclusion of the 1990s Serb—Bosnian conflict will particularly care about finding the exact doorway (if indeed the building still stands) where Archduke Ferdinand was assassinated to start World War I? (For decades this was an important landmark visited on a Sarajevo city tour.) Similarly, how many cruise passengers can name the year and the victim of the terrorist attack aboard the *Achille Lauro*? Parenthetically, visitors to areas where terrorist activities have occurred against tourists should know the dates of those prior attacks because sometimes "anniversary" remembrances are a repeat occurrence.

In perspective, when considering the tourist impact of crime and terrorism the relative desirability of the attraction influences the rate of tourist recovery and outweighs all but the most serious threats to personal safety. Random attacks on a few German tourists motoring in Florida did not deter most other Germans from their planned charter flights from snowbound Frankfurt to sunny Miami (possibly with a planned extension to the Mayan ruins of Yucatan). As a contrasting example, India has never been a high-profile destination for Americans because of adverse images of poverty, beggars and disease. The outbreak of armed conflict in the fabled Vale of Kashmir or a newscast reporting cases of pneumonic plague in Bombay almost immediately curtails American tourist travel to the sub-continent, even if these events do not directly affect Americans or their destination cities.

Turney-High (1981: 19) summarized his life-long interest in violence and conflict by examining it in the context of behavioral science theory, in which "war is a state of mind and a legal condition. The violent means of waging war is called warfare . . . the essence of war and warfare is to introduce turbulence and crisis into another social system while attempting to prevent a lack of equilibrium within the we-group." It is this penetration into an alien social network that gives special meaning and memory to the places and events, and links warfare to tourism.

To demonstrate its pervasive social implications, four criteria in combination define true warfare (Turney-High, 1971): (1) a group motive; (2) a body of warriors among whom exist individuals with authority to lead, and others to take orders; (3) military strategies, to bring fighting units to positions where battle objectives can be attained; and (4) material and logistics to sustain a campaign to victory, or to withstand siege, until the goals are realized (including essential supplies for an affected civilian population). Turney-High clearly distinguishes between warfare as a military engagement distinct from "police actions" such as urban riots and gang wars.

War permeates every segment of society for both aggressor and aggrieved. As military analysts know, to initiate a war successfully implies (1) the presence of an economic stockpile adequate to meet all needs: and (2) that the labor of each member of the armed forces is expendable or not needed to (a) sustain the home communities for the duration of the conflict and/or (b) to produce the armaments necessary to engage in successful combat. The ability to remove personnel from an active labor force and, in the event of their death, to sustain post-war society without them, points to surplus population, particularly if one of the war aims — the annexation of more territory — is achieved and must be administered. A defeated nation usually faces still greater problems in loss of its stockpile, manpower, territory, resources, and administration plus a burden of war debt, reparations, reconstruction, and possible imposition of slavery. It is these factors, many of which are seldom articulated to a civilian public prior to engaging in war (but which become evident after the fact) that extend the battlefield to every hearth. The penetration of war into the very fabric of human life makes it *the time-markers of society*. People know that life has changed perceptibly, and they chronicle the differences in their lives as three eras: "before the war," "during the war" and "after the war." This pervasive impact of warfare figures prominently in the tourist involvement with memories and monuments.

Warfare and culture change

Before examining the "attractions" of war, one must speak of the actors — the men and women who participate in warfare, abroad or at home, for they are agents of cultural transmission. Throughout history war has stimulated technological innovations, soon followed by adaptive social change, almost all of it through human contact. Except for the impetus of war and the need for armies to travel, most people living on subsistence economies remained close to home base: hunters in the range they knew and farmers on the land they tilled. Leisure travel (as distinct from exploration and religious pilgrimages) is essentially an outgrowth of the Industrial Revolution, when machines replaced manpower, and individuals began selling their hours of labor at a price commensurate with their skills, generating discretionary time and money for travel.

In the pre-leisure era, the Crusaders provide a well-documented example of acculturation associated with warfare. With their accompanying armies, retainers, cooks and prostitutes, the Crusaders constituted a significant body of people, traveling long distances for a decade or more, to and from the Holy Land. *En route*, these individuals camped and lived among alien tribes, shopped for trinkets in native bazaars, ate different foods and learned new crafts. Once home they introduced many Asian customs to their families and incorporated them into their life-style. To name just one, accompanying troubadours entertained Europeans with Persian songs of *romantic love*, a theme then virtually unknown on the Continent. Subsequently romance appeared in the early novels, also in theater and opera. However, romantic love became the basis for marriage in Europe only after World War II, when arranged marriages were no longer practical due to changed social mobility.

The overseas experience of the American GI during World War II is a major (and unpublished) factor in the development of American mass tourism. Aside from the actual battlefields on the Continent, many soldiers were billeted in England for training, then "toured" parts of Europe in the course of military occupation, where many found "roots" of their heritage. Troops in the Pacific "discovered" South Sea islands, India, China, and later, Japan. The insular, previously isolated society of America was changing. Of those who returned home as victors, many were imbued with a desire to see the war-time sites under peace-time conditions. Meanwhile their wives and sweethearts had worked in defense plants, and after the war, many moved to civilian jobs. The wages of working wives became the discretionary income to make leisure travel possible (Smith, 1979). Moreover, only the US (of the industrial nations) emerged from World War II without destruction and the consequent need to rebuild infrastructure. Because Americans — then the world power-brokers — took vacations abroad, and virtually established the principle of paid vacations as a "human right," the industrialized world has gratefully imitated that trend. Nations now termed Third World may be predicted ultimately and similarly to conform.

Thus, of today's soldiers, Diller and Scofidio (1994: 20) observe, "travel is no longer simply a provision of war; it has become a fringe benefit, even an incentive. Advertisements for the armed forces promise military service as a way to 'See the World'."

Tourism and commemoration

The consequences of warfare have contributed a staggering array of physical memorabilia, events and obligations which are clustered below into five warfare—tourist genres. Common to all of them is a single theme — commemoration. Schwartz (1982: 377) is instructive here:

> Our memory of the past is preserved primarily by means of chronicling, the direct recording of events and their sequence. However, the events selected for chronicling are not all evaluated in the same way. To some of these events we remain morally indifferent; other events are commemorated, i.e., invested with an extraordinary significance and assigned a quantitatively distinct place in our conception of the past . . . commemoration lifts from an ordinary historical sequence those extraordinary events which embody our deepest and most fundamental values . . . [it is] in this sense a register of sacred history.

For any one society, the military time-markers of society are of two types: the wars whose outcome benefited the group and those that did not. This dichotomy is usually victory or defeat but not necessarily. Some wars are better not fought than lost, as most observers would hold true for Vietnam. The reasons underlying American involvement in that conflict were never clearly articulated to the public (or the soldiers) probably to avoid exacerbating a Cold War with China. The resulting lack of time and status markers perpetuates the controversy that will forever cloud that period of world history. The commemorative symbols for both victory and defeat may be externally the same, but internally the sense of "sacred history" and the associated values can be polarized. A third and different level of commemoration surrounds the heroes, both living and deceased, and is discussed below.

Success in war supposedly improves socio-economic conditions for the victors, albeit at a cost of lives and resources, and therefore victory reinforces group identity and national pride (Elshtain, 1991). Commemoration builds cohesion, even as the military recognizes that men from widely divergent backgrounds meld in battle to a "buddy system," founded on mutual respect and trust. Heroes emerge from those bonds, in the individuals who, at great personal sacrifice or risk, save comrades from imminent life-threatening dangers. Higher on the hierarchical scale are the officers, especially commanding generals and admirals, whose strategies change the course of history. Respect, even hero worship, form part of their commemoration. Overall, a victory reinforces self-worth, in the belonging to a winning team, and the satisfaction of knowing that "we've done something right." Americans shared all these sentiments during World War I when they fought and won the "war to end all wars," and set aside November 11 as a national Armistice Day (now Veterans Day) to honor the "last war." The Treaty of Versailles (November 11, 1919) instantly turned an old palace into a major tourist destination, forcing the French as a matter of national pride to restore its fountains and renovate the property. But the chronicle of life moves on; that generation of soldiers dies, and their victory markers lose some luster. After World War II, tourists still visit Versailles, but travel promotions now advertise it as the home of Marie Antoinette and her glorious ballroom and not the former political venue.

Victory in World War II still "lives" in public consciousness because many participants are active senior citizens. The 50th Anniversary ceremonial has deep-seated and special meaning on two counts: (1) the glow of remembrance for the big victory in 1945 partially glosses over the Vietnam defeat; and (2) the recent victory in the 1991 Gulf War clearly demonstrated that America is still a great power with a military to be respected. The technology of the Gulf War was different from World War II, but the will to win, and the ability to do so, is intact and the nation is prideful.

To lose a war (eg, Germany and Japan in World War II) symbolizes both defeat and national shame, coupled with international distrust. Defeat is divisive, as individuals seek scapegoats to explain away the demands of a now-dead leadership. With infrastructure and the economic system in shambles, it is a long material road back — especially if reparations are a condition of surrender.

In defeat there is little sacred history to commemorate, and monuments to a leader such as Hitler would be a mockery. Germany had no funds to bring her war dead home; many are buried in cemeteries on foreign soil, in France and the Low Countries. To maintain pride of nation, Volksbund Deutsche Kriegsgraberfursorge e.V. organizes German youth groups who spend two weeks each summer in one of some 16 European countries, on-site at a memorial cemetery. In the summer of 1993, these groups tended graves at 109 sites, 52 within France alone (and also vacationed as tourists!).

And the Japanese lost "face" in their humiliating defeat. The Japanese also left many of their war dead where they fell. The author was traveling with a group of friends in Saipan in 1975, 30 years after the war. Among guests in the hotel were groups of older/aged Japanese who were spending day-after-day digging in the mud at the base of Suicide Cliffs, probing for remains of family members who, as soldiers, were either killed or committed *hara-kiri* there. We chanced upon one such group holding a Buddhist cremation and decided to opt for the participant – observer mode. At first the Japanese participants seemed embarrassed by American presence, but as we lighted candles and joined their procession, a sense of closure prevailed.

Saipan and Guam are now popular Japanese honeymoon destinations. These young Japanese transcend national shame as they visit the various war sites and shrines, with an attitude that connotes "that was their war" — "their" being two generations and political eons ago. Older Guamanians, however, and others (eg, Filipinos, Trukese and Palauns) who suffered under Japanese occupation prior to and during World War II, are not yet ready to forgive, let alone forget. Ingenuous smiles and perfunctory service greet these conquerors-turned-tourists, but true hospitality is often lacking.

Many classification systems could be created to describe the vast array of military – warfare – tourism relations. The choice selected here is not all-inclusive. Rather, it is suggested by the nature of the site(s) and their tourism – cultural attributes.

The heroic phase

Names of great warriors dominate history books because they are important military time-markers, only a few of them are named here: Alexander the Great, Julius Caesar,

Genghis Khan, William the Conqueror, George Washington, Lord Nelson, Napoleon, and Dwight Eisenhower. Heroes all, their tourist legacies are stone and bronze, to be photographed and admired. In centuries past, victorious armies marched beneath great stone arches which served as visible symbols of successful conquest. The Romans built many which still stand at their conquered cities as far distant as Ephesus. The Arch of Triumph, with details of victorious battles inscribed on each side, is a Paris landmark. Begun in 1806 when Napoleon was at the height of his power, most construction and completion took place between 1825 and 1836, a decade after his defeat at Waterloo in 1815. Through this symbol of the Heroic Phase, the French commemorate their military history: first, the short-lived Empire of Napoleon (which ended in defeat!); and second, when the arch became the "altar to our country" and returning armies from World War I marched through it in 1918. Assured that the 1918 victory had ended war for all time, France closed the structure to further mobile military but heightened its honor by consecrating in 1920 the Tomb of the Unknown Soldier beneath its arch. Not to be outdone, in the same era the USA built an almost identical arch in honor of George Washington at Valley Forge. London's Trafalgar Square with its Nelson's Column is equally famous and an important tourist rendezvous.

The Roman Emperor Hadrian marked his conquest of Britain with the Wall that bears his name; every year thousands of tourists climb its few remaining parapets. The Chinese have reconstructed easily accessible portions of their Great Wall as a tourist attraction, so impressive that individuals are known to have successfully delayed their death until after a tour to Beijing to fulfill a final sightseeing quest (Smith, 1992:2).

Booty from war is traditionally expressed by the adage, "to the Victor belongs the Spoils," and for the most part, they have been treasures indeed. Hadrian's Villa, in the Tivoli Gardens just outside Rome, once housed his trophies from the Graeco–Roman Wars. The extensive British Museum contains the Rosetta Stone from Egypt and countless other valuable curios that were incidental to colonial expansion. Other types of museums specialize in collections of uniforms, armaments, medals and, post World War II, interactive museums such as Portsmouth (England) have rooms devoted to civilian life during an air raid. Another important Portsmouth exhibit is the Overlord Tapestry which required five years to complete and in meticulous embroidery chronicles the events of World War II (as did the Bayeux Tapestry for the invasion of England by William the Conqueror in 1066 AD). Tourists may also visit Lord Nelson's flagship, *Victory*. American tourists sometimes complain about a European itinerary which visits too many cathedrals as if they were solely of religious import. Many gold altars of Spain, and the gold chalices and jeweled crosses found in many church treasuries are booty from the conquest of Peru, piracy on the Spanish Main and the Crusades. Wars inspired by religion are found throughout history, commencing with primitive tribes who engaged in blood feuds or sought relief from illnesses by killing the shaman in the "tribe across the river."

The Heroic Phase includes the men who made it so — the political figures who either provoked war or had to mobilize defense and the military architects whose duty was to obey a commander-in-chief as head of state. Until recently, success was a bronze statue of the general on a fine horse, and an elaborate lore exists among sculptors as to the appropriateness of a raised right hoof *vis-à-vis* a left front hoof etc. Such details must be correct! It is also worth noting the number of successful military leaders who have attained high public office, in a change of leadership style and military-to-civilian status.

General George Washington became the Father of his Country, General Simon Bolivar is the Liberator of Latin America with a country named for him; and General Eisenhower moved from the office of Allied Supreme Commander in World War II into the White House, with a popular election slogan, "I Like Ike".

Failed leaders rate no figures. The many statues of Lenin and Stalin that once accented their hero worship in the Soviet Union are no longer in vogue in the Consolidated States of the 1990s; instead, many of these status-marker figures now lie, broken and screened from public view, in a field near Gorky Park in Moscow. Their final resting place is as ignoble as those of their victims: the Poles, Lithuanians and others who were committed to mass graves some 50 years ago in a process the 1990s termed "ethnic cleansing," partly a euphemism for death for civilian prisoners of war. These erstwhile leaders and their followers also systematically annihilated millions of Ukrainians and others who refused to give up their private farms to collectivization under communism. Warfare can be internecine as well as external.

The Heroic Phase is identified by monuments, about which Hubbard (1984: 28) writes:

> Monuments traditionally "embody an idea important to those who erected them . . . a monument endures beyond its time, holds that idea before us, in our time, and asks us to contemplate that idea — turn it over in our heads, stand it next to our own experienced and ask if it still applies . . . Monuments thus set before us the task of reassessing our own values.

In this context, the Vietnam War Memorial was fraught with much controversy (Wagner-Pacifici and Schwartz, 1991) and conflicting values associated with the ambivalence about the war itself. As James Mayo (1988: 170) observes,

> defeat . . . cannot be forgotten and a nation's people must find ways to redeem those who died for their country to make defeat honorable. This must be done by honoring the individuals who fought rather than the country's lost cause.

Most governments "erect monuments" but consistent with defeat, this Memorial is constructed of black granite, and lies below the street level of the Washington DC government mall. Tourists at this popular attraction walk down a path to view its long slabs engraved with the names of the 57 939 war dead. Termed by some veterans the "ditch of shame," its ethnographic symbolism is visibly evident — as a "black hole" it is the sacred memory of the first major defeat in America's military history.

Remember the fallen

The adage "no one is ever dead as long as someone remembers" succinctly defines the roles of battlefields and military cemeteries. No people — nation or tribe — wants to lose its young men (and women) to war. Although old people and babies are also victims of war, society is fueled by the energy of youth; and most commonly, it is youth who lies beneath the sod.

Battlefields are of particular interest to two diverse groups: history buffs and military strategists, both real and armchair, who tramp over the areas with books in hand, studying details of the battle as it relates to terrain, to ground cover and to troop movements. Secondly, battlefields are hallowed ground, to be memorialized and to remember "the Fallen." For many visitors, an eerie sense of the supernatural lingers in the air — the mystery of the souls (or spirits) of those who died there. Even members of the post-Industrial generation share some of the wariness of the Arctic Inuits who avoid traveling across the battlegrounds of long ago, lest they disturb the *inua* (spirits) of the deceased. Battlefields confirm the earlier statement that wars are the ultimate time-markers of society.

Organized commercial tours to visit battlefields, with lecturers to explain the nature of the engagement, are popular tourist activities. The US National Museum, the Smithsonian, has sponsored tours of this type for several years, and in 1995, offers two new destinations: *Petersburg to Appomattox* is a four-day itinerary that traces "the longest siege campaign in American military history . . . and features the battlefields, private homes and museums associated with this decisive campaign;" and *The Civil War in the Southwest*, in a five-day seminar, notes that "though located far from Civil War primary theaters of military activity, New Mexico was the site of two ferocious battles, at Valverde and Glorieta. For the Confederacy, these engagements were a desperate attempt to distract Union forces from battles in the East, and to reach the West's gold fields to replenish their war chest . . . visit the Glorieta Battlefield and attend a re-creation of this dramatic event" (Smithsonian Seminars, 1994—95: 20).

In England, excerpts from a mailed solicitation advertised Major and Mrs Holt's Battlefield Tours (1993), as follows:

7—9 August: Waterloo I; lecturer Colonel Cyriel Desmet
21—24 August: Waterloo II. "The actions that sealed the fate of Napoleon's 100 days adventure"
6—18 September: "Drums in the Wilderness", Canada. "This memorable tour looks at the Seven Years War of 1756—63".
11—18 September: "The Battles of the Crimea taking in the battles of the Alma, Inkerman and Balaclava where the battlefields themselves are marvelously untouched"
13—26 November: "The Zulu and Boer Wars". The epic battles of Isandlhwana and Rorke's Drift will be studied in depth with the help of local experts.
"The First World War" — in this special 75th anniversary year of the Armistice, there are a number of fascinating options:
31 July—2 August: "Retreat from the Mons"
17—19 July: "Three Days in Ypres"
18—20 September: "Tanks at Cambrai and the Hindenburg Line"
14—18 August: "The Royal Flying Corps"
4—10 August: "Battles of the Isonzo"
10—12 November: "75th Armistice Commemoration Tour"

The geographical range of battlefield visits coincides with British overseas military activities. The battle years in the Canadian, Russian and South African locations preclude veteran attendees and the tours are historical commemorations. A guidebook to World War I sites has also been published in Flemish/Dutch (Brants, 1969).

Cemeteries, usually landscaped in green (lawns, shrubs and trees), symbolize the living eternity and the "rest in peace" from one's labors. And surprisingly, they have become consistent tourist destinations. Alerted to visitor counts as noted at the National Cemetery of the Pacific (Table 17.1), in 1993 the author mailed a survey instrument to 16 national cemeteries and battlefields in the USA. The 100 per cent response to the survey was not unexpected given the organizational structure of these federal parks and memorials. Because most of the battlefields are related to the Civil War (1861−5), the data reflected the media emphasis on the 125th anniversary of its termination and the subsequent Civil Rights movements. Every site reported significant increases in attendance, as much as 75 per cent in the last ten years for the Fredericksburg, Virginia memorial. To meet public demand and as an educational service, in 1992 the US National Park Service published a brochure, *Visiting Civil War Battlefields: How to Have a Quality Experience*, and other printed materials outlined methods to research Civil War ancestors (Webb, 1992).

Gettysburg National Military Park receives the largest number of visitors to military memorials in the US and had undertaken an extensive 1992 self-survey as a prerequisite to planning for future tourism increases. Their data closely parallels that of the other parks and is generalized here to illustrate the war-site tourist interest. Gettysburg receives around 1.4 million visitors per year. The age breakdown shows 28 per cent children (1−15 years); 5 per cent teenagers (16−20 years); 52 per cent adults (20−60 years); 15 per cent senior citizens (60+ years). Summer visitation was seasonally important and almost 75 per cent of the visitors came as family units; only 1 per cent arrived on tour buses. Of the visitors, 5 per cent were disabled, 9 per cent were non-English speaking (in ranked order, the main languages represented were Spanish, French, German, Japanese, Chinese), and only 3 per cent were minority members — dominantly Blacks and Hispanics. Of the visitors, 51 per cent were regional residents, 12 per cent local residents, 35 per cent national residents and only 2 per cent were international in origin. Gettysburg is a large complex and differs from other parks because 51 per cent of its visitors stay overnight in the area; elsewhere the military parks are almost exclusively used by day-trippers or pass-through tourists.

Public relations staff in each of the 16 surveyed sites attributed their increased visitation to two factors: the parks had instituted more effective marketing campaigns because operating funds are often linked to attendance figures; and the Ken Burns *Civil War* mini-series on Public Broadcasting (PBS) television had stimulated great national interest (video copies have been widely sold for home viewing). In addition, the national interest in developing rural tourism (Edgell, 1993) prompted individual states to design advertising campaigns around their tourist attraction resources, some of which are military (see Figure 17.1).

The surge of Civil War tourism interest was also supported by numerous travel articles in the leading magazines, *Travel Holiday, National Geographic Traveler* etc as well as travel sections in newspapers such as the *Boston Globe, New York Times* etc. A comparable media phenomenon accompanied the 50th anniversary of Europe's D-Day (June 6, 1994) accompanied by many hours of TV and repeated showings of the film *The Longest Day*. This was followed by media coverage of the 50th anniversary of MacArthur's invasion of the Philippines (October 20, 1944) and the Battle of the Bulge (December 16, 1944).

Lest we forget

The theme, Lest We Forget, turns homeward to the lives of civilians and their war-time problems and losses. *The Diary of Anne Frank* (Frank, 1989) recounts the poignant story of a Jewish girl hiding in Amsterdam during the Nazi regime, and her home is still a much-visited tourist attraction. A Holocaust site — the Nazi concentration camps at Auschwitz, Buchenwald and Dachau to name just three — is "not a museum, even though it seems on the surface to be a museum; is not a cemetery, even though it has some features of a cemetery; it is not just a tourist site, even though it is often full to overflowing with tourists. It is all these things at once" (Webber, 1992). Above all, it is a place to remember, "lest we forget." Since the end of World War II, more than 20 million visitors have viewed Auschwitz, an impressive number given its location in Poland and some difficulty of access during the Cold War era. The Holocaust Museums maintain this theme. In Washington DC, the United States Holocaust Memorial Museum is regarded as one of the most popular attractions in the nation's capital. During the 18 months following its opening (April 26, 1993), the visitor count was 3 381 000 or an average of over 6500 persons per open day (Brian Page, personal communication).

The Resistance Museum in Oslo commemorates the years of Nazi occupation and the activities of the "underground" acting as saboteurs against railroads, bridges and other strategic sites. The emphasis here is directed principally toward Norwegian school children, about 45 000 of whom visit the museum annually. To come a second or third time during elementary school years is not inappropriate because, according to age and grade level, each student is handed an assignment sheet of questions to be completed from the exhibit and graded by their teachers. The message intended for these young citizens is simple: "never forget what it means to lose your freedom."

When we were young

Anthropologists who have studied primitive warfare, including Turney-High and Hoebel, remind us that warfare offers many opportunities for young men — excitement, adventure, the chance to demonstrate their courage or prowess and to obtain status that often leads to upward mobility. Depending on customs in some cultures (including the pre-Columbian Aztec and modern Islam), death on the battlefield may assure the deceased a place in a "higher Heaven." Among the Plains Indians, membership in military societies was both expected and honored. And as young warriors grew older, their position in the community often was commensurate with their military leadership and skills. When youth waned, aging soldiers shared their tales with eager-eyed children, perpetuating the nobility of war.

World history can recount many parallels, especially in cultures where inheritance by primogeniture excluded younger siblings from family lands, and their status became dependent on serfdom or military service. Brass buttons, braid and medals often replaced fields and farms. Twentieth-century examples include the years of the Great Depression (the 1930s) when joblessness soared and numbers of young Americans served as mercenary soldiers in the French Foreign Legion or found adventure fighting in the Spanish Civil War. And in the 1990s as higher education becomes ever more expensive, the promise of education money and/or valuable technical training are important enlistment inducements.

Old soldiers do go back to the battlefields, to revisit and remember the days of their youth. This author has spent many hours at sea, traveling with veterans who served in the Pacific Theater of World War II, from Guadalcanal in the Solomon Islands to Truk in the

Caroline Islands, and to remote Peleliu and Angaur — all scenes of very bloody battles. They laid ceremonial wreaths on the waters above sunken vessels, climbed over rusting landing craft half-buried in mangrove swamps, inched through overgrown jungles to find broken aircraft bodies and even occasionally meet a local resident beside whom they had once fought. Their memories (and those of accompanying wives) are wrapped in this nostalgia. Military reunions have become a rich market in the American and European travel industry, and many military units have held reunions every five years since the end of World War II. It was generally agreed by veteran groups that the 50th Anniversaries would be the last, because of the age factor, hence the effort to make them outstanding events. The 1994 celebration of D-Day at Normandy was by all yardsticks a world class celebration. Veterans returned *en masse* to the beachheads to reminisce and also to watch some of their over-70 peers once again parachute "behind enemy lines." Unexpected among the attendees at this event, given the relative expense of a European trip for many American couples, were the numbers of veterans attending who had fought in the Pacific. Identifiable by his shoulder patches and battle ribbons, one graying veteran summed it well, "those of us who have been in combat share something very special . . . I simply had to be here, to honor those men."

Reliving the past

Military re-enactments have been quite commonplace in the USA and Canada: small repetitive encampments are staged at a number of historic forts and battlegrounds, especially during periods of maximum tourism. Such displays are often adjuncts to the living history concept popular at many museums, as the great Canadian fortress at Louisburg holds hourly parades of "redcoats" in the British style; and Americans honor the bridge at Lexington "where the shot was fired heard round-the-world" to mark the beginning of the American Revolution. A historical purist might question authenticity of costume, firearms, even narration, but the visual reinforcement of honor and sacrifice to country are ennobling goals. Organizations devoted to the study of individual wars, especially the US Civil War have become widespread across the nation, and involve the acquisition and collection of uniforms, armaments and other memorabilia. Periodically these special interest groups form units of the Union and Confederate armies, and complete with cannons and horses they go into battle, some of which may last for an hour or an afternoon. Realism requires that the wounded be littered to field hospitals, while the air thickens with smoke and fumes. The outcome of the battle is sometimes arranged, sometimes left to chance, but the event is usually part of a larger festival, with food booths, handicrafts, carnival rides and a general "fair-like" atmosphere.

Nevada City, California is a small community of some 6000 nestled in the Sierra Nevada foothills, along State Highway 89, known as the "Mother Lode" route. Several blocks of historic 19th-century homes and businesses create a much visited Victorian ambience, and tourism income is an asset to the stores which serve a diversified farming and retirement hinterland. This small community now sponsors an annual two-day weekend event in mid-September, described as Constitution Day celebration in the West, and featuring one of the largest Civil War re-enactments on the West Coast. Individual Masonic Lodges in the US sponsor a Constitution Day anniversary each year, and a Lodge member in Nevada City proposed in 1965 that the town hold a parade which would broaden community participation instead of the rather customary Lodge dinner. The innovator and World War II veteran, Colonel William Lambert, tirelessly rounded up marching bands from nearby high schools, veterans units, members of various Shrine groups with their miniature cars etc, until the parade became a successful one-day gala, all in honor of the signing of the Constitution. In 1989, Nevada City received a national commendation as a Bicentennial City for this event and the City Fathers, aware of Col. Lambert's failing health, decided to assume community responsibility and expand the activities to a two-day format. Meanwhile, members of the Civil War Association had been seeking a suitable venue, and approached Nevada City leaders for permission to join and augment the occasion with a re-enactment. Given the apparent polarity of their goals: the commemoration of the Constitution to *join* the states, and the Civil War an attempt to *divide* the states, it was only after considerable discussion that permission was granted. The basis for the decision was the fact that the Civil War, while divisive, had not destroyed the Union. The Constitution emerged stronger than ever, in the motto, "in Union there is Strength." The concluding sequence of the battle as staged here always includes the Confederates laying down their arms but walking away from the scene, leading their horses home to plow (historically true and here a symbol of unification).

This Nevada City festival attracts an estimated 10 000 visitors many of whom reserve accommodation a year or more in advance and overflow the bed-and-breakfast establishments into nearby towns and highway motels. Hundreds of Civil War "buffs" bring their cannons on truck beds and trailer their horses, then camp for two or three nights on the site. The Saturday morning parade has floats, marching bands and equestrian groups as well as Civil War units. The afternoon features a Civil War battle. Sunday celebrations include a re-enactment of the Signing of the Constitution, a non-denominational Church service and another Civil War battle. Nevada City does not maintain visitor attendance or revenue records because city officials deem this a hometown patriotic and historical gathering of which they are very proud, not a theatrical event staged for outsiders or profit.

Tourism and war: a viable tourism "alternative"

The rapid rise of tourism following World War II, fostered by a war-time technology that gave birth to airplanes with transatlantic capability, has irrevocably transformed global perspectives. Wars were once fought over boundaries on contiguous terrain to satisfy some local need or command. As the Julian calendar marks the near-end of the 20th century, wars are now fought in the air and beneath the sea as well as on land. Logistics permits troop deployments literally halfway round the world, and engagement may occur to satisfy some international agenda such as, ironically, peace-keeping. All these innovations notwithstanding, warfare remains more a sociological phenomenon than a military occurrence.

A tribal uprising, an internecine war, in tiny Rwanda in the 1990s has affected the entire Western world, and set into motion a world-wide network of social service and medical agencies to curb life-threatening outbreaks of contagious disease; the stock market became wary; military planes were loaded with relief supplies and water purification equipment (all at a substantial cost to the taxpayer); adjacent countries were overwhelmed with refugees. Television networks brought "graphic scenes" of the starved and dying into homes everywhere and we grieved for their pain. Most of the world was physically untouched by this event, but life in Rwanda will never be the same. Half-a-million people have died, and for those who live, there will always be the trilogy of life "before the war," "during the war" and "after the war."

Wars are the time-markers of society, and the effects of war covertly invade our cultural beliefs and human behavior. We commemorate events and heroes, if victorious; in defeat, we seek ways to maintain dignity. Wars reinforce group identity and foster nationhood and pride, and hold up to public view our social, political and economic aspirations and their fulfillment. We honor the living as we honor the dead. Tourism becomes enmeshed in all these activities. Scarcely a town exists in Western Europe, North America, or Australia and New Zealand (also in Latin and African communities as well) that does not have a World War I marker, inscribed with the names of the war dead, placed conspicuously in the town square. Many such monuments are pointed out by local guides. As the visitor moves out from the local scene, the array of potential tourism sights and sites related to the military and war seems almost endless. The reasons are simple but clear: we honor the event, the place and the person who created each tiny segment of our sacred history. Remembrance and commemoration are the essence of the past that fashioned today. Tourism to war-related sites is honorific, not maudlin; and by our knowledge of war, its meaning and mechanisms, we better understand our roles in the global society.

References

Balandier, G. (1968). An anthropology of violence and war. *International Social Science Journal*, **38**, 4: 499−511.

Boilsi, T. (1984). Ecological and cultural factors in Plains Indian warfare. In R.B. Ferguson (ed.), *Warfare, culture and enviornment*. Orlando, FL: Academic Press, 141−68.

Brants, C.E. (1969). *Velden van weleer: Reisgids naar de Eerste Wereldoorlog*. Amsterdam: Nijgh & Van Ditmar.

Cohen, E. (1987). The tourist as victim and protegé of law enforcing agencies. *Leisure Studies*, **6**: 181−98.

Diller and Scofidio (1994). *Back to the Front: Tourisms of War*. Basse-Normandie: FRAC.

Edgell, D.L. (1993). *World Tourism at the Millennium*. Washington DC: US Department of Commerce, US Travel and Tourism Administration (USTTA).

Elshtain, J.B. (1991). Sovereignty, Identity, Sacrifice. *Social research*, **58**, 5: 545−64.

Farrell, B. (1982). *Hawaii: The Legend That Sells*. Honolulu: University of Hawaii Press.

Frank, A. (1989). *Anne Frank: A Critical Edition*. New York: Doubleday.

Fried, M., Harris, M. and Murphy R. (eds) (1968). *War: The Anthropology of Social Conflict and Aggression*. New York: Doubleday.

Haas, J. (1990). *The Anthropology of War*. London: Cambridge University Press.

Hoebel, E. (1954). *The Law of Primitive Man: A Study in Comparative Legal Dynamics*. Cambridge: Harvard University Press.

Holt, Major and Mrs (1993). Battlefield Tours, Ltd., Golden Key Bldg., 15 Market St., Sandwich, Kent CT13 9DA, England.

Hubbard, W. (1984). A meaning for monuments. *The Public Interest*, Winter, 17−30.

Jansen-Verbecke, M. and Go, F. (1994). Tourism development in Vietnam: The opportunities and threats. Paper presented at the IIPT Second Global Conference, *Building a Sustainable World Through Tourism*, September 12−16, Montreal.

Khan, M., Olsen, M. and Var, T. (eds) (1993). *VNRS Encyclopedia of Hospitality and Tourism*. New York: Van Nostrand Reinhold.

Malinowski, B. (1941). An anthropological analysis of war. *The American Journal of Sociology* **XLVI**, (4): 521−50.

Mayo, J. (1988). War memorials as political memory. *Geographical Review*, January: 62−75.

Mead. M. (1965). *And Keep your Powder Dry: An Anthropologist Looks at America*. New York: William Morrow.

Page, B. (1994). Personal communication. Washington DC: US Holocaust Memorial Museum, Education Section.

Pospisil, L. (1958). The Kapauku Papuans and their law. *Yale University Publications in Anthropology*. New Haven: Yale University Press.

Schwartz, B. (1982). The social context of commemoration: A study of collective memory. *Social Forces* **61** (2): 327−401.

Smith, V. (1979). Women: The taste-makers in tourism. *Annals of Tourism Research* **VI** (2): 49−60.

Smith, V. (1992). The quest in Guest. *Annals of Tourism Research*, **19**(1): 1−18.

Smithsonian Museum Smithsonian Seminars 1994−95 (1994). Washington DC: US National Museum.

Time Magazine (1994). Russia's secret spoils of World War II. October 17: 17.

Turney-High, H.H. (1971). *Primitive War: Its Practice and Concepts*. Columbia: University of South Carolina Press.

Turney-High, H.H. (1981). *The Military: The Theory of Land Warfare as Behavioral Science*. West Hanover, MA: The Christopher Publishing House.

Volksbund Deutsche Kriegsgraberfursorge e.V., Referat Reisen. Kassel: Werner-Hilpert-Strasse 2, 3500, Germany.

Wagner-Pacifici, R. and Schwartz, B. (1991). The Viet-Nam Veterans Memorial: Commemorating a difficult past. *The American Journal of Sociology* **97**, (2): 376−420.

Webb, R.A. (1992). Visiting Civil War battlefields: how to have a quality experience. *National Parks* (March/April): 46−8.

Webber, J. (1992). *The Future of Auschwitz: Some Personal Reflections*. Oxford: Centre for Postgraduate Hebrew Studies.

18 Wars, tourism and the "Middle East" factor

YOEL MANSFELD

Introduction

One of the most destructive impacts on the tourism industry can be the effect of security situations on potential tourists' propensity to visit a given destination, country or region. A turbulent security environment, caused by wars, coups d'état, civil wars and terrorist attacks, has already demonstrated its negative impact on tourism development in many countries around the world (Taylor and Quayle, 1994). The propensity to visit tourist destinations diminishes once tourists realize that their holiday, and sometimes their lives, may be jeopardized (Kurent, 1991). The nature of security events, their duration, location, level of severity, frequency and the way they are perceived by the tourist can determine the level of the negative impact on the travel industry. The most problematic effect is that resulting from the decline of inbound international tourist flows to a given affected country (Bar-On, 1989; Brent Ritchie, 1992; Ryan, 1991).

Security situations in the Middle East have affected not just those countries directly involved but, in some cases, also the rest of the eastern Mediterranean basin, including those countries which have never taken an active part in the regional conflict (eg Turkey, Greece and Cyprus). As a result of on-going conflicts in the Middle East, international tourist flows to this region have been occasionally affected while over the same period, world tourism arrivals have grown steadily, attaining new records every decade (Go and Frechtling, 1991). Between the beginning and the end of the 1980s, world tourist arrivals grew by 62 per cent, meaning an average annual growth of 6.2 per cent (Mansfeld, 1993). At the same time, tourism to Middle East countries has grown by only 52.9 per cent, an average annual growth of 5.29 per cent (World Tourism Organization, 1992).

This chapter will evaluate the impact of security situations on the propensity of tourists to visit the Middle East between 1967 and 1992. As official and reliable data on tourist flows to Middle East countries in 1993 and 1994 is still unattainable for most of the region's countries, this analysis will have to ignore the current transition period from war to peace. The chapter will focus on two major research questions: (1) to what extent has the on-going Middle East conflict affected tourist flows to the region? And (2) has this impact been geographically differentiated? If the answer to these questions is negative, a regional model of marketing strategies is needed to promote tourism despite occasional violence. If, however, the negative impacts on inbound tourist flows are geographically

Tourism, Crime and International Security Issues, edited by
A. Pizam and Y. Mansfeld. © 1996 John Wiley & Sons Ltd.

differentiated, alternative market- and country-specific policies are needed to overcome the negative impacts of violence on the tourist industry of the region.

Theoretical framework

Security problems and international tourism

A change in the political and security stability of a destination country can paralyze tourism-based economic activities at least until the period of unrest is over (Richter and Waugh, 1986; Conant et al., 1988; *Economist* Intelligence Unit, 1988; Millman, 1989; Department of Economic Development, 1989; Ankomah and Crompton, 1990; Mansfeld, 1993). This calls for an understanding of the causal relations between political-security instability and inbound tourist flows (Norton, 1987). On the one hand, there is an evident necessity to understand these relationships; on the other hand, empirical studies measuring these relations are very limited and, in most cases, of a diachronic rather than a synchronic nature, making it difficult to generalize about the characteristics of these effects (Richter, 1983; Burnett and Uysal, 1990; Mansfeld, 1993). Various issues concerning the impact of security situations on tourist flows, however, have already been raised by the literature.

One factor is the role of negative images associated with tourist regions hit by wars and terror (Hall, 1994). Image is formed by the interaction of values, attitudes and the individual's comprehension of the real world (Chaliand, 1987). This comprehension is strongly shaped by signals communicated from the tourist's own environment (Muir and Paddison, 1981). If these signals are channeled through various "media filters," inconsistencies could develop between the actual and the perceived situation (Dilley, 1986).

The second factor is the issue of market sensitivity to turbulent situations. This sensitivity has been examined both horizontally (ie, a comparative examination of the sensitivity of various markets to a given security situation) and vertically (ie, by looking at the response of one market to a security situation affecting various tourist destinations). Thus the US market, when compared to a number of European countries, was found to respond differently to the security situation caused by Libyan-backed terror attacks against targets in Western Europe in 1986. The number of American tourists visiting Europe at that time dropped significantly compared to Europeans visiting their neighboring countries (Ryan, 1991). When the American market is examined on a vertical basis in light of the 1986 events, the drop in the number of visitors to Europe does not appear to be evenly distributed (Brady and Widdows, 1988). These trends suggest that various markets can react differently to a given security situation and that each of these markets might behave differently when the affected region is comprised of more than one country.

Another issue is the relationship between the severity of security events and the pattern of inbound tourist flows to the affected country. Chaliand (1987) and Moorhead (1991) both claim that in any case terrorism has a major effect on the volume of tourist flows to any affected destination. This is attributed by them to the role of the media in covering these events. However, they did not try to compare the effect of terrorism with the effect of wars or continued unrest situations (such as the *Intifada* taking place in the occupied

West Bank or the occasional terror attacks in Northern Ireland). Ryan (1991), on the other hand, in summarizing his study on tourism, terrorism and violence, concluded that different types of security situations have a varying effect on the tourist industry's situation, particularly on its attraction potential. For example, minor security events can result in a drop in tourist flows that is confined to a particular destination country. Major crises, on the other hand, can create a spill-over effect, with adjacent countries also affected through loss of potential inbound flows (Hollier, 1991).

Moreover, the impact of security instability in a given region may be far-reaching, even producing world-wide economic hardship. The Yom Kippur War in 1973 and the 1990 Gulf War, for example, each brought about a rise in oil and insurance prices, and a consequent slowdown in economic activity in many of the major tourist-generating countries (Lieber, 1987; *Economist* Intelligence Unit, 1990). The high insurance prices during the Gulf War and high fuel prices following the Yom Kippur War caused a sharp rise in travel costs (mainly airline fares), thus diminishing the ability of tourists to travel abroad (British Tourist Authority, 1990). If security and political instability in a given tourist destination sometimes place even global tourist interaction in jeopardy, there is a need to study these effects in order to help reduce the negative impact of such events on the international scene, let alone on the country or region concerned.

The Middle East: a fragile tourist system

The Middle East is regarded by the major tourism-generating countries as a relatively unsafe place to visit (Hall, 1994). In some studies this situation has been called "the Middle East Factor" (*Economist* Intelligence Unit, 1989b). This region has a long history of intensive terror, warfare and political instability (Taylor and Quayle, 1994). However, these events started to become of interest to the tourist industry towards the end of the 1960s when the Six-Day War changed the political as well as the tourist map of the region. The majority of security situations that had any bearing on inbound flow of international tourism resulted from the Arab–Israeli dispute. As a result of these events other countries located in the region were also affected in terms of a decline in the number of tourists who visited them. In the case of the Yom Kippur War and the Gulf War, the conflicts had negative impacts on the entire tourist world in spite of the fact that the Middle East share in world tourism arrivals is minimal — 2.2 per cent in 1990 (Brent Ritchie, 1992). This phenomenon of innocent countries that suffer from other countries' disputes is quite common. Thus, Indian and Maldives tourism have suffered from Sri Lankan terrorism, Pakistani tourism was negatively affected by the war in Afghanistan and the Uganda coups deterred East African tourism (Richter and Waugh, 1986; Richter, 1987; Mansfeld, 1993).

However, the case of the Middle East conflict is different because of its long-lasting nature, the intensity of violent activities and their frequency. Thus, Herbert (1985), in characterizing the level of risk for travelers to Middle East destinations, concluded that in terms of numbers of active terrorist groups and airport safety measures, all Middle East countries are basically "no go" places. Today, a decade after Herbert published his work, the situation has not improved. The Middle East still represents a high level of risk for tourists, yet this risk is more a result of terror rather than full-scale wars. The recent terror activities of the Islamic extremists in Egypt were targeted officially and effectively towards tourists. The same pattern has emerged in the case of the Kurdish People's Liberation Army, the military wing of the Kurdish Workers' Party (known as the PKK). These terrorist groups have declared that tourists as a target are used to harm the economic interests of some Middle East countries (Taylor and Quayle, 1994). Despite the recent activities of these terrorist groups the "Middle East" factor, ie, the negative tourist image of this region, is primarily a result of the Arab—Israeli conflict. Table 18.1 demonstrates the key role of the Arab—Israeli conflict in shaping the so-called "Middle East" factor.

Nearly every year since the Six-Day War either one or a combination of major security events has taken place in the Middle East. It appears that since 1967, Israel has been associated with nearly all security events occurring either in the Middle East region or outside it. Within the time frame analyzed here (1967—92) 10 out of 23 years of major security events showed a decline in inbound tourist flows to Israel. One of the questions to be dealt with in this chapter is to what extent the decline occurring in Israeli inbound tourism corresponded with a similar decline in other Middle East countries. A comparative analysis of this question follows. At this stage, though, it is possible to conclude that the Arab—Israeli conflict has played a major role on occasion in deterring tourists from visiting the Middle East region.

Methodology

A geographical definition of the "Middle East"

The Middle East as a geographical research unit for this study is the region which includes Israel and all Arab countries neighboring Israel and located in the eastern Mediterranean basin. For this study the countries located in this region have been divided into two major groups. The first group contains "inner-ring" countries that have been part of the Middle East conflict during the period 1967—92, ie, Israel, Syria, Jordan and Egypt (Lebanon was excluded from the analysis due to its long-lasting civil war and the lack of relevant time-series data on tourist arrivals).

The second group, the "outer-ring" countries, are those located in the eastern Mediterranean but which have never played any role in this regional conflict. However, on some occasions terrorism related to the Arab—Israeli dispute has taken place on their land, and on other occasions (such as the Gulf War) security situations in the Middle East "spilled over" and affected the inbound tourist flows to these countries. This group includes Turkey, Greece and Cyprus.

Data evaluation

Various sources of data were used in order to establish time series of inbound tourist flows to the studied countries (eg, the World Tourism Organization, *The Economist* Intelligence Unit, *The Middle East Review* and *World Travel and Tourism Review — Indicators, Trends and Forecasts; Statistical Abstracts of Israel* etc). Obtaining the data for the comparative analysis of tourist flows was quite complicated as the classification of data in each country is slightly different, and definitions of tourists, excursionists and

Table 18.1 A profile of Middle East security events and their impact on inbound tourist flows to Israel

Year	Type of Major Security Event	No. of ME Countries Involved	Location	No. of Visitor Arrivals[1]	Change over Previous Year (%)
1967	War — The Six-Day war	4	Within the ME region	268 000	−7
1970	War — War of attrition between Israel and Egypt	2	Within the ME region	441 000	+8
1971	Terror — Sabena hijack	1	Both within and outside	657 000	+49
1972	Terror — against pilgrims in Tel Aviv and against Israelis in Munich	1	Both within and outside	728 000	+49
1973	War — Yom Kippur war, Israel, Egypt and Syria	3	Within the ME region	661 000	−9
1974	Terror — events in Israel and in Rome	1	Both within and outside	625 000	−6
1975	Terror — events in Israel	1	Within the ME region	620 000	−1
1976	Terror — Air France hijack to Entebbe	1	Outside the region	797 000	+24
1977	Terror — events in Israel	1	Within the ME region	987 000	+9
1978	War and Terror — Litani campaign in Lebanon; terror attacks in Israel and Europe	1	Within the ME region	1 071 000	+6
1979	Terror — events in Israel	1	Within the ME region	1 176 000	−3
1981	Bombing and Terror — Israel destroys Iraqi reactor; terror events in Israel	2	Both within and outside	1 139 000	−12
1982	Terror and War — Israeli ambassador killed in London; war in Lebanon	2	Both within and outside	998 000	−12
1983	War — partial occupation of Lebanon	2	Within the ME region	1 167 000	+17
1984	Terror — attacks on Israeli embassies in Cairo and Nicosia	3	Within the ME region	1 259 000	−8
1985	Terror — international terror (*Achille Lauro* cruise ship; TWA hijack)	1	Both within and outside	1 436 000	+14
1986	Terror — Libyan terror in Europe	None	Outside the region	1 196 000	−17
1987	Uprising — start of the Palestinian *Intifada* in December	1	Within the ME region	1 518 000	+27
1988	Uprising and Terror — *Intifada*; attack in Nicosia	2	Within the ME region	1 299 000	−14
1989	Uprising and War Threats — *Intifada* continues	1	Within the ME region	1 425 000	+10
1990	Uprising and War Threats — *Intifada* continues; Iraqi threats	1	Both within and outside	1 342 000	−6
1991	Uprising and War — *Intifada* continues; the Gulf war	1	Both within and outside	1 118 000	−17
1992	Uprising and Terror — *Intifada* continues; attacks on Israeli embassies in Argentina and Turkey	2	Both within and outside	1 805 000	+61

Source: Israel, Central Bureau of Statistics (1969). *Statistical Abstracts of Israel* (selected years). Israel, Army Spokesman, *Terror Events and Casualties in Israel: June 68–September 92*. World of Information (1988). *The Middle East Review*. Saffron Walden: World of Information.

visitors also tend to have slightly different meanings in each country. Moreover, a breakdown of the total flow into market segments was in some cases impossible because some of the countries use different regional classifications of the generating markets. In order to overcome the incompatibility of the data, this study has used yearly figures referring to international arrivals at frontiers. Apparently, this was the only variable that could be used for comparison and which allowed a breakdown of the data into two distinct markets: regional Arab tourism, which covers travel among the Arab countries of the Middle East; and the non-Arab international market, which is comprised mainly of West European tourists. It is assumed here that the former market, being part of the region and aware of its cultural as well as its political situation, would be less sensitive in terms of travel propensity than the latter market, which is heavily reliant on the media and the images it conveys with respect to the Middle East. By isolating the Arab market from the total flow to each country, one is also able to eliminate the problem of data based on visitors rather than real tourists. Thus, if a country such as Jordan supplies data on a number of visitors it includes in its tourism statistics those who stayed less than 24 hours in the country, usually workers or pilgrims in transit or crossing the country to and from Saudi Arabia.

Analysis

The research questions formulated in the introductory section of this chapter were as follows:

1. To what extent has the on-going Middle East conflict affected tourist flows to the region?
2. To what extent has the impact of turmoil in terms of decline in tourist arrivals been geographically differentiated?

The Arab—Israeli conflict and its impact on tourism to the Middle East — a macro perspective

The general trend of inbound tourist flow to Israel compared with that of the countries involved in the Middle East conflict is similar. The upward trend in tourist arrivals is evident from Figure 18.1. However, when decrease in inbound flows to Israel as a result of security situations is compared to the corresponding figures of the Arab countries involved in the conflict, one observes some variations. Thus, a year after the Six-Day War in 1967, inbound tourist flows to Israel recovered while the surrounding Arab countries faced an on-going decline of tourist arrivals which continued for three consecutive years (Figure 18.1).

On the other hand, the Yom Kippur War (1973), which caused a three-year decline in tourist arrivals to Israel, affected the Arab countries differently as tourists' propensity to visit them declined only during 1973. From 1974 onwards, the Arab countries enjoyed an on-going interest as tourist destinations, in spite of the emergent oil crisis that caused a slowdown in international tourist movements around the world. The same situation occurred as an outcome of the Lebanon—Israel conflict in 1982. While there was a decline in arrivals to Israel, the neighboring Arab countries faced a recovery trend. This

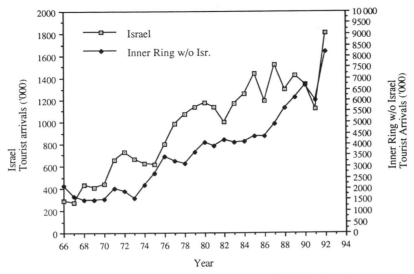

Figure 18.1 Inbound tourist flows — Israel vs. "inner-ring" Middle East destinations

trend followed a decline both in Israel and the Arab countries in 1981 when the Israelis bombed the Iraqi nuclear reactor and following a number of terrorist attacks within Israel. The latest mutual downward trends are found in 1986 when international terror in Europe backed by the Libyan government resulted in a retaliation by the Americans, causing a major crisis in terms of tourist arrivals to Europe and the whole of the Middle East region. Since 1987, a boom year in incoming tourist flows, Israel has faced two major periods of decline: (1) emerging in the wake of the outbreak of the *Intifada* at the end of 1987 and (2) from the start of the Gulf crisis in August 1990. At the same time, Syria, Egypt and Jordan together faced a substantial growth of tourist arrivals. Even in 1990, when the Gulf crisis started to deter people from travel, these countries managed on a regional level to keep a growing interest in the Arab part of the region. Only the Gulf War, which commenced at the beginning of 1991, "managed" to cause a mutual decline in the number of tourists visiting the entire inner ring of the Middle East. The conclusion is that if the situation in Israel is compared to the overall volume of tourists visiting the Arab countries which are involved in the conflict, not every decline in tourist flows to Israel has affected these countries. In other words, from a macro perspective, the Arab—Israeli conflict has not caused a systematic negative impact on tourists' propensity to visit the "inner ring" part of the region. Therefore, it may be concluded that over the 1967—1992 period, inner-ring Middle East countries have been negatively affected in terms of levels of inbound tourist flows. However, when Arab inner-ring countries are compared to Israel, the impact of security events has, in most cases, been time and place differentiated.

Security situations in the Middle East and their spill-over effect

Those countries defined here as the "outer ring" of the Middle East region are not part of the Arab—Israeli conflict. Yet being part of this region might drive potential tourists to

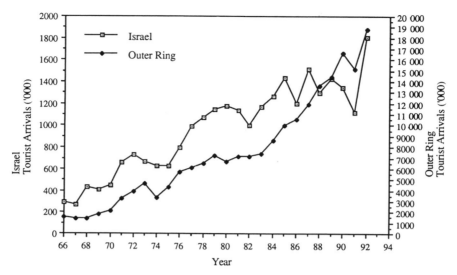

Figure 18.2 Inbound tourist flows — Israel vs. "outer-ring" Middle East destinations

associate them with the deterring tourist image of the Middle East. A comparison of tourist flows to Israel between 1967–92 with those of the "outer-ring" countries demonstrates that both share a general upward trend along this period. However, while Israel has faced numerous declines as a result of security situations, only twice has this spilled over to the "outer-ring" countries. A corresponding diminution occurred as a result of the Yom Kippur War in October 1973. This war resulted in a world oil crisis which affected the global tourist movement and not just the Middle East destinations. Nevertheless it took the "outer-ring" countries only one year to recover, and in 1975 the volume of tourists visiting Turkey, Cyprus and Greece nearly reached the 1972 figures. At the same time, Israel was struggling to regain tourists' interest in the country but failed to do so until 1976 (see Figure 18.2).

The second decline took place as a result of the Gulf War. As a result of this conflict, insurance costs and oil prices rose sharply and hit "outer-ring" countries which had nothing to do with it were also affected. When tourist flows to all "inner-ring" countries are compared to the inbound tourist flows to the "outer-ring" destinations, the same pattern emerges (see Figure 18.3).

Both in the 1973 case and the Gulf War it took less than 12 months for the "outer-ring" countries to recover from the downward trend. This suggests that a spill-over effect seen in these rare cases was primarily a result of the rise in fuel and insurance prices. Once these prices went down the recovery trend started. Thus, in the case of the influence of security situations in Israel and/or all "inner-ring" countries, with regard to the propensity to visit the "outer-ring" countries, a spill-over based on risky image played only a marginal role. The conclusion is that the "outer ring" in the Eastern Mediterranean tourist region faced spill-over effects in terms of inbound tourist flows only after those security events in the Middle East which produced an international crisis. Otherwise, these countries have been immune from the conflict and perhaps even gained from it, as tourists would most probably visit the "quiet" side of the East Mediterranean as an alternative to those countries involved in the conflict.

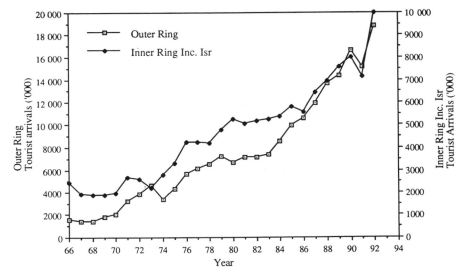

Figure 18.3 Inbound tourist flows — "inner-ring" vs. "outer-ring" Middle East destinations

Table 18.2 Correlation analysis of tourist arrivals: Israel compared to other Middle Eastern countries[1]

Countries examined	Correlation coefficient (r)
Inner Ring	
Israel — Egypt	0.86
Israel — Jordan	0.89
Israel — Syria	0.54
Outer Ring	
Israel — Cyprus	0.77
Israel — Greece	0.91
Israel — Turkey	0.72

[1] $N = 26$ and $\alpha \leq 0.01$

Source: Based on data base of international tourist flows to the Middle East, 1967 — 92.

The effect of security situations on tourism demand — Is it geographically differentiated?

From both the results of the correlation analysis in Tables 18.2 and 18.3 and Figure 18.4, it appears that, with the exception of the Gulf War, fluctuations in the overall inbound tourist flows resulting from regional security events have a differential pattern. When declines in arrivals to Israel were compared with the "inner-ring" countries, relatively high correlation coefficients were obtained for Egypt and Jordan, but a low one obtained for the relations between flows to Israel and flows to Syria (see Table 18.3). When the effect of a security event is compared in terms of percentage of growth or decline in tourist arrivals on the previous year, the nature of this impact is detected (Table 18.3). Two kinds of differential impacts in tourist flows are observed. The first is a difference in

Table 18.3 Fluctuations in tourist arrivals resulting among the "inner-ring" countries: relative changes on previous year[1,2] (%)

Event \ Country	Israel	Egypt	Jordan	Syria
The Six-Day War, 1967	−7.0 (1)	−45.0 (2)	−52.0 (5)	−17.4 (2)
The Yom Kippur War, 1973	−14.89 (3)	−1.1 (12)	+5.3	−31.6 (1)
The Lebanon War, 1982	−13.0 (1)	+3.4	−29.5	−24.1 (2)
International terror, 1986	−17.0 (1)	−13.6 (1)	+2.6	+5.0
Intifada 1988	−15.0 (1)	+3.8	+26.0	+4.8
Iraqi threats (1990)	−5.0 (2)	+3.8	+16.2	+5.8
Gulf War 1991	−17.0 (1)	−15.0 (1)	−15.4 (1)	+8.8

[1] Only the major security events were included.
[2] Figures in brackets refer to the number of decline trend years after a security event has happened.
Source: Based on data-base of international tourist flows to the Middle East, 1967–92.

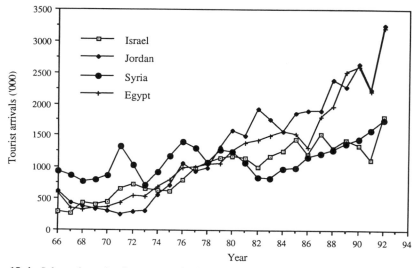

Figure 18.4 Inbound tourist flows to each "inner-ring" country of the Middle East

the relative reaction in terms of number of arrivals as a result of a given Middle East conflict event. The second is the direction of this reaction (negative or positive) as taken by the tourists (see Table 18.3).

The Six-Day War in 1967 affected all "inner-ring" countries because they all took part in this war. Although the direction was in all cases a negative one, ie, a decline in tourist arrivals, the level of decline in each country was variable. While Israel lost only 7 per cent of its inbound tourist flow, Egypt and Jordan faced a major decline and Syria a more moderate one. The large loss of 52 per cent in Jordan reflects not only the fact that it lost the war and, like Syria and Egypt, could be regarded as an aggressive and unstable country, but also because it lost a substantial number of tourist attractions situated in the West Bank. As this area has been occupied by Israel since 1967, this loss to Jordan, which continued for five consecutive years, became a bonus for Israel as it immediately promoted those attractions in its potential markets.

The Yom Kippur War in 1973 also yielded differential patterns of inbound tourist flows to "inner-ring" countries (see also Table 18.3). While the countries involved in the conflict, ie, Egypt, Israel and Syria, all suffered from relative decline in tourist arrivals, Jordan, which did not participate in the war, managed to gain 5.3 per cent on the previous year. This finding already suggests that a country that does not take an active part in conflict is not regarded by potential tourists as a threat. Among those countries participating in the war there were also differences in the level of reaction. Egypt, on the one hand, was not substantially damaged, having a decline of only 1.1 per cent. On the other hand, Israel and Syria lost a considerable number of potential tourists (see Table 18.3). Israel's loss was more moderate, though, spread over a three-year period; Syria's was more pronounced, but it managed to recover from the crisis after one year. The fact that only in Israel's case did it take three years to recover from the after-effect of this war should be regarded as a problem related to the poor image which tourists have of this country. Tourists have realized that even in Israel major security events can have a destructive result and that Israel's security reputation should not be taken for granted in the future. The results of the war between Israel and Lebanon in 1982 were quite similar. Only Israel, which took part in this event, suffered a decline in tourist arrivals.

The case of the impact of international terror in 1986 on the "inner-ring" countries is interesting, as it took place within neither of these countries' boundaries. Yet again, the reaction of potential tourists to these events was differential. While Israel and Egypt faced a decline in tourist flows, Jordan and Syria enjoyed a relative gain on the previous year. These unexpected results raise the question as to whether unaffected Syria and Jordan were manifesting ceased flow.

The *Intifada* (the uprising of the Palestinians in the West Bank and Gaza strip), as a conflict that is confined to the territories occupied by Israel alone, could not change the upward trend in tourist arrivals in Egypt, Jordan and Syria. The prolonged effects of the *Intifada* and the Iraqi threats aimed directly at Israel as the Gulf conflict emerged in 1990, resulted in a drop in inbound tourist flows only in Israel.

However, the Middle East faced a totally different situation when the Gulf conflict turned into a full-scale war in the beginning of 1991. While Israel, Jordan and Egypt suffered a major decline in tourist arrivals, Syria gained 8.8 per cent over 1990 figures. This supports the hypothesis made earlier, regarding the large proportion of intra-regional Arab market in Syrian overall tourist arrivals which was hardly affected by the Gulf threat.

The inevitable conclusion is that when the overall tourist flow to the "inner-ring" countries is examined, differing patterns of impact are detected. Tourists' propensity to visit "inner-ring" countries is a discriminate one and decreases in most cases only when a country is directly involved in a given security event. Moreover, involvement in a given security event does not lead to similar levels of relative decline among the "inner-ring" countries as this was also found to be country differentiated.

Conclusions

This chapter has examined two main research questions: (1) to what extent the Arab−Israeli conflict has affected inbound tourist flows to this region? And (2) is this effect geographically differentiated? With respect to the first question, the analysis showed that, although the general trend over the 1967−92 period was similar, not every security event that caused a decline in tourist arrivals affected the Arab countries in the same way. This conclusion refers not just to the level of impact caused by a security event on tourists' propensity to visit the "inner-ring" countries but also to cases where "outer-ring" destination countries faced a spill-over effect when the cause of the security event originated in the "inner-ring" section of the Middle East. Such spill-over effects took place only when the security conflict produced an international crisis. Otherwise, these countries have remained immune from the conflict and perhaps even gained from it, as tourists preferred to visit the "quiet" side of the East Mediterranean as an alternative to those countries involved in the conflict.

The second research question was intended to find out if the "Middle East" factor is a poor tourist image and results in a similar impact on tourist arrivals in each of the region's countries. Or could it be that this effect is geographically differentiated? This question was examined with respect to the "inner-ring" countries only. Results of the analysis show that the Middle East is variably affected from security situations. It appears that not every security event leads directly to a drop in the number of tourist arrivals in each country. Declines are very much correlated with the level of involvement of each Middle East country in a given security situation. If it took an active part in a security situation, its ability to attract tourists was weakened. However, if it did not participate in any kind of direct security activity, it will not encounter a decline in tourist arrivals because of security events in other parts of the region.

This study has shown that the "Middle East" factor, ie, the regional perception of a no-go area, does not exist in practical terms. However, further detailed research is required to substantiate these results on the basis of more refined data and evaluation of other possible interfering variables that could explain fluctuations of tourist arrivals. In order to eliminate the possibility that changes in travel behavior would have occurred as a result of non-security factors, the analysis here was based on the most crucial security events in the region between 1967–92. Such an approach is legitimate if the study remains on a level of regional evaluation. But, if the research focus were to be directed toward a study of each Middle East country separately, it would be necessary to examine the relative effect of security situation *vis-à-vis* other internal and/or external factors that could have shaped the pattern of tourist arrivals.

While this study followed the hypothesis that each country within the troubled region of the Middle East is perceived variably in terms of its risk to tourists, it is important in future studies to produce further profiles of market segment sensitivity to security events. This has to be done both on a regional and country scale. If such a profile is achieved, a given country affected by a security situation will plan and allocate its financial resources more efficiently by investing in promotion according to its various markets' level of sensitivity to security situations and their level of severity.

Another lesson from this analysis is that the tourist sector in destinations which are occasionally exposed to security situations should use the most effective means of communication in order to convey to their markets a clear message regarding the scale of risk and its geographical distribution. This is also relevant to countries that are not regularly involved in security situations, yet are located within the perceived range of the image spill-over effect.

References

Ankomah, P.K. and Crompton, J.L. (1990). Unrealized tourism potential — The case of Sub-Saharan Africa. *Tourism Management*, **11**(2): 11 — 22.

Bar-On, R. (1989). The Effect of International Terrorism on International Tourism, unpublished paper presented at the *First International Seminar on Aviation Security — "Terror in the Skies,"* The Centre for Special Studies, Gelilot-Tel Aviv, February 5 — 9, 83 — 104.

Brady, J. and Widdows, R. (1988). The impact of world events on travel to Europe during the summer of 1986. *Journal of Travel Research*, **26**(3): 8 — 10.

Bregha, F. (1989). Tourism, development, peace. *World Leisure and Recreation*, **31**(4): 5 — 8.

Brent Ritchie, J.R. (1992). Global tourism policy: An agenda for the 1990s. In D.E. Hawkins and J.R. Brent Ritchie (eds), *World Travel and Tourism Review — Indicators, Trends and Forecasts*. Oxon: CAB International, 149 — 58.

British Tourist Authority (1990). Factors affecting the slow of international tourism. *Tourism Intelligence Quarterly*, **12**(2): 14.

Burnett, G.W. and Uysal, M. (1990). On the nature of peace in relationship to tourism: Three cases. *The Tourist Review*, **1**, 2 — 6.

Chaliand, G. (1987). *Terrorism from Popular Struggle to Media Spectacle*. London: Sagis Books.

Conant, J.S., Clark, T. Burnett, J.J. and Zank, G. (1988). Terrorism and travel: Managing the unmanageable. *Journal of Travel Research*, **26**(4): 16 — 20.

Crandall, L. (1987). The social impact of tourism on developing regions and its measurements. In J.R. Brent Ritchie and C.R. Goeldner (eds), *Travel, Tourism, and Hospitality Research — A Handbook for Managers and Researchers*. New York: John Wiley & Sons, 373 — 83.

Crelinsten, R.D. (1989). Images of terrorism in the media. *Terror: An International Journal*, **12**(2): 167 — 98.

Department of Economic Development (1989). *Tourism in Northern Ireland: a View of the Future*. London: HMSO.

Dilley, R.S. (1986). Tourist brochures and tourist images. *The Canadian Geographer*, **30**(1): 59 — 65.

Economist Intelligence Unit (1988). Fiji, *International Tourism Reports* **2**, 50 — 67.

Economist Intelligence Unit (1989a). Tourism and developing countries, *Travel and Tourism Analyst* **6**, 76 — 87.

Economist Intelligence Unit (1989b). Cyprus, *International Tourism Reports* **4**, 56 — 68.

Economist Intelligence Unit (1990). Lebanon, Cyprus, *Country Profile — Annual Survey of Political and Economic Background*. London: *The Economist* Intelligence Unit Ltd.

Go, R. and Frechtling, D. (1991). World travel and tourism review, part one: Indicators. In D.E. Hawkins and J.R. Brent Ritchie (eds), *World Travel and Tourism Review — Indicators, Trends and Forecasts*. Oxon: CAB International, 3 — 5.

Grotewold, A. (1990). Searching for core area growth. *Geojournal*, **22**(4): 399 — 407.

Hall, C.M. (1994). *Tourism and Politics: Policy, Power and place*. Chichester: John Wiley & Sons.

Herbert, A.B. (1985). *International Travelers' Security Handbook* New York: Hippocrene Books.

Hollier, R. (1991). Conflict in the Gulf — Response of the tourism industry. *Tourism Management*, **12**(1): 1 — 4.

Iglarsh, H.J. (1987). Fear of flying: Its economic costs. *Terror: An International Journal*, **10**(1): 45 — 50.

Israel, Central Bureau of Statistics (1969). *Statistical Abstracts of Israel 1969*, No. 20.

Israel, Central Bureau of Statistics (1975). *Statistical Abstracts of Israel 1975*, No. 26.

Israel, Central Bureau of Statistics (1982). *Statistical Abstracts of Israel 1982*, No. 33.

Israel, Central Bureau of Statistics (1987). *Tourism and Hospitality Services Quarterly*.

Israel, Central Bureau of Statistics (1989). *Statistical Abstracts of Israel 1989*, No. 40.

Israel, Central Bureau of Statistics (1991). *Statistical Abstracts of Israel 1990*, No. 42.

Israel, Army Spokesman (1986). *Terror Events and Casualties in Israel: June 68 — September 86*.

Kurent, H.P. (1991). Tourism in the 1990s: threats and opportunities. In D.E. Hawkins and J.R. Brent Ritchie (eds), *World Travel and Tourism Review — Indicators, Trends and Forecasts*. Oxon: CAB International, 78 — 82.

Lieber, R.J. (1987). Middle East oil and the industrial democracies: conflict and cooperation in the aftermath of the oil shocks. In S.F. Wells and M. Bruzonsky *Security in The Middle East — Regional Change and Great Power Stategies.* Boulder and London: Westview Press, 217–35.

Mansfeld, Y. (1993) Turbulent security environment and variable propensity to travel — the case of Israel, 1948–1989. TESG, *Journal of Economic and Social Geography*, **84**(2): 132–43.

Millman, R. (1989) Pleasure Seeking -v- the "Greening" of World Tourism. *Tourism Management.* **10**(4): 275–8.

Moorhead, P. (1991). An Examination of the Relationship Between Terrorism, the Media and Tourism, with Reference to the Northern Ireland Tourism Product. Unpublished M.Sc. thesis, Department of Management Studies for Tourism and Hotel Industries, University of Surrey.

Muir, R. and Paddison, R. (1981). *Politics, Geography and Behaviour.* London and New York: Methuen.

Norton, G. (1987). Tourism and international terrorism. *The World Today* **43**(2): 30–3.

Richter, K.L. (1983). Tourism politics and political science: A case of not so being neglect. *Annals of Tourism Research*, **10**(3): 313–35.

Richter, K.L. (1987). The political dimensions of tourism. In J.R. Brent Ritchie and C.R. Goeldner (eds), *Travel, Tourism, and Hospitality Research — A Handbook for Managers and Researchers.* New York: John Wiley & Sons, 215–27.

Richter, K.R. and Waugh, W.L. (1986). Terrorism and tourism as logical companions. *Tourism Management.* **7**(4): 230–8.

Ryan, C. (1991). *Tourism, Terrorism and Violence — The Risks of Wider World Travel.* Conflict Studies, London: Research Institute for the Study of Conflict and Terrorism, 244.

Taylor, M. and Quayle, E. (1994). *Terrorist Lives.* London and Washington: Brassey's.

World of Information (1988). *The Middle East Review.* Saffron Walden: World of Information.

World Tourism Organization (1992). *World Travel Statistics.* Madrid: World Tourism Organization.

World Tourism Organization (1993). *World Travel Statistics.* Madrid: World Tourism Organization.

Part 4

Crime and the hotel industry

19 Tourist-related crime and the hotel industry: a review of the literature and related materials

SUSAN A. BACH

Introduction

The 1990s is a period of major change in the hotel industry, particularly in the area of guest security. Prior to this time, the issue of guest security in hotels was rarely discussed (Biagini, 1992; Raterman, 1994). Hotels with security departments tended to downplay the presence of security personnel in order to avoid guest concern about the possibility of danger to their well-being. However, a series of events in the past few years has changed the nature of hotel security and the awareness many travelers have about their safety.

Several international tourists murdered in Florida in the early 1990s brought crime against travelers to national and international attention, especially through major coverage in the press and media. In Florida, which is so dependent upon the tourism industry, this negative publicity has had a serious effect on the numbers of international visitors coming to the state (Blum, 1993; Donoho, 1993b), as well as on conferences booked and hotel occupancies (Dodd, 1993; Griffin, 1993).

The negative publicity was further exacerbated by television coverage portraying a nation with criminal activity out of control and news exposés about lax hotel security. Crime against tourists was no longer an issue the hotel industry could minimize or ignore because the traveling public was aware of the potential dangers they faced. The national crime problem had directly affected industry and indeed all aspects of the hospitality and tourism industries.

In the early 1990s, a frequent topic on national television was serious and violent crimes against hotel and motel guests. Nationally broadcast news, investigative print journalism, and talk shows featured reports about crimes against travelers, interviews with victims, and perhaps the most damaging to the hotel industry, a *20/20* segment on the ABC television network in October 1992 about lax hotel security. This segment profiled the ease with which a guest could obtain a room key from the front desk with no identification; how an intruder, posing as an employee, might identify rooms occupied by a female traveling alone; the negligent way in which some hotels exercise key control;

Tourism, Crime and International Security Issues, edited by
A. Pizam and Y. Mansfeld. © 1996 John Wiley & Sons Ltd.

and how easy it is for someone to take a key when checking out of a hotel and return to the same room at a later time as an intruder.

This type of national media coverage was represented on other networks as well. CBS aired a program on *48 Hours* entitled "State of Fear" about crime out of control in Florida. The prime time program interviewed youngsters who had terrorized travelers and showed no remorse and little regard for human life or property. Their prison sentences were cut short due to overcrowded prison conditions. Citizens were interviewed on the program and complained that money to fight crime appeared to be unavailable until international travelers were murdered, suggesting that law enforcement and the legislature were more concerned about the effects of crime on tourism than on residents of the state.

Some of the other programs which aired features on crime in America and the social causes and consequences of crime included *Eye on America, Inside Edition, Montel Williams, Geraldo*, and *Larry King Live*. While not all the programing on crime aired during this period was hospitality and tourism related, the negative impact on the industry was felt as fewer international travelers came to the United States. Concerns about safety were expressed by frequent travelers, and conference groups canceled their bookings or changed venues to locations perceived to be more safe. The impact was quickly obvious in lower occupancies and rates.

One thing has become certain, the traveling public is much more aware of its vulnerability and more sensitive to security provided by hotels and motels. This concern appears to have further sensitized some hoteliers to their responsibilities in the area of guest security.

Innkeepers' legal responsibility

In the United States, innkeepers are responsible for providing a safe and secure environment for their guests. Over the years, the court system has demonstrated that hoteliers can be held liable for damages when they fail to carry out their responsibility. This responsibility starts with the concept of *foreseeability*, which holds hoteliers responsible for foreseeing, or anticipating, the possibility that criminal activity might occur, causing loss or injury to guests. If a hotel has previously experienced any criminal activity on its property or is located in an area that has criminal activity, the courts hold that the hotelier should anticipate that these situations may adversely effect the well-being of a hotel guest. Consequently, hoteliers are responsible for exercising *reasonable care* to protect guests from the harm of "foreseeable" criminal activity (Townsend, 1988). While this approach appears reasonable, in fact, it is imprecise and open to interpretation by the courts. Therefore, hoteliers do not have clear guidelines which define the expected security measures they should take to foresee injury or loss to guests and the steps necessary to exercise reasonable care to prevent what is perceived to be foreseeable.

The laws which govern hoteliers' responsibilities are part of the body of common law, which has evolved from the early English system of judicial practice and social custom. Not only have these laws continued to evolve, but they are also influenced by the structure of the American judicial system, in which each state is able to develop its own laws and precedents, thus further complicating the issue. Examining the outcomes of previous court cases could provide hoteliers with some knowledge about responsibility in exercising reasonable care, but legal precedent may not be consistent from state to state. Therefore, case law alone provides insufficient guidelines for hoteliers.

Frequently therefore, hoteliers turn to the literature as a source of information regarding the security strategies available to fulfill their responsibility to provide a secure environment. This chapter is a review of the hospitality literature related to hotel crime prevention and guest security.

The broad subject of guest protection is an area which includes not only crime prevention, but also addresses fire and life safety, the proper response to bomb threats and terrorism and accident prevention. Each of these areas is important for hoteliers to consider in terms of the overall well-being of guests. This discussion however, focuses solely on crime prevention.

Until the unfortunate crimes against tourists mentioned earlier, hotel crime prevention did not receive as much attention as that precipitated by guest injury and loss caused by hotel fires. Following a series of hotel fires, Congress passed a law in 1990 which prohibits the reimbursement of hotel expenses for government employees who stay in properties which do not meet fire codes. Many corporations also discourage their employees from staying in properties that do not meet fire codes. As a result, fire safety in the hospitality industry has improved significantly (Prestia, 1993).

As yet, there has not been a similar national effort to increase hotel security in order to protect guests from crime. In fact, the American Hotel and Motel Association (AH&MA) specifically states that it does not believe there should be national security standards for hotels or motels since no two are alike (Ellis, 1986). As a result of the diversity in physical plant, location, staffing, operational practices and types of guests, the AH&MA contends that standards would not be feasible (Ellis, 1986: Educational Institute, 1993). However, there is disagreement with this position: (CFHMA recommended security, (1993); Prestia, 1993). For example, in response to the negative impact of crimes against tourists, the Central Florida Hotel and Motel Association (CFHMA) developed 19 recommended safety and security standards for its membership, 11 of which are no or low-cost measures (CFHMA recommended security, 1993). In addition, the new security technology developed and adopted by hotels informally creates and continuously updates an informal standard. It is too soon to say the tide has changed regarding the issue of standards, but there is little doubt that the traveling public is concerned about their safety when they stay in a hotel or a motel (Hayward, 1994).

Attention to guest security is not new, although the focus was originally on "the detection and apprehension of room burglars, the attempted prevention of prostitution on premises, and dealt largely with obstreperous cocktail lounge patrons" (Burstein, 1985: 1). Frequently, the "house detective" was a retired law enforcement officer, with little knowledge of how a hotel operated and an orientation of apprehension rather than prevention.

However, modern hotel security has begun to take a proactive posture by adopting an attitude of prevention. This change has come about in part as the result of well-publicized liability claims and in part because the hotel industry has begun to develop a security function specifically to meet the unique needs of the lodging industry (Burstein, 1985; Ellis, 1986; Prestia, 1993; Smith, 1993).

A theoretical component

Another factor contributing to the increased sophistication of hotel security is the incorporation of knowledge from the field of criminology. One theory the hospitality industry has adopted from criminology is that of Crime Prevention Through Environmental Design (CPTED), which suggests that the physical design, security hardware and electronics and behavioral security measures incorporated into the operation of a facility can do much to deter or displace criminal activity from an environment (Jeffrey, 1977; Newman, 1972). This theory lends support to the issues of foreseeability and reasonable care by suggesting that carefully thought out security strategies can provide increased guest safety.

The National Crime Prevention Institute (NCPI) (1986) presents a model which classifies various types of crime prevention strategies into two CPTED categories: *physical* devices include both mechanical hardware and electronic devices purchased and installed to protect people and their property; *behavioral* measures include written policies and procedures, employee training, and strategies instituted and followed to protect people and property.

The NCPI model is applicable to crime prevention in the hotel industry, and the security strategies it recommends can be used as a framework by which to review the literature available to hoteliers. In the literature, there are a vast number of articles suggesting a myriad of different security strategies for hoteliers to incorporate. What is most noted by its absence is the lack of independent empirical evidence to support any strategy.

This lack of empirical evidence based upon research may be one reason why there are no minimal standards of hotel or motel security. Also, the potential costs of installing mechanical or electronic hardware, and the extensive array of technological options available, may have lead to confusion about which security strategies offer the best return for a hotel's security dollar. While the need for independent empirical research is critical, neither the lack of research to date, nor the potential cost of developing or upgrading an existing security program, are a reasonable defense for a hotelier. The public does not expect the hotel industry to correct the national crime problem, but they do expect to be safe in a hotel or motel (Merkin, 1993).

Literature review

The literature provides hoteliers with an array of articles that are either descriptive, outlining what is available in the security marketplace, or prescriptive, suggesting strategies that have been incorporated by another lodging facility or group of properties. Although this information offers suggestions for hoteliers to consider, it does not provide empirical data supported by research. Nevertheless, since the journal articles are one source of information currently available to hoteliers to consider in their decision making, this literature merits review. The review which follows is categorized according to the NCPI's model.

Physical security devices

Physical security devices represent items of both a mechanical and electronic nature that are installed to protect guests and their property. According to the NCPI these types of devices include *boundary markers* such as fences, gates, and shrubs; *perimeter access barriers* such as doors, locks and windows; *internal barriers* such as safes and restricted floors, *electronic security systems* which include *surveillance systems* such as lighting and surveillance cameras, coupled with human observation; and *intrusion detection systems* such as sensors and alarms.

Technological advances have been instrumental in increasing the sophistication of physical devices. Hotel journals abound with articles reviewing what is new and available in the marketplace. It is important to note in this discussion of physical devices that the CPTED literature supports using physical security devices in conjunction with behavioral security procedures to provide comprehensive security strategies. This approach is also recommended in the hospitality literature.

New technological advances are obvious in the types of locks available for guest room doors (Biagini, 1992, 1993, 1994). The trend is toward electronic locks, activated by plastic cards which have codes randomly assigned at check-in (Johnson, 1992; Merkin, 1993; Wagner, 1991). However, it is estimated that these locks are currently in use in only about 30 per cent of hotels (Lambert, 1993). Nevertheless, electronic locks using plastic card keys offer advantages unavailable with traditional locks. These advantages include an investigatory capacity to print out a list of the keys used to enter a room during a particular time period and the ability to easily reprogram a single lock or all the locks on property in the event that a pass key is lost (Baum, 1992; Biagini, 1992, 1994; Johnson, 1992; Kohr, 1991; Straub, 1992). This type of sophistication is not available with traditional brass keys.

Locking systems include additional, or secondary locks, to enhance the effectiveness of the primary lock. Included in secondary locks are deadbolt locks and latch bars or chains on guest room doors (Ellis, 1992; Rusting, 1993b). These types of locking devices are designed to provide additional protection while guests are in their rooms. The American Automobile Association (AAA) now requires that all hotels listed in their 1995 *Tourbooks* provide guest room doors with deadbolt locks as well as an additional secondary locking device and view ports in the door, commonly referred to as "peepholes." The AAA estimates that this policy change affects over 19 000 hotels and motels in the United States and approximately 3000 properties in Canada and Mexico (American Automobile Associate, March 16, 1993). The AAA further estimates that 79 per cent of all properties listed in their *Tourbooks* already meet these standards (Automobile Association of America, January 1, 1994). Locking systems are also a concern on sliding glass doors in guest rooms. Consequently, the installation of "Charlie bars" to prevent the door from being pushed open from the outside is advisable.

Johnson (1992) and Kohr (1991) discuss the expense of retrofitting a property with electronic locks. Kohr suggests considering the cost of rotating or replacing cylinders should be considered in relation to the cost of upgrading a locking system to the new technology (Kohr, 1991). Several major hotel chains have mandated electronic locks for all their properties. For example, Holiday Inns Worldwide has directed that all their hotels install electronic locks by 1996 (Holiday Inn locks, 1993). Choice Hotels

International installs electronic locks in all its budget properties, and Budget expects all its motels to convert to electronic locks by 1996 (Wolff, 1993). Electronic locks are likely also to be installed in most new construction. While locking systems are part of a physical strategy, this security approach is often coupled with behavioral measures such as removing the room number and the hotel name from the key or tags (Rusting, 1993b; Smith, 1993).

The NCPI recommends the strategy of using internal barriers to protect people and property. These physical devices control access to protect guests from intruders, as well as from people who have legitimate reason to be on property such as other guests or employees (NCPI, 1986). In the hotel industry, in-room safes are an example of internal barrier devices installed to protect guest property (Biagini, 1992, 1993, 1994; Company offers tips, 1993; Finkelstein, 1990; Rowe, 1991; Saied, 1992). The use of safety deposit boxes available through the front desk is an alternate option but one less convenient for the guest. Other internal barriers such as restricting floors for women traveling alone and preventing or discouraging access to specific locations within the hotel are behavioral strategies which support internal barriers.

Surveillance systems constitute another strategy recommended by the NCPI and include human observation, as well as the use of closed circuit cameras, adequate lighting and intrusion detection systems. This category of security strategies combines physical and behavioral measures to monitor the activity in and around a hotel on the theory that crime is minimized if the criminal believes he or she can be seen and potentially identified (Walpole, 1991; Wolff, 1992). George (1993) reports on the adaptation of guard tour technology to monitor patrol check points as security officers walk about a property in order to increase the effectiveness of security patrol observation.

Surveillance cameras and closed circuit television have been used as part of a hotel's overall security program. The literature stresses that it is important that the equipment be monitored by trained employees (Kohr, 1991; Salomon, 1993; Selwitz, 1990). The use of dummy cameras or un-monitored closed circuit television cameras can provide a false sense of security to a guest and can be an invitation to criminal activity, guest injury and, ultimately, financial liability (The National Shopping Center Security Report, 1993; Selwitz, 1990).

Adequate lighting is essential in an overall security program as a deterrent to crime (Henry, 1994; Selwitz, 1990). While "adequate" is a relative term, industry experts suggest that exterior lighting should be one foot candle, or enough illumination to read a newspaper while standing outdoors on a dark night (Ellis, 1992; Kohr, 1991).

Human observation is another essential element in the CPTED theory. While human observation has behavioral components, the NCPI classifies it as part of the overall physical category of surveillance. Human observation can take the form of social observation by all the people in a building or facility, as well as inspection by patrolling security officers (George, 1993; NCPI, 1986; Ronan, 1993). Social observation should be part of the required behavior by all since it means employees making eye contact with guests and initiating light social conversation. Although this hospitality practice is used in some hotels and motels to make visitors feel welcome, it can also serve as a strong deterrent to crime because criminals and intruders do not want to be seen. Recognition potentially increases the chance of later being identified.

The hospitality literature also addresses the NCPI strategies of erecting and maintaining boundary markers such as fences, gates, and landscaping as a physical and psychological crime deterrent (Wolff, 1992). Another deterrent recommended by the NCPI model is intrusion detection systems with alarms that are activated when a wired door is opened. These can be silent alarms that are detected in the security department or at local law enforcement headquarters and many hotels use these systems to secure doors in remote areas of the facility (Lattin, 1993). Guest rooms with windows which may offer easy access from the outside should have special locks installed to protect the windows from being pried open.

Ideally, physical crime prevention strategies should be considered during the planning, design and construction stage of a hotel or motel. It is at this stage that NCPI's suggestions for eliminating alcoves in a hallway, dark corners and external stairways hidden from view behind which someone may hide are easily incorporated into a new facility.

The literature stresses that each hotel and motel is unique and security strategies must be evaluated on a property by property basis (Ellis, 1986; Henry, 1994; Kennedy, 1992; Rusting, 1993c). Not only does this suggest that knowledge of available physical security hardware is important for the hotelier, but that the hotelier must also know about the types of crimes that are prevalent in a specific area in order to determine what strategies are most appropriate to consider (Kohr, 1991; Magenheim, 1993; Talley, 1991; Walpole, 1991). This strategy brings us to the discussion of behavioral security procedures and the benefit of behavioral measures as a complement to physical devices.

Behavioral security procedures

Behavioral security procedures are operational security practices implemented to provide safety and security for guests. The strategy of incorporating behavioral procedures to support physical security devices is reflected in the security policies developed by management. These security policies represent the standards by which employees are expected to carry out their duties from a security perspective. The use of behavioral measures is encouraged by the NCPI (1986) model as well as by hospitality literature. These strategies are procedures which are generally inexpensive to incorporate into a security program but require management diligence in monitoring to insure that adherence to policies is consistent.

The proper development of security policies requires significant foresight and an understanding of how guests might be vulnerable to criminal activity. The development and implementation of these policies impels management decisions to exercise reasonable care and emphasizes the importance of guest security (Henry, 1994; Kavanaugh, 1992; Keller, 1993; Kohr, 1991). In order to understand how guests might be vulnerable to crime, it is important for hoteliers to establish open lines of communication with law enforcement (Ellis, 1992; Henry 1994; Kohr, 1991; Magenheim, 1993; Ronan, 1993; Rusting, 1993c; Talley, 1991).

In addition to providing information about criminal activity in the area, law enforcement can also assist a hotelier by conducting a security survey of the property (Gillette, 1994; Henry, 1994; Ronan, 1993; Talley, 1991). A security survey, which can also be conducted by a liability insurance representative or a consultant, identifies areas of a hotel which are vulnerable to crime. Implementing changes recommended in a security survey can positively influence liability insurance rates, and instituting corrective measures becomes a matter of record in the event a guest lodges a claim against a property. Should a hotelier determine it is in the best interest of the property not to institute a corrective security measure suggested as part of a survey, the rationale behind this decision should be documented as well, since non-action on a recommendation is also considered a matter of record (Gillette, 1994). Foreseeing the possibility of criminal activity and instituting reasonable policies and procedures to protect against such incidents, as well as training employees to follow policy, is central to the concept of behavioral strategies.

Ongoing training is critical to the effectiveness of behavioral measures (Donoho, 1993a; Kavanaugh, 1992). Training in the hotel industry includes training of front office staff, security officers and all the employees on a property. Numerous references suggest the importance of front office employees trained to follow security procedures (Donoho, 1993a; Giovanetti, 1993; Kennedy, 1992; Wagner, 1991; Wolff, 1992). At the front desk specifically, the literature suggests practices such as writing down the room number for guests rather than announcing it out loud at check-in, providing instruction on how to use the key so guests do not have to fumble at their door, requesting that guests return keys at check-out, verifying guest identity prior to replacing lost guest room keys and requesting that a security officer or manager escort a guest to the room to verify the guest's identity prior to issuing a replacement key (Chervenak, 1993; Donoho, 1993a; Hayward, 1994; Kennedy, 1992; Merkin, 1993).

Women traveling alone pose additional safety concerns for hotels and motels. In order to minimize their vulnerability, it has been suggested that women be assigned to rooms within view of or near the front desk, near an elevator to avoid having to walk down a long corridor, or to a room not in a remote area of the property. Women can also be assigned to rooms on specifically designated floors which require a special key for access (Donoho, 1993a; Giovanetti, 1993; McGreevy, 1992; Wolff, 1993). Giovanetti (1993) also points out that some hotels provide free limousine service early in the morning and late in the evening in business districts where a female guest may be vulnerable because the area is deserted during off hours.

Wolff (1993) points out the importance of training hotel telephone operators in order that they not divulge guest names or room numbers. Further, he suggests that callers should be asked to identify a guest by name, and not just by room number, before being connected. In addition, some hotels have discontinued direct dial to guest rooms from lobby house phones and now require that calls to guest rooms be directed through the switchboard.

Industry experts support an in-house security department in hotels where the size of the property warrants this strategy. The unique requirements of each property dictate the necessity for and size of a full-time security presence on property (Burstein, 1985; Rusting, 1993c, Smith, 1993). Smith (1993) recommends a minimum of one officer for each of the three shifts for every 300 rooms. He further suggests that staffing be based on room size rather than occupancy because of occupancy fluctuations and unpredictability. In addition, it is his contention that hotels with 300 or more rooms require a full-time security director, responsible for supervision and management of the hotel's security activities. Burstein (1985) suggests that several factors in addition to the number of rooms be considered in determining staff size. Among them he includes acreage upon which the property stands, the extensiveness of parking facilities, recreational amenities available on property, the overall complexity of the property based upon the other services and facilities available, as well as proximity to other facilities.

Effectively managing a security department includes careful screening, hiring, and training of staff (Burstein, 1985; Rusting, 1991; Smith, 1993). Kohr (1991), Rusting (1991), and Smith (1993) stress the importance of carefully screening potential security officers through the use of references and background checks. Ellis (1986) recommends bonding security staff in light of their access to almost every area of the property. Once on board, security staff must be continuously trained and updated in topics such as life support, guest relations, employee relations, innkeepers' laws, emergency procedures, crisis management, report writing and communication and investigative techniques (Burstein, 1985; Ellis, 1986; Smith, 1993).

As referred to in the earlier discussion on human observation, many properties now consider all their employees part of their security effort. However, this strategy requires appropriate staff training (Baum, 1992; Henry, 1994; Keller, 1993; Kohr, 1991; Marshall, 1992; McGreevy, 1992; Rusting, 1993a; Talley, 1991; Walpole, 1991). Educating employees to be sensitive to security issues and instructing them in how they are expected to respond to a problem or crisis situation can help a property limit the potential of guest loss or injury (Ellis, 1992; Henry, 1994; Kavanaugh, 1992; Keller, 1993; Kohr, 1991; McGreevy, 1992; Miller, 1993; Rusting, 1992a; Talley, 1991). This security strategy increases the effectiveness of any security program, but to be effective training must be ongoing and well documented.

The literature suggests several strategies which combine the use of physical devices and behavioral measures to increase guest security. An example of this strategy is locking side doors after hours. For this strategy to be effective, hoteliers should provide signs on both sides of the door outlining the hours during which the door is locked and directing visitors to the main entrance. Other areas of a hotel where access can be restricted include parking facilities or hotel facilities that are locked to the general public and require a guest room key for access such as a fitness room.

Although adequate lighting is considered a physical strategy, this strategy is enhanced by the inexpensive behavioral measure of implementing a procedure for regular inspection of lights. These inspections should cover all outdoor areas, requiring that burnt out bulbs be immediately replaced and ensuring that outdoor lamps are not obstructed by trees, shrubs, or other objects (Ronan, 1993).

According to the NCPI (1986), effective key control and lock maintenance procedures are an essential component to any security program. This critical behavioral strategy includes maintaining a key log, strict control over passkeys and master keys, and rotating or replacing cyclinders when brass keys are missing (Burstein, 1985; Ellis, 1986; Smith, 1993; Wolff, 1993). All key control activities should be regularly documented both as part of monitoring and control and as evidence in the event of a claim (Ellis, 1992; Johnson, 1992; Kavanaugh, 1992; Kohr, 1991; Ronan, 1993; Wolff, 1992, 1993).

Smith (1993) addresses the strategy of key coding. This is a relatively new technique adopted by some hotels that continue to use brass keys. These properties have removed the room number and hotel identification from the key, but have engraved a number or number and letter sequence on keys so that they may be identified by the front desk staff. This practice permits the continued use of brass keys and helps in preventing unauthorized use of lost room keys. However, this system does not preclude rotating or changing cylinders if keys are missing, since a guest can purposefully check into a hotel to obtain a key to be used in committing a crime at a later time.

Behavioral strategies also include the behavioral modification of guests to increase their security. Guest education has become an important consideration of the AH&MA, the AAA and conference planners (Barker, 1993; Donoho, 1993a, b; Fried, 1993; Lambert, 1993; PCMA, 1994; Radigan, 1993; Thomas, 1993). Organizations such as the AH&MA and the AAA offer printed material to be distributed at the front desk. Some hotels have begun to provide their own security information in guest rooms. These brochures instruct guests about common sense practices to follow. The recommendations include suggestions such as not opening a guest door without being certain who is on the other side, calling the front desk to verify that an employee was sent up to the room when the guest has not requested service, refraining from announcing the name of the hotel in which they are staying, taking precautions about showing large sums of money or jewelry in public and getting directions prior to leaving the hotel in order to travel only in areas considered safe. The AH&MA has also developed a short information video which can be shown on the television in the guest room. The video instructs guests in the same common sense precautions available in brochures.

Rutherford and McConnell (1991) point out that a property can be held liable for not informing guests about criminal activity not only in the hotel but also in the immediate vicinity. While it might appear that even suggesting the possibility of criminal activity in or around a hotel would raise concern among guests, a shift in perception about guest security has changed this notion (Hayward, 1994; Rusting, 1992a). When properly presented, guest education can actually make guests feel more secure because it implies that the hotel gives high priority to their security.

Several authors suggest that hotels offer to escort guests to isolated areas where they may be vulnerable such as parking lots (Donoho, 1993a; Kennedy, 1992; McGreevy, 1992; Meeting planners must eye, 1993). When a hotel provides this service, a carefully screened and trained service addresses an area of concern of some meeting planners, as well as corporate travel managers who make arrangements for company employees who travel frequently. Needless to say, properties which make security services available should educate guests about these amenities.

The meeting and travel industry have also expressed concern about the issues of guest security (Barker, 1993; Boisclair, 1993; Hayward, 1994; PCMA, 1994; Raterman, 1994; Wolff, 1993). Meeting planners are asking questions about security issues as part of their site inspection and assessment of a facility (Meeting planners must eye, 1993). Sharing a concern for traveler security, the American Society of Travel Agents (1989) (ASTA) published a brochure for distribution to customers which includes security and safety tips.

As with any program, regular maintenance strategies are essential to insure that security equipment is functional. In terms of a comprehensive hotel security program, not only must equipment be maintained, but behavioral measures should be monitored as well. Documentation is a very important aspect of a comprehensive security program because it demonstrates the priority placed on maintaining security. Security policies should be reviewed periodically to insure that they are current. In addition, managers should supervise employees to verify that they are adhering to written policies (Burstein, 1985; Ellis, 1986; Smith, 1993).

Additional sources

In addition to journal articles, several reference books address hotel security. In *Hotel Security Management*, Burstein (1985) discusses the concepts of physical security and behavioral security practices. He offers an extensive review of the structure and policies of a "protection department" as well as providing insights about guest protection. The book provides several checklists with particularly insightful questions for consideration in the hotel or motel development stage for protecting information and for conducting a property survey. These checklists can be valuable in planning security programs.

Smith (1993), in *Hotel Security* offers an in-depth discussion about investigation of room thefts, including information on how to set up a guest room to conduct an integrity test of a suspected employee using a hidden camera. He also addresses the importance of detailed and accurate incident reports, which are essential to any investigation, and reminds hoteliers that all records can be subpoenaed in the event a property is sued. The chapter on report writing stresses the importance of documentation to a comprehensive security program.

Security and Loss Prevention Management (Ellis, 1986) was developed under the auspices of the Educational Institute of the American Hotel and Motel Association. This book presents a broad view of hotel security, including legal aspects, physical hardware, behavioral measures, internal controls and safety and loss prevention. Summaries of several lodging court cases are included in the text.

Another volume from the Educational Institute (1993) is *S.A.F.E: Security Awareness for Everyone*, a training packet which includes several manuals: a manager's manual, with excerpts from *Security and Loss Prevention Management*; an employee handbook, which can be self-paced or used in a workshop setting; a trainer's guide with basic group training suggestions; and an implementation and resource guide for trainers. While the manuals are basic, they provide a foundation springboard for setting up a security awareness training program on property.

Accident Prevention for Hotels, Motels, and Restaurants (Kohr, 1991) focuses primarily on the safety of a hotel from the perspective of preventing accidents, but refers to several security issues as well. From a security perspective, the sections on factors to consider in hotel or motel design raise important points for architects and developers.

Chocolates for the Pillows, Nightmares for the Guests: The Failure of the Hotel Industry to Protect the Traveling Public from Violent Crime (Prestia, 1993) exposes the hotel industry's negligence in the area of guest safety by examining lax hotel security and its effect on guests. References and excerpts from several liability cases decided in the plaintiff's favor suggest that the industry has not done enough to police itself. Prestia also writes about some of the key reasons why crimes, particularly violent crimes against guests, have been downplayed by the hotel industry.

Each of these sources provides hoteliers with critical information about equipment and practices that help to promote guest security and limit a property's liability. Further, they offer valuable information to use in security planning and decision making. Since each property is unique, management must assess the needs of their property and its guests to determine what combination of security measures is most appropriate. However, what is essential for any security program to be effective is commitment from management and ownership. A well thought out program requires money, time and human resources and cannot depend upon occupancy levels or whether room rates increase.

Where do we go from here?

All hoteliers are expected by guests and the courts to provide a safe and secure environment. Hoteliers operating on a limited budget should be aware that failing to provide for guest security because of high costs does not constitute a reasonable defense, particularly since many effective strategies require little or no cost. In addition, the literature is clear in its recommendation that physical security devices alone are insufficient to protect a hotel from the liability associated with guest injury or loss. In fact, the less costly strategy of incorporating behavioral procedures to support physical devices is stressed by both the hospitality industry experts and by the NCPI (1986) classification model of the CPTED theory.

Although numerous recommendations for establishing safety and security procedures are available in the literature, the most striking issue is the fact that no empirical evidence is available to validate the extensive crime prevention strategies recommended by hospitality industry experts. While empirical data would inform a hotelier about preferred strategies, the lack of such data forces hoteliers to rely on descriptive information to guide them in combating criminal activity in a hotel.

In view of the critical impact crime has on the hospitality industry, research in lodging crime prevention is warranted and the results should be made readily available to academicians and the industry. The types of research which would make a significant contribution include assessing the effectiveness of specific strategies in installing crime prevention, evaluating the types of crimes most prevalent in different hotels and locales and measuring guest and hotelier perceptions of security and safety. However, regardless of the current lack of research, hoteliers are still responsible for taking reasonable measures to provide their guests with a safe and secure lodging environment.

Crime is a serious issue which affects every aspect of society and its organizations. While the hospitality industry is not responsible for curing the national crime problem, the industry is responsible for protecting its guests and exercising social responsibility. As one of the largest employers, not only in the United States, but world-wide, the hotel industry impacts on many lives and communities. There is a positive role each hotel can play in its own community to minimize crime.

As a microcosm of society, hotels and motels serve many diverse customers. Since properties are frequently located in the same community as many of their employees, vendors, and suppliers, as well as some of their customers, hotels and motels can demonstrate their commitment to the well-being of their local community by being a good neighbor and responding to the needs of the neighborhood.

Hotels and motels are in the advantageous position of being able to educate their neighbors in the services provided to the community. This education process can be accomplished by interacting with various community agencies which serve a neighborhood. For example, local hotels and motels can establish a partnership with a local school at any level from preschool through high school and offer field trip opportunities through different departments. Not only do these experiences serve an educational purpose for the students, but they can also create an awareness about career alternatives that many students may not have considered because of their limited knowledge of these choices. Hospitality industry supervisors and managers can be called upon to speak to classes about subjects within their own expertise. For example, a chef might be an appropriate speaker in a high school chemistry or home economics class, an engineer could address the merit of recycling, and a front office manager could speak about the effects of technology on customer service. These same managers can also volunteer to coach sports teams, tutor students and serve as mentors. Hotels and motels can provide excellent internship or work study experiences for students interested in a career in any field which is represented on property. In many communities, this type of management involvement is as important to the health of a property as is involvement in professional and business organizations.

Other activities in which lodging facilities can be involved include donating unused food prepared for banquets to homeless shelters. In addition, gifts and donations collected prior to holidays can be given to children in local hospitals and schools. Sponsoring neighborhood events, such as sports teams, charity functions or providing meeting space on an "as available" basis for neighborhood watch meetings or similar community functions, positions the property in the minds of its neighbors as a concerned partner, interested in the welfare of the area, its residents, and businesses. The possibilities can be limitless and should be dictated by community needs and business constraints.

This type of involvement in the community is not only good for business, but can also assist in deterring crime because the hotel or motel is seen as part of the community. Since many crimes are committed in areas well known to perpetrators, such as the areas surrounding their own neighborhoods, being positioned as a valuable partner in the community can make a hotel or motel a less desirable place to commit a crime because of positive neighborhood sentiment toward the enterprise.

References

American Society of Travel Agents (1989). *Hotel Tips*. Alexandria, Virginia: ASTA World Headquarters.

Automobile Association of America (1993). AAA will require stiffer security at approved lodgings. Press release, March 11.

Automobile Association of America (1994). *AAA Revised Tourbook Listing for Guest Security*. Heathrow, FL: American Automobile Association Travel Publishing Department.

Automobile Association of America (1994). 99% of AAA approved lodgings to comply with stiffer safety requirements in U.S. and Canada. Press release, January 1.

Baratta, A. (1993). NY police dept. updates safety pamphlet for tourists. *Travel Weekly*, October 4, **52**, 25.

Barker, J. (1993). Safe and protected. *Successful Meetings*, **42**: 57−9.

Barone, M. (1993). Commentary snares of a lost paradise. *U.S. News and World Report*, October 11, **115**: 53.

Baum, C. (1992). Security directors discuss guest protection. *Hotels*, **22**: 61−4.

Beck, M., Kael, P., Smith, V. and Carroll, G. (1993). In a state of terror. *Newsweek*, September 27: 41−2.

Biagini, D. (1992). Guest-room security: Making it a priority. *Hotel and Resort Industry*, **10**: 38−9.

Biagini, D. (1993). Locking in on safety and security. *Hotel and Resort Industry*, **11**: 39−46, 56.

Biagini, D. (1994). Give your property a safety net. *Hotel and Resort Industry*, **12**: 44−9, 54.

Blum, E. (1993). Small percentage of groups cancel Florida meetings over safety issue. *Travel Weekly*, **52**: 1, 4.

Boisclair, M. (1993). In wake of Florida attacks traveler safety a hot topic. *Meetings & Conventions*, **28**: 29.

Burstein, H. (1985). *Hotel Security Management*. New York: Praeger Publishers.

CFHMA recommended security and safety standards (1993). *CFHMA News and Views*, September: 1.

Carper, J. (1993). Security is a requirement, not an amenity. *Hotels*, **27**: 56.

Chervenak, L. (1993). Tech trends: Are you wired to win? *Hotel and Resort Industry*, **16**: 34–40.

Company offers tips on the proper way to choose in-room safes. (1993). *Hotel and Motel Management*, **208**: 73.

Dodd, W. (1993). A tough decision in a difficult situation. *AAA World*, **13**: 40.

Donoho, R. (1993a). On guard. *Successful Meetings*, **42**: 58–67.

Donoho, R. (1993b). In search of a safe haven. *Successful Meetings*, **42**, 15.

Doolittle, L. (1993). *Orlando Sentinel*, September 18: C-5.

Doolittle, L. (1993). Tourism industry fails reality check. *Orlando Sentinel*, October 1: C-1.

Duffy, B. (1993). Florida: The state of rage. *U.S. News and World Report*, October 11, **115**: 40–51.

Eddings, J. and Witken, G. The most dangerous state: How long will Florida fiddle? *U.S. News and World Report*, October 11, **115**: 51.

Educational Institute. (1993). *S.A.F.E.: Safety Awareness for Everyone*. East Lansing, Michigan: Educational Institute of the American Hotel and Motel Association.

Ellis, R. (1986). *Security*. East Lansing, Michigan: Educational Institute of the American Hotel and Motel Association.

Ellis, R. (1992). The security challenge. *Lodging Hospitality*, **48**: 38–42.

Finkelstein, A. (1990). A safe bet: Vault makers target hotel room market. *Orlando Business Journal*, December 21, **7**: 1, 11.

Fried, L.I. (1993). Protecting your travelrs. *Corporate Travel*, **9**: 24–8, 37.

George, S. (1993). Check-in touring. *Security*, **30**: 14.

Gieseking, H. (1993). Preventing hotel crime. *Travel Weekly*, **52**: 47.

Gillette, B. (1994). NJH&MA seminar focuses on security. *Hotel and Motel Management*, **11**: 1, 31.

Giovanetti, T. (1993). Hotels beckon to women with security programs, services. *Hotel Business*, **2**: 3, 30.

Griffin, E. (1993). The traveler safety issue: Let's get real. *Meetings and Conventions*, **28**: 9.

Hayward, P. (1994). The hotel industry and the great American crime wave. *Lodging*, **19**: 26–8, 45–6.

Henry, D. (1994). Good safety plan critical to defend against lawsuits. *Hotel and Motel Management*, **209**: 46.

Holiday Inn locks in security (1993). *Hotel and Resort Industry*, **16**: 11.

Jeffrey, C.R. (1977). *Crime Prevention through Environmental Design*. Beverly Hills: Sage Publications, Inc.

Johnson, B.A. (1992). Card-keys reduce liability concerns. *Hotels*, **26**: 122–3.

Kavanaugh, R.R. (1992). Security: everyone on guard. *Hotels*, **26**: 39.

Keller, S.R. (1993). Cross training isn't just for sports. *Security Management*, **37**: 66–7.

Kennedy, D.B. (1992). The violent gender gap. *Security Management*, **36**: 56–8.

Koentopp, J. (1992). The mirage concerning hotel security. *Security Management*, **36**: 54–60.

Kohr, R.L. (1991). *Accident Prevention for Hotels, Motels and Restaurants*. New York: Van Nostrand Reinhold.

Lambert, M. (1993). Are your guests really safe? Steps to improving security. *Hostmark AAA*, **29**: 4–5.

Lattin, T. (1993). Factory outlet: Hotel wakes owners to basic needs. *Hotels and Motel Management*, **208**: 28, 54.

Magenheim, H. (1993). Orlando area hotels focus efforts on protecting their guests. *Travel Weekly's Guide to Florida, section 3*: F4.

Marshall, A. (1991). Document hotel's patron-safety policies in writing. *Hotel and Motel Management*, **206**: 16.

Marshall, A. (1992). Keep employees current on safety procedures. *Hotel and Motel Management*, **207**: 16.

McConnell, J.P. and Rutherford, D.G. (1993). Why innkeepers go to court: An update. *The Cornell Hotel and Restaurant Administration Quarterly*, **34**: 23–7.

McGreevy, M. (ed.), (1992). Security off premises: The boundaries are fuzzy. *Hospitality Law*, **7**: 1.

McGreevy, M. (ed.) (1993a). Juries won't accept excuses for security shortcomings. *Hospital Law*, **8**, 1−5.

McGreevy, M. (ed.) (1993b). Security: It's the law. *Hospitality Law*, **8**: 8.

Meeting planners must eye security (1993). *Hotel and Motel Management*, **208**: 6.

Merkin, J. (1993). Hotel security: Much more is needed to shut down critics. *Hotel Business*, **2**: 5.

Miller, R. (1993). The people problem. *Security Management*, **37**: 49−50, 58.

Mullins, R. (1991). Rising crime concerns force motel chains to be more security conscious. *The Business Journal of Milwaukee*, **8**: 4−5.

National Crime Prevention Institute. (1986). *Understanding Crime Prevention*. Boston: Butterworths.

The National Shopping Center Security Report. (1993). *Chain Store Age Executive*, 84−114.

Newman, O. (1972). *Architectural Design for Crime Prevention*. Washington, DC: Law Enforcement Assistance Administration.

Professional Convention Management Association (PCMA) (1994). *Enjoy your meeting — safely!* Birmingham, Alabama: Professional Convention Management Association.

Prestia, K.L. (1993). *Chocolates for the Pillows, Nightmares for the Guests: The Failure of the Hotel Industry to Protect the Traveling Public from Violent Crime*. Silver Spring, Maryland: Bartley Press.

Radigan, M. ,(1993). AAA intensifies security standards. *Hostmark AAA*, **29**: 5.

Raterman, K. (1994). Travel industry reacts to growing concern about crime. *Meeting News*, **18**: 1, 15.

Ronan, T.O. (1993). The hospitality of hotel security. *Security Management*, **3**: 38−40.

Rowe, M. (1991). Security smarts: The insurance industry is forcing lodging security to modernize. *Lodging Hospitality*, **47**: 50.

Rowe, M. (1992). Security and self-serve: In the wake of negative publicity, new awareness. *Lodging Hospitality*, **48**: 34.

Rusting, R. (ed.) (1991). Security guards who commit crimes: What's being done to weed out the rotten apples and improve performance? *Hotel/Motel Security and Safety Management*, **9**: 5.

Rusting, R. (ed.) (1992a). Educating guests about crime. *Hotel/Motel Security and Safety Management*, **10**: 6.

Rusting, R. (ed.) (1992b). Survey finds wide approval of certification program for hotel security. *Hotel/Motel Security and Safety Management*, **10**: 1−2.

Rusting, R. (ed.) (1992c). Upgrading security in smaller properties: What operators can do. *Hotel/ Motel Security and Safety Management*, **10**: 5.

Rusting, R. (ed.) (1993a). How Ritz-Carlton hotels apply "TQM" to guest security and safety. *Hotel/Motel Security and Safety Management*, **11**: 1−3.

Rusting, R. (ed.) (1993b). Motel 6 takes the lead in economy lodging security. *Hotel/Motel Security and Safety*, **11**: 2−3.

Rusting, R. (ed.) (1993c). Need for security in all suite hotels recognized by major chains. *Hotel/ Motel Security and Safety Management*, **11**: 1−3.

Rusting, R. (ed.) (1993d). NYC security directors tackle new guard laws, renewed terrorism fears. *Hotel/Motel Security and Safety Management*, **11**: 1−2.

Rutherford, D.G. and McConnell, J.P. (1991). De facto security standards: operators at risk. *Cornell Hotel and Restaurant Administration Quarterly*, **31**: 107−17.

Safety, cost of travel will be major concerns in 21st century. (1989). *Hotels and Restaurants International*, **23**: 29−30.

Saied, J. (1992). Safe at any speed. *Lodging*, **18**: 38−41.

Salomon, A. (1993). Concern for safety spawns new products. *Hotel and Motel Management*, **208**: 8, 26.

Selwitz, R. (1990). Focusing on security: surveillance systems keep an eye on crime. *Hotel and Motel Management*, **205**: 37, 40.

Slepian, C.G. (1993). Setting standards for hotel security. *Hotel and Resort Industry*, **2**: 48−51.

Smith, H. (1993). *Hotel Security*. Springfield, Illinois: Charles C. Thomas, Publishers.

Straub, J. (1992). A safe solution for hotel rooms. *Security Management*, **36**: 51−2.

Talley, L. (1991). Pay attention to the security. *Lodging Hospitality*, **47**: 46.

Thomas, C. (1993). AH&MA spearheads new safety coalition. *Hotel and Motel Management*, **206**; 4, 11.

Townsend, R. (1988). Reasonable care: How safe is safe? *Lodging Hospitality*, **44**: 106–8.

Wagner, G. (1991). Technology meets tomorrow. *Lodging Hospitality*, **47**: 103–4.

Walpole, J.T. (1991). The brave new world of hotel security. *Security Management*, **35**: 83–5.

Wolff, C. (1992). Looking over your shoulder. *Lodging Hospitality*, **48**: 52–4.

Wolff, C. (1993). Setting security straight. *Lodging Hospitality*, **49**: 30–2.

20 Legal aspects of tourism and violence

STEPHEN M. LeBRUTO

Introduction

English social customs and judicial decisions from the Middle Ages formed the basis for United States common law. For example, an early common law rule that applied to places of public accommodation attached liability to the innkeeper as an insurer, with certain exceptions, for the loss of guest property. Although federal, state and local legislation, administrative rules and court cases have modified this particular innkeeper liability, numerous additional laws, rules and cases have attached additional legal responsibilities for the innkeeper (Sherry, 1993).

This chapter addresses the legal aspects of providing tourism services as related to violent acts. Hospitality operations are generally considered quasi-public places, therefore negligence on the part of the service provider is often used as a basis for determining liability for injuries. Injuries suffered can be the result of negligent acts by employees, guests, non-guests, invitees, licensees and trespassers. There is a duty to provide safe premises. Disclaimers and delegation of duties do not relieve liability (Jefferies, 1990).

Hotels, restaurants, and other providers of tourism services are often victims of crime and criminal activity (Jefferies, 1990). Among these crimes are: guests skipping out on their bills; credit card fraud; the passing of bad checks (both travelers and personal); and the passing of counterfeit money. Providers of hospitality services need to know their legal rights relative to these crimes and develop internal policies and procedures to minimize the establishment's loss. This chapter addresses these legal issues.

The sale of food and beverage attaches certain liabilities to providers of hospitality, including civil liability as a result of the illegal sale of intoxicating liquor, which could result in a violent act (Goodwin and Gaston, 1992). Disorderly conduct, detention and eviction of guests, non-guests and others is an issue that has potential to become a violent act affecting tourism.

When a guest dies in a hotel, special procedures must be undertaken. This is especially true with violent deaths. Should proper procedures not be followed, the innkeeper is liable to legal actions (Jefferies, 1990).

Tourism, Crime and International Security Issues, edited by
A. Pizam and Y. Mansfeld. © 1996 John Wiley & Sons Ltd.

Limited liability statutes

Under the common law, unless the guest was negligent, innkeepers were liable for property stolen from guests. This made the innkeeper practically an insurer of guest property. The reasoning behind this English common law was that travelers during the Middle Ages were offered accommodation that usually consisted of one large room where all the guests of the inn slept (Bellucci, 1987). The lack of physical controls associated with this arrangement necessitated the innkeeper to accept responsibility for guests' personal property. Early innkeepers furthermore had reputations implying that they were not to be trusted with one's property. This assumption of liability, on the innkeeper's part, was an attempt to change public opinion.

As the hospitality industry evolved, physical security measures improved, and guests were offered secure private accommodations. Changing modes of transportation permitted the traveling public to carry more personal property than what was only necessary for the trip. Salespeople brought samples of their products into the inn, and merchants carried goods for sale at distant locations. Clearly, it was necessary for the liability of innkeepers for personal property of guests to change (Bellucci, 1987).

Most states have adopted laws limiting the liability of innkeepers for guests' personal property. Generally speaking, hotels are not liable for the loss of guest property unless the hotel was negligent, provided the establishment has adhered to the statute, which usually requires a posting of the laws of limited liability (Cournoyer et al., 1993). Guests do not have to be notified verbally or in writing of the hotel's limited liability. In some states, innkeepers are required to provide safes, or access to a safe, at all times (Jefferies, 1990). Even when property is placed in a safe and there is a loss, the hotel is liable only up to the statutory limits, provided it was not negligent (Cournoyer et al., 1993).

The state of Florida is regarded as an innkeeper-friendly state. With respect to its statutes on limited liability, innkeepers are not required to accept anything for safekeeping, nor are they required to provide safes for guests (Bellucci, 1987). In the event that an innkeeper accepts guest valuables for safekeeping and they become lost, the innkeeper has no liability, unless he/she was negligent. If it is proven that the innkeeper was negligent, in this state, his/her liability is limited to $1000, provided the guest has a receipt from the innkeeper stating the value of the goods left for safekeeping and a notice to the guest that the loss is limited to $1000 in the event of negligence on the part of the innkeeper has been properly posted (Florida Statutes 509.101 and 509.111).

For personal property stolen from a guest room, the liability for an innkeeper in Florida is limited to $500, again only if there is negligence on the part of the innkeeper and the notice is properly posted (Florida Statutes 509.101 and 509.111). The liability can be extended to $1000, if, prior to the loss, the innkeeper inspected the goods and furnished the guest with a receipt. If an innkeeper does not comply with the statutes regarding limiting liability fully, he/she may become, under common law, an insurer of the guest's property (Florida Statutes 509.101).

In the Florida case Rose H. Garner v. Margery Lane, Inc., (242 So. 2d 776, Fla. 4th Dist. Ct. App. 1970) the plaintiffs, upon arriving at the hotel signed registration cards stating: "Money, jewels and other valuable packages must be deposited at the office to be kept in the safe, otherwise the management will not be responsible for any loss." No space was provided on the card for an estimate of the value of the property. The hotel did not inquire as to the value of the goods. There was an armed robbery of the hotel resulting in the loss of the plaintiff's property.

The original decision was in favor of the defendant. The court did not interpret the language on the registration card as having created the hotel's status as an insurer. Upon appeal, the court found in favor of the plaintiff because a reasonable person would believe that the hotel waived its right of limited liability in order to provide better service. In addition, by not inquiring as to the value of the contents placed with the innkeeper for safe keeping, the hotel did not comply fully with the statutes (Sherry, 1993).

In another case where the hotel did not comply with the requirements of the statute, Fennema v. Howard Johnson (559 So. 2d 1231 Fla. App., 1990), the defendant guaranteed that the vehicle and trailer would be safe in the parking lot. Limited liability can only be claimed if the hotel provided a copy of the statute in a prominent place. In this case it was inside a closet door. Since the defendant had prior knowledge of criminal activity in the parking lot, it had a duty to take necessary precautions for the safety of the guest. Instead, the defendant guaranteed the safety of their property (Cournoyer et al., 1993).

In the Florida case Aniballi v. Sonesta Beach Hotel (Fla. 3rd Dist. Ct. App., 1985), the plaintiffs deposited $85 000 in jewelry in the hotel's safety deposit box. On the fourth day of their visit, the property was stolen. The court held that the hotel was not in violation of the statute and therefore was protected by limiting its liability to $1000. Aniballi appealed to two higher courts where the decision was upheld (Bellucci, 1987).

Negligence

A tort is an unlawful act done in violation of someone. There are two types of torts: voluntary and involuntary. Voluntary torts are deliberate and perhaps violent acts such as assault and battery. Involuntary torts are best categorized as accidents (Cournoyer et al., 1993).

In order for a plaintiff successfully to bring a tort action (voluntary or involuntary) based on negligence against an establishment four elements need to be proven: a duty of care was required by the establishment; this duty of care was breached; the proximate cause of the damages was due to the breach of duty; and there were damages sustained (Cournoyer et al., 1993).

Duty of care owed

Hospitality operations are quasi-public places. As such, four groups of people may be on the premises: guests, invitees, licensees and trespassers. A guest is defined as a person who is on the premises for the purpose for which the establishment is open to the public. An invitee is a guest or visitor of a guest, accepted by the proprietor, who is also on the premises for the purpose for which the establishment is open to the public. A licensee is a person who does not qualify as a guest or an invitee but has the permission of the owner to be on the premises such as an off-duty employee. Trespassers are persons on the premises without the permission of the proprietor (Sherry, 1993).

The operator has a duty of care to guests and invitees to inspect the premises for dangerous conditions and correct these dangerous conditions exercising reasonable care.

Liability may result when the operator fails to correct, or adequately warn, guests and invitees of dangerous conditions that are known, should have been known or are brought to the establishment's attention (Sherry, 1993). For example, in a hotel, the owner/operator has a duty of care to guests and invitees to provide locks in good working order on guest room doors (Townsend, 1988).

In Kveragas v. Scottish Inns, Inc. (733 F. Supp. 2d 409 6th Circuit, 1984), intruders broke down the door to the plaintiff's guest room. The plaintiff was shot and $3000 was taken from the room. The door was hollow and the lock was third rate. If adequate locks had been installed, the door would not have been broken down so easily (Rutherford and McConnell, 1991).

Garzilli v. Howard Johnson Motor Lodges (419 F. Supp. 1210l E.D. N.Y., 1976) involved an assault on a celebrity guest, Connie Francis. The intruder gained access through sliding glass doors that could be opened from the outside without much difficulty. Judgment was affirmed to the plaintiff (Sherry, 1993).

The duty of care for a licensee is less. There is no requirement for the operator to inspect for dangerous conditions. The only duty is to warn licensees of dangerous conditions that are known. The operator cannot act in a way to increase peril to licensees.

The least duty is owed to trespassers. Trespassers are on the property without the permission of the operator. The only duty of care that is owed to trespassers is to refrain from arranging the premises in a manner that would cause harm to the trespasser. In a 1975 Florida case, Pedone v. Fontainebleau Corporation, Pedone died as a result of a pool accident. Pedone was a trespasser, and as such the hotel was only responsible not to commit a willful or wanton injury to him.

The duty of care can be further explained by addressing who may be permitted to enter a guest room. The innkeeper has a duty not to allow anyone access to a guest room unless he/she is a registered guest of that particular room. Allowing a non-registered guest access to a guest's room is a frequent request innkeepers receive. Entrances by an innkeeper to the guest's room are limited to routine housekeeping and emergencies (Cournoyer et al., 1993).

Breach of duty

The second element necessary to bring a tort action based on negligence is that a breach of the duty of care owed needs to occur. This would mean that in a case of guest room door locks that were defective or improper, the operator must fail to repair the devices; or in a restaurant or bar situation with standing water on the floor, the proprietor must not act as a reasonable person would, perhaps by allowing large pools of water to remain accumulated. For licensees, a failure to warn of dangerous conditions would be a breach of the duty. The creation of hazards would be considered a breach of the duty owed to trespassers. There is no further duty owed to trespassers (Cournoyer et al., 1993).

Breach of duty as the proximate cause

In negligence cases, a third element is the most difficult to prove. It requires the plaintiff to establish that the breach of duty by the proprietor caused the injury. A guest attacked in a room with a faulty door lock would not have a successful tort action based on negligence if the intruder entered the room through a properly secured window. In a restaurant situation with a wet floor, a fall on a dry portion of the floor would probably not be sufficient for the plaintiff to prevail (Cournoyer et al., 1993).

Damages

A negligence suit based on torts will not be successful unless the plaintiff suffers damages. Operating an automobile at high speeds in a congested area may be a negligent act, but without damages, a judgment based on negligence cannot be made against the defendant. Juries have a tendency to treat negligence suits in the same manner as malpractice suits. With a plaintiff who has suffered visual damages, it is common that the jury is sympathetic (Cournoyer et al., 1993).

Defenses

A defense often used by the defendant is contributory negligence. Contributory negligence states that the defendant did not exercise reasonable care and this lack of reasonable care on the part of the plaintiff led to his or her damages. An example would be a guest in a hotel walking through unmarked sliding doors, where the hotel can demonstrate that the guest had used these doors in the past. In states that recognize contributory negligence, the plaintiff cannot collect if he/she was partially negligent. Some states that follow the contributory negligence rule are: Alabama, Kentucky, Maryland, North Carolina, South Carolina, Tennessee, Virginia and the District of Columbia (Cournoyer et al., 1993).

The vast majority of states follow the rules of comparative negligence. Under comparative negligence, the liability is allocated between the plaintiff and the defendant. The plaintiff is only allowed to recover from the defendant that portion of the damages attributed to the defendant. For example, the plaintiff may have been 40 per cent negligent and therefore would only be entitled to a recovery of 60% of the total damages (Cournoyer et al., 1993).

Many of the states that follow the rule of comparative negligence further restrict awards to the plaintiff by exercising the 50 per cent rule. The 50 per cent rule states that if the plaintiff is more than 50 per cent negligent, he/she cannot collect any of his/her loss (Cournoyer et al., 1993).

Another defense to tort actions brought in negligence could be the Assumption of Risk Doctrine. The three elements necessary under this doctrine are: the plaintiff had knowledge of the risk; the plaintiff appreciated the risk; and the plaintiff could have avoided the risk. Examples of where the Assumption of Risk Doctrine can be applied are: attendance at a baseball game where the attendee could be injured by a baseball; a guest entering a construction area clearly marked off limits to the general public and there is a defined alternative path; and a guest of a hotel going for an evening walk when he/she had been advised that the area was unsafe. In the last example, the innkeeper is reminded that if the evening walk is being taken within the walls of the hotel, the hotel has a responsibility to provide a safe environment (Cournoyer et al., 1993).

Other relief for the plaintiff

The Doctrine of Last Clear Chance provides relief for a plaintiff when the plaintiff: has clearly been negligent; has put him/her self in a position of peril, from which he/she cannot escape; can prove that the defendant was aware or should have been aware of the plaintiff's peril and had the opportunity to avoid injury to the plaintiff. Under this Doctrine, the plaintiff can be awarded damages due to negligence for failing to act (Cournoyer et al., 1993).

The Latin phrase *"Res ipsa loquitur"* means "the thing speaks for itself." Under this Doctrine, the plaintiff needs only to prove: that the injury must have been caused by an accident that does not happen without negligence in normal situations; that the object that caused the injury was within the defendant's control; that the plaintiff did not engage in any activity that could have caused the accident; and that the plaintiff had no prior knowledge of the cause. Examples where this Doctrine can be applied include situations where bricks from a building have fallen on guests, ceiling fans have dropped and window shades have fallen while operating. The best defense for the defendant is to show regular inspections and compliance with all codes (Cournoyer et al., 1993).

In McCleod v. Nel-Co Corp. (112 N.E. 2d 501 Ill., 1953), the plaster from the ceiling fell while the plaintiff was sleeping. This does not occur without negligence in normal situations, the ceiling was totally under the control of the defendant, and the plaintiff was unaware of the problem and did nothing to cause its failure (Cournoyer et al., 1993).

Violent acts by employees

Under the Doctrine of Respondeat Superior, "let the master answer," employee negligence is imputed to the employer. The rationale for this Doctrine is that the employer controls the employee and therefore should be responsible for the employee's actions. In addition, it protects the plaintiff by attaching liability to the employer who, presumably, has greater assets than the employee. The Doctrine does not apply in cases where the employee's act is personal in nature. Employers could be liable if new employees were not checked to determine if they have a history of fighting, anti-social behavior or excessive aggressiveness (Cournoyer et al., 1993). Some states have passed legislation charging employees who steal from guests with felonies rather than misdemeanors. In Florida, any tourism employee convicted of theft faces a felony penalty of up to five years' imprisonment and/or fine of $5000 (Florida Statutes 509.162).

Failure to exercise reasonable care in the selection of employees can be costly. An airline company lost a suit when one of its ticket agents bit a passenger. Another company was found guilty of negligent hiring practices when it hired a convicted rapist to work in its mailroom. Employees of the firm were attacked off duty by this individual who had access to their home addresses (Karger, 1990).

The Employee Polygraph Protection Act of 1988 prohibits employers subjecting employees to polygraph examinations (lie detector tests). The only exception is if the employee had access, and there is a reasonable suspicion that he/she was involved. In these cases, the employee must be furnished with a written statement detailing the loss, confirmation that he/she had access and there is reasonable suspicion that he/she was involved. A report must be filed with the local authorities. One procedure mistake on the part of the employer could lead to a costly lawsuit (Jefferies, 1990).

Violent acts by other guests or invitees

The operator of hospitality enterprises has a duty to protect guests and invitees from their guests and invitees as well. The operator can be found negligent if he/she allows fighting on the premises or permits aggressive people to enter the establishment and remain. Being warned about certain individuals is enough to require the operator to exercise additional care. The operator is also negligent if he/she fails to provide additional security when warranted (Jefferies, 1990).

Under common law hospitality operators are required to accept all who apply, with certain exceptions. An operator may refuse to accept a potential guest: if there are no accommodations available; the guest is not willing to pay; the applicant is drunk or disorderly; is bringing in unallowable items or has a contagious disease (Jefferies, 1990). In Florida, innkeepers are permitted to eject or refuse service to a guest if the individual is: intoxicated, immoral, profane, lewd, brawling, disturbing the peace of others, injures the establishment's reputation, fails to pay, acts in a detrimental way or deals in controlled substances. This refusal of service or ejection can be written or oral. However, if it is written it must be in the following specific language:

> You are hereby notified that this establishment no longer desires to entertain you as a guest and you are hereby requested to leave at once. To remain after receipt of this notice is a misdemeanor under the laws of this state.

This statute provides the operator with the right to remove persons provided the action is not based upon race, creed, color, sex, physical disability or national origin. Clearly, the innkeeper can remove persons who could cause harm to other guests (Florida Statutes 509.141).

Duty to provide safe premises

Safety is a major concern of guests in hotels. Availability of dead bolts in guest rooms and well-lit parking lots are in the top 20 reasons why business persons choose a hotel. Operators of hospitality facilities are often asked tough safety-related questions by their guests such as: what is the crime rate in your community? Have there been any muggings or other assaults near your facility? What are your front office procedures for key control? Guests are concerned about the possibility of monetary losses or physical harm. A major selling point of the Millennium Hotel in the Wall Street area of New York City is the level of security in the hotel (Angelo, 1992).

The American Automobile Association (AAA) places security and safety high on its list when rating hotels and will not include a facility in its publications if the security is less than an established minimum. For example, properties are required to have dead bolts and view ports on all guest room doors, deadbolts on all connecting room doors and adequate locking devices on sliding glass doors to be listed in the 1995 publications of the

AAA. If, however, a property has not completed the requirements by the time of its inspection for the 1995 publications, listing will not be denied provided the property furnishes the AAA with an affidavit certifying that they have met the guest room security requirements after the inspection. Affidavits are due in the AAA offices at various times in 1994, depending on the property's geographical location (Hine, 1994). The AAA has 35 million members, and as such helps effect changes in the industry.

There are six major safety issues that need to be addressed (Angelo, 1992). The first issue is foreseeability. Foreseeability is a growing trend in the courts resulting in negligence cases with punitive awards. The basis for these decisions is that the operator knew or should have known. Foreseeability liability can be reduced by requesting the local police to patrol the parking lots, conducting thorough follow-up investigations of all incidents, the maintenance of complete and accurate written records and management staying informed of industry court cases.

Door lock systems are the second hotel safety issue. In addition to providing dead bolt locks and 180-degree door viewers on all guest room doors, the locking systems should be electronic programmable locks. Electronic programmable locks are the industry standard, and many hotel associations have passed resolutions requiring member properties to have them installed. Hotel properties that are delinquent in changing their locking systems and retain key systems with the room number engraved on the key, in an effort to contain costs, are certain to pay out more in lawsuits than the conversion cost. The testimony usually follows these lines: the hotel maintains a par stock of keys for each room; room attendants put keys left in the room in an open container on their hallway cart; and when the supply of keys drop below a certain level, replacement keys are made. What happened to the missing keys? Nobody knows. Why does the hotel not use programmable electronic locking systems? Too expensive. This is the wrong answer.

The term "*infra hospitium*" translates as "within the walls of the hotel." What this means is that the duty to protect guests and to provide safe premises extends to areas that the guest may use ancillary to the hotel. This could be the passageway between the hotel and the designated parking garage even if the walk takes the guest off hotel property. These perimeter areas are the third safety concern. Outside areas, such as parking lots, require lighting that will permit the reading of a newspaper.

The fourth issue relative to the duty to provide safe premises is the education of guests. The most important aspect of this issue rests in answers to the first two questions presented in this section: what is the crime rate in your community? Have there been any muggings or other assaults near your facility? When an operator is asked these questions, the response must be truthful. Do not provide the guest with false information or underestimate the level of safety in the neighborhood.

Food delivery vendors are licensees; however, it may not be in the property's best interest to allow vendors freedom to roam the property and deliver their products to individual guest rooms. The property should establish procedures to handle outsiders to the property. The most common safeguard is to instruct guests not to provide vendors with their guest room numbers and require the guest to come to the front desk to pick up his/her order. This is the fifth safety issue.

The sixth major safety issue involves the use of trained security guards. Employing professional security guards who are properly trained, and knowledgeable about the legal use of force and the statutes relative to the right to detain are the best defense. Regarding the use of force, the general rule is that one may use only that amount of force necessary to neutralize the act. Although state statutes differ on the right to detain, Florida's law states "an operator may take a person into custody and detain that person in a reasonable manner and for a reasonable time if the operator has probable cause to believe that the person was engaged in disorderly conduct" (Florida Statutes 509.143). It furthermore becomes incumbent upon the operator to call for a law enforcement officer immediately.

Hotel associations have accepted the fact that properties have a responsibility to provide safe premises. The Central Florida Hotel and Motel Association published in 1993 (CFHMA, 1993) 20 recommended minimum security and safety standards for its member properties. This association has also established a seminar program for security and safety. Proactive management by professional organizations such as the Central Florida Hotel and Motel Association in areas of safety and security can help reduce the negative effect that violence and crime has had on the tourism industry.

Crimes committed by guests

Hotels, restaurants, and other providers of services can be victims of crimes committed by their guests, invitees, licensees and trespassers. Some examples of these criminal acts are guests leaving without paying, the fraudulent use of credit cards, the passing of stolen or counterfeit travelers checks, presenting payment with worthless personal checks and the passing of counterfeit money.

When guests don't pay

Florida Statutes provide for up to five years in prison and a $5000 fine or both for skipping out on a bill. This is a felony in Florida as long as the amount of service was greater than $300. If it was less than $300, then it would be a misdemeanor in the second degree (Florida Statutes 509.151).

Perhaps the most difficult aspect of cases where the guest did not pay is the establishment of intent. Generally speaking, the law is on the side of the proprietor as long as he/she can demonstrate "*prima facie*", or at first sight (Jefferies, 1990). This means that in the eyes of a reasonable person, it seemed that the patron did not intend to pay.

In Florida, if the operator has probable cause to believe that any person has obtained services with the intent to defraud him/her, or has taken personal property from the establishment, the operator may take the person into custody (Florida Statutes 509.162). This custody or detention is permitted for a reasonable period of time as necessary to take him/her to the nearest magistrate. The key phrases of this statute are probably "cause and a reasonable period of time."

The downside risk of exercising one's rights under this statute could be allegations made against the proprietor for false imprisonment, slander, or malicious prosecution (Jefferies, 1990).

In the Florida case Hamilton v. State, the defendant was found guilty of obtaining lodging with the intent to defraud. Upon appeal appellant pleaded not guilty and filed a motion to dismiss on the basis that Florida Statutes 509.151 and 509.161 were unconstitutional. Hamilton contended that these statutes "(1) create an impermissible presumption violative of the Fourteenth Amendment of the Federal Constitution; (2) violate the privilege against self-incrimination contained in the Fifth Amendment; and (3) violate the constitutional proscription against imprisonment for non-payment of debt.'' The motion to dismiss was denied with the judge stating that these statutes were constitutional.

Credit card fraud

Credit cards have become a way of life, and use of them continues to grow. With annual charges in excess of $120 billion, and outstanding balances of the same approximate amount, this is a large business (Goodwin and Gaston, 1992). Unfortunately, this legitimate growth has also spawned another growth industry, credit card fraud. It was estimated that credit card fraud might exceed $1.5 billion in 1994 (Scott, 1994). Credit card systems are a contract where there is an offer and acceptance for a service, not a sale. Therefore, Article 2 of the Uniform Commercial Code does not apply to credit cards.

Credit card companies are either three-way contracts or two-way contracts. In a three-way contract, the card issuer and an individual enter into an agreement where the applicant agrees to terms as stated by the issuer. The second phase of this contract is when the cardholder offers the card for payment of goods or services in lieu of cash. The acceptance on the part of the merchant of the card completes the transaction. The final aspect of the three-way contract is when the evidence of the sale is presented by the merchant to the issuer for payment. This also creates a contract between the issuer and the cardholder establishing payment due to the issuer from the cardholder. The card issuer generates revenue by discounting the proceeds of the sale to the merchant by anywhere between 3 and 10 per cent. It also generates income from those holders who do not pay their entire balance when due, thus generating interest expense (Goodwin and Gaston, 1992).

In a two-way contract, the merchant is the card issuer. This is essentially an accounts receivable system. Credit is granted certain customers who can make purchases by presenting a card. The extension of credit is a method to stimulate sales, and create brand loyalty. In certain situations it may be beneficial for an organization to manage its own card system. Department stores and gasoline service stations are examples where two-way contracts are often used (Goodwin and Gaston, 1992).

When a card issued to a holder is lost, stolen or misplaced by the holder, the issuer must be notified at once. Under federal law, a cardholder is limited to $50 in unauthorized charges made on a card before notice is given to the issuer that the card is lost. There is no liability for the card holder if the issuer is notified before the card is used (Goodwin and Gaston, 1992).

A merchant is generally not liable for accepting a credit card in lieu of cash for a sale unless he/she has been negligent. Negligence can be established if the merchant accepted a card that was expired, obviously altered or was on a list of invalid cards. If an authorization is required, the merchant could also be negligent if he/she failed to obtain the authorization, or permitted a sale in excess of the authorized amount (Goodwin and Gaston, 1992).

When a card is presented and is subsequently denied, the merchant's responsibility is to inform the customer that the card has been denied and to furnish the name and address of the credit agency refusing to accept the charge. It is not within the merchant's domain to explain why the credit was refused (Goodwin and Gaston, 1993). Some companies offer rewards to persons who, when in the course of business, come across an invalid card and retain it.

Travelers checks

Travelers checks are another form of payment used by patrons of hospitality businesses. Generally, the merchant is not liable for the acceptance of forged or fraudulent travelers checks unless he/she was negligent. The holder is required to endorse the check in the presence of the cashier. The cashier then matches the two signatures on the check. If a reasonable person would conclude that they are identical, and the check is not on a list of unacceptable checks, then the transaction can be completed. If the cashier is in doubt as to the matching of the signatures, he/she should ask to see other identification. If the holder refuses, the check should not be accepted (Scott, 1994).

Although there are people in society who continually find new ways to create fraudulent travelers checks, a proprietor can protect him/herself by being knowledgeable about a couple of basic characteristics of travelers checks. Most travelers checks begin with an 8000 code. In addition, American Express travelers checks will smudge the denomination value on the left side of the back when wet. Since this is the only part of the check that will smear, and it will smear only once, when in doubt the cashier should apply this technique (Scott, 1994).

Personal checks

The most common negotiable instrument used in the United States is the personal check. Close to 90 per cent of the daily business transactions in the United States involve checks. The number of checks processed in 1993 was about 100 billion, with 2 per cent returned. Returned checks experience an approximate recovery rate of 50 per cent. The Federal Bureau of Investigation estimated in 1992 that 54 000 fraudulent checks were passed every hour (Scott, 1994). It is not a requirement for hospitality enterprises to accept personal checks from guests. However, most operations in the spirit of good customer service, accept personal checks. Caution, awareness, experience and common sense should be the rules in check acceptance procedures (Scott, 1994). In addition, there are check guarantee firms that will insure personal checks. This insurance can be purchased at various levels of coverage under different fee structures (usually around 4 per cent). The check recipient telephones the insurance company and furnishes information such as driver's license number, check amount and the type of check. An authorization number is then furnished by the check guarantee company. It is good management practice to inform guests when they arrive if checks are not accepted so that they can make other arrangements.

In the state of Florida, in order to prosecute a person for passing a bad check, the acceptor is required to obtain the following information: full name, current residence (not post office box), home telephone number, business telephone number, place of employment, sex, date of birth, height, race and driver's license number. Other requirements for the payee are to insist that the check be signed in the presence of the cashier and to indicate on the check the initials of the accepting person. Post-dated checks should not be accepted, nor should checks where the numerical and written amounts do not match. In addition, a list should be maintained of persons who have a history of bad checks (Lamar, 1992).

The procedures in the state of Florida for filing a complaint against a person for passing a bad check are explained below (Lamar, 1992). The first step is to present the check for payment. Assuming payment is denied, a certified letter, return receipt requested, needs to be sent to the person who passed the check. This is required for checks returned for insufficient funds. If the check was returned because the account has been closed, this step is not necessary. The person who passed the bad check has seven days to tender payment in full, plus $20, or 5 per cent of the check, whichever is greater. If full restitution is not made after the seven days, criminal prosecution can begin. The Worthless Check Division of the State's Attorney General's office requires the payee to furnish the original check. This check must be stamped by the bank. In addiition, a notarized worthless check affidavit must be included in the packet along with a copy of the certified letter and the identification of the checkwriter. Worthless checks cannot be prosecuted when the recipient accepted post-dated checks, was asked to hold the check or had reason to believe that the check was not good. The maker of the check also cannot be prosecuted if insufficient information was obtained (Lamar, 1992).

Counterfeit money

If an establishment accepts counterfeit money, its only recourse is to the person from whom it was received. When it is included in the deposit, it will be reduced from the day's receipts. The currency is not returned to the depositor. Therefore, all personnel who handle money need to be trained in cash receipt procedures and basic tests of counterfeit money. It is also suggested that ongoing training be maintained to keep employees informed of the latest developments in this criminal activity (Scott, 1994).

Alcohol and violent acts

There are a minimum number of lawsuits where hotels are sued by non-guests for injuries caused by guests. However, lawsuits as a result of injuries suffered due to accidents related to alcohol or drunkenness are increasing. Relief is being sought from providers and servers of alcoholic beverages (McConnell and Rutherford, 1993).

The 21st Amendment to the United States Constitution states that each state has the right to control the sale of alcohol within that state. The sale of alcohol products is therefore governed by state liquor authorities (Jefferies, 1990).

Under common law, vendors are not generally liable for the actions of customers who were sold beverages for damages caused while they were intoxicated. The reason for this is due to the fact that the damages were caused by the intoxication rather than the sale of the alcoholic beverage (Goodwin and Gaston, 1992).

Liquor liability laws are generally referred to as Dram Shop Acts, and have existed since the 1800s. Dram Shop Acts modify common law and permit third-party recovery against the vendor. It is not the sale of the liquor that attaches the liability but rather the service. Most state Dram Shop Acts prohibit sale or service of alcohol to minors, service to intoxicated persons and to habitual drunkards. Even if a specific state does not have a Dram Shop Act, modified common law can attach liability to the server (Goodwin and Gaston, 1992).

In the 1800s, public drunkenness was a major problem. Wisconsin, in 1849, was the first state with a Dram Shop Act. Indiana, Ohio, New York and Maine followed soon after the Wisconsin law. After the Civil War, Dram Shop Acts were enacted practically nation-wide. The basics of the early acts were to prohibit sale or service to minors, habitual drunkards and obviously intoxicated individuals. These laws were not enforced and, by the end of Prohibition, most were repealed or simply not enforced (Boyd et al., 1991).

Currently 41 states and the District of Columbia have some form of Dram Shop Act or apply modified common law to the extent that liability is attached to the server. Florida and 24 other states recognize both statutory and common law cases regarding enforcement against third parties. Florida requires written notice with regard to the sale or service to habitual drunkards (Florida Statutes 768.128). About 20 states limit the liability of sellers by requiring proof of the seller's negligence or illegal service (Boyd et al., 1991).

Death of a guest

Unfortunately, there is a possibility that a person may die while a guest at a hotel. The innkeeper's responsibility falls into one of two broad categories. If the deceased was under the care of a doctor, the doctor is responsible for notifying the local health department and relatives. The body is removed from the hotel by an authorized undertaker. When a guest dies and is not under the care of a doctor, the police are notified, and the body is taken to the morgue (Jefferies, 1990).

If the death is natural, generally there is no problem and the innkeeper's involvement ends. The only other requirement, in Florida, is to notify the Division of Hotels and Restaurants within five days of the fatality, providing the date of death, circumstances and name of establishment (Florida Statutes Administrative Rule 7C-1.005).

If the death is unnatural, the police will continue with the investigation. The innkeeper has a duty to keep the premises sealed. All personal property should be turned over to the police, or an inventory should be made and the property secured. To avoid liability, the innkeeper needs a tax waiver from whomever the personal property is turned over to (Jefferies, 1990).

References

Angelo, T. (1992). Security: Guests demand to feel safe and secure. *Play it Safe, 1*. Philadelphia: CIGNA Business Communication.

Bellucci, E. (1987). Florida's limited liability statutes provide no free security hugs! *Florida Hotel & Motel Journal*, **10**(11): 13–16.

Boyd, J.A., Vickory, F.A. and Maroney, P.F. (1991). The trends in dram shop laws and how they affect the hospitality industry: Balancing competing policy considerations of tort reform and curbing drunk driving. *Hospitality Research Journal*, **15**: 25–42.

CFHMA Board of Directors (1993). *Central Florida Hotel and Motel Association Recommended Minimum Security/Safety Standards.*

Cournoyer, N., Marshall, A. and Morris, K. (1993). *Hotel, Restaurant and Travel Law: A Preventative Approach.* Fourth Edition. Albany, NY: Delmar Publishers.

Florida Statutes Chapter 509 Public Lodging and Food Service Establishments.

Goodwin, J. and Gaston, J. (1992). *Hotel & Hospitality Law: Principles and Cases.* Fourth Edition. Scottsdale, AZ: Gorsuch Scarisbrick.

Hine, K. (1994). *The 1994 AH&MA 83rd Annual Convention & Show.* Denver, CO: American Hotel and Motel Association.

Jefferies, J.P. (1990). *Understanding Hospitality Law.* Second Edition. East Lansing, MI: Educational Institute of the American Hotel and Motel Association.

Karger, J. (1990). Hiring: Your first opportunity to blow it. *The Meeting Manager*, **10**(10): 27–8.

Lamar, L. (1992). *Minimize your risk of bad checks.* Orlando, FL: Worthless Check Division, Office of the State Attorney General.

McConnell, J. and Rutherford, D. (1993). Why innkeepers go to court: An update. *The Cornell Hotel and Restaurant Administration Quarterly*, **34**(5): 23–7.

Rutherford, D. and McConnell, J. (1991). DeFacto security standards: Operators at risk. *The Cornell Hotel and Restaurant Administration Quarterly*, **31**(4): 107–17.

Scott, J. (1994). White collar crime: Serial killer of American businesses. Unpublished work.

Scott, J. (1994). Defensive check acceptance procedures: A guide for businesses. Unpublished work.

Scott, J. (1994). A guide to recognizing counterfeit checks. Unpublished work.

Sherry, J.E.H. (1993). *The laws of innkeepers.* Third Edition. Ithaca, NY: Cornell University Press.

Townsend, R. (1988). Reasonable care: How safe is safe? *Lodging Hospitality*, **44**(2): 106–8.

Conclusions and recommendations

ABRAHAM PIZAM AND YOEL MANSFELD

The evidence presented thus far shows beyond any doubt that acts of violence occurring at or *en route* to tourism destinations, and especially violent acts specifically aimed at tourists, threaten the existence and well-being of the tourism industry. Crimes, terrorism, civil unrest and war have caused serious damage to the tourism industries of afflicted destinations and in some cases totally decimated a whole industry.

The question that we must ask ourselves is whether these acts should be considered as factors caused by wider social and political circumstances and therefore uncontrollable by tourism destinations, or whether the public sector and the tourism industry can take steps to prevent these acts and minimize their effects. While we strongly believe that the ultimate cause of acts of violence against tourists is rooted in deep social and political motives, we also profess that through the administration of proper measures it is possible to decrease the occurrence and minimize the damage caused by such incidences.

Based on the accumulated experiences of many tourism destinations and some of the case studies described in this book we propose the following recommendations to the tourism industry and the public sector.

Tourism industry

Tourism enterprises must recognize the fact that their properties and guests might become victims of crimes and violent acts. Therefore, rather than denying the existence of such crimes or constantly attacking the media for creating panic and negative publicity, tourism plants should invest significant resources in increasing awareness, guest education and crime prevention measures.

1. The evidence shows that crimes against tourists tend to occur in geographical areas that have a higher level of general crimes. Therefore, wherever possible hotels and other tourist attractions should not be built in such areas.
2. When designing tourism plants such as hotels, restaurants and tourist attractions, crime prevention through environmental design (CPTED) should be practiced. Very often architects and developers put little if any emphasis on safety and security issues

Tourism, Crime and International Security Issues, edited by
A. Pizam and Y. Mansfeld. © 1996 John Wiley & Sons Ltd.

and are mostly concerned with aesthetics and functionality. Building hotels or motels with unlimited open access to guest rooms, having no physical boundaries to the property, creating alcoves and hidden corridors and not providing sufficient lighting in corridors and public spaces invites criminal acts.

3. Not only should the function of safety and security be considered as critical to the success of the tourism enterprise and its chief be elevated to the executive level, but all employees should be trained in security measures. The ultimate aim is to make every tourism employee a security employee.

4. Tourists must be made aware of the possibility of criminal acts against them and educated in prevention and security measures. Proper instructions must be provided both in written and audio-visual form (ie, through TV sets) to all tourists at each tourism plant (ie travel agencies, airports, car-rental agencies, hotels, tourist attractions etc).

5. Tourism enterprises must be constantly involved in researching and evaluating the effectiveness of crime prevention measures — such as security hardware and security policies — in their properties.

6. To be able to evaluate the effect of crime prevention measures on crime reduction in their properties, tourism enterprises must collect and keep accurate and honest records of all crime incidences occurring on their properties. Furthermore, for the benefit of the whole industry, these statistics should be shared with local and national law enforcement agencies. Very often misguided tourism managers believe that by not collecting this information at all, or by not reporting it to law enforcement agencies, they are guarding their reputation and protecting themselves from future litigation.

7. Tourism trade associations should consider the establishment of national or regional security accreditation commissions that will certify tourism enterprises for meeting minimum security measurements.

8. Tourism enterprises must have contingency "crisis plans." Such plans ought to address such issues as overcoming negative publicity as a result of violent incidences, marketing and promotional plans to increase attendance etc.

9. The tourism industry must monitor and measure the short- and long-term effects of terror and warfare on the propensity of tourists to visit affected destinations. This will enable a development of more effective contingency plans to minimize the economic damage emerging in the wake of such events.

10. Marketing strategies aimed at resuming inbound tourist flows after terror and/or warfare activities should target the less sensitive market segments first, thus ensuring a quick recovery from the downward trend.

11. In countries suffering from an on-going, yet unjustified, poor tourist image due to terrorist or warfare activities in the past, the tourism industry must adopt a "destination-specific" marketing policy. A successful example of such an approach has been the winter sun resort of Eilat which always remained in the shadow of major terror and/or warfare activities taking place in Israel. A decision by the industry to market Eilat as "Eilat," without associating it with Israel, ensured a steady growth of visitors to this resort even in periods of turmoil in the rest of the country.

12. Once turmoil periods resulting from terrorism or warfare activities end, the tourism industry should consider turning these affected war zones into favorable tourist destinations selling war and political unrest as a tourist attraction.

Public sector

National, regional and local authorities must recognize that prevention of violent acts against tourists is not the sole responsibility of the tourism industry. Such acts not only affect the well-being of the tourism industry at the destination but the image and reputation of the entire locality. Being perceived as a dangerous destination not only deters tourists from coming and affects the livelihood of countless numbers of people who work for this industry but also deters investors and potential residents from moving into the area. Public authorities should put their energy and resources into action plans rather than blaming the media for "blowing the incidents out of proportion." These action plans should aim at preventing violent crimes from occurring and/or minimizing their damage. Following are a number of steps that in our opinion should be instituted by public authorities on a local, regional or national level.

1. Law enforcement agencies must institute uniform methods of classifying criminal incidences, separate the incidences against tourists from the rest of the criminal incidences and publicly report these statistics on a periodic basis.
2. State and national legislatures should make criminal acts against tourists a major criminal activity that is severely punishable.
3. The reporting of all criminal activities in tourism enterprises should be made mandatory.
4. Local authorities should embark on a public education program intended to increase the awareness of all citizens as to the grave damage that criminal activities against tourists cause to a community. The ultimate objective of such a program would be to make the entire community a "neighborhood watch" community, where each resident is on the lookout for potential criminals and reports any suspicious acts to law enforcement agencies.
5. Tourist information services in cooperation with local authorities should provide proper tourist-signage and distribute free written information about security-risk areas.
6. Whenever possible, large tourist destinations should consider the establishment of tourist police units. Such units would handle not only tourist-related crimes but would help to train and educate the tourism industry and the general public in tourist-crime prevention.
7. The public sector should underwrite the conduct of several comprehensive research programs intended to measure the long-term effectiveness of crime prevention measures in the tourism industry.
8. Public tourist promotion agencies should have contingency "crisis tourism promotion plans" to be put in operation immediately following a major security incident such as murder, terrorism or civil unrest. The aim of such plans would be to change the perception of the area as an unsafe and dangerous destination.
9. National governments should issue security warnings to the general traveling public whenever such information is received from intelligence sources.
10. Governments should be highly involved in financing promotion of their tourist destinations after terror or warfare activities come to an end and resuming tourist inbound flows becomes possible. Such a policy would prove to the private sector that

its government is not just responsible for damaging the tourist industry but also committed to its reactivation and reconstruction.

11. Governmental agencies should publish up-to-date information on risk to travelers which should be distributed through official intergovernmental communication systems to ensure that such information reaches all potential tourists.

12. International cooperation on a governmental level seeking preventive measures to reduce the negative effects of terrorism against tourists should be promoted and institutionalized. Such needs have become more relevant in recent years as tourists occasionally become a direct target for extremists and terrorist groups.

13. Research guided by international bodies such as the World Tourism Organization should monitor the global effects of political instability, terrorism and warfare on the world tourism industry. This would add a global dimension to the existing research on national or regional levels.

Index

Index compiled by Geoffrey Jones